C000145508

The
World Atlas of
Musical Instruments

The World Atlas of Musical Instruments

Illustrations
Anton Radevsky

Text
Bozhidar Abrashev & Vladimir Gadjev

Design
Krassimira Despotova

h.f.ullmann

The measures given in this book are metric measures. For conversion into American measures, please see the following table:

1 mm = 1 millimeter = 0.04 inches
1 cm = 1 centimeter = 10 millimeters = 0.39 inches
1 m = 1 meter = 100 centimeters = 39.37 inches
1 km = 1 kilometer = 1,000 meters = 0.62 miles
1 kg = 1 kilogram = 2.2 pounds = 35.27 ounces
1 metric ton = 1,000 kilograms = 1,102 short tons

Original title: *Ilyustrovana Entsiklopedia na Muzikalnite Instrumenti*

ISBN of the original edition: 954-474-224-7

© 2000 by Kibea Publishing Company (Bulgarian edition)
bl. 329, entr. J, k. Lulin, BG – 1336 Sofia

© for this English edition: h.f.ullmann publishing GmbH

All rights reserved. No part of this publication may be reproduced,
stored in a retrieval system, or transmitted in any form
or by any means, electronic, mechanical, photocopying,
recording or otherwise, without the prior written permission of the publisher.

Editor: Ivanka Nikolova
Assistant editor: Geoffrey Dean
Translation from Bulgarian: Janeta Shinkova
Editors of the English translation: Laura Davey and Geoffrey Dean
Project coordinator: Kirsten E. Lehmann
Project assistants: Tanja Krombach and Teofila Issidorova
Computer processing: Ludmil Tassev and Jordan Angelov

Cover design: Simone Sticker
Overall responsibility for production: h.f.ullmann publishing GmbH, Potsdam, Germany

Printed in China

ISBN 978-3-8480-0051-7

10 9 8 7 6 5 4 3 2 1
X IX VIII VII VI V IV III II I

www.ullmann-publishing.com
newsletter@ullmann-publishing.com

CONTENTS

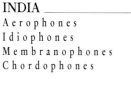

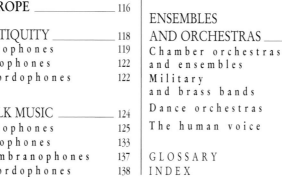
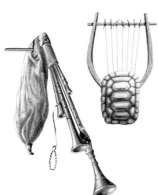

FOREWORD

MUSIC WAS BORN IN THE HUMAN BRAIN: first as a sound, then as a succession of sounds organized in a certain way. Man then sought a way of communicating through these sounds, of discovering their true place within a human community, however small it may be. Essentially, music is a form of communication.

The human voice was the first medium of musical communication: the most natural and most expressive instrument, though somewhat limited. Observing and imitating nature in their daily struggle for survival, the first humans began to be aware of the sounds around them. They could hear the wind hissing in the reeds, old trees groaning and creaking, stones clashing against each other, birds singing. They began to imitate these sounds, sometimes to protect themselves, sometimes to become one with nature and its divine harmony. This was how the first primitive "musical instruments" appeared: a blade of grass or a hollow reed, adding a new nuance to the expressiveness of the human voice.

Recent historical sources give evidence of our ancestors' customs: singing and dancing around the fire, beating primitive drums, shouting and chanting, offering sacrifices. Born as a crucial element in their developing sense of community, this must have been the most ancient music.

The ancient peoples of the Mediterranean, the cradle of European civilization, perceived music as an integral part of their syncretic folk traditions. Unfortunately, our knowledge of the most ancient cultures is minimal, and sounds were too ephemeral to give us a clear idea of the first steps in the long history of music that were made in those distant times.

It seems that sound preceded speech, which, in its turn, appeared thousands of years before writing. Thus, our knowledge of music from the time before it became an art can only be drawn from images of instruments and from the collective human memory that has preserved a wealth of ancient traditions.

By studying the history of musical instruments, we, the people of the third millennium A. D., can learn a great deal about our origins and come to know ourselves better. By following the evolution of musical instruments, their migration into different regions of the world, and by comparing their construction and playing techniques with those of their modern equivalents, we can speculate as to how they must have sounded in their original cultural contexts. With some imagination, and with a certain amount of knowledge, we can even guess what sort of music they played.

Ancient philosophers included music among the "seven liberal arts": grammar, rhetoric, and logic formed the first part of the curriculum, known as the trivium, while geometry, arithmetic, music, and astronomy formed the quadrivium (the terms referring respectively to the three and four paths of knowledge). As a result, music continued in the succeeding centuries to be highly regarded, not only as a form of art, but also as a significant and ever-expanding body of knowledge. As the search for musical knowledge became more systematic and organized, the need for more sophisticated musical instruments became increasingly imperative. Particularly during the Renaissance, advances in music theory and the invention of improved musical instruments ran parallel. In fact, whenever important musical developments have taken place, the instruments themselves have been a significant contributing factor.

During the 20th century our cultural horizons have expanded as never before, establishing closer connections between Eastern and Western peoples. Our way of thinking has changed, and we now regard the world as one large community to which we all belong. The process of globalization and the rapid development in information and communication technologies have also influenced our outlook, opening our eyes in relation to the "esoteric" cultures. In view of this, we have tried to collect and present in this encyclopedia an information base as broad as possible to provide a similarly global perspective on musical instruments, from the dawn of human civilization to the present day. It is our hope that this volume will enrich the knowledge of music lovers in today's open and inquisitive world.

Yehudi Menuhin and Ravi Shankar.

THE CLASSIFICATION OF INSTRUMENTS

THE STUDY OF MUSICAL INSTRUMENTS, their history, evolution, construction, and systematics is the subject of the science of organology. Its subject matter is enormous, covering practically the entire history of humankind and includes all cultural periods and civilizations. The science studies archaeological findings, the collections of ethnography museums, historical, religious and literary sources, paintings, drawings, and sculpture. Organology is indispensable for the development of specialized museum and amateur collections of musical instruments. It is also the science that analyzes the works of the greatest instrument makers and their schools in historical, technological, and aesthetic terms.

The classification of instruments used for the creation and performance of music dates back to ancient times. In ancient Greece, for example, they were divided into two main groups: blown and struck. All stringed instruments belonged to the latter group, as the strings were "struck" with fingers or a plectrum. Around the second century B. C., a separate string group was established, and these instruments quickly acquired a leading role. A more detailed classification of the three groups – wind, percussion, and strings – soon became popular.

At about the same time in China, instrument classification was based on the principles of the country's religion and philosophy. Instruments were divided into eight groups depending on the quality of the sound and on the material of which they were made: metal, stone, clay, skin, silk, wood, gourd, and bamboo.

In neighboring India, the system included fewer and larger categories, generally corresponding to the modern European classification: tata, sushira, avanaja, and Ghana – strings, wind, membranophones, and idiophones.

Around 1880, Victor Mahillon, the founder of the famous Brussels collection, published a full classification including non-European and folk instruments, the *Catalogue descriptif et analytique du Musée instrumental du Conservatoire Royal de Musique, Bruxelles.* In 1914, his study was followed by the publication of *Systematik der Musikinstrumente* by Erich von Hornbostel and Curt Sachs. Hornbostel and Sachs focused on the sound-generator: an air-column, a string, a membrane, or a hard surface. This standard was adopted in the science of organology, and serves as a basis for both teaching and research, although the classification of the symphony orchestra (strings, wind [woodwind and brass], and percussion) is still popular in musical circles.

Today, there are many systems of classification for musical instruments, based on their different characteristics. Each system has its own sphere of application.

The scientific classification of musical instruments, based on the principle of sound-generation, includes five groups:

aerophones (the sound is generated by an air-column),

idiophones (the material itself generates the sound),

membranophones (the sound is generated by a stretched membrane made of skin or other material),

chordophones (the sound is generated by a stretched string), and

electrophones (the sound is generated by electronic means).

The European tradition is somewhat different. Instead of aerophones, European musicians use the term wind, more particularly woodwind and brass. Chordophones are referred to as strings. Membranophones and idiophones are united under the name of percussion. Keyboard instruments form a separate category. A keyboard allows the player to produce several tones simultaneously. Thus, this group unites very different instruments, such as the piano and the harpsichord (in which the sound is generated by vibrating strings), the organ (by a vibrating air-column), and the accordion (by vibrating metal tongues). This category also includes modern keyboards.

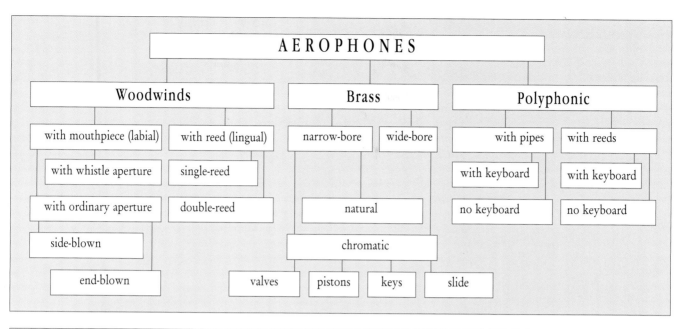

AEROPHONES

Woodwinds
- with mouthpiece (labial)
  - with whistle aperture
  - with ordinary aperture
    - side-blown
    - end-blown
- with reed (lingual)
  - single-reed
  - double-reed

Brass
- narrow-bore
- wide-bore
  - natural
  - chromatic
    - valves
    - pistons
    - keys
    - slide

Polyphonic
- with pipes
  - with keyboard
  - no keyboard
- with reeds
  - with keyboard
  - no keyboard

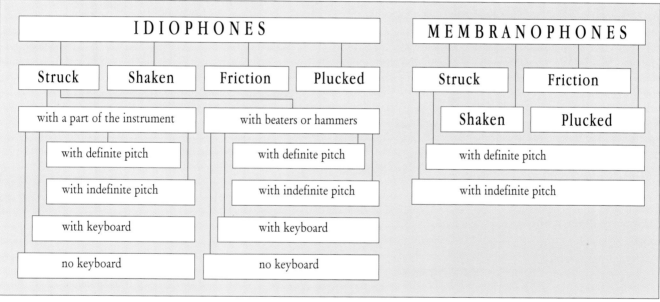

IDIOPHONES

Struck   **Shaken**   **Friction**   **Plucked**
- with a part of the instrument
  - with definite pitch
  - with indefinite pitch
  - with keyboard
  - no keyboard
- with beaters or hammers
  - with definite pitch
  - with indefinite pitch
  - with keyboard
  - no keyboard

MEMBRANOPHONES

Struck   **Friction**
Shaken   **Plucked**
- with definite pitch
- with indefinite pitch

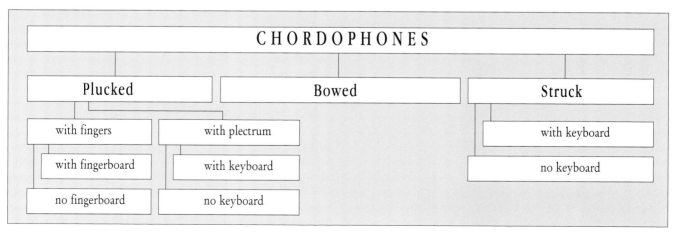

CHORDOPHONES

Plucked
- with fingers
  - with fingerboard
  - no fingerboard
- with plectrum
  - with keyboard
  - no keyboard

Bowed

Struck
- with keyboard
- no keyboard

Aerophones

The aerophone group includes a wide variety of instruments in which the sound is generated by a vibrating air mass. They are divided into free aerophones and aerophones proper, depending on whether or not the air mass is enclosed in a tube. The former type appeared in early primitive cultures, while the latter had a long evolution and played an important role in the development of musical traditions.

The range of wind instruments in which the air mass is enclosed in the instrument depends on the length, diameter, shape, and construction of the tube (or more specifically, of its bore). The smaller these specifications are, the higher the instrument's range.

Wind instruments are divided into woodwind and brass, according to the vibrating medium and the method of sound-generation (the categories indicating the method of sound-generation rather than the material of which the instrument is made).

In woodwind and brass instruments, which constitute the majority of modern aerophones, the change of pitch is achieved by changing the length of the vibrating air-column in the tube. This can be done by "overblowing" – that is, by increasing the pressure of the air mass to obtain a certain natural tone of the harmonic series.

Natural trumpet.

An important factor determining an instrument's pitch is the ratio between the tube length and its interior diameter. Thus, instruments can be narrow-bored (with a relatively long and narrow tube), or wide-bored (relatively short and wide).

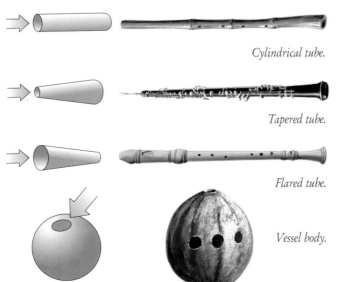

Cylindrical tube.

Tapered tube.

Flared tube.

Vessel body.

The pitch may also be changed by opening or closing fingerholes positioned on the tube, or by connecting or disconnecting additional sections of tubing by means of a special mechanism, such as valves, pistons, or a slide.

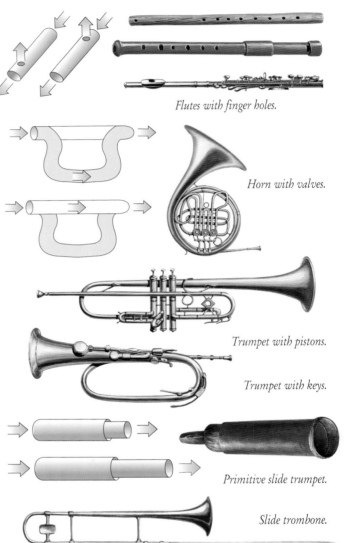

Flutes with finger holes.

Horn with valves.

Trumpet with pistons.

Trumpet with keys.

Primitive slide trumpet.

Slide trombone.

On the basis of the tones contained within their range, brass instruments are divided into natural (without valves, pistons, or slides, and capable of producing only overtones) and chromatic (capable of sounding all chromatic tones).

All woodwind instruments are wide-bored. Their tubes are most often straight, and lower-pitched versions may be bent once or twice in various shapes.

Brass instruments consist of tubes of conical or cylindrical bore (or a combination of the two). A flared bell connects the instrument with the outside air, improving the sound projection and influencing the instrument's sound quality. Because of the length of their tubing, modern brass instruments are always coiled in circular or oval shapes.

According to the classification of Hornbostel and Sachs, aerophones are divided into three main groups, some of which can be further subdivided:

Flutes:

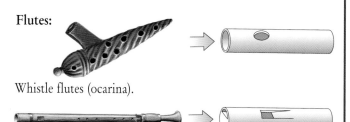

Whistle flutes (ocarina).

End-blown flutes (recorders, panpipes, folk instruments).

Transverse flutes (flute, piccolo).

Trumpets with cup mouthpiece (trumpets, trombones, tubas, serpents).

Reeds:

Single-reed (clarinet, saxophone, bagpipe).

Double-reed (oboe, bassoon, surna).

Metal reeds (mouth harmonica, accordion, harmonium).

Like other instruments, the timbre or tone colour of aerophones is determined by the presence of overtones, their number, loudness, and relation to the fundamental tone. The richer an instrument is in overtones, the more resonant and expressive its sound; the poorer it is in overtones, the drier the sound. In some instruments, lower overtones predominate, and their sound is full and deep but not very penetrating. In others, higher overtones predominate, producing a shrill, penetrating sound. Yet others are characterized by medium overtones, giving softness and roundness to the sound.

Idiophones

Percussion instruments are the earliest musical instruments, dating back to the dawn of human civilization.

In terms of the sound they produce, tones or noises, they are divided into two main groups: of definite and of indefinite pitch.

The sound effects for which the human body can be used are considered the first prototypes of percussion instruments. Objects found in nature or produced by man began to serve as sound generators: stones, sticks, jagged pieces of wood, hollow vessels, primitive wooden drums, pots, and so on. The use of percussion instruments was related to celebrations, feasts, funeral ceremonies, dances, and other such events. They are found in all cultures and continents.

Idiophones are divided into the following groups, according to the way in which the vibrations are generated:

Struck idiophones: two or more sonorous parts clash together.

Claves.

Struck idiophones with beaters.

Slit drum.

Shaken idiophones: small pellets are enclosed within an object.

Maracas.

Friction idiophones: the instrument's surface is rubbed.

Glass harmonica.

Sapo cubana.

Plucked idiophones:

Sansa.

The two main acoustic elements of idiophones, the sound generator and the vibrating medium, may be non-differentiated (parts of the same object), differentiated and connected, or quite separate. Usually, idiophones have resonators, and some have a special amplifying system.

The European system of instrument classification combines the idiophone group with the membranophone group in a single category of percussion instruments.

Membranophones

These are instruments in which the sound is produced by the externally generated vibration of a stretched membrane. Almost all membranophones have resonators: the instrument's shell and the air enclosed in it.

Struck membranophones: all single- and double-head drums, regardless of their shape and membrane material (skin, metal, plastic, etc.).

Snare drum.

Friction drums: sounded with a stick or a cord

African friction drum with a rod.

Russian friction drum with horse hair.

With singing membranes:

Mirliton.

Chordophones

These are instruments in which the sound is produced by vibrating strings stretched between fixed points.

The tone sounded by a string depends on its length, thickness, mass, and tension. The shorter, the thinner, and the tighter a string, the higher the frequency of its vibration and respectively the pitch obtained.

A string's fundamental (lowest) tone is obtained when it vibrates at its entire length. When pressed at a certain point and thus shortened, the tone is higher. The string vibrates simultaneously in its entire length and in equal sections (halves, thirds, fourths), thus producing overtones. If the frequency of the vibration of the fundamental tone is 1, the overtones form a simple arithmetic progression of the type 1:2:3:4:5:6:7:8. An instrument's timbre is determined by the combination of overtones and their number, frequency, and loudness in relation to the fundamental.

With the exception of a few primitive instruments, chordophones are equipped with resonators of varying shape, size, and construction whose function is to amplify and enrich the sound. The resonator is of primary significance for an instrument's sound quality; this is why the great luthiers paid particular attention to its material, size, and proportions.

Chordophones are divided into three main groups:

Plucked:

With fingers (guitar, lute).

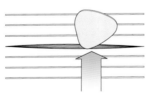

With plectrum (mandoline, shamisen).

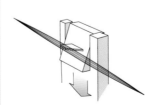

Keyboard-controlled mechanism as on the harpsichord.

Struck:

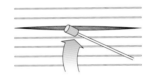

With beaters (dulcimer).

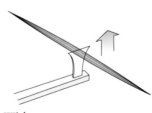

With tangents (clavichord).

With hammers (piano, grand piano).

Bowed:

All folk fiddles, viols, the whole violin family.

Other classifications focus on other characteristics of stringed instruments. A widely popular one divides them as follows:

Chordophones with no resonator:

Musical bow.

Chordophones with resonators:

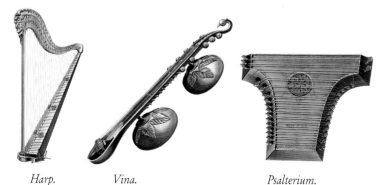

With a frame but without a keyboard.

Harp.   *Vina.*   *Psalterium.*

Clavichord.   *Harpsichord.*   *Piano.*

With both frame and keyboard.

With a fingerboard; the strings are plucked with fingers or plectrum.

Lute.   *Guitar.*   *Mandolin.*

With a fingerboard, bowed (a huge variety of folk instruments around the globe, the whole classical violin family, the viols).

Rebab.   *Sarangi.*   *Erh-hu.*   *Viola.*

Electrophones

Musical development during the 20th century made necessary an important new category in the Hornbostel and Sachs classification: the electrophones. Their unifying characteristic is that the sound is generated by means of vacuum valves or semiconductor devices.

Electronic piano.

Electronic violin.

Electric guitar.

Synthesizer.

AFRICA

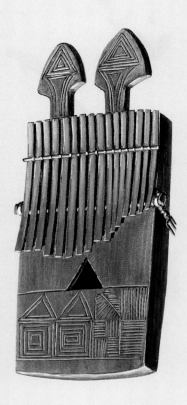

THE MUSICAL CULTURE OF AFRICA is as diverse as its people, who speak about 700 different languages and dialects, more than on any other continent. The musical heritage of the African continent includes the original contribution of the ancient inhabitants of the Nile valley. In ancient Egypt, the predominating instruments were the harps (shoulder-held, knee-held or placed on tables), the flutes (end- or side-blown, one- or two-duct), the wooden pipes, the single- and double-head drums, the tambourines with jingles, the hemispherical metal cymbals, the wooden castanets, and so on. The music of ancient Egypt was mystical, soft and gentle. The Islamic countries north of the Sahara Desert (such as Morocco, Tunisia, Algeria, and Egypt) have musical traditions related in many ways to those of the Middle East, while the music of the sub-Saharan countries, where large communities spread out over vast territories still lead a simple, traditional life, is more practical in character. Here music is inseparable from dancing and singing, and in fact few Africans use the abstract term "music," referring instead to songs, dances, and poetry.

Music and dance are central to many ceremonies and rites that mark important occasions such as birth, initiation, marriage, and funerals. Similarly to African folklore and history, musical traditions are passed on orally; no system of notation exists. Music also plays a significant role as a means of communication in Africa, through the "talking drums" that convey signals and messages, sometimes over great distances. But the most noticeable features of the music of sub-Saharan Africa are its incredible speed and rhythmic complexity in polyrhythmic structures often led by percussion instruments.

The close connection between African music and dance helps explain the domination of rhythm and percussion (idiophones and membranophones). Musical ensembles, ranging in size from two to twenty or more players, almost invariably include drums, xylophones, and clappers. There are instruments both of indefinite pitch, such as bells and some types of drums, and of definite pitch (flutes, trumpets, xylophones, primitive harps). While keeping a fast tempo, the ensemble musicians play contrasting rhythmic patterns with almost complete independence among the parts, giving this music an unforgettable sense of excitement.

African vocal music is based on the question-and-answer pattern, similar to the call-and-response later found in the African-American spiritual. In short phrases that are often repeated with slight variations, a soloist asks a question, and the chorus answers. The melodic richness of African music, often based on tetrachords and the pentatonic scale, is also due to polyphonic singing in parallel intervals (thirds, fourths, fifths), expressive semitone and sliding effects, and careful attention to subtle nuances in tone color, to which African vocalists are particularly sensitive. Also typical of African singing are the frequent interruptions for spoken or recited passages.

In the early 20th century, when Europeans began to break away from traditional approaches to painting and music, they became more receptive to so-called "primitive" art, and African music began to arouse the interest of an expanding circle of musicians and music lovers. First African-American jazz and later the direct borrowing of African musical models popularized the rhythmic intensity and the timbral potential of traditional African instruments.

AEROPHONES

In Africa, the most frequently used aerophones are flutes, simple whistles, horns, and primitive trumpets. They are generally less popular than the other instrument groups. Flutes are made of bamboo, cane, or wood; horns and trumpets are made of animal horn, ivory, bamboo, or wood.

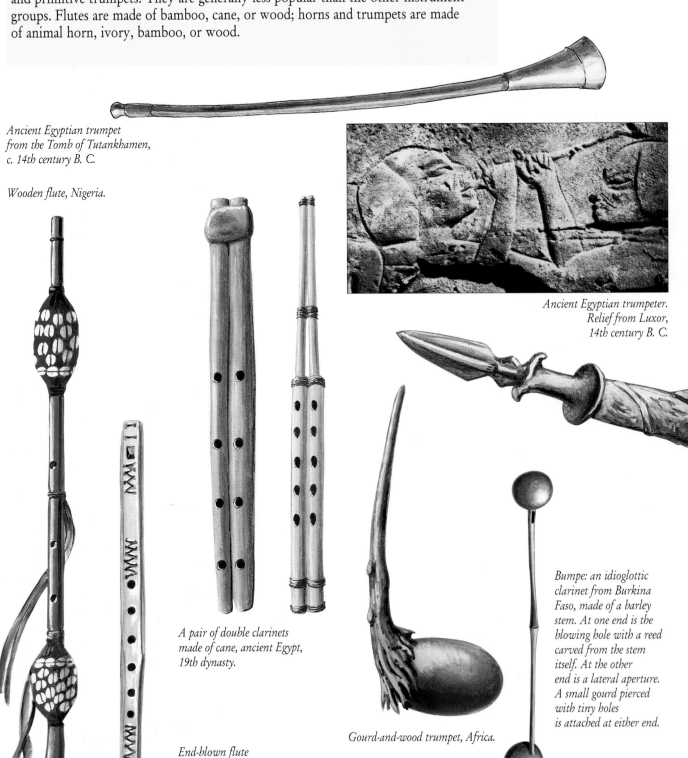

*Ancient Egyptian trumpet
from the Tomb of Tutankhamen,
c. 14th century B. C.*

Wooden flute, Nigeria.

*Ancient Egyptian trumpeter.
Relief from Luxor,
14th century B. C.*

*A pair of double clarinets
made of cane, ancient Egypt,
19th dynasty.*

*End-blown flute
with six fingerholes, Morocco.*

Gourd-and-wood trumpet, Africa.

*Bumpe: an idioglottic
clarinet from Burkina
Faso, made of a barley
stem. At one end is the
blowing hole with a reed
carved from the stem
itself. At the other
end is a lateral aperture.
A small gourd pierced
with tiny holes
is attached at either end.*

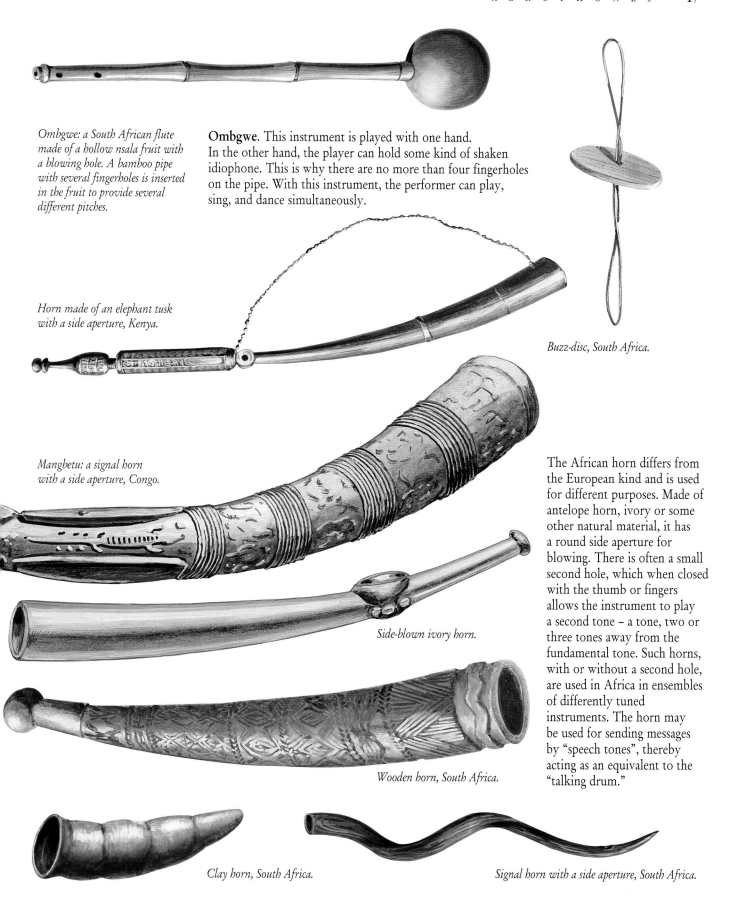

Ombgwe: a South African flute made of a hollow nsala fruit with a blowing hole. A bamboo pipe with several fingerholes is inserted in the fruit to provide several different pitches.

Ombgwe. This instrument is played with one hand. In the other hand, the player can hold some kind of shaken idiophone. This is why there are no more than four fingerholes on the pipe. With this instrument, the performer can play, sing, and dance simultaneously.

Horn made of an elephant tusk with a side aperture, Kenya.

Buzz-disc, South Africa.

Mangbetu: a signal horn with a side aperture, Congo.

The African horn differs from the European kind and is used for different purposes. Made of antelope horn, ivory or some other natural material, it has a round side aperture for blowing. There is often a small second hole, which when closed with the thumb or fingers allows the instrument to play a second tone – a tone, two or three tones away from the fundamental tone. Such horns, with or without a second hole, are used in Africa in ensembles of differently tuned instruments. The horn may be used for sending messages by "speech tones", thereby acting as an equivalent to the "talking drum."

Side-blown ivory horn.

Wooden horn, South Africa.

Clay horn, South Africa.

Signal horn with a side aperture, South Africa.

IDIOPHONES

Idiophones are the simplest African instruments, and the most widely used since ancient times. These include bells, clappers and scrapers, xylophones, and drums carved of a single piece of wood. Many of them are of indefinite pitch, such as the struck idiophones, the shaken idiophones and the lithophones. Others are of definite pitch, such as the xylophone and the mbira (thumb-piano). In this group, the xylophone plays a particularly important role as a solo instrument in both small groups and ensembles of up to 30 players. Some tribes of southeastern Africa are famous for their xylophone ensembles, which also include instruments of other families.

An important idiophone is the mbira (sansa, kalimba), a melody instrument capable of playing complex themes. Another leading idiophone is the slit drum, which varies greatly in size from very small to very large. It is used both as a "talking drum," (i.e. for transmitting signals and messages), and as a musical instrument, in combination with membranophone drums.

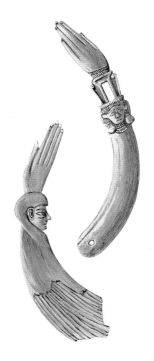

Ancient Egyptian clappers made of hippopotamus teeth.

Struck, Shaken and Friction Instruments

These are instruments that are sounded by striking two parts together. They produce a characteristic clatter of indefinite pitch. Found in all continents, they vary enormously in their design and material: wood, bamboo, stone, bone, metal, and so on. Some of the struck idiophones are intended to imitate the clapping of hands.

Ancient Egyptian clappers made of elephant tusks.

Ritual naosistrum used in a religious ceremony. Relief from Abydos.

Ancient Egyptian naosistrums, the New Kingdom, 16th – 11th centuries B. C.

Metal castanets, Algeria.

A native of Togo with a time-beating idiophone made of a gourd.

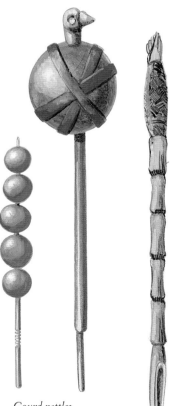

These idiophones are rattles made of hollow containers with small hard objects inside. The sound is produced by shaking. These instruments have been used since ancient times in various parts of the world. They may be made of dried gourd, bamboo, wood, bast, tortoise shell, horn, bone, skin, clay, and metal. Modern versions are made of plastic.

Gourd rattles.

Ivory clapper from Nigeria.

Some of the oldest idiophones found in nature or made by man out of wood, bamboo, stone or bone, these instruments are used to beat time for dancing. They are sounded by being hit against each other, against the ground, or against a resonating object.

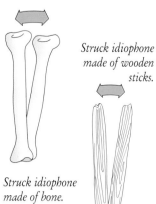

Struck idiophone made of wooden sticks.

Struck idiophone made of bone.

Time-beating idiophone made of a gourd, Ghana.

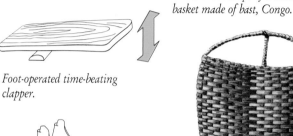

Foot-operated time-beating clapper.

Rattle in the shape of a double basket made of bast, Congo.

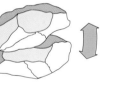

Struck idiophone of stones.

Rattle made from donkey's jaw.

Basket rattle made of bast, Congo.

Double rattle made of interlaced stems, Congo.

Cabaza

This is an instrument of African origin that later spread to Latin America. In its original form it was made of a dried gourd, either round or, less often, egg-shaped, with a handle affixed; modern cabazas are made of wood or of Bakelite. It is covered with a network of beads, beans, or pebbles threaded together.

African cabaza with external rattling devices.

The cabaza is held in the right hand and shaken, or hit with the left hand; the sound is produced by the beads scraping against its surface.
In West Africa, the dance tradition and its rhythmic basis involve the use of the cabaza in combination with metal bells. Instead of beads, some instruments are strung with snake vertebrae.

Cabaza made of a gourd, Nigeria.

Sistrum

A metal idiophone, it was used in ancient Egypt in the cult of Isis, and was also found in other countries of the Mediterranean, in northeastern Africa, and in South-East Asia. The instrument consists of a metal frame bent to form a long loop with a handle. Metal rods pass loosely through holes in the frame and cross it at a slight angle, their ends bent outside the frame. In some sistrum varieties metal rings are strung on each rod, which jingle when shaken. Sistrums were used by Egyptian priests in rites.
Modern sistrums are of simpler construction.

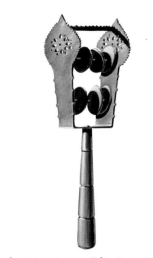

Abyssinian sistrum, Ethiopia.

Ancient Egyptian sistrum.

Girl playing the sistrum. Ancient Egypt, mural from the Necropolis in Thebes, the New Kingdom.

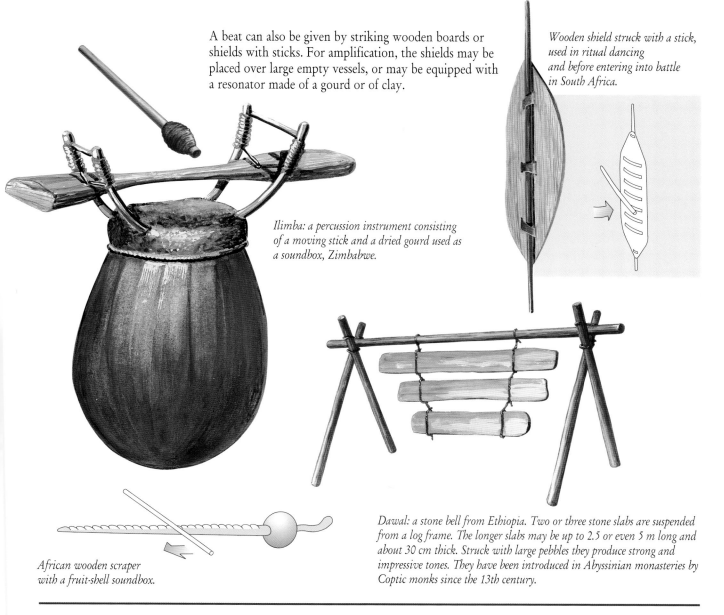

A beat can also be given by striking wooden boards or shields with sticks. For amplification, the shields may be placed over large empty vessels, or may be equipped with a resonator made of a gourd or of clay.

Wooden shield struck with a stick, used in ritual dancing and before entering into battle in South Africa.

Ilimba: a percussion instrument consisting of a moving stick and a dried gourd used as a soundbox, Zimbabwe.

African wooden scraper with a fruit-shell soundbox.

Dawal: a stone bell from Ethiopia. Two or three stone slabs are suspended from a log frame. The longer slabs may be up to 2.5 or even 5 m long and about 30 cm thick. Struck with large pebbles they produce strong and impressive tones. They have been introduced in Abyssinian monasteries by Coptic monks since the 13th century.

Sonorous Vessel

These are hollow vessels of a variety of materials, shapes, and sizes: pots, fruit shells, mugs, bowls, and bottles, may be used as percussion idiophones. The sound is produced by shaking or striking with beaters or hands. In some cases, water is used to adjust the tuning.

An African water drum: two halves of dried gourds of different size, with water poured into the larger one and the smaller one placed inside.

Sonorous vessel with pebbles.

Sonorous vessels: gourds filled with water.

Sansa

The sansa is an African plucked idiophone. It consists of a varying number of metal or reed tongues attached side by side to a wooden base – a board or a resonator box. The sound is produced by plucking the free ends with the thumbs or index fingers. The pitch of each tongue depends on its length, which can be adjusted by pushing it backwards or forwards beneath the bracket that holds it in place.

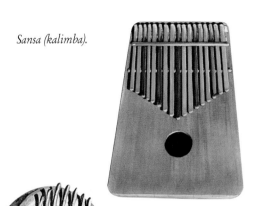

Sansa (kalimba).

Sansa with a soundbox, Cameroon.

Sansa (mbira), eastern Nigeria.

Sansa (mbira).

Sansa with a soundboard, South Africa.

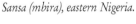

In Europe, the sansa is known as thumb piano. The instrument's original name is mbira; sansa is a word of Babylonian origin, used by ethnomusicologists and exhibition organizers. The largest instrument of this group is the gwenambira. It has 32 tongues, the lower-pitched being to the left of the centre, and the higher-pitched to the right.

Sansa with a dried gourd as a resonator, South Africa.

Bell

African wooden bell.

Ethiopian temple bell with a triple beater.

Hollow wooden bells are often richly decorated, and can have one, two, or even three beaters.

Wooden bell, Gabon.

Bells cast in metal are covered with fabric. The sound produced when the bell is struck with a beater varies according to the diameter of the bell and the point at which it is struck.

Double bell (aporo) with a beater, Cameroon.

Wooden Drum, Slit Drum

The authentic African slit drum is a signalling instrument, sometimes enormous in size. It is also found in South-East Asia, Oceania, and South America. The instrument is made of a hollowed wooden trunk, with two rectangular slits of different widths along the flat upper side. When the slit drum is struck on the thinner side (around the slits), the sound is lower in pitch; when the drum is struck on the thicker side, the sound is higher. This instrument can be struck with fingers, hands, or wooden beaters. The sounds produced are about a third or a fourth apart.

Set of African slit drums.

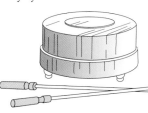

Modern slit drum with beaters.

African wooden drum from Congo, shaped like a human body. This instrument is played by moving the stick up and down in the slit.

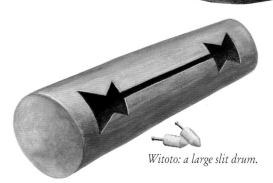

Witoto: a large slit drum.

Xylophone

In xylophones, the sound source is a set of tuned wooden bars struck with beaters. The name derives from the Greek words *xylon* (wood) and *phone* (sound). The bars are often placed on a frame, and arranged in order of pitch. Resonators are placed below them to amplify, enrich, and prolong the instrument's brief and fairly dry sound.

Primitive as well as more sophisticated xylophones are found in Africa, South-East Asia (as part of the Indonesian folk-orchestra, the gamelan), Oceania, and South America.

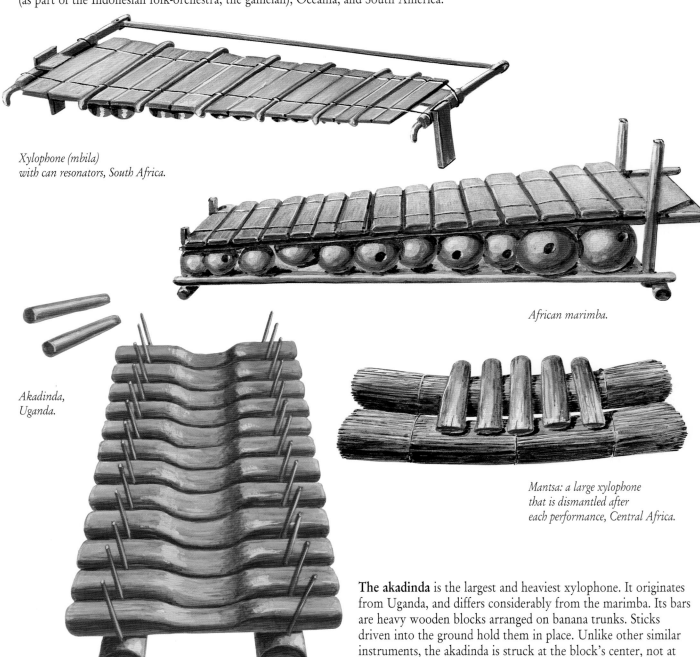

Xylophone (mbila)
with can resonators, South Africa.

African marimba.

Akadinda,
Uganda.

Mantsa: a large xylophone
that is dismantled after
each performance, Central Africa.

The akadinda is the largest and heaviest xylophone. It originates from Uganda, and differs considerably from the marimba. Its bars are heavy wooden blocks arranged on banana trunks. Sticks driven into the ground hold them in place. Unlike other similar instruments, the akadinda is struck at the block's center, not at the rim. The instrument may have between 12 and 17 bars, and a set of akadindas may cover a range of four to five octaves. The bass akadinda is usually placed in a shallow pit in the ground.

MEMBRANOPHONES

Drums are membranophones that are known all over the world. They have been used by shamans and fortune-tellers, in pagan rites, as signal and military instruments, and for accompanying songs and dances. They are still widely popular as folk instruments. In the 18th century, many improved versions were introduced into European orchestras. Drums have membranes made of skin (now increasingly often of plastic) at one or both ends. The shells can be made of wood, clay, metal, or thick paper. The variety of shapes and sizes is immense: cylindrical, conical, barrel-shaped, cup-shaped, bowl-shaped, hourglass-shaped, standing on legs, elongated, stretched on a frame, rubbed, and so on. Drums can be sounded with hands, beaters, brushes, or various other implements. Drum ensembles exist in various sizes, from small groups of two to four drummers to large ones of up to 15 (in Burundi, Uganda, Rwanda, and other countries of Eastern Africa). The drums are tuned to different pitches, allowing large ensembles to play melodies.

Drum

Long drum, Nigeria.

With their shells of different shapes and depths, African drums allow not only the playing of complex rhythmic combinations but also the expression of a wide range of nuances and tone colors. In that respect, African drums are the most sophisticated in the world. Within the ensembles, drummers have different roles: the leader is a soloist who is free to improvise on the traditional structures and rhythmic patterns, while the other drummers repeat the rhythmic patterns. There are dozens of types and hundreds of varieties of African drums.

African wooden drum shaped like an hourglass, Dahomey.

Some membranophones are of a definite pitch, while others (such as the hourglass-shaped pressure drum above) are capable of producing different tones of indefinite pitch. This drum's two heads are connected with straps that can be tightened or loosened with the hands. Thus, the drummer can control the tension of the membranes and change the pitch as desired. This drum imitates human "tonal speech." Sometimes, seeds or beads may be placed inside the shell or jingles may be strung at the rim for more interesting effects.

Dancers with hourglass drums, Tanzania.

In African culture drums are used in all spheres of everyday life: to regulate the rhythm of labor, as an accompaniment to dancing, and in all kinds of religious and political ceremonies. "Talking drums" are capable of conveying signals over a large distance. Africans attribute magical powers to their drums. They believe that these instruments house the sacred spirits of their drummer predecessors. The making of a drum is a special ritual, and the instruments are often kept in richly decorated containers, not unlike Christian shrines. The drums are often perceived as a symbol of power and authority. This is why African leaders are often accompanied by official drummers on their visits.

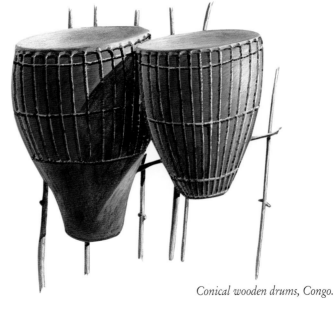

Conical wooden drums, Congo.

"Talking" drum (kalungu), Nigeria. It is struck with a curved beater with a hemispherical tip. The pitch can be modified by adjusting the tension of the membrane by tightening or loosening the tensioning ropes, and thus the intonation of the human voice can be imitated.

Some drums are used in pairs. Female qualities are attributed to the lower-pitched instrument, and male qualities to the higher-pitched one. Drums that are capable of producing pitches within the range of at least an octave are suitable for the imitation of the intonations of the Yoruba language in West Africa.

Single-head cylindrical wooden drum, Ivory Coast.

Single-head cylindrical wooden drum, North Africa. The shell is covered with skin.

Naqqara, Egypt.

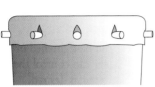

Primitive and uneven tensioning of the single-head drum's membrane.

Single-head conical wooden drum (itenga), Uganda.

Wenda ngoma drum, South Africa. This kind of drum is often played by women.

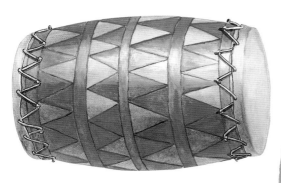

Large barrel-shaped double-head
wooden drum, Nigeria.
It is played resting on the ground,
struck with the hands
on the two heads.

Mukupiela drum.

Double-head cylindrical wooden
drum, with rope-tensioned skin
membranes, Nigeria.

South African drum (isigubo),
carved of a single piece of wood,
with two rope-tightened heads.
The isigubo is struck with beaters
on both heads.

Tensioning with zigzagging cord
used on double-head drums.

Set of small goblet-shaped
wooden drums, Ivory Coast.

Goblet-shaped single-head
wooden drum, Ivory Coast.

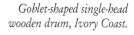

Goblet-shaped single-head
wooden drum, Nigeria.

Timpani (kettle drums) are single-head membranophones of definite pitch. The name derives from the Latin "tympanum" (drum), and suggests a connection with the Greek "tympanon" and the European "thop."

Timpani prototypes were used by the earliest humans. Similar instruments have been found in Asia, the Mediterranean, and among African tribes and American Indians. They were used in rites, rituals, and games, as well as for military purposes.

Two main types of timpani were known in older times: small, portable ones, and large, mighty noise-makers. Perhaps the large variety best correspond to our own notion of this instrument.

African drum standing on "human" legs.

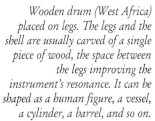

Conical wooden drum (kobago), Ethiopia.

Wooden drum (West Africa) placed on legs. The legs and the shell are usually carved of a single piece of wood, the space between the legs improving the instrument's resonance. It can be shaped as a human figure, a vessel, a cylinder, a barrel, and so on.

Wooden kettle-drum, Central Africa.

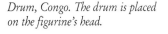

Drum, Congo. The drum is placed on the figurine's head.

Friction Drum

This is a drum of average size, found in Africa, North America, and Europe. The body may have the shape of a pot, a vase, a cylinder, a cone, a barrel, or a ball, and may be made of wood, fruit shell, clay, metal, or cardboard. A membrane is stretched across the top, and in its center a rope, a thick string, or horsehair is tied in a knot. Sometimes the string is replaced by a wooden stick. The sound is produced by rubbing the rope or stick with the hands. The vibrations are transferred to the membrane and it produces fairly long and loud hoarse sounds of indefinite pitch, resembling a lion's roar.

Ingungu: friction drum made of a gourd, South Africa.

Friction drums.

CHORDOPHONES

Chordophone instruments are found all over the continent, in a variety of types and shapes. Most of them are plucked: either simple harps developed from hunting bows or mwets (musical bows with one or more soundboxes and varying numbers of strings), lyres, various zithers, lutes and fiddles.

Musical Bow

Prototypes of the most primitive stringed instruments, musical bows have been found around the world and are still in use in Africa, Asia (India, Indonesia), America, Australia and Oceania. They developed from the hunting bow and largely preserved its shape.

Musical bows usually have one or two strings stretched between the ends of a long flexible stick, curved like a hunting bow. More developed variants also include a soundbox, which may be part of the body or separate.

The strings are either plucked with fingers or a plectrum or bowed. Players sit or stand, using their mouths as a resonator, or supporting the musical bow on a hollow object to improve the resonance.

Several musical bows joined together and with a common soundbox, Central Africa.

Several musical bows joined together and with a common soundbox, West Africa.

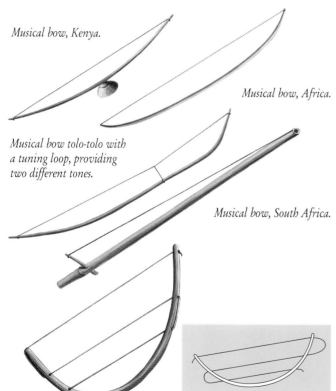

Musical bow, Kenya.

Musical bow, Africa.

Musical bow tolo-tolo with a tuning loop, providing two different tones.

Musical bow, South Africa.

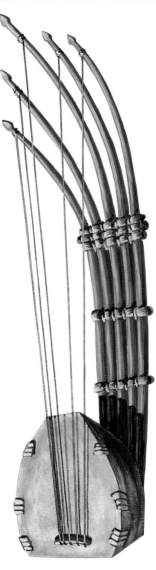

Pluriarc: a set of several musical bows tuned to different pitches, with a common soundbox, South Africa.

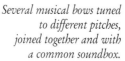

Musical bow with a single zigzagging string providing three different tones. The mouth cavity is used as a resonator.

Several musical bows tuned to different pitches, joined together and with a common soundbox.

Lyre

The African lyre is similar to the ancient one and has the same specifics. It developed in two shapes, round and quadrangular, and is used as an accompanying instrument in a number of rituals and religious feasts. African lyres vary regionally in construction, decoration, and tuning. In ancient Egypt, the lyre was widely used in the royal court.

*Ancient Egyptian lyre.
A mural at the Necropolis in Thebes, 18th dynasty, 16th-14th centuries B.C. Detail.*

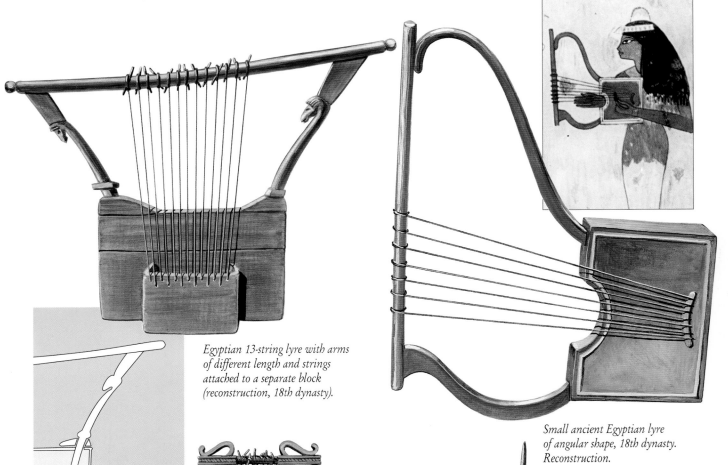

Egyptian 13-string lyre with arms of different length and strings attached to a separate block (reconstruction, 18th dynasty).

Cross-section of an Egyptian lyre. Detail.

Small ancient Egyptian lyre of angular shape, 18th dynasty. Reconstruction.

Ethiopian lyre (bagana), used by aristocrats and priests (an interesting comparison can be made with the round kerar).

Kerar: primitive Ethiopian six-string lyre. The soundbox is made of tortoise shell or of a pot. The two arms are connected with a crossbar to which the strings are attached. Often richly decorated, the kerar is used by tribal healers to chase evil spirits away from the sick. The instrument is regarded as having magical properties, and this is reflected in the decoration (which often includes mirrors and amulets).

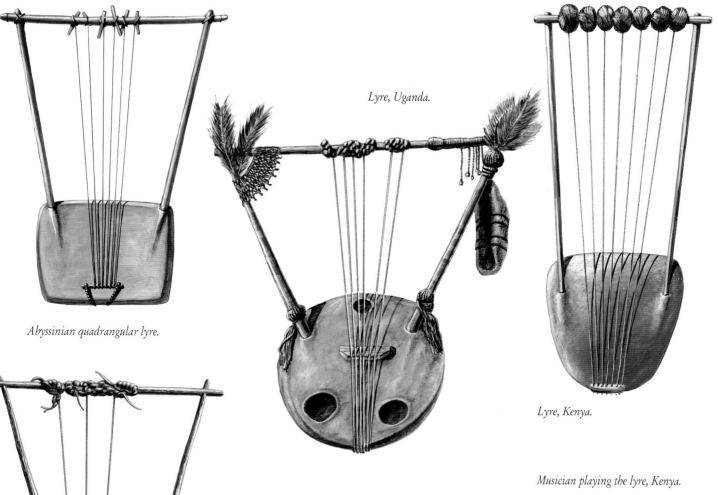

Abyssinian quadrangular lyre.

Lyre, Uganda.

Lyre, Kenya.

Three-string kissar, Sudan.

Musician playing the lyre, Kenya.

The African lyre is often played as accompaniment to a vocal performance. The player plucks the strings with the right hand, close to the cross-bar, with a plectrum made of skin or bone. The instrument is supported by a strap on the left hand, the fingers of which are spread out over the strings. The strings are tuned to a pentatonic scale. The instrument is found under different names in different parts of the continent: kerar in Ethiopia, tanbur in Sudan, kissar, rebaba, and so on. In Ethiopia, a very high-pitched lyre known as bagana is found, with a massive body and ten strings.

Harp

The main difference between the harp and the lyre is that the harp's strings run at an acute angle from the soundbox to the neck, while the lyre's strings are perpendicular to both the soundbox and the crossbar. As compared to the majority of plucked instruments, a characteristic feature of the harp is the vertical plane of strings and the lack of a bridge and fingerboard.

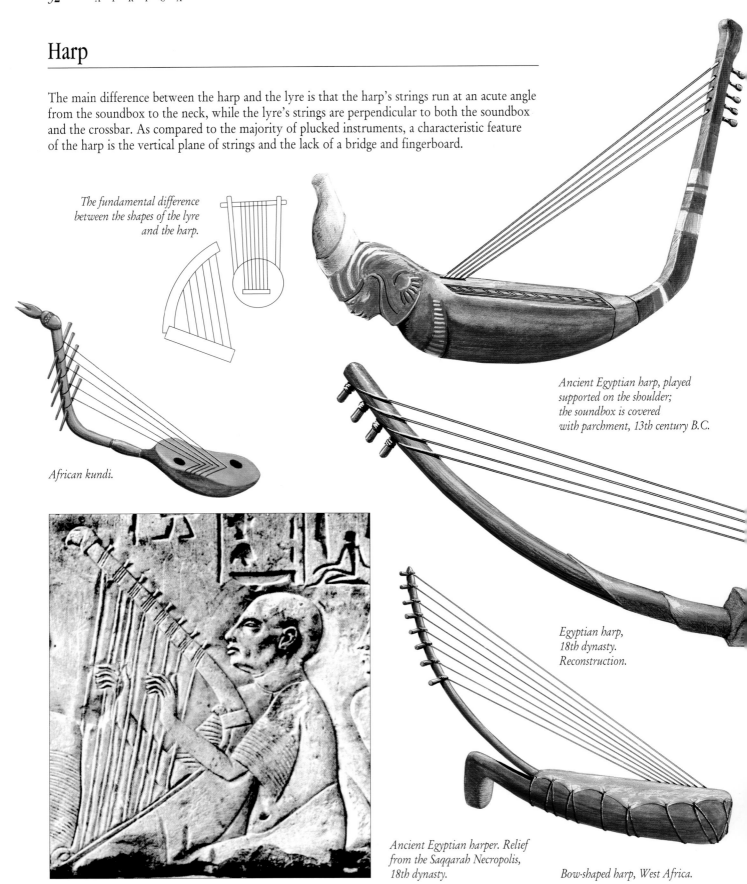

The fundamental difference between the shapes of the lyre and the harp.

African kundi.

Ancient Egyptian harp, played supported on the shoulder; the soundbox is covered with parchment, 13th century B.C.

Egyptian harp, 18th dynasty. Reconstruction.

Ancient Egyptian harper. Relief from the Saqqarah Necropolis, 18th dynasty.

Bow-shaped harp, West Africa.

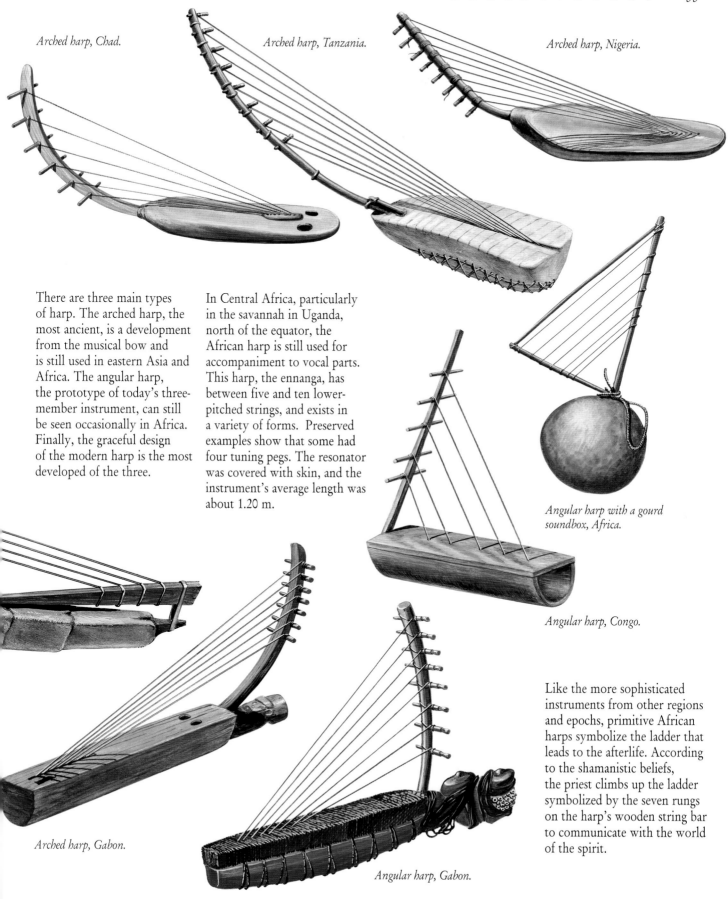

Arched harp, Chad.

Arched harp, Tanzania.

Arched harp, Nigeria.

There are three main types of harp. The arched harp, the most ancient, is a development from the musical bow and is still used in eastern Asia and Africa. The angular harp, the prototype of today's three-member instrument, can still be seen occasionally in Africa. Finally, the graceful design of the modern harp is the most developed of the three.

In Central Africa, particularly in the savannah in Uganda, north of the equator, the African harp is still used for accompaniment to vocal parts. This harp, the ennanga, has between five and ten lower-pitched strings, and exists in a variety of forms. Preserved examples show that some had four tuning pegs. The resonator was covered with skin, and the instrument's average length was about 1.20 m.

Angular harp with a gourd soundbox, Africa.

Angular harp, Congo.

Arched harp, Gabon.

Angular harp, Gabon.

Like the more sophisticated instruments from other regions and epochs, primitive African harps symbolize the ladder that leads to the afterlife. According to the shamanistic beliefs, the priest climbs up the ladder symbolized by the seven rungs on the harp's wooden string bar to communicate with the world of the spirit.

Zither

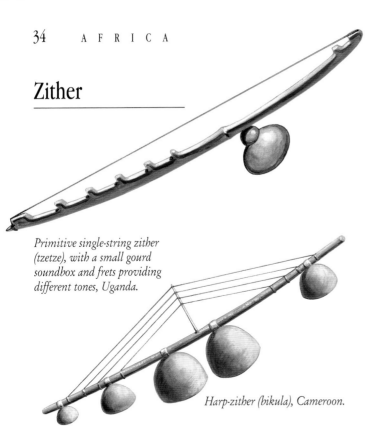

Primitive single-string zither (tzetze), with a small gourd soundbox and frets providing different tones, Uganda.

Cradle-shaped African zithers, made from a single hollowed piece of wood with a single long string zigzagging over it. The soundbox is often covered with skin. The strings may be made of silk, gut, horsehair, or metal – whatever is available.

Harp-zither (bikula), Cameroon.

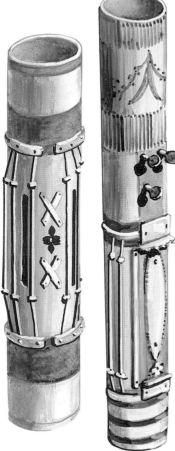

The valiha, a round zither of Madagascar, has 14 or more "strings" separated from the bamboo piece itself. It is 80 cm long and about 7.5 cm wide. The "strings" are tuned with a small movable bridge. The instrument is held at an angle, and the strings are plucked with the fingernails. The valiha probably arrived from South-East Asia five or six centuries ago. It is an interesting fact that this music shows a pronounced European influence. The metal strings of the 20th-century valiha have changed the quality of its sound. Modern valihas are made of a variety of materials.

Elegant cradle-shaped zither, Uganda.

Two valihas: multi-string bamboo-tube zithers, Madagascar.

Totombito zither, Congo.

Fiddle

African fiddles are made of wood; they are either carved from a single block, or the back is made separately. The player sits on the ground. The bow position and the playing technique are completely different from those used for stringed instruments in the modern European orchestra.

Egyptian rebab used for accompaniment. Its soundbox is trapezoidal, its sides made of wood, and its belly and back of parchment.

Rebab, Morocco.

Four-string fiddle with a resonator made of a cardboard box, South Africa.

African fiddles are made in many varieties. Some are carved of a single piece of wood, with an attached neck/fingerboard of a different wood. Others have long necks, slightly projecting below the soundbox, to accommodate the long strings. Still others have a spike like a cello and the instrument can be turned so that the bow touches different strings without changing its plane. Some fiddles are goblet-shaped.

Rebab, northwestern Africa. This instrument has a narrow, elongated soundbox, concave in its lower part, and with soundholes in the upper part. The pegbox is bent back. The two strings are made of gut and rest on a low bridge. Under various names, the rebab is found in Egypt, northwestern Africa, India, the Malay Archipelago, Java (heart-shaped), Sumatra, and Central Asia.

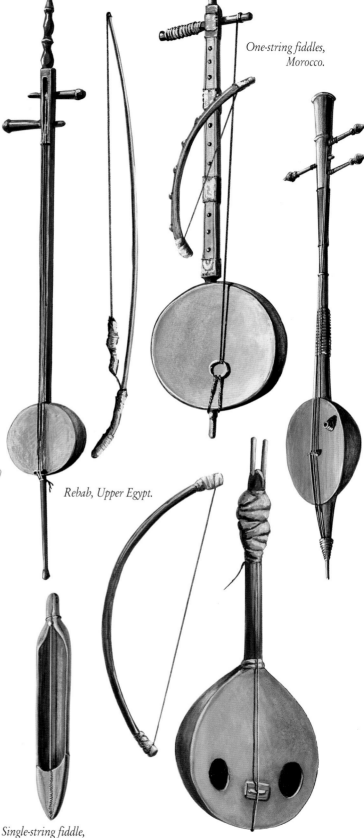

One-string fiddles, Morocco.

Rebab, Upper Egypt.

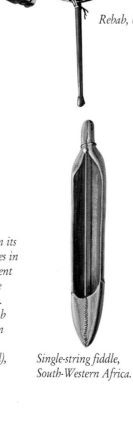

Single-string fiddle, South-Western Africa.

One-string African fiddle.

Lute

Ramkie: primitive guitar from South Africa, with a soundbox made of a gourd or a can and covered with pelt.

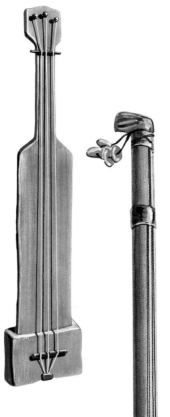

Ancient Egyptian lute, 16th – 14th centuries B. C.

Lute with a skin resonator, skin membranes, and sonorous metal plates in the upper part of the neck, Burkina Faso.

Ancient Egyptian lute. Reconstruction.

Egyptian lute, very similar to the ancient Egyptian model: a long wooden body with a resonator made of skin, a stick for a neck, and tightly attached strings.

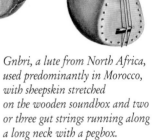

Gnbri, a lute from North Africa, used predominantly in Morocco, with sheepskin stretched on the wooden soundbox and two or three gut strings running along a long neck with a pegbox.

Ancient Egyptian lute player. Relief from the Saqqarah Necropolis, 18th dynasty.

Senegalese musician playing the kora.

Harp-lute kora, West Africa.

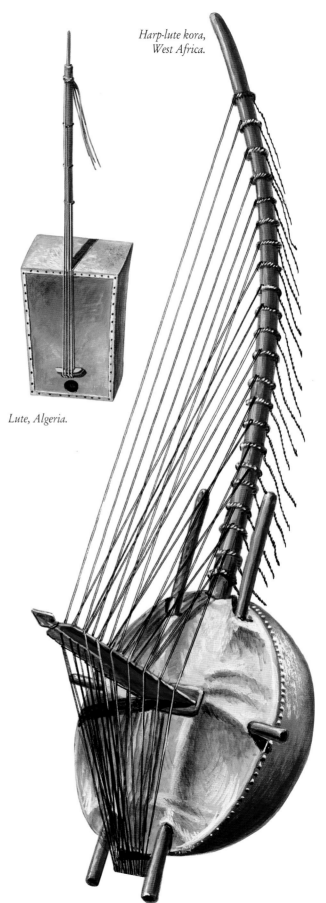

Lute, Algeria.

The stringed instrument called kora is a harp-lute used by the Mandinka people in Mali, Guinea, Senegal, Gambia and the northeastern part of the Ivory Coast. It has been in use for at least 200 years, and was first described in the literature on African music as "a large 18-string harp". Today's kora has 21 strings divided into two parallel groups running parallel to the soundbox. There are eleven strings on the left and ten on the right, passing through a bridge with the respective number of slits. The player plucks the strings with his thumbs and forefingers. As with some other African instruments, the notes of the scale are distributed between the two hands.

Part of the repertory of this instrument was inherited from professional musicians who played two older instruments: the balo (an 18-block xylophone) and the konting (a small five-string lute). The kora is usually used to accompany singing, though solos and duos are not unusual. One such solo is the theme of the Gambian national radio, which can be heard twice daily.

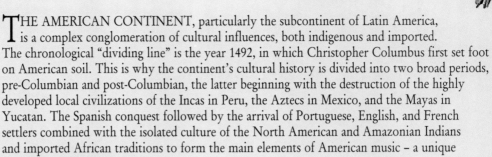

AMERICA

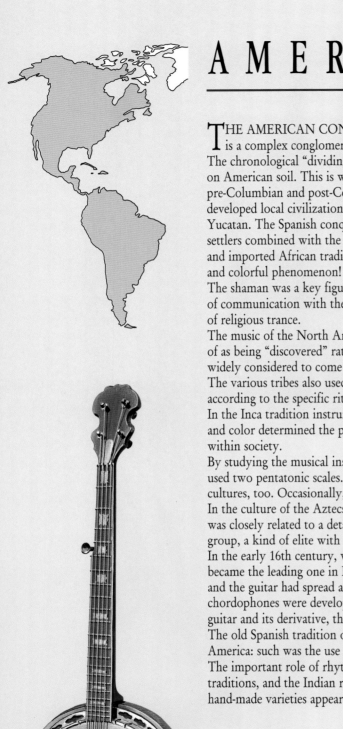

T HE AMERICAN CONTINENT, particularly the subcontinent of Latin America, is a complex conglomeration of cultural influences, both indigenous and imported. The chronological "dividing line" is the year 1492, in which Christopher Columbus first set foot on American soil. This is why the continent's cultural history is divided into two broad periods, pre-Columbian and post-Columbian, the latter beginning with the destruction of the highly developed local civilizations of the Incas in Peru, the Aztecs in Mexico, and the Mayas in Yucatan. The Spanish conquest followed by the arrival of Portuguese, English, and French settlers combined with the isolated culture of the North American and Amazonian Indians and imported African traditions to form the main elements of American music – a unique and colorful phenomenon!

The shaman was a key figure in the culture of Amazonian Indians. Music was his chief means of communication with the spirits of the past and the future and helped him to achieve a state of religious trance.

The music of the North American Indians was primarily vocal, and songs were thought of as being "discovered" rather than willfully composed: the "discovery"of a new song was widely considered to come from the subconscious or through supernatural intervention. The various tribes also used instruments, particularly drums and rattles, which were chosen according to the specific rite or ceremony, and also had a spirtual significance.

In the Inca tradition instruments were divided into "male" and "female." The classification and color determined the player's social status. Trumpeters, for example, were highly respected within society.

By studying the musical instruments of the Incas, experts have been able to ascertain that they used two pentatonic scales. The use of two pentatonic scales can be traced to other Indian cultures, too. Occasionally, seven-tone scales were also found.

In the culture of the Aztecs in Mexico, musicians had a very high social status. The repertory was closely related to a detailed religious calendar, and the musicians formed a special privileged group, a kind of elite with enormous professional responsibilities.

In the early 16th century, when the colonization of America began, the Spanish lute school became the leading one in Europe. By the early 16th century, the lute, the rebab, the harp, and the guitar had spread across America. Over the next two centuries, a number of plucked chordophones were developed on the basis of the lute. In America the lute was replaced by the guitar and its derivative, the Portuguese guitar, a close relative of the mandolin and the banjo.

The old Spanish tradition of using stringed instruments for rhythmic purposes continued in America: such was the use not only of the guitar, the lute and the harp, but also of the banjo. The important role of rhythm was common to the Spanish folklore, the African musical traditions, and the Indian religious rituals. Thus, beside the existing instruments, improvised hand-made varieties appeared.

AEROPHONES

The aerophones of North and South America are made of wood, bamboo, clay or bone (including human bone). Research has uncovered a precursor of the ancient double clarinet (aulos) among the instruments of the Urua Indians, consisting of two cane pipes, one longer than the other, and equipped with vibrating reeds.

The aerophone group also includes primitive trumpets as well as free aerophones such as bull-roarers and buzz-discs.

Bull-roarer

Bull-roarers are among the most ancient sound-making devices, dating back to the Stone Age and are known all over the world. They belong to the free aerophone group, producing vibrations in the surrounding air when agitated. A bull-roarer is a piece of wood (occasionally of bone), of various shapes and sizes, tied to a string. When whirled round above the head, it produces a screaming sound, softer or louder depending on the speed of rotation. The pitch can also be adjusted by changing the speed. Bull-roarers are used as toys or in magic rites.

Bull-roarers, Brazil.

Eskimo bull-roarers.

Bull-roarer, Canada.

Bull-roarer, North America.

Canadian Eskimos used this bull-roarer to imitate the voices of spirits and bring about conception. It might have also been used to announce social events and gatherings. The notched edge makes the sound louder.

Buzz-discs, South America.

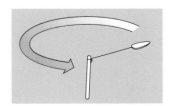

Whirling a bull-roarer.

Buzz-disc

A disc of wood, bone, paper, or plastic is pierced twice in the center, and a string is passed through one hole and back through the other and tied. The disc is rotated to wind up the string, and when the string unwinds it makes a whirring noise. This can be repeated, using the momentum that winds the string up again.

Whistling top, South America.

Whistling Top

These are made of hollow objects (fruit shells, small gourds, metal boxes, reels) pierced with holes and sometimes equipped with a mechanism (as in the case of the humming top), which are spun by a string or by a spiral handle. Where there is a string it is wound around the object, setting it spinning when pulled. The air passing through the holes produces a whistling sound. In the case of the humming top, the toy is pumped with a spiral handle and the toy spins, emitting a sound of relatively definite pitch.

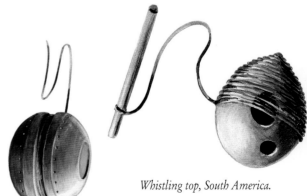

Yo-yo, the U. S.

Whistling top, South America.

Flutes in Unusual Shapes

These instruments belong to the end-blown flute group. They either have a simple blowing hole or a lip-plate. Some have no fingerholes and play a single tone, while others are equipped with a varying number of fingerholes and are thus capable of producing different pitches.

Although continually threatened by the Aztecs, neighboring tribes adopted many of their customs and musical traditions. Even today, for example, the Cuna Indians in Panama make an ocarina-shaped wind instrument of clay or stone. This instrument is found in most pre-Columbian cultures in Central and South America.

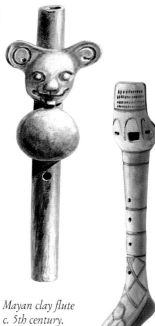

Mayan flute in the shape of a man playing a polyphonic flute, 5th century.

Mayan clay flute c. 5th century.

Leg-shaped Aztec flute made of clay.

Peruvian clay flute made of two connected vessels, each half-filled with water. When air is blown into the opening of the rear vessel, the water level in the front one rises, forcing air through the whistle.

Peruvian clay flute in the shape of a seated flautist.

Flute made of a fruit shell that produces a single tone, South America.

The pot whistle is an ingenious instrument that uses the pressure of water to send air through the whistle. The same principle is applied in the ancient Greek and Roman hydraulis or water organ.

Clay flutes, Ecuador.

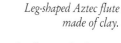

Wooden flute, British Columbia. This flute of anthropomorphic shape and complex construction plays four different tones. To prevent the wood from splitting during the insertion of the side tubes it is tied with bast. This instrument is used in magic rites and ceremonies.

Clay flute, Costa Rica.

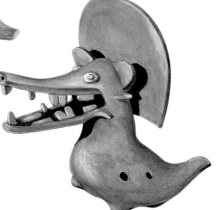

Chipaktli: Aztec flute made of a dragon-shaped pot.

End-blown Flute

End-blown flutes with simple holes exist in various sizes
and have a varying number of fingerholes. They are usually
cylindrical in bore, and may be made of bone, horn, wood,
bamboo, or metal. The notch may be held at an angle to the
player's mouth, and may have a sharp or rounded edge, be
narrower or wider, v-shaped, quadrangular, or u-shaped. This
instrument is found in all continents.

Clay flutes, Mexico.

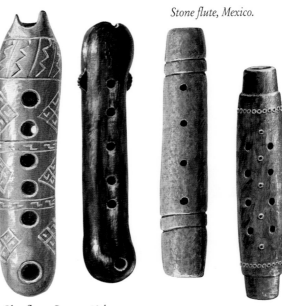

Stone flute, Mexico.

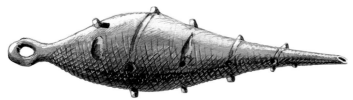

*Spindle-shaped copper flute
that produces a single tone,
Columbia.*

Flutes made of bone, Peru.

Unlike the Amazonian tribes, the Incas in Peru had a highly
developed civilization, the remains of which bear witness
to a relatively rich musical tradition. Many instruments were
made of clay and bone, including panpipes (antaras) and
pot whistles. In the culture of the native Peruvian population
aerophones dominated and there were no chordophones.

Clay flutes, Peru, c. 13th century.

*Stone flute, North America.
The eight fingerholes in two
parallel rows are decorated with
inlaid shells, the same decoration
forming a circle at each end
of the flute. As the instrument
is bored throughout, we can only
guess how it was played.*

Cane flute, Cuba.

*Cross-section of a primitive
transverse flute.*

Folk musician, Brazil.

Clay flute, Mexico.

Clay flute, Mexico, 14th century.

Transverse flute made of clay, Mexico, 4th – 8th centuries.

Ornamented clay flute, Panama.

Flute made of jaguar bone, British Guyana.

Mayan clay flute, c. 5th century.

Transverse flute made of wood, with six fingerholes, Bolivia.

Flute, Peru.

North American Indian from Missouri, holding a flute.

Aztec transverse flute, c. 5th century.

Wooden flute, Dakota, North America.

The flute played an important role in the musical traditions of North American Indians. It was most often used for love songs. The instrument in the illustration is about 60 cm long and decorated with leather straps. The fingerholes are skillfully and meticulously carved to facilitate the fingering.

Clay flute, Mexico, 7th century.

Flute made of human bone, Ohio. It was used in funeral ceremonies and in other rites of the Hopewell Indians of North America. A copper ring facilitates playing. The two grooves by the notch were probably used to tie the flute to a string for easier carrying.

Polyphonic Flute

These are primitive instruments in which air is blown into two or more tubes simultaneously. The tubes are usually joined side by side, tied with string. There are also instruments in which air is blown into several channels from a single mouthpiece. These flutes may be blown through an ordinary blowing hole or through a mouthpiece, and there may be two or more notches below it, depending on the number of tubes. Polyphonic flutes are made of stone, clay, bamboo, wood, metal, or plastic.

Triple flute made of limestone, Mexico, 5th century.

Mexican polyphonic flute made of clay, with two tubes, the longer one curved, 7th century.

Double transverse flute made of clay, Mexico, 6th – 8th centuries.

Double clay flute, Mexico, c. 5th century.

Bolivian double flute with notches, one of its tubes melodic and the other a drone.

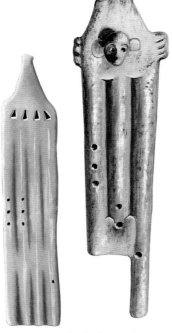

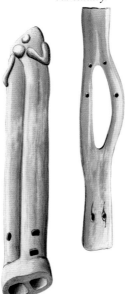

Mexican quadruple flute made of clay. The four notched tubes are played through a single blowing hole. As the instrument is fairly wide, the blowing hole is relatively narrow so that the air may be distributed equally between the tubes.

Mexican polyphonic flute made of clay, 7th century.

Primitive flute apertures.

Shapes of primitive polyphonic flutes.

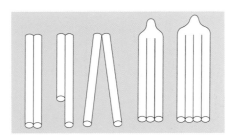

South American flute consisting of three separate pipes tied with bast, with notches almost at the pipes' center.

Double clay flute, Honduras.

Panpipe

Panpipes date back to at least 2000 years ago, and were
a feature of all early civilizations. They were made of various
materials: clay, stone, wood, and cane. In more recent times
they have also been made of metal and plastic. The variety
of tuning is immense. In Central America, the typical panpipe
had two rows of pipes, one pitched higher than the other,
providing a full chromatic scale.

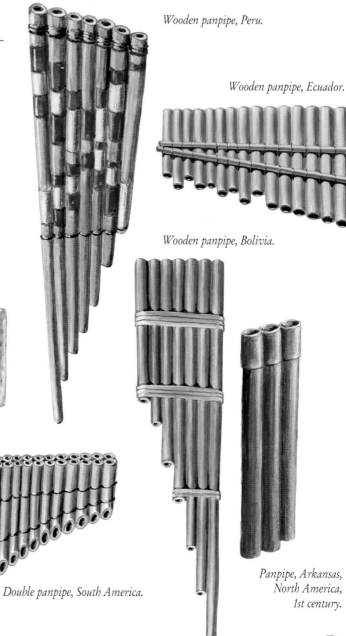

Wooden panpipe, Peru.

Wooden panpipe, Ecuador.

Wooden panpipe, Bolivia.

*Peruvian stone panpipe,
2nd century B. C.*

Double panpipe, South America.

*Panpipe, Arkansas,
North America,
1st century.*

*Peruvian musicians,
Nasca culture, 4th – 6th centuries.*

*Panpipe, Ohio, North
America, c. 2nd century.*

Clarinet

The clarinet group includes instruments in which the air column is caused to vibrate by the vibrations of a single reed, either carved from the tube itself (idioglottic clarinets), or inserted into it (heteroglottic clarinets). The reed may be inserted in the upper end of the instrument for the player to hold in his mouth, or in the lower end. Instruments of this type were made in ancient Egypt; from there, they spread to North Africa and Europe. They are found throughout Africa, in Asia and in America in a variety of sizes and designs. Clarinets may be made of cane, wood, bone, or plastic.

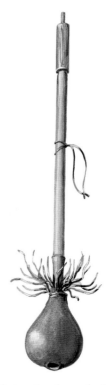

Primitive clarinet (guajiro) with an idioglottic reed, South America.

Clarinet made of human bone, California, 11th – 16th centuries.

Double clarinet (urua) of the Camajura Indians of Brazil: a giant instrument consisting of two tubes of different lengths with idioglottic reeds.

The construction of some primitive wooden clarinets.

Heteroglottic clarinet, North America.

South American clarinet: a tube with a reed inserted into a cow's horn.

South American heteroglottic clarinet with a gourd resonator.

Double clarinets, British Columbia. This instrument is found only on the northwest coast of North America. The double clarinet is used in ceremonies related to the winter solstice as well as in ritual dances.

Metal trumpet shaped like an animal horn, Bolivia.

Trumpet

The primitive trumpet was known around the globe as a military, hunting, shepherding, ritual, and cult instrument, made of bone, horn, wood, bamboo, gourd, coiled bark, clay, or metal. The blowing hole could be at the narrow end or in the instrument's side.

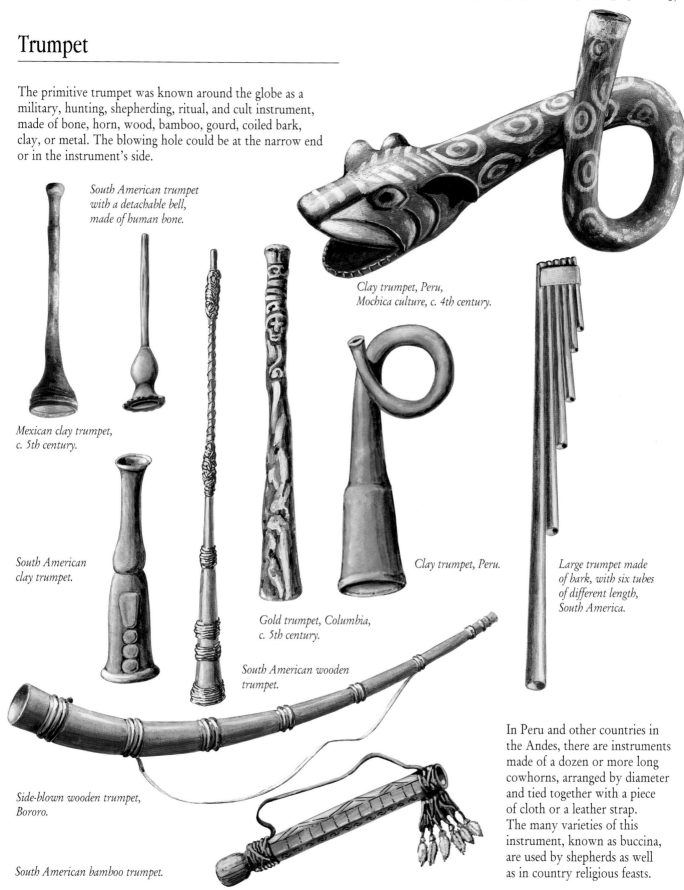

South American trumpet with a detachable bell, made of human bone.

Clay trumpet, Peru, Mochica culture, c. 4th century.

Mexican clay trumpet, c. 5th century.

South American clay trumpet.

Gold trumpet, Columbia, c. 5th century.

South American wooden trumpet.

Clay trumpet, Peru.

Large trumpet made of bark, with six tubes of different length, South America.

Side-blown wooden trumpet, Bororo.

South American bamboo trumpet.

In Peru and other countries in the Andes, there are instruments made of a dozen or more long cowhorns, arranged by diameter and tied together with a piece of cloth or a leather strap. The many varieties of this instrument, known as buccina, are used by shepherds as well as in country religious feasts.

IDIOPHONES

Like other early cultures that have existed for a long time in isolation, the Amazonian Indians have preserved ancient traditions in their music. Percussion instruments are the dominating group, and include a variety of friction idiophones made of wood or bone, shaken idiophones made of animal claws, fruit shells or nuts, struck idiophones, and, of course, a great variety of drums.

Time-beater made of cane, Hawaii.

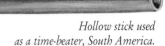

Hollow stick used as a time-beater, South America.

Struck, Shaken and Friction Idiophones

Primitive struck idiophones:

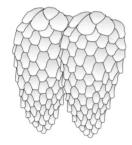

Pine cones.

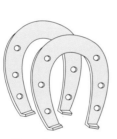

Horse-shoes.

Wooden spoons.

Rough wooden blocks with straps.

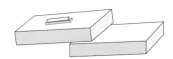

Polished wooden blocks with straps.

Struck idiophone, British Columbia. This instrument of the Indians from the northwest coast is a fine example of Indian art. The anthropomorphic carving uses the wood's natural shape. The handle is wound round with a leather strap for more comfortable handling. The shaman, an Indian healer, used this idiophone in rituals to call up the spirits of ancestors, the dead, and the gods.

Musician playing the aiotl, a struck idiophone made of tortoise shell, Mexico, c. 8th century.

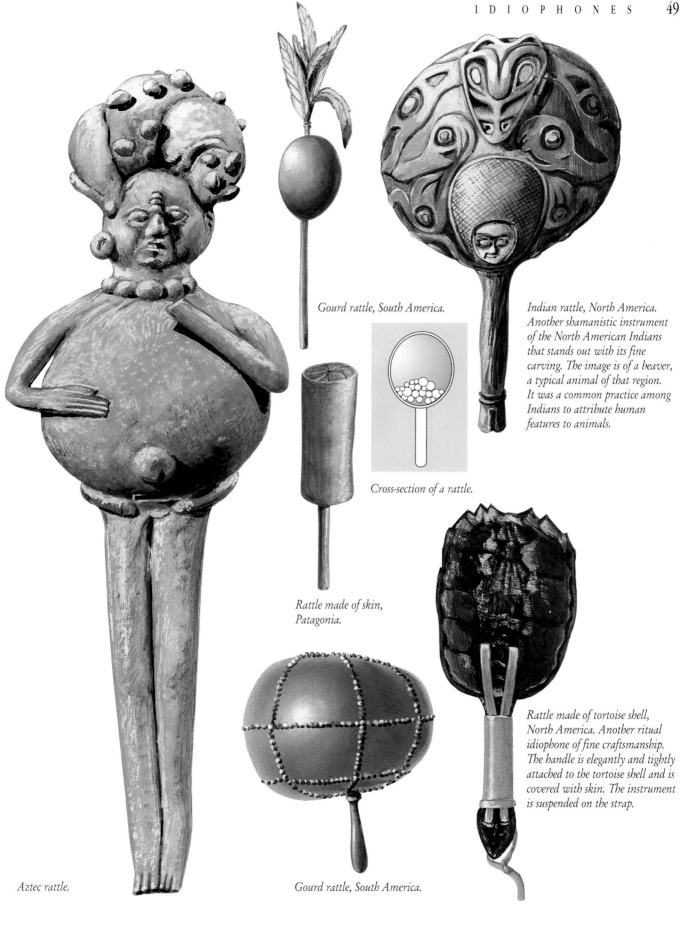

Gourd rattle, South America.

Cross-section of a rattle.

Rattle made of skin, Patagonia.

Indian rattle, North America. Another shamanistic instrument of the North American Indians that stands out with its fine carving. The image is of a beaver, a typical animal of that region. It was a common practice among Indians to attribute human features to animals.

Rattle made of tortoise shell, North America. Another ritual idiophone of fine craftsmanship. The handle is elegantly and tightly attached to the tortoise shell and is covered with skin. The instrument is suspended on the strap.

Aztec rattle.

Gourd rattle, South America.

The modern cabaza (pearl-maracas) is a hollow wooden cylinder with a handle, covered with a rough metal sheet and a network of metal beads. The instrument is held in the right hand and sounded by striking with the fingers of the left hand, or by rotating the instrument's body while the beaded net remains relatively still, or by holding the net with the left hand and turning the body with the right.

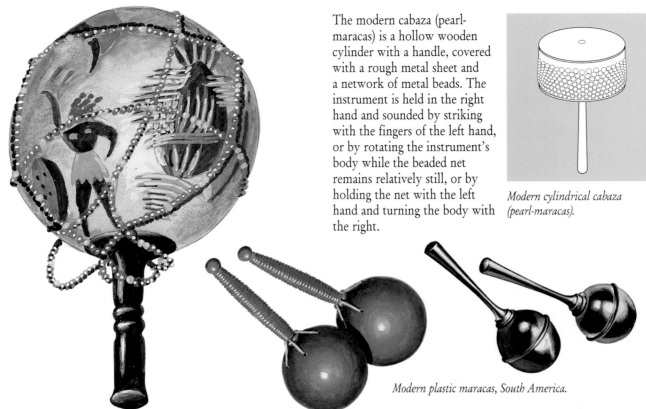

Modern cylindrical cabaza (pearl-maracas).

Modern plastic maracas, South America.

Modern plastic cabaza (pearl-maracas), South America.

Tubular Rattle (Chocalho)

A type of maracas made of a thick piece of reed, wood, or aluminum tube, closed at both ends, with seeds, pits, or lead shot inside. It is held either with both hands, one at each end, or with one hand, in the middle, and shaken to produce a rattling sound.

Ornamented bamboo chocalho, South America.

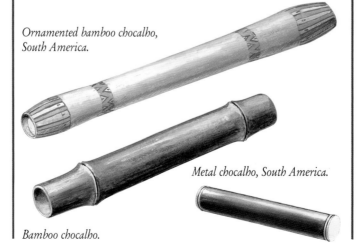

Metal chocalho, South America.

Bamboo chocalho.

Modern wooden maracas, South America.

Mexican sistrum (sonajero).

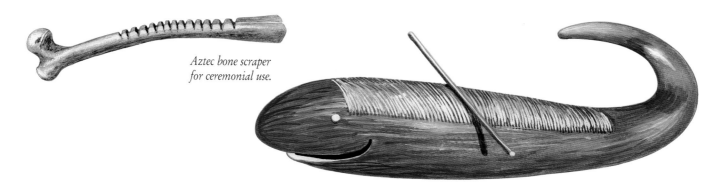

Aztec bone scraper for ceremonial use.

Gourd guiro in the shape of a whale, Cuba.

Guiro (Gourd scraper)

A friction idiophone of Cuban origin, the guiro is used in Latin America by dance bands and in various rites. The guiro is made of an elongated gourd cut with transverse notches along the surface of the curve. Slits are cut down one or both sides to emit air resonance; these are narrower towards the neck. The guiro is held in the left hand and scraped or struck with a thin metal rod or stick held in the right hand.

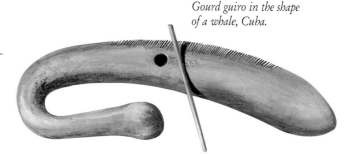

Gourd guiro, Cuba.

Gourd guiro.

Sapo Cubana

A Cuban and Brazilian version of the guiro, made of a bamboo pipe open at one end (resonator opening). A single longitudinal slit and numerous transverse cuts are made along the body of the pipe. The sound is produced by scraping with a fork-shaped stick.

Reco-reco (Scratcher)

This instrument was created to replace the sapo cubana in European musical practice, in view of the continent's climatic conditions. It is spindle-shaped, made of hardwood, with circular cuts and several resonator openings.

Sapo cubana.

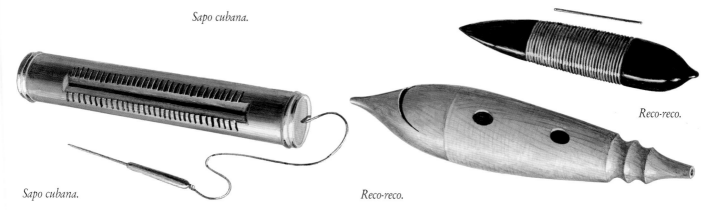

Sapo cubana.

Reco-reco.

Reco-reco.

Mexican bell.

Tambourine frame with jingle discs and no membrane, Brazil.

Wooden Drum (Slit Drum)

Aztec slit drum (teponaztli). This anthropomorphic drum is admirably proportioned. Its ornamentation is in the best traditions of the Mixtec Indians of ancient Mexico. The H-shaped slit is typical of these drums and responsible for their characteristic sound.

Slit drum, Costa Rica.

Wooden drum carved from a single piece of wood, with a tongue, Costa Rica. The form of this drum suggests an African influence.

Aztec slit drum (teponaztli), with carved tongues.

Barrel used as a folk drum.

Sonorous Vessel

Indian metal drum (pejote) filled with water, New Mexico. This sort of drum was used for magical and cult purposes. As the drum is filled with water, the skin membrane stays moist and can be frequently retuned. The bulges on the shell facilitate the tensioning, making it more even.

Xylophone

Primitive xylophone with gourd resonators, Guatemala.

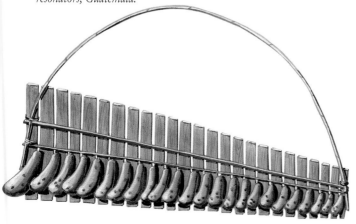

Xylophone with wooden resonators, Guatemala.

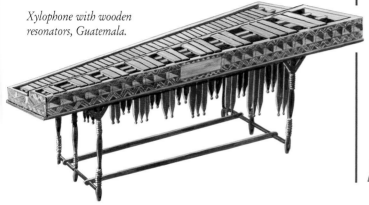

Steel Drum

Steel bands first appeared in the 1930s, when the black population of Trinidad sought an inexpensive way of taking part in festive carnivals. At first they used pots, cans, dustbin lids, and other such makeshift "instruments." Later, they turned to used oil barrels, which were ingeniously perfected by heating up and water-cooling until the desired tone was obtained. The highest-pitched steel drums were called ping-pong; their role within the band was to play the melody. Lower-pitched ones were divided into alto, tenor, and bass. The beaters were similarly made of whatever was available, usually wood with a rubber end (made from old bicycle tyres). Steel bands also included a number of smaller percussion instruments. They played calypso and other folk genres from Trinidad and the Caribbean islands. In time, some of these instruments (the steel drums, for example) were adopted by American jazz and used by a number of dance bands.

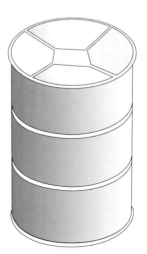

Three steel drums viewed from above: ping-pong (playing the melody), guitar pan (accompaniment), and bass (for the bass part). Sets often include four instruments, covering a range of 20 tones, and are capable of playing rhythmic figures of indefinite pitch.

Vibraslap: a modern American substitute for the jawbone. The instrument consists of a thin, springy metal rod, bent at the middle, with a small wooden box at one end and a wooden ball at the other. When the wooden ball is hit it shakes the rod, causing the loose end inside the box to vibrate.

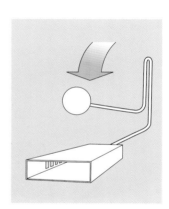

MEMBRANOPHONES

Aztec drum with carved legs and a membrane made of jaguar skin, Mexico. A ritual instrument, beautifully carved in the traditions of ancient Mexican cultures. It was often played together with the teponaztli drum, as they sounded very similar. The images include a priest of the god of dance, a priest of the jaguar order, and a priest of the eagle order to whom the symbol of war belonged. A calendar sign is recognizable in the middle. The trapezoidal cuts appear to have a merely decorative function.

As early as in the Mayan and the Incan cultures, the drums played an important role and predominated in the large ensembles of that time of up to 100 musicians. Thus, the multitude of African American drums and typical percussion instruments of the continent's later folk ensembles are a natural continuation of ancient traditions. In colonial chronicles these ensembles are described as "menistrels", and the rich set of percussions rivalled in variety today's widely used one. Without this wealth of instruments, the creation of a fundamental modern work such as Edgard Varese's *Ionisation* would have been impossible.

Singer shaking a rattle and beating a huehuetl drum, Mexico, 9th century.

Double-head cylindrical wooden drum, Panama.

Three netted conical wooden drums, Cuba.

Wooden drum, Argentina.

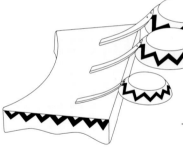

Sartene: a Latin American folk instrument consisting of different-sized pans.

Conga and Tumba

These are single-head drums of African origin. Primitive examples consist of a hollowed-out piece of wood with a skin membrane stretched over the top by means of cords. Black slaves took the instrument to Latin America, where it was made in two forms, barrel-shaped (tumba) and tapered (conga). The body is carved from wood and the skin membrane stretched with nails. The instrument is carried on a strap on the player's shoulder. Modern models have a long wooden body. The conga is more popular than the tumba, being easier to make and having undergone certain structural improvements. The ring is pushed down from the rim for the player's convenience. The instruments now stand on legs and are played in combinations of two or three congas and tumbas of different sizes. The player stands, striking the membrane with hands or beaters.

Congas.

Tumba.

Three bongos.

Modern conga.

CHORDOPHONES
Musical Bow

Musical bows with a bridge producing two different tones, Alaska.

Musical bow, Brazil.

The decoration shows that the Eskimo musical bow was not merely a household object, but was probably used for ritual purposes.

Fiddle

Apache fiddle, Oklahoma, North America. An instrument of solid construction, bored throughout almost the whole of its length. Several hoops prevent it from splitting. The single peg is surprisingly efficient: by pushing it further in or pulling it out the string can be tuned approximately, while fine tuning is effected by turning the peg. The restrained decoration is characteristic of North American Indians. A tassel is attached to the end of the instrument.

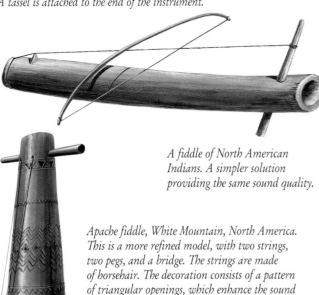

A fiddle of North American Indians. A simpler solution providing the same sound quality.

Apache fiddle, White Mountain, North America. This is a more refined model, with two strings, two pegs, and a bridge. The strings are made of horsehair. The decoration consists of a pattern of triangular openings, which enhance the sound produced.

Harp and Guitar

The harps and guitars came to America from Europe via the colonizers and then via the pioneers and settlers. They were of folk origin and were used for domestic playing. Definitely the most popular were the Spanish and Portuguese guitars in Latin America and the Irish harps in North America.

Charango: South American guitar with a body made of armadillo skin.

Latin American harp-lute.

Apache Indian playing the fiddle.

Ukulele

The ukulele is a popular four-string instrument resembling a small guitar. Its size is about half that of the guitar, and it has 12 frets. It is plucked with the fingers or nails. If no special ukulele strings are available, violin strings may be used. The ukulele was brought to Hawaii by Portuguese immigrants in the 19th century. Its precursor was an instrument called kavakuito. The ukulele became popular in the U.S. in the early 20th century.

Ukulele.

The banjolele (or banjo ukulele) is an instrument that developed as a combination of the mandolin (hence it is also known as the banjo mandolin) and the banjo. It has the banjo's soundbox and the strings of the ukulele, with the number of frets increased to 16.

Banjo

A stringed instrument of African-American origin, popularized in American folk and popular music and in early jazz. It consists of a round wooden resonator onto which a vellum belly is secured with a hoop and screws (between eight and 24). There are between 17 and 20 frets on the fingerboard, the long neck ending in a slightly bent pegbox. The banjo usually has four strings but a five-string variety has recently gained popularity. The strings of the banjo in C are tuned c, g, b, d1 (the music is notated an octave higher than it sounds). In the banjo in G, there is a d string instead of a c string, and the fifth g1 string is only about three quarters of the length of the others. It is played with the left thumb.

Banjolele.

Banjo.

Banjo-mandolin with four double strings.

Guitar-banjo

A relatively rare hybrid of the guitar (body shape) and the banjo (round hole on the belly, covered with snake skin and serving as a resonator). The guitar-banjo has only three strings.

Guitar-banjo.

Dobro guitar.

"Dobro" Guitar

Inside the instrument's body is a round metal resonator. It is played with a special thimble. The "Dobro" guitar was particularly popular with early blues musicians.

AUSTRALIA AND OCEANIA

BEFORE THE EUROPEAN COLONIZATION of Australia in the 18th century, which pushed the Aborigines into the desert regions of the continent, the culture of the native population had existed almost unchanged for centuries. The music of the Aborigines, like that of Amazonian Indians, is based mainly on the human voice and singing. The finest performers are capable of producing double notes. Songs and dances to the accompaniment of musical instruments play an important part in the life of Australia's native population, in its labor, rites, and celebrations. The glissando is a feature of the traditional singing style, with intervals as small as a quarter or even an eighth of a tone. Later, melodic patterns using intervals of a second or a third became established.

Unlike the Australian Aborigines, the Maori of New Zealand are a Polynesian people, like the inhabitants of most Pacific islands. Their songs and dances are more vigorous and express a greater variety of moods. While in Australia the native population has two main musical forms – the sharada (a love song performed antiphonally by groups of male and female singers) and the korobori (a ritual dance performed by the tribe when young men come of age) – in New Zealand music accompanies many different human activities. The typical instruments include the wooden gong, trumpets made of conch shells or wood (also used for signaling), and primitive flutes which are sometimes made of a whale's or a shark's tooth. The Maori have a curious technique of playing their primitive flutes: blowing through the nose which has a special significance in their ritual practice.

The white settlers of the 18th century, most of whom were British, brought to Australia and the nearby islands their own folk music and songs, which served as the foundation of the continent's present-day musical culture.

AEROPHONES

Bull-roarer

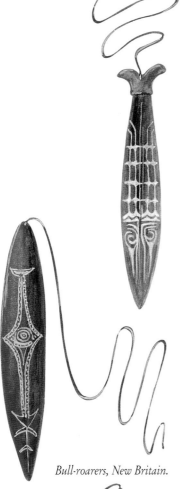

Bull-roarers, New Guinea.

Bull-roarers, New Britain.

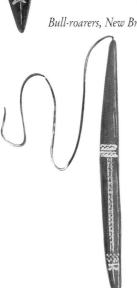

These instruments are about 50 cm long. They are held by the string and whirled in the air, producing a roaring sound. Bull-roarers are used in rites intended to induce conception, in which women are not allowed to participate. Bull-roarers are taboo for women. When a baby is about to be born, a new bull-roarer is made. It is placed in the baby's cradle as a mythical connection between the newborn and its ancestors. In Australia, the sound of the bull-roarer is associated with a child-abducting monster but also with the spirits of the dead. When whirled above the tribe's chieftain, it is believed to drive away evil forces.

Vessel-shaped Flute

Vessel flute made of a fruit shell, Oceania.

Gourd flute, Oceania. This is a simple and primitive nose-blown instrument.

Clay flute, New Guinea. Clay flutes derived from even more primitive instruments made of fruit shells.

Wooden (Bamboo) Flute

Wooden flute, New Guinea.

Nguru wooden flute, New Zealand.

The flute is narrower at the upper end so that the player may carry it on a string on his neck. This particular example is richly carved with admirable taste and sense of proportion, turning a simple instrument into a work of art. It would probably be nose-blown, though, it might also be mouth-blown. Its owner is likely to have been of high social status. Some instruments have what appear to be useless fingerholes, suggesting that they were made empirically, by boring holes until the desired tones were obtained.

Nose-blown flute made of bamboo, Tahiti. The sound is produced by blowing gently through one nostril, while closing the other.

Nose-blowing was a relatively rare technique. According to the Maori and other island peoples, it had a more powerful spiritual effect than mouth-blowing.

Wooden flute, Australia. Although simpler in construction, this flute was a powerful weapon in a skillful player's hands: its magic sounds gave him a clear advantage in the struggle for a girl's heart. A local saying has it that the sound of the flute makes men extremely jealous.

Bamboo flute, Tahiti.

Musicians playing side-blown flutes, New Guinea.

Wooden nose-blown flute, Fiji. The decoration helps to find the fingerholes (bored with hot iron) more easily.

Panpipe

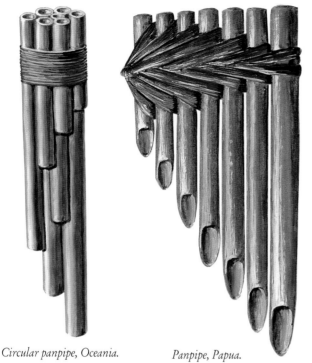

Circular panpipe, Oceania.   *Panpipe, Papua.*

In most cases, though not always, panpipes are played in ensembles. Panpipes vary in size, resulting in a significant difference in pitch. When used to accompany a solo, the panpipe can be tapped rhythmically like an idiophone. The tuning is relatively easy: the length of each pipe is adjusted until the desired pitch is obtained. Circular panpipes allow for the playing of chords.

Panpipe player, New Guinea.

Trumpet

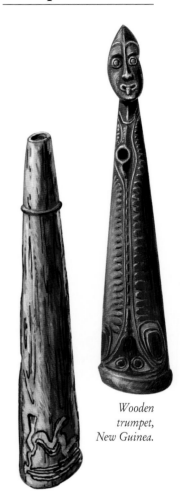

Wooden trumpet, New Guinea.

An older and more primitive wooden instrument, following the ordinary horn shape prior to the creation of the real trumpet – an instrument capable of a piercing and impressive sound.

Trumpet with a telescopic skin cover, New Guinea. A rare and ingenious solution of the problem of insufficient length. The similarity to the modern slide trombone is self-evident. Despite its primitive design, the instrument is perfectly functional.

Wooden trumpet, New Guinea. The instrument's zoomorphic shape is typical of this and other regions. The original shape of the wood has been used skillfully and elegantly in the decoration. The trumpet is side-blown probably because it would have been much more difficult to bore an axial opening.

Wooden trumpet consisting of two tubes carved from a single piece of wood, with a blowing hole halfway along each tube, New Zealand. This is a rare example, of unusual shape, following the piece of wood used. A handy hole at the left end allows the instrument to be carried on a string around the player's neck. Depending on the strength of blowing, it can sound softer, like a clarinet, or more penetrating, like a trumpet.

Didgeridoo: an Australian wooden trumpet. Essentially, it is a kind of megaphone, about a meter and a half long and 5 – 10 cm in diameter. The edge of the blowing hole is covered with wax to provide more comfort for the player. The instrument plays a single tone but experienced musicians are capable of producing a second, higher-pitched one. The didgeridoo's name derives from a word that is said before performance at various ceremonies.

Sea-shell blown through a side opening, Marquesas Islands. The conch was used for military signals, for announcing important seasonal events, and for cult purposes. Before blowing the conch the musician would recite a charm, as this instrument was believed to possess magical powers.

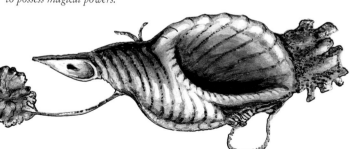

Didgeridoo. Aboriginal instruments are made of a variety of materials: wood, bamboo, tree bark, reptile or fish skin, or various kinds of stick. The most famous Australian instrument, however, which has become a symbol of the continent along with the boomerang and the kangaroo, is the didgeridoo: a trumpet of considerable length made of a sapling that has been hollowed out by termites. It produces a continuous penetrating sound, though skilled players are capable of occasionally interjecting short vocal phrases. The didgeridoo is thus a kind of "storyteller." The technique of experienced players is particularly interesting: by inhaling briefly through the nose and blowing continually into the instrument, they actually practice the "circular breathing" that was adopted by many musicians around the world in the second half of the 20th century. This technique was first introduced by jazz instrumentalists, and was later adopted even by vocalists such as Frank Sinatra.

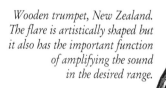

Wooden trumpet, New Zealand. The flare is artistically shaped but it also has the important function of amplifying the sound in the desired range.

IDIOPHONES

Struck, Shaken and Friction Instruments

The wooden struck idiophones from Australia's northern coast are quite unusual. Their fish-like shape is believed to have magical significance, since these instruments are supposed to bring about rain and fertility. In Australia, the fish is a commonly used symbol identified with both water and fertility.

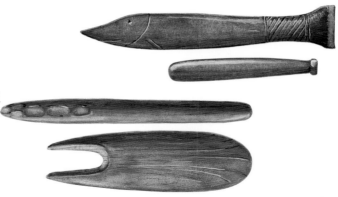

Struck idiophones, Australia.

Struck idiophone (kalaau), Hawaii.

Bamboo clapper (pu-ilu) used in ritual dances, Hawaii.

Time-beating stick, Australia.

Struck idiophone (poi), whirled in dances.

Ulili: gourd rattle, Hawaii. This idiophone has a cord wound round the axis that, when pulled, makes the two side gourds spin and the seeds inside rattle, producing a special sound effect. It is used in ritual dances.

Australian rattle made of a pod.

Wooden drum played by rubbing the surface with moist hands, Papua. Before playing, palm oil is rubbed into the "tongues." When rubbed, they produce different pitches. The instrument is used in ceremonies dedicated to the dead, and may neither be seen nor heard by women and children.

Sonorous Vessel

Hawaiian water drum (hula-ipu).

Water drum with a lid, New Guinea. The sound is produced by striking the lid with the hands. When played, the drum is immersed in water and struck on the lid, which produces rather distinctive sounds.

Wooden jew's harp, Australia.

Primitive jew's harp of African origin with a wooden blade attached, Hawaii. This instrument is held close to the mouth, which acts as a resonator, and is played with the fingers.

The jew's harp is a delicate instrument. About 15 cm long, it produces a soft but charming sound. According to travelers, young men would play it outside the huts of their chosen girls, hoping to attract their attention gently.

Wooden Drum, Slit Drum

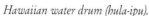

Wooden drum, Fiji. With its shape and the slit in the middle, the instrument resembles a canoe. The slit is short to make the drum sturdier. This drum is usually placed in the player's lap, but it may also be held at chest level, which modifies its sound slightly.

Primitive xylophone (tutupele), New Britain. The frame consists of two parts. The double beaters make it possible to play different notes.

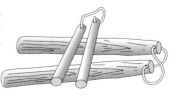

Slit drum, New Guinea. This is also canoe-shaped, but unlike the simple lali-ni-meke, it is richly ornamented. The two handles and the carved abstract shapes have ritual significance.

MEMBRANOPHONES

Long Drum

The shape of the drums – two opposed cones – is symbolic, reflecting the dualism of nature (fire – water, sky – earth). The use of the skin of sacrificial animals for the membranes enhances the ritual importance of the drums.

This drum impresses with its simple design. It is symmetrical, and the handle is tightly fixed to the shell.

Single-head wooden tubular drum, Papua, New Guinea. The membrane is tightened by driving numerous wedges into the tensioning cord at the rim.

Long single-head wooden drum, Papua, New Guinea. Drum from the southwestern coast of New Guinea. Its long and finely carved handle represents a human figure.

Large single-head wooden drum in the shape of a long vase, Papua, New Guinea.

Two long single-head drums, New Guinea. The membranes are stretched and glued to the shell. The beautifully carved bird-shaped handles also have a ritual meaning.

Long wooden drum, Oceania.

Long wooden drum, Oceania.

Goblet-shaped drum, New Guinea. The skin membrane has been stretched over the maker's knees or over a hole in the ground before being stretched on the shell. The wooden shell is decorated with carved images typical for the region. The handle has nothing to do with the drum's musical qualities but is convenient for carrying. The apparent variety of shapes – conical, tubular, barrel, or a combination of these – is responsible for the variety of sounds produced.

CHORDOPHONES

The string of the Australian musical bow may be tensioned by an additional loop, bending the bow further. The tightly attached gourd resonator amplifies the sound and improves its quality.

The musician puts the end of the bow in his mouth and sounds the string by plucking it with his fingers or by bowing it. The pitch can be adjusted by opening and closing the mouth.

Musical bows, Australia.

Goblet-shaped drum, Hawaii. In this type of drum, perhaps the most ancient in the region, the membrane tension is controlled by cords running to the bottom of the shell. This drum can be played with both hands, or with one hand and a beater.

Primitive zither made of corn and bast, New Guinea.

Zither, Australia.

The primitive Australian bamboo zither is not a true stringed instrument. The bamboo stick is first peeled longitudinally, and then, once it is dry, wooden blocks are inserted at both ends. The zither may have more than one "string." These zithers (which may also be regarded as members of the idiophone group) are not widely used in Australia. They probably evolved under African influence through the valiha of Madagascar.

Goblet-shaped drum, New Guinea. This example demonstrates the evolution of the drum shell. The membrane is accurately tensioned by the wedges distributed evenly around the rim. In modern drums, this is achieved by means of keys.

Friction drum made of a gourd, New Guinea. The hole on the gourd is important for the tone quality. The instrument is believed to originate in India. Its ritual role is to imitate the voices of ancestors.

A musical bow player, New Guinea.

THE FAR EAST

WHEN THE TRAVELER MARCO POLO returned from China around 1297, the Europeans refused to believe in the existence of a strange civilization as old as the pyramids in Egypt. It was only when the sea routes to the Far East were discovered in the 16th century that an encounter with Chinese culture became possible. Historians and musicologists later discovered that a collection of ritual songs known as *Li Chi,* and the *Shih Ching* anthology of poetry, containing about 300 songs, date back to 1100 years before Christ. Even before Plato and Aristotle, the Chinese philosophers Lao-tzu and Confucius had emphasized the moral value of music, seeing in it a means to moral perfection. On a metaphysical level, Chinese philosophers mystically maintained that music was an inseparable part of the universe, of the rhythm of nature, and that it thus provided a balance between the skies and the earth, between the female "yin" and the male "yang."

The metaphysical and mystical meaning attributed to musical instruments was related to the material of which they were made, to the mood of the different seasons, and to natural phenomena such as fire, water, thunder, and earth. The silk strings of the ch'in, for example, symbolized the spirit of summer and fire, and the pan-pipe the spring and the pure mountain air.

The organic connection between Chinese music and speech naturally determined the priorities within the Chinese musical tradition: melody and the sound of the instrument were more important than rhythm and harmony.

Korea's close contacts with China and Buddhism exerted a considerable influence on its culture, particularly on its music and musical instruments: zithers, flutes, woodwinds, gongs, and drums. Korean music in its turn had an influence on the music of Japan. From ancient times, Korean musicians have been invited to Japan as teachers and organizers of royal and religious musical ceremonies.

The music of Japan represents a special case within the civilization of the Far East. Because of its location, the island nation had regular contacts with China, Korea, and Manchuria, and was thus subjected to strong cultural pressure. On the other hand, Japan was situated away from continental Asia and the Silk Route, and thus managed to distance itself somewhat from its neighbors and to prevent linguistic and other influences.

As in China, the musical theatre in Japan had strong ancient traditions. The No theatre, combining singing and reciting, was the most sophisticated theatrical form in Eastern Asia. The Kabuki theatre (ka signifying "song"; bu, "dance"; and ki, "skill") emerged around the 16th century and was the most popular form of theater for ordinary people. In European terms, it was an amalgam of opera, pantomime, and circus. Kabuki used musical ensembles both off- and onstage. The dances were accompanied by drums and flutes, or by samisen and voice. Drums, gongs, bells and clappers announced the beginning of the show and of every new scene.

The roots of Indonesian music go back to the 4th to 6th centuries, though Europe's first encounter with it did not occur until he 16th century. Of all musical cultures of the Far East, it is the one most closely related to dance and to the theatre of masks and shadows. As elsewhere in the Far East, it is based on a pentatonic scale developing into a seven-tone scale. Paradoxically, despite the rhythmic variety and the wealth of percussion instruments used in the music of Indonesia, it is the melody that plays the leading role. The main theme and the developing melodic and rhythmic material are known as "stem" and "flowers."

AEROPHONES

A legend has it that a scientist of the name of Lin Lun was the first to use 12 bamboo pipes as a standard of pitch for the steps of the chromatic scale. The system was finally established in the last millennium B.C. The basic sound corresponded to the E of the European scale. The length times the width equal 81, a number that the Chinese believe to possess magical properties. The length of each subsequent pipe was two thirds that of the previous one, thus forming a circle of fifths containing all 12 steps of the chromatic scale. The Chinese realized this long before it was discovered by Pythagoras. Five tones of that circle form a pentatonic scale, which was typical not only of Chinese music but of ancient music in general.

Musician playing the flute.

Flute

The Far-Eastern flutes are end-blown flutes with a mouthpiece. They are equipped with a simple mouthpiece through which air is directed towards a sharp-edged notch below. These flutes are found in various sizes and with a varying number of fingerholes, and can be made of bamboo, wood, bone, or clay. In Western Europe the most common form of the end-blown flute is the recorder.

Japanese bamboo flute. The end-blown flute, or shakuhachi, is one of the most popular wind instruments in Japan. It is made of a piece of bamboo cut close to the root, and is equipped with a mouthpiece and six fingerholes. This instrument is used in Japanese solo and chamber music and is one of the original instruments of Zen Buddhism. Its tone is soft and clear in the low register; the other registers are less stable. The shakuhachi acquired its present form in the 17th century.

Transverse flute made of bamboo, with a membrane stretched close to the blowing hole that gives an interesting quality to the sound.

Wooden flute, Thailand.

Vessel-shaped clay flute, China, 13th century B. C.

Japanese panpipe (pai-hsiao).

Chinese flute (lung-ti). This unusual flute is used for religious ceremonies. It is made of bamboo, with a carved wooden dragon at each end. The fine dragon figures bring a certain elegance to the beautifully decorated and varnished pipe. The mouth hole is covered with thin paper, which produces a buzzing sound.

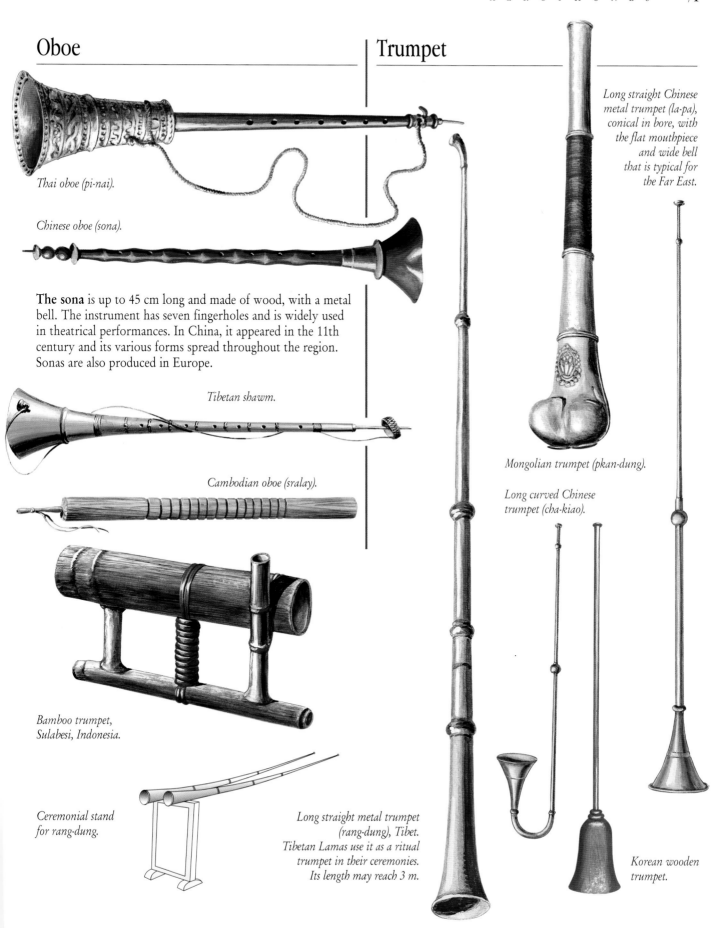

Oboe

Thai oboe (pi-nai).

Chinese oboe (sona).

The sona is up to 45 cm long and made of wood, with a metal bell. The instrument has seven fingerholes and is widely used in theatrical performances. In China, it appeared in the 11th century and its various forms spread throughout the region. Sonas are also produced in Europe.

Tibetan shawm.

Cambodian oboe (sralay).

Bamboo trumpet, Sulabesi, Indonesia.

Ceremonial stand for rang-dung.

Trumpet

Long straight Chinese metal trumpet (la-pa), conical in bore, with the flat mouthpiece and wide bell that is typical for the Far East.

Mongolian trumpet (pkan-dung).

Long curved Chinese trumpet (cha-kiao).

Long straight metal trumpet (rang-dung), Tibet. Tibetan Lamas use it as a ritual trumpet in their ceremonies. Its length may reach 3 m.

Korean wooden trumpet.

Mouth Organ

The khen mouth-organ
of Laos is made of 18 pipes
arranged in two parallel rows.
The longest, lowest-pitched
pipe is up to 3.5 m long and
the highest- and the lowest-
pitched pipes are often tuned
an octave apart. The khen is
used as a solo instrument,
or several khens are played
in an ensemble.
The dyak mouth-organ of
north Borneo belongs to the
same family. It consists of
between five and nine bamboo
pipes affixed to a gourd.
The mouthpiece may be made
of palm-wood but some are
metal. This instrument
is chiefly used for playing
serenades.

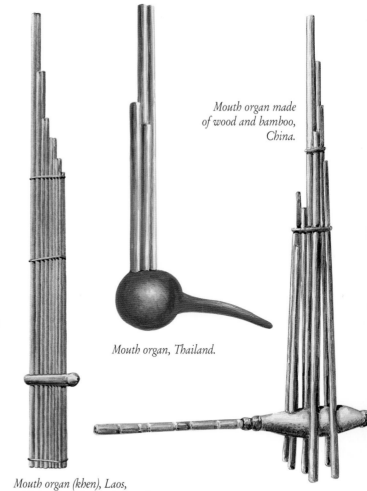

*Mouth organ made
of wood and bamboo,
China.*

Mouth organ, Thailand.

*Mouth organ made of a gourd
and bamboo, Borneo.*

*Mouth organ (khen), Laos,
with bamboo pipes and a wooden
sound-chest.*

*Tibetan horn (lings-dun)
made of copper.*

Playing the mouth-organ khen, Laos.

Conch horn, Japan.

Chinese mouth organ (sheng).

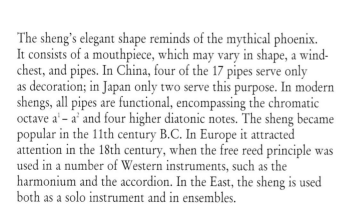

Chinese mouth organ (sheng).

Sheng

The mouth organ sheng was designed in China about 3000 years ago. The pipes are stopped with the fingers. When the pipes are not stopped, the air causes the free metal reeds to vibrate. In more modern instruments, the reeds are made of brass and tuned with wax.

Chinese mouth organ (sheng).

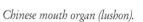

Chinese mouth organ (lushon).

The sheng's elegant shape reminds of the mythical phoenix. It consists of a mouthpiece, which may vary in shape, a wind-chest, and pipes. In China, four of the 17 pipes serve only as decoration; in Japan only two serve this purpose. In modern shengs, all pipes are functional, encompassing the chromatic octave $a^1 - a^2$ and four higher diatonic notes. The sheng became popular in the 11th century B.C. In Europe it attracted attention in the 18th century, when the free reed principle was used in a number of Western instruments, such as the harmonium and the accordion. In the East, the sheng is used both as a solo instrument and in ensembles.

Chinese mouth organ (sheng).

IDIOPHONES

Bin-sasara: a Japanese strung clapper, consisting of thin wooden strips strung by their ends on a cord, with a hand-grip at each end. The instrument is held up in a horseshoe shape, while a deft movement of the hands makes the strips clatter against each other in one direction and then in the other.

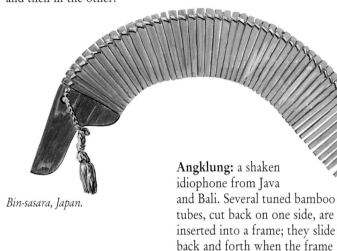

Bin-sasara, Japan.

Korean bak: six pieces of hard wood strung together and struck against each other with both hands.

Angklung: a shaken idiophone from Java and Bali. Several tuned bamboo tubes, cut back on one side, are inserted into a frame; they slide back and forth when the frame is shaken. The pitch depends on the length and diameter of the tubes.

Angklung, Java.

Modern Japanese castanets.

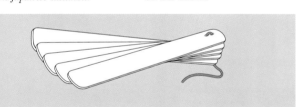

Bamboo pipes suspended from a wooden bar.

Modern bamboo pipes.

Bamboo pipes, wood chimes: a Japanese instrument, consisting of a set of suspended dried bamboo pipes of varying length and width. There are two main forms: pipes suspended on strings from a rod, or pipes suspended from a metal ring that is itself suspended on a string. The sound is produced by shaking the instrument, by striking the pipes with a beater, or by hitting the pipes against each other with the hands.

Bell

Chinese bell,
part of a set of 16.

In ancient China, bells were used for both theoretical studies and for establishing scale proportions. The strong influence and the fast expansion of Buddhism in the 3rd century A. D. in China, Korea and Japan gave bells an important role in religious ceremonies. At about the same time, their significance for Christianity in Europe increased, too. Buddhist bells produce a deep and pleasant sound, similar to the sacred mantra "Om". This encouraged the casting of larger and larger bells, some of them weighing as much as 70 t. They were placed in temples and monasteries. Unlike European bells, they had no beaters and were struck with hammers.

Small Chinese bell.

Large Chinese bell.

Chinese bell (po-chung).

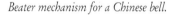

Beater mechanism for a Chinese bell.

Chinese bronze bell,
9th – 6th centuries B. C.

Chinese bell (po-chung). Bells were widely used in the music of Confucianism. Unlike smaller instruments, which are usually played in sets, the po-shung is suspended on its own.

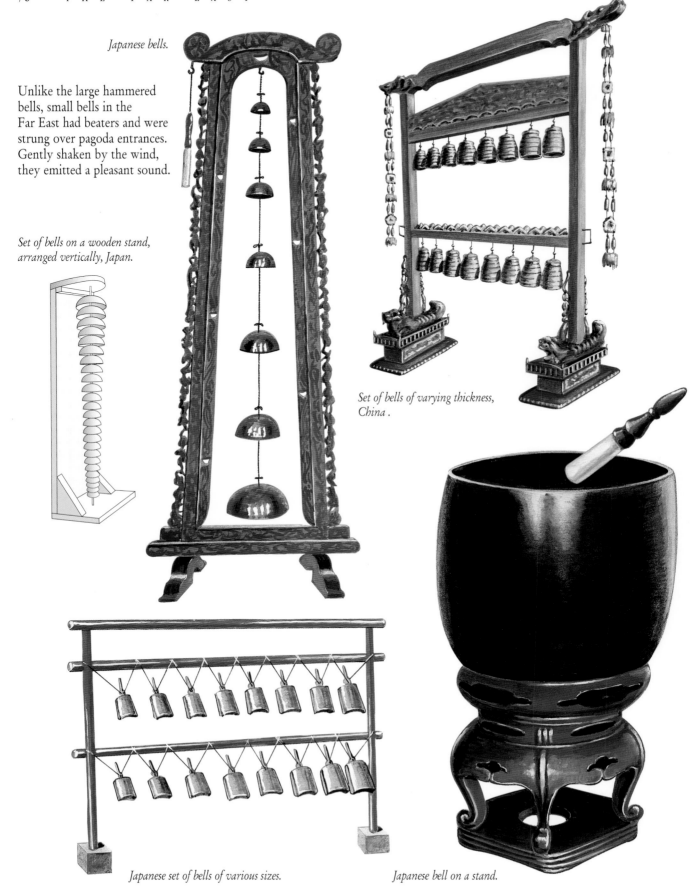

Japanese bells.

Unlike the large hammered
bells, small bells in the
Far East had beaters and were
strung over pagoda entrances.
Gently shaken by the wind,
they emitted a pleasant sound.

*Set of bells on a wooden stand,
arranged vertically, Japan.*

*Set of bells of varying thickness,
China .*

Japanese set of bells of various sizes.

Japanese bell on a stand.

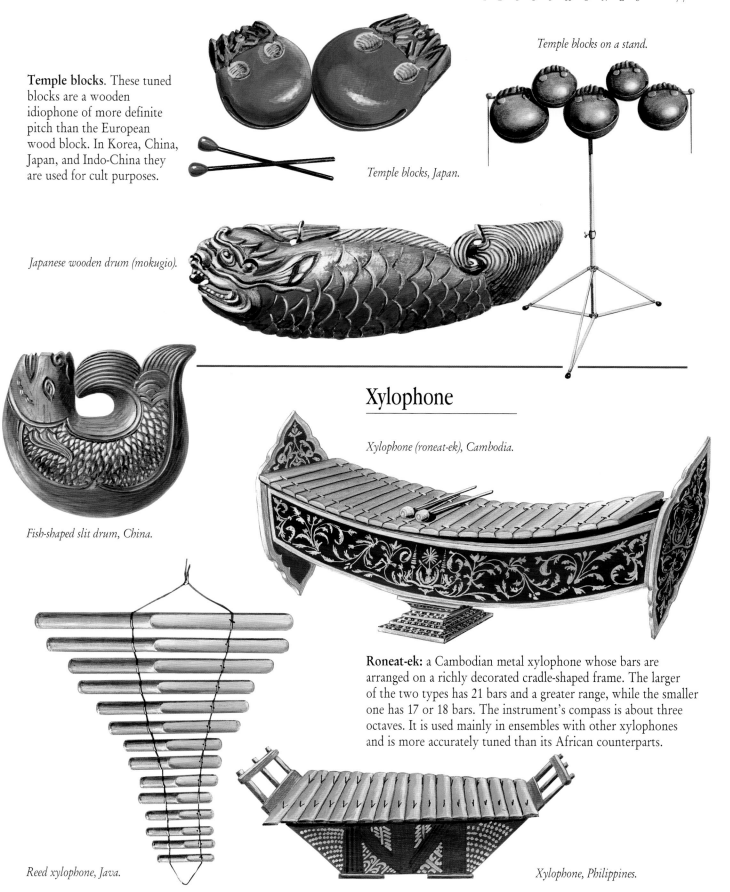

Temple blocks. These tuned blocks are a wooden idiophone of more definite pitch than the European wood block. In Korea, China, Japan, and Indo-China they are used for cult purposes.

Temple blocks on a stand.

Temple blocks, Japan.

Japanese wooden drum (mokugio).

Fish-shaped slit drum, China.

Xylophone

Xylophone (roneat-ek), Cambodia.

Roneat-ek: a Cambodian metal xylophone whose bars are arranged on a richly decorated cradle-shaped frame. The larger of the two types has 21 bars and a greater range, while the smaller one has 17 or 18 bars. The instrument's compass is about three octaves. It is used mainly in ensembles with other xylophones and is more accurately tuned than its African counterparts.

Reed xylophone, Java.

Xylophone, Philippines.

Lithophone

In their most primitive form, Chinese lithophones consist either of two sonorous stones, held one in each hand and struck together, or of a set of stones of different sizes that are hit with smaller stones. Lithophones can still be found occasionally in folk and professional music in China.

Chinese framed lithophone.

Pien ch'ing: a Chinese instrument made of two rows of stone plates on a frame; of varying thickness, the plates produce tones of different pitches.

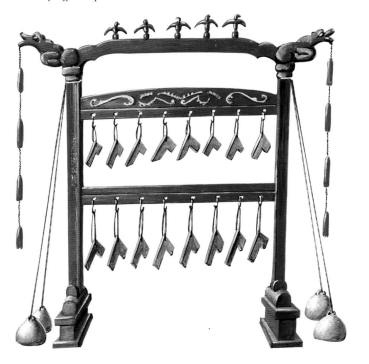

Metallophone

Saron, Java.

Saron and Gender

The saron is a very characteristic Javanese instrument, and an important member of the gamelan orchestra. Seven polished bronze bars are arranged on a cradle-shaped frame. The bars are about 2 cm thick, slightly thicker at the ends. They are struck with a beater made of horn or wood. The instrument is richly decorated with dragon figures. Though of a relatively limited compass, it plays the melody in the gamelan orchestra.

Gender is a metallophone from Java, used in the gamelan orchestra. It is a set of polished metal plates, each supplied with a separate bamboo resonator.

The gender differs from the saron not only in the separate resonators for each block but also in their larger number (up to 14).

Gender, Java.

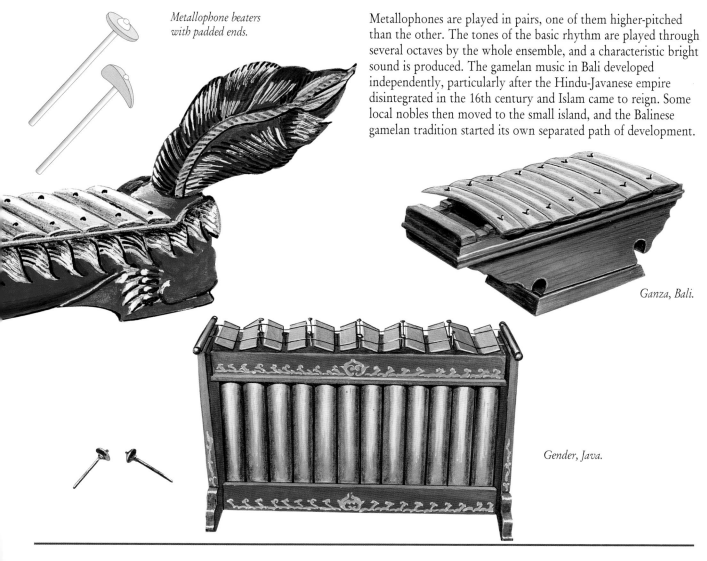

Metallophone beaters with padded ends.

Metallophones are played in pairs, one of them higher-pitched than the other. The tones of the basic rhythm are played through several octaves by the whole ensemble, and a characteristic bright sound is produced. The gamelan music in Bali developed independently, particularly after the Hindu-Javanese empire disintegrated in the 16th century and Islam came to reign. Some local nobles then moved to the small island, and the Balinese gamelan tradition started its own separated path of development.

Ganza, Bali.

Gender, Java.

Cymbal

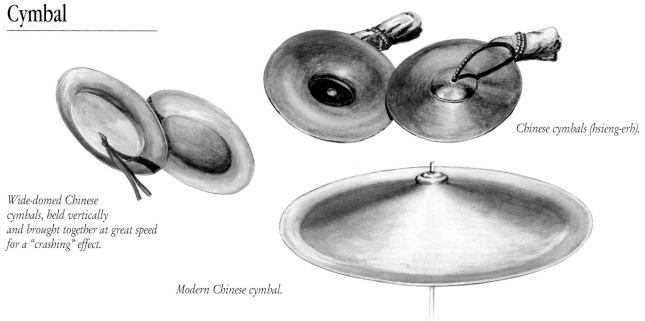

Chinese cymbals (hsieng-erh).

Wide-domed Chinese cymbals, held vertically and brought together at great speed for a "crashing" effect.

Modern Chinese cymbal.

Gong

A metal idiophone of relatively definite pitch, depending on the instrument's size, the gong's onomatopoeic name originates from the Malay Archipelago, and more particularly from Java, where it is still used in the gamelan orchestra. The gong is widely popular in East and South-East Asia. In Africa it is found in Ethiopia. It came to Europe from Asia. The gong is a flat bronze disc, 40 to 80 cm in diameter. Its rim is turned back, and the flat central part is often decorated with dragon figures or floral motifs. Suspended on a frame by the rim, the gong is struck with a soft-ended mallet, at or near the center, but not near the rim as the sound there is weaker and of more indefinite pitch. In the Far East gongs are produced in a variety of shapes.

Chinese gong.

Chinese set of gongs (chon-lo).

Modern gong.

Gong-player, Kalimantan.

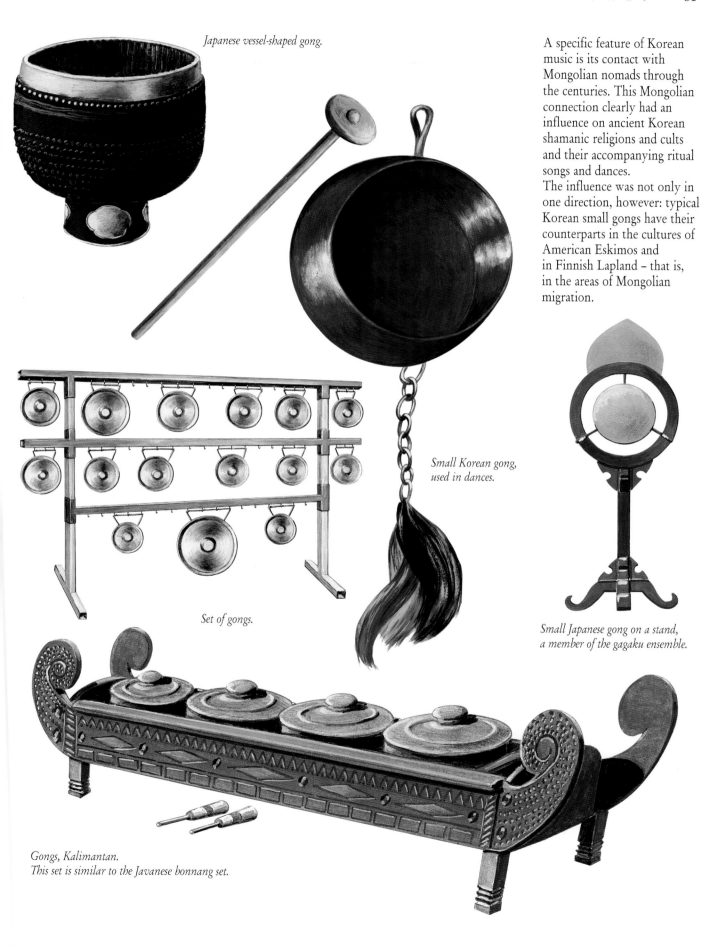

Japanese vessel-shaped gong.

A specific feature of Korean music is its contact with Mongolian nomads through the centuries. This Mongolian connection clearly had an influence on ancient Korean shamanic religions and cults and their accompanying ritual songs and dances.

The influence was not only in one direction, however: typical Korean small gongs have their counterparts in the cultures of American Eskimos and in Finnish Lapland – that is, in the areas of Mongolian migration.

Small Korean gong, used in dances.

Set of gongs.

Small Japanese gong on a stand, a member of the gagaku ensemble.

Gongs, Kalimantan.
This set is similar to the Javanese bonnang set.

Javanese Gong

This type of gong is hollow and domed, with a much larger diameter than the Chinese gong. The sound is produced by striking the "boss" of the gong with a soft-ended beater. The instrument is widely used in Java and Borneo. Javanese gongs are placed horizontally or suspended vertically from frames; in Thailand and Burma they are arranged in a circle, with the player in the center.

Among the Javanese gongs two specific types stand out.
The bonnang is an instrument with two horizontal rows of five to seven gongs each, and placed on a low stand. The gongs in one row are tuned an octave higher than the gongs in the other row. They differ in size as well as in the width of the flat rim surrounding the "boss." The other type, the kenong, is high-pitched and hollow, it is played on its own, supported on cross-wires on a box-shaped frame. Both gongs are part of the gamelan ensemble.

Set of Javanese gongs, suspended from a frame.

Gong with gold ornaments, Burma.

Javanese gong (kenong).

Siamese set of Javanese gongs, placed horizontally on a circular frame around the player.

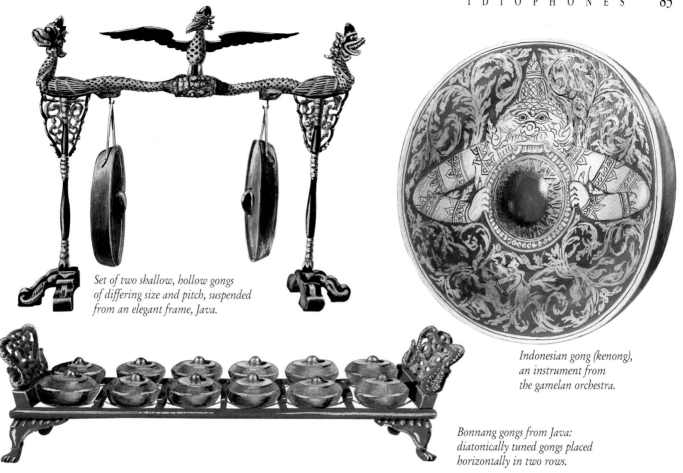

Set of two shallow, hollow gongs
of differing size and pitch, suspended
from an elegant frame, Java.

Indonesian gong (kenong),
an instrument from
the gamelan orchestra.

Bonnang gongs from Java:
diatonically tuned gongs placed
horizontally in two rows.

Tam-tam

A close relative to the gong, the tam-tam can be regarded
as one of its larger forms. The tam-tam is characterized by
a considerably deeper sound, a different timbre, and indefinite
pitch. The name is of Indian origin. The tam-tam originated
in the Far East and came to Europe through China, where
it has been a sacred instrument since ancient times. It consists
of a disc of pressed, forged, or turned bronze, between 60 and
180 cm in diameter. Its center is slightly domed and the rim is
thicker and turned back. The tam-tam is suspended on a thick
wire from a circular or rectangular metal frame, and struck with
a heavy mallet with a rounded, felt-covered end.
Tam-tams of different sizes are sometimes assembled into sets.

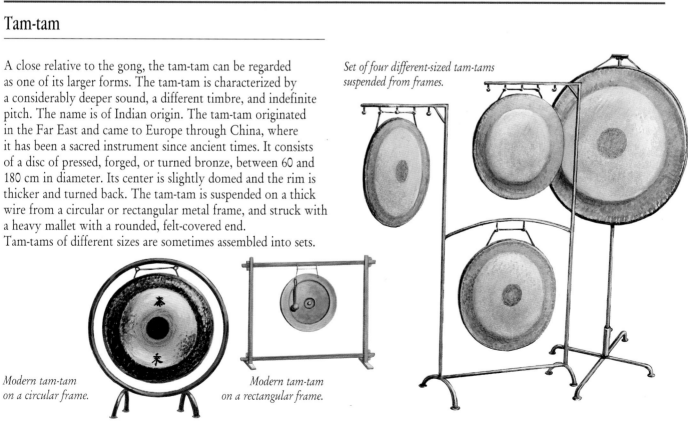

Set of four different-sized tam-tams
suspended from frames.

Modern tam-tam
on a circular frame.

Modern tam-tam
on a rectangular frame.

MEMBRANOPHONES

Like all other musical cultures of the world, the ancient and rich musical culture of the Far East has made extensive use of percussion instruments, and more particularly of membranophones. Varying in size, construction, and tuning, these instruments have always been related both to religious rituals and to secular culture (folk music, dance, theater, and so on).

Hourglass-shaped drum (changko), Korea.

Japanese hourglass-shaped wooden drum. Its pitch may be modified by pulling the ropes with the fingers, thereby tightening the membrane.

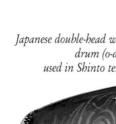

Double-head wooden barrel drum, Laos.

Double-head wooden barrel drum, struck with hands on both heads, Cambodia.

O-daiko

The giant barrel-shaped drum, o-daiko, is an important member of the famous Japanese gagaku ensembles. Two meters in diameter and weighing about 300 kg, it is supported on a wooden platform and played by two drummers, one for each head. They strike the skin membranes with heavy wooden clubs, providing rhythmic support for the ensemble. Ko-daiko is similar though much smaller in size: just 76 cm in diameter. When played in processions, this drum is carried by two men on a post. The drummer strikes it with two heavy wooden beaters.

Japanese double-head wooden drum (o-daiko), used in Shinto temples.

Goblet-shaped wooden drums, Indonesia.

Indonesian netted goblet-shaped wooden drum (nias).

Tsuri-daiko drum on a stand, an instrument used in the Japanese gagaku ensemble.

Japanese shallow wooden drum (dool).

Tekbang drum, Java.

Double-head wooden drum used in the Indonesian folk orchestra gamelan, Bali.

Japanese double-head wooden drum (okedo).

Tambourine without jingles, Java.

Barrel-shaped single-head wooden drum (skor-tom), Cambodia.

Ku or **gu** is the Chinese generic term for a double-head drum. It has rings attached to the shell, by which it can be suspended from a wooden stand. The stand has three or four legs, which surround the drum. In the Chinese theater, this drum is struck with two wooden beaters on the upper head.

Javanese rattle drum (kelontonga): a double-head drum with a small handle. Two wooden or metal pellets hang on the instrument's two sides. When the drum is shaken, the pellets strike the membranes.

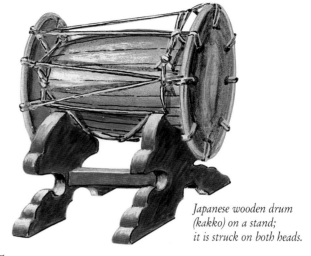

Japanese wooden drum (kakko) on a stand; it is struck on both heads.

Tom-tom

The construction of these tom-toms is similar to that of the snare drum. It differs only in the height-diameter ratio of the shell, the larger size, and the absence of a snare. The name is of Chinese origin. Tom-tom prototypes have existed in Africa and the Far East for centuries. European tom-toms are a modification of the Chinese instrument. In its original form, the tom-tom consisted of a barrel-shaped wooden shell with two skin membranes nailed to it.

Chinese barrel-shaped wooden drum (ku).

Old Chinese tom-tom.

Three different-sized Chinese tom-toms.

CHORDOPHONES

Chordophones are particularly important in the Far East. They correspond to one of the eight "sound categories," defined according to the material of which the instruments are made (in this case, the "silk" of the strings). The immense variety of harps, zithers, fiddles, lutes, and other stringed instruments originates in China, more particularly from the northern school established in the 14th century. The wide use by ladies of the high class, and for accompaniment to singing, further increased the popularity of these instruments. They are also frequently used in ensembles of various composition and function.

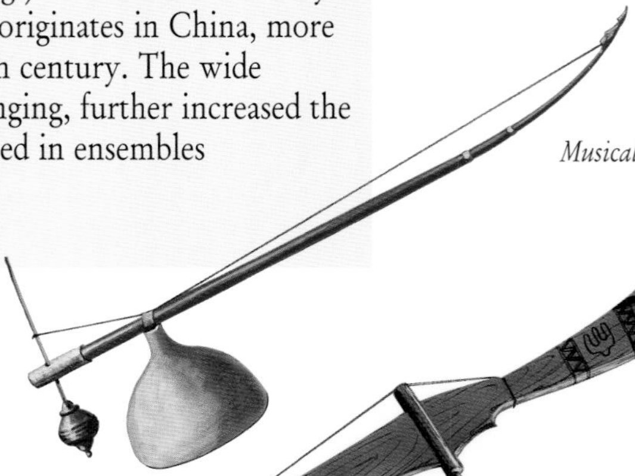

Musical bow (sa-din), Cambodia.

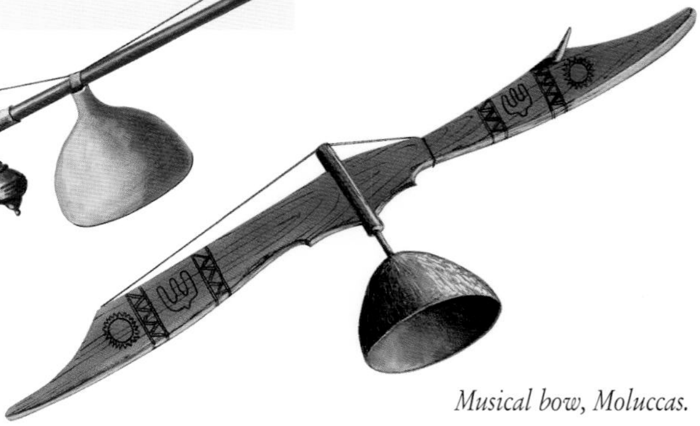

Musical bow, Moluccas.

The saung-gauk is a classical Burmese arched harp. It usually has 13 silk strings running through rings on a bow. The strings are tuned by rotating the rings and by moving them up and down the bow. Built for use in the royal court, the saung-gauk is richly decorated and varnished in red and gold. Today it is used mostly in Burma, though it was once popular all over Indochina.

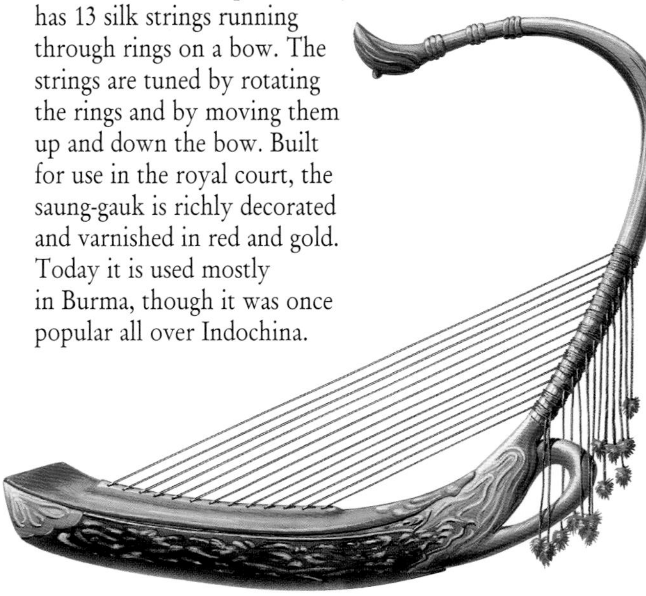

Saung: a bow-shaped harp, Burma.

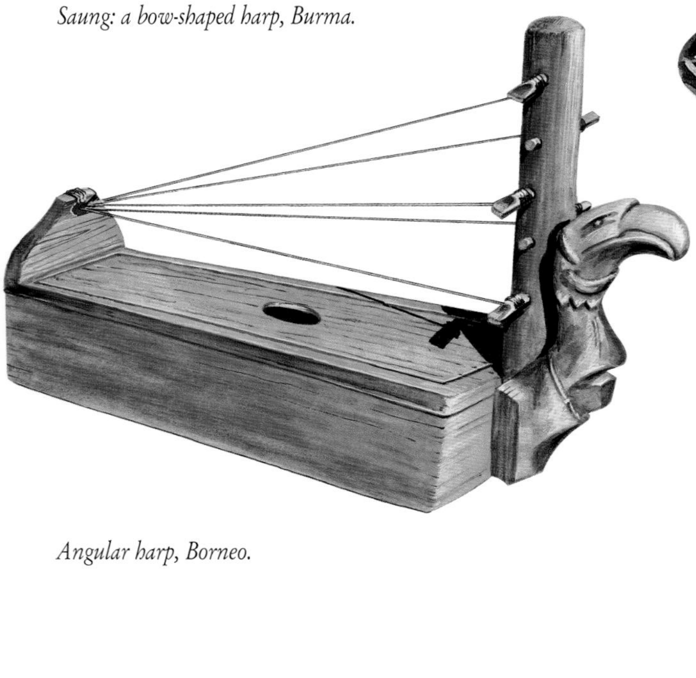

Zither

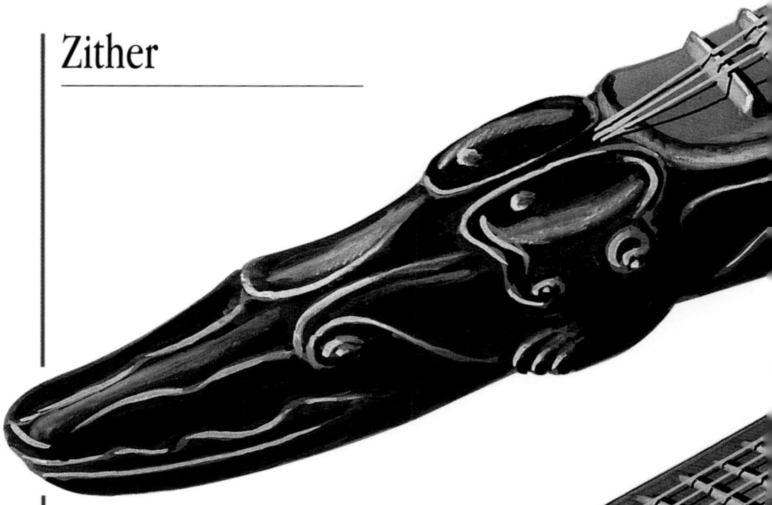

Small three-string crocodile-shaped zither (mi-guan), Burma.

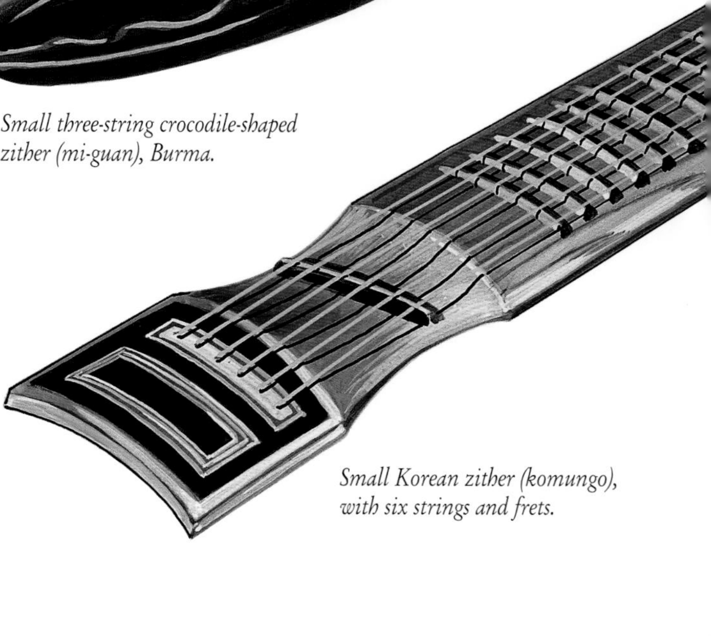

Angular harp, Borneo.

Small Korean zither (komungo), with six strings and frets.

Chinese zither (ku ch'in), with seven strings shortened by the fingers. The places to press the strings are marked with inlaid ivory circles.

Koto

Along with the samisen and the straight pipe from the Japanese theater, for which a rich solo repertory exists, Japanese music is symbolized by the koto. Most classical koto pieces were composed during the Edo period (1615 – 1867), when Edo (today's Tokyo) was the country's capital. Koto is a 13-string instrument with movable bridges and a soundboard that is about 1.8 m long. It is played by moving the bridges, one for each string, and plucking the strings with an ivory plectrum. For centuries, koto was the favorite instrument of the imperial court and the aristocracy, and a common cultural pastime of noble ladies. Different schools modified the instrument's construction and design and established their own styles of playing. Songs were written that demanded koto accompaniment. Along with the samisen and the flute, the koto was a member of the sankyoku chamber ensemble, and its basic repertory is known as danmono.

Japanese koto player.

Japanese zither (koto), with 13 silk strings that can be shortened by moving bridges and are plucked with a plectrum.

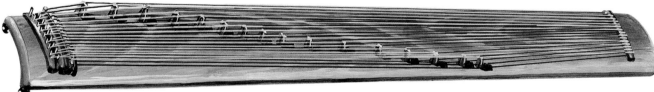

Koto zither, Japan.

Fiddle

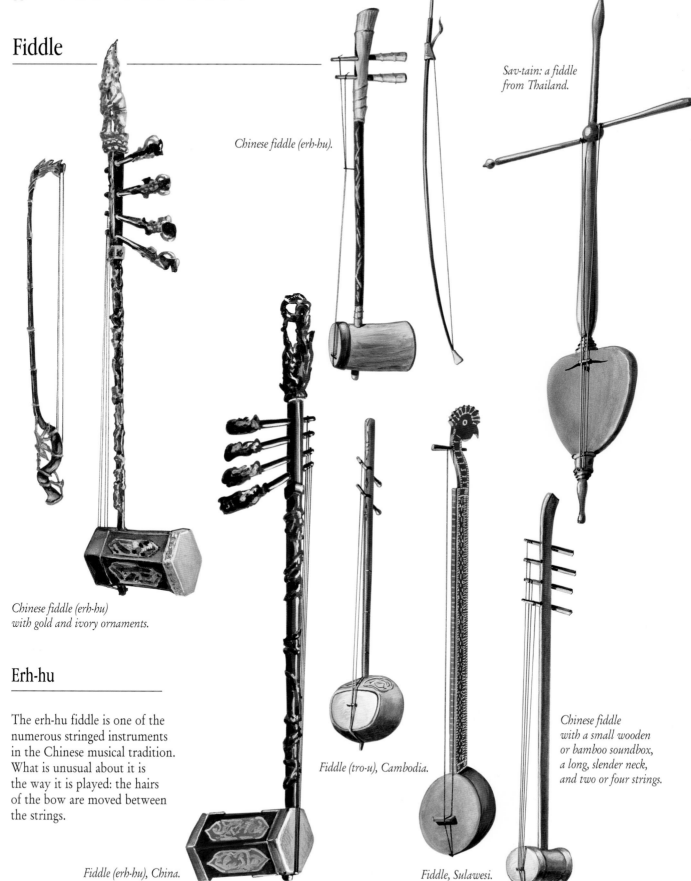

Chinese fiddle (erh-hu).

Sav-tain: a fiddle from Thailand.

Chinese fiddle (erh-hu) with gold and ivory ornaments.

Erh-hu

The erh-hu fiddle is one of the numerous stringed instruments in the Chinese musical tradition. What is unusual about it is the way it is played: the hairs of the bow are moved between the strings.

Fiddle (tro-u), Cambodia.

Fiddle (erh-hu), China.

Fiddle, Sulawesi.

Chinese fiddle with a small wooden or bamboo soundbox, a long, slender neck, and two or four strings.

Lute

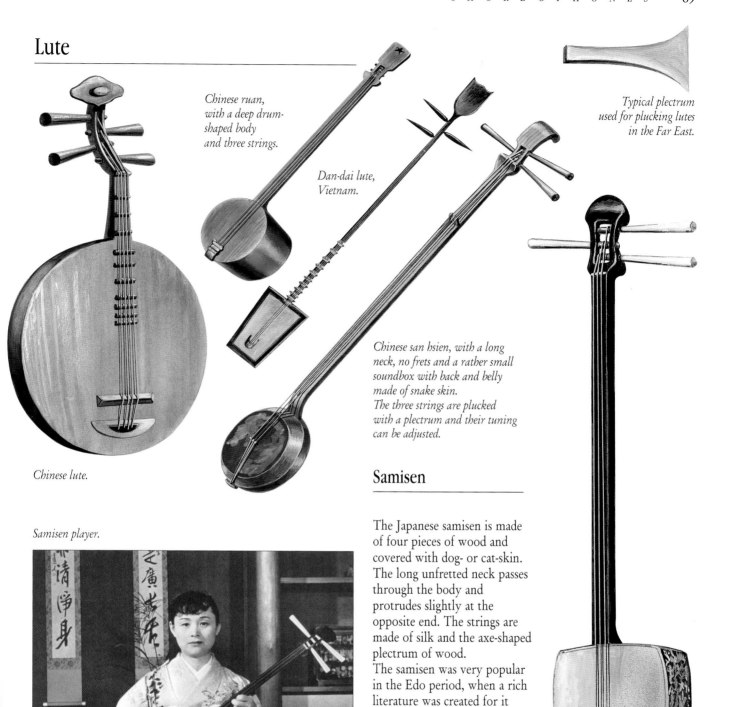

Chinese ruan, with a deep drum-shaped body and three strings.

Dan-dai lute, Vietnam.

Typical plectrum used for plucking lutes in the Far East.

Chinese san hsien, with a long neck, no frets and a rather small soundbox with back and belly made of snake skin.
The three strings are plucked with a plectrum and their tuning can be adjusted.

Chinese lute.

Samisen player.

Samisen

The Japanese samisen is made of four pieces of wood and covered with dog- or cat-skin. The long unfretted neck passes through the body and protrudes slightly at the opposite end. The strings are made of silk and the axe-shaped plectrum of wood.
The samisen was very popular in the Edo period, when a rich literature was created for it (usually for samisen and voice). In contemporary chamber music, it featured in ensembles with the shakuhachi flute. In the Kabuki theater, the samisen was accompanied by a flute and percussion instruments.

Japanese samisen, with a rounded rectangular soundbox, a belly and back made of skin, a very long unfretted neck, and three silk strings to be plucked with a plectrum.

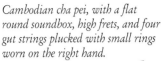

Japanese biwa with a pegbox that is perpendicular to the neck.

Japanese lute (ku).

Cambodian cha pei, with a flat round soundbox, high frets, and four gut strings plucked with small rings worn on the right hand.

Japanese lute (biwa).

Lute, Kalimantan.

Chinese yueh ch'in ("moon ch'in"), with a flat round soundbox, short neck with rather high frets, and four silk strings.

Lutes, Philippines.

Chinese lute (p'i p'a), an instrument favored by women players, with four gut strings plucked with a plectrum, and frets. There is a metal string inside the flat pear-shaped soundbox.

TRADITIONAL ENSEMBLES

The court music gagaku
in Japan, the equivalent of the Chinese "elegant music", was played by ensembles of the same name, performing outdoors, at temples, and at palaces. The gagaku ensemble usually consisted of two orchestras performing on a special platform. The one on the left played Indian or Chinese works, while the one on the right performed Korean and Manchurian works. The two orchestras took turns playing, and offered their audience a very rich repertory indeed, in terms of style as well as of time span.

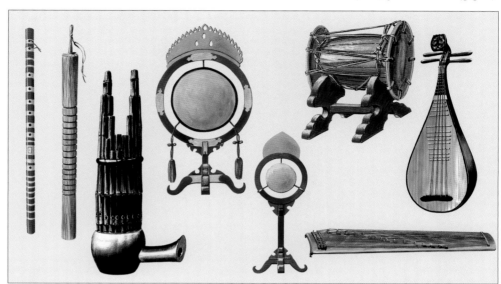

Instruments of the Japanese ensemble (gagaku).

Instruments of the Gamelan orchestra, Java.

The gamelan ensemble has become synonymous with the music of Indonesia and Java. Gamelan means "a strike with a hammer." A legend has it that the Javanese god Sang Hyang Guru used gongs to summon the other gods, thus creating the first gamelan music.
The traditional gamelan orchestra may include up to 75 different percussion instruments grouped in 20 families. The dominating role is taken by gongs of all shapes and sizes. The largest one, the ageng, has a diameter of 90 cm. Interesting instruments in the ensemble include the bonang, the double-head kendang drum (played with both hands), and a variety of xylophones. The debut of the gamelan orchestra in Europe was in 1889, at the World Exhibition in Paris. Thousands of Parisians and tourists gathered next to the newly built Eiffel tower, to listen to the exotic music of far-away East Asia. One of the listeners was the 27-year-old composer Claude Debussy, whose works were influenced by the East Asian music.

INDIA

INDIA'S MUSICAL TRADITIONS date back to the third millennium B. C., and are thus among the most ancient in the world. In India, music and musical instruments are believed to be of divine origin, and their classification according to the European system is only approximate. Classical Indian music uses about 500 different instruments, which are deeply rooted within the country's philosophy, religion, and mythology.

It was in India that the first system of notation was developed, as were the syllables denoting the steps of the scale, sa, ri, ga, ma, pa, dha, ni, corresponding to the familiar descending fa, mi, re, do, si, la, sol. A number of musical texts written on palm leaves have preserved hymns, religious pieces, and cult music.

Between the 12th and the 16th centuries two separate musical styles developed: karnatak in southern India, and Hindustani in northern India and today's Pakistan. The latter was strongly influenced by Persian music and absorbed many of its elements. This was inevitable, given that Hindustani music developed chiefly in the courts of princes, most of whom came from Persia and were Muslims. Karnatak music developed in the temples, and followed its own path.

A variety of vocal styles emerged in India's many provinces, the different types including sacred hymns, rural songs, greeting songs, dance melodies (Bengal), and fishermen's and boatmen's songs. Each type had its own name and unique features.

The establishment of British rule in India in the 18th century did not seem to affect the centers of musical composition and development in northern India; that is to say, the aristocratic circles. However, after 1947, with the pronouncement of the country's independence, aristocratic patronage of the arts lost its significance, and, as in Europe in the 18th and 19th centuries, music began to change its orientation and to address a broader section of the population.

Indian music is characterized by a fusion of dance, song, and instrumental accompaniment. Each style of dance has its own characteristic form of accompaniment, provided by well-established ensemble types. This close connection between music and dance is largely responsible for the wealth and complexity of rhythmic patterns. There may be three, four, five, six, seven, perhaps even as many as 24 beats per measure. The rhythm is usually double, with a sophisticated rhythmic pattern unfolding against the background of a continual pulsating one. Abrupt changes of rhythm are found only in religious music.

Indian music is based on the human voice and is predominantly monophonic. There are five-, six-, and seven-tone scales; scales consisting of seconds are typical. The scales used determine not only the size of the intervals but also the character of the ornamentation, the playing techniques, and the "mood" of a given work, known as the raga. The range of Indian music is no more than four octaves. Instrumentalists imitate the vocal style, and songs are used as a framework for improvisation, which plays an important role in the Indian musical tradition and has helped attract the attention of the West in the second half of the 20th century. Another characteristic feature of Indian music is the rich ornamentation of both vocal and instrumental music.

The melody often passes through microtones (intervals smaller than a semitone), and the parts are delicately, carefully, and richly ornamented.

AEROPHONES

Bamboo Flute

In India, as in all other parts of the world, the transverse flute made of bamboo is widely used. In India it is found under different names: bansi, bansuri, murali, zamsi, and venu in northern India, and kolalu, pilankuzhal, and pilanagrovi in southern India. There is also a great variety of folk flutes.

Pungi (Tiktiri)

The pungi (tiktiri) is an instrument consisting of two reed pipes glued together and inserted into a gourd. The mouthpiece is at the other, smaller end of the gourd. One of the pipes is a drone playing a single note, while the other, with fingerholes that can be adjusted with wax, plays the melody. The pungi is used by snake-charmers and in folk music.

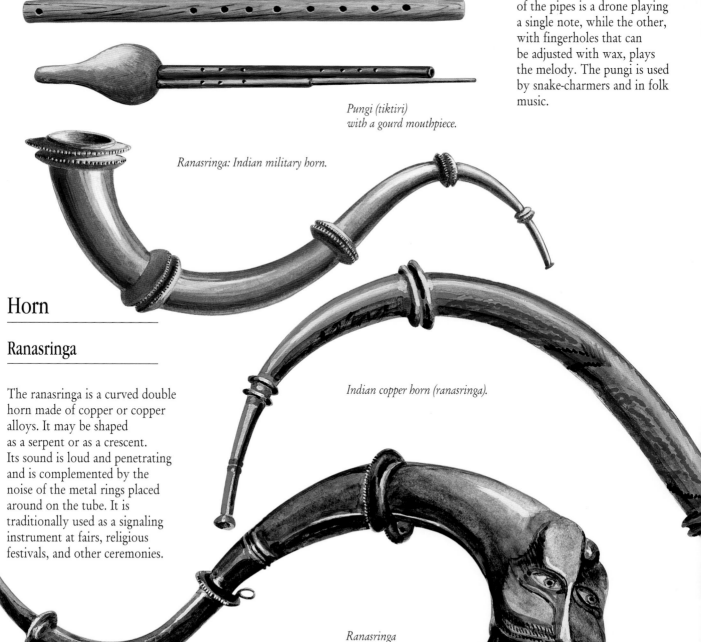

Classical Indian side-blown flute with eight fingerholes.

Pungi (tiktiri) with a gourd mouthpiece.

Ranasringa: Indian military horn.

Indian copper horn (ranasringa).

Ranasringa with two bells, Nepal.

Horn

Ranasringa

The ranasringa is a curved double horn made of copper or copper alloys. It may be shaped as a serpent or as a crescent. Its sound is loud and penetrating and is complemented by the noise of the metal rings placed around on the tube. It is traditionally used as a signaling instrument at fairs, religious festivals, and other ceremonies.

Clarinet

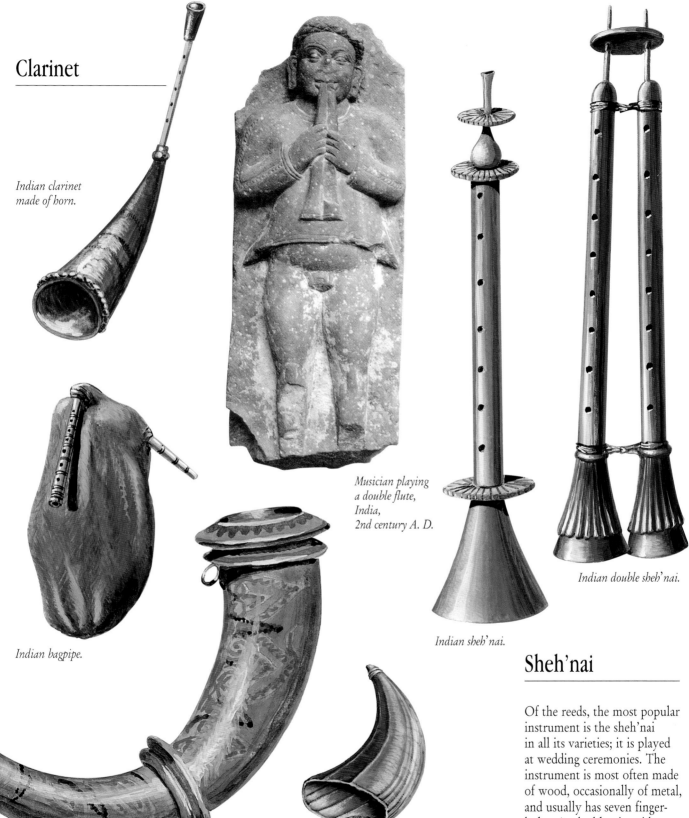

Indian clarinet made of horn.

Musician playing a double flute, India, 2nd century A. D.

Indian bagpipe.

Buffalo horn.

Indian sheh'nai.

Indian double sheh'nai.

Sheh'nai

Of the reeds, the most popular instrument is the sheh'nai in all its varieties; it is played at wedding ceremonies. The instrument is most often made of wood, occasionally of metal, and usually has seven finger-holes. At the blowing side, two flat reeds are inserted with a small space between them.

IDIOPHONES

In India the instruments that serve to keep time, in addition to the drums, are chiefly bells and clappers. In classical Indian music, as well as in religious and dance music, small cup cymbals serve this purpose. These can often be seen in the nagasvaram ensemble in the south. Also in southern India, the earthenware pot (ghatam) is used for rhythmic accompaniment. It is struck with the fingers and is especially convenient for quick tempos.

Jew's harp.

Longitudinally split piece of bamboo which serves as a cult instrument in India.

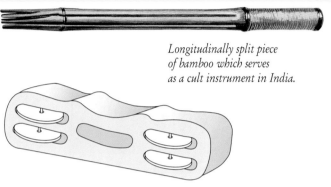

Kartal, India.

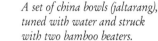

A set of china bowls (jaltarang), tuned with water and struck with two bamboo beaters.

Bells on a belt.

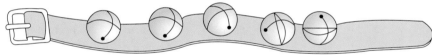

MEMBRANOPHONES

In India, the membranophone family is rich and varied. In the music of southern India, karnatak, the horizontal two-headed mridanga (one of the oldest instruments in that region) is noteworthy; in the north a larger version of this instrument is called pakhavaj.

The dominating northern drum is the tabla, the most popular instrument in Hindustani music. In solo performances, these vertical drums offer an excellent opportunity for the player to display his virtuosity. Within an ensemble, they function as accompaniment, one tabla played with the right hand to supply the tonic and one played with the left hand for the bass part. The tabla is struck with the hands or fingers. It is made in different pitches and timbres. The same playing technique is also used for the popular barrel drum (dholak).

In northern India, the function of the drums is to repeat a rhythmic formula. In the south, the drummer follows the rhythm set by the soloist and interjects occasional vocal phrases. Drummers take turns at playing quick variations (improvisations), adding new rhythmic formulas to the solo melody.

Mridanga: the two membranes are tied to the shell with a network of leather straps. It is tuned by inserting wooden blocks under the straps. For finer tuning, the blocks may be hammered further in.

Long barrel-shaped wooden drum, southern India. This is one of the oldest musical instruments in India with great importance in karnatak music.

Indian tambourine without jingles. The membrane is stretched with cords.

Indian double-head barrel drum (dholak), with cloth-covered shell, used mainly in folk music in northern India. Dholak has a cylindrical or barrel-shaped body about 50 cm long and 30 cm wide. Usually held in a horizontal position, it is played with beaters or with the hands. This instrument is a close relative and an apparent predecessor of the Turkish davul.

Bengali hourglass-shaped double-head drum (dugdugi).

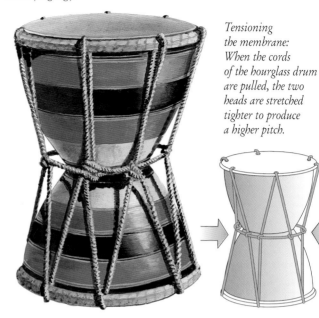

Tensioning the membrane: When the cords of the hourglass drum are pulled, the two heads are stretched tighter to produce a higher pitch.

Banja and Tabla

The banja and the tabla are single-head Indian folk drums. The banja is ball-shaped and made of metal. The tabla is a wooden drum of tubular shape. Its tensioning and consequently its pitch are adjustable with wooden blocks inserted between the shell and the tensioning straps. The head of the banja is tensioned by pulling the cords. In the membranes of both instruments, a circular hole is cut and covered with a round piece of thick, hard skin. Both are struck with the fingers and can produce a variety of rhythmic patterns, pitches, and tone colors.

Drummers, India.
Relief, 1st century B. C.

Tabla.

Banja.

Flat wooden kettle-drum, India.

Indian tudum.

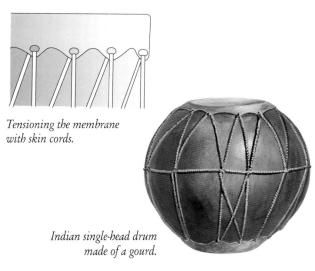

*Tensioning the membrane
with skin cords.*

*Indian single-head drum
made of a gourd.*

Indian tikora drum.

CHORDOPHONES

In the long history of Indian music, plucked
stringed instruments have always been next
in importance after the human voice.
In some regions, such as northern India, they are
even equal in status, whether played solo or as an
accompaniment to the voice. Like instruments from
other groups (aerophones, idiophones,
and membranophones), they are perceived
as incarnations of deities.

Zither

Vina

The vina is the oldest musical instrument in southern India.
It is believed to be a symbol of the goddess Sarasvati. The vina
has two or four melodic strings, with three unstopped strings
running next to the fingerboard, acting as drones and
providing rhythmic figures. The instrument is about a meter
long. Behind the fingerboard, at both ends, there are two
symmetrical gourd soundboxes. Unlike the adjustable sitar
frets, vina frets cannot be moved.

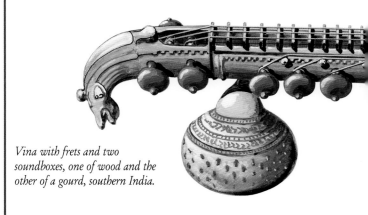

*Vina with frets and two
soundboxes, one of wood and the
other of a gourd, southern India.*

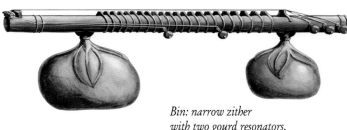

*Bin: narrow zither
with two gourd resonators,
northern India. This is one
of the two main vina types.*

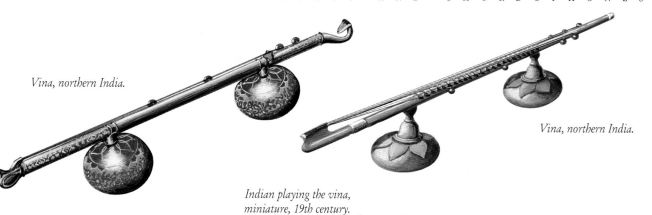

Vina, northern India.

Vina, northern India.

Indian playing the vina, miniature, 19th century.

Fiddle

Sarangi: a traditional bowed instrument, about 60 cm long, with a skin-covered soundbox and a short, broad fingerboard. The bow is heavy. The three melody strings are stopped with the nails from the side. In addition, there are between 11 and 24 sympathetic strings running under the playing strings. In southern India, the sarangi has been superseded by the violin.

Sarinda: a popular folk instrument in India, Nepal and Afganistan. Similar to the sarangi this is a fiddle with three strings, a short fingerboard, and a strange skull-like shape.

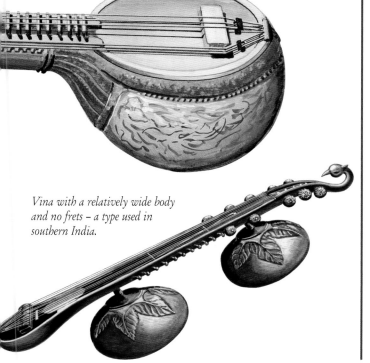

Vina with a relatively wide body and no frets – a type used in southern India.

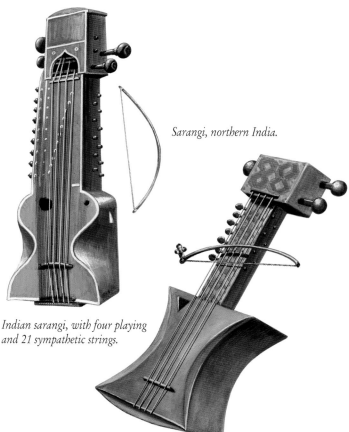

Sarangi, northern India.

Indian sarangi, with four playing and 21 sympathetic strings.

Indian sarinda.

Indian fiddle.

Indian sringara.

The neck of the "peacock" gets open to allow the adjusting of the strings.

Southern Indian mayuri (peacock sitar), with four playing strings and 18 frets. The melodic strings are plucked or bowed.

Lute

Sarod, India.

The tanbur is a lute up to 130 cm long, with a large soundbox made of a gourd and covered with a thin wooden board, and a long fingerboard with four metal strings running over it. The tanbur can be held upright or placed horizontally. The continuous sound of the drone strings functions as a unifying element, and contributes to the special atmosphere created by this instrument.

Tanbur with a fretted fingerboard and four strings, Kashmir.

The sarod is a plucked stringed instrument originating from the Afghan rabab. It is played with a plectrum of ivory or coconut shell. The sarod has six strings, four melodic and two drones, which provide the rhythmic background. There may be between 11 and 16 sympathetic strings.

Surbahar from northern India with melodic and drone strings and 18 frets.

Sitar

The sitar is a plucked stringed instrument of the lute type, which is widely used in northern India. It has developed from the Iranian long lute, and its name derives from the Persian setar. Some of its technical features have been borrowed from the vina. The sitar has a long fingerboard with 19 – 23 metal frets arching over it. The seven strings include five principal playing strings and two drones providing rhythmic accompaniment. Another 8 – 13 sympathetic strings run below the frets, almost parallel to the playing strings. The instrument is played with a wire loop worn on the right index finger.

The legendary musician Amir Khusru (13th / 14th century) was a great reformer of the sitar.

He made a number of changes in the instrument's construction that have been preserved to the present day. He also initiated the introduction of movable frets that could be moved up and down the fingerboard. The fingerboard was thus divided according to the seven-grade octave, and the modes were eliminated. The player could obtain additional tones or semitones by changing the position of these frets.

Today, the most famous sitar player is Ravi Shankar (b. 1920), whose first concerts in Europe and the United States in 1956 – 1957 contributed much to the rediscovery of classical Indian music by the West, and later had a powerful influence on jazz and rock music.

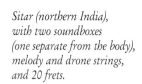

Sitar (northern India), with two soundboxes (one separate from the body), melody and drone strings, and 20 frets.

Instruments of an Indian orchestra.

Despite the great diversity of instruments and musical traditions, the tanbur and the sitar stand out as the basic national instruments in India.

In a set along with the struck tabla, these instruments form the ensemble which is probably best known to westerners. It was this ensemble as well as some sitar players that arose the interest to traditional Indian music in both Europe and America after World War II. These modern influences remind that the great invention of producing sounds of different pitches by means of rubbing the string with a bow and shortening or lengthening it with fingers is connected with the Indian musical tradition.

Indian sitar player.

MIDDLE EAST

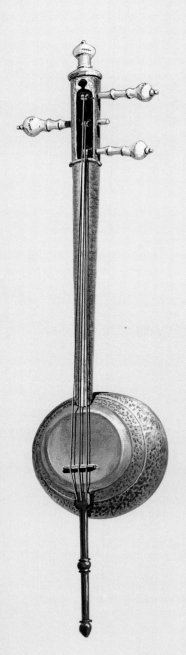

THE MIDDLE EAST IS A CROSSROAD OF CULTURES. The ancient, no longer existing cultures of Assyro-Babylonia, Phoenicia, and Palestine had a rich musical heritage and a great variety of stringed, percussion, and wind instruments: Sumerian sistrums, harps and lyres, Hebrew shofars, metal triangles, and multi-pipe flutes. The Bible mentions the orchestra of Babylonian king Nebuchadnezzar and the exceptional talent of Hebrew king David as a harp player and psalm composer.

Later, the Arabic music exerted a dominating influence. Its roots can be traced back to the 2nd century B. C., to the nomadic Bedouin tribes. Their singers and poets handed down a tradition of rites, songs, dances, and magic spells. The huda singing style (caravan intonations and rhythms, which set the pace of the caravan) dates back to those times, as do the buka funeral chants. In both these forms, music was closely related to text, rhythms were simple, and the range of the melody was no more than a fourth (though the scales included microtones, unlike the scales of traditional Western music).

Another characteristic of Arabic music was its nasal sound. The old instruments used to accompany the traditional singing style included the duff tambourin, the girbal frame drum, the nay flute, the qussaba, a primitive oboe, and the mizmar.

The "golden age" of Arabic music started in the first century of the reign of the Abbasids. The capital was moved from Baghdad to Damascus, bringing the Arabic and Persian cultures closer together. The Arabs adopted the Persian notation system, the 17-tone scale was developed, and the first collection of songs was compiled.

The mosque was an important center for the Islamic musical tradition. The muezzin, who called the faithful to prayer from the top of the tall minaret, was the most experienced and skillful vocalist in religious practice. Believers also participated in the singing: divided into several groups, they performed fine vocal improvisations. The free rhythm and intonation based on chanting had a much greater influence than the Jewish cantilena style that also originated from the ancient Middle East.

The influence of Islam was not restricted to sacred music. Songs were performed by pilgrims on their way to the sacred town of Mecca, and dancing dervishes performed ecstatic dances to the accompaniment of flutes, fiddles, and drums, whirling quickly in a mystical trance.

Arabic art also flourished in Spain (Cordoba, Andalusia) around the end of the 10th century. New musical forms evolved and Moorish instruments were widely used (for example, the rebab and the surna). Adopted and perfected by the Gypsies in Andalusia, their influence led to the development and popularization of flamenco singing and dancing. Arabic music also exerted an unquestionable influence on the art of the troubadours and trouveres in southern France during the Middle Ages. It was from Arabic music that they took the idea of singing to accompaniment and the alternation of vocal and instrumental phrases. Some of the Arabic song genres were also adopted.

Many studies discuss the transmission of Arabic instruments and musical styles to Europe through the Moors in Spain. Few, however, acknowledge the role of the crusaders and their expeditions to the Holy Land. Returning to their homes in Europe, the crusaders brought with them many Arabic instruments and musical practices and styles, and established them within their own cultural environment. Later in the Middle Ages, new instruments evolved from these Arabic prototypes, such as the bowed rebec, tambourines and drums, lutes, zithers and dulcimers, new woodwind instruments, and the long slender trumpet. Gradually, the crusaders adopted the practice of marching to the sound of Turkish percussion and pipes, establishing a new "vogue" in military music and bands.

AEROPHONES

Flute

Turkish flute with two ducts, one of which is a drone.

Tutek: end-blown flute with a mouthpiece from the Caucasus region.

Turkish flute with a mouthpiece.

Flute with a mouthpiece, Iraq.

Wooden flute, Turkey.

Dilli-tujduk, a flute made of cane, with four fingerholes on each of the two tubes, Central Asia.

Clarinet, Oboe and Trumpet

Heteroglottic clarinet made of elder, Near East.

Idioglottic clarinet, with six fingerholes in front and one at the back, made of cane, Near East.

Double clarinet made of bird bone, Palestine.

Arabic double clarinet (arghul el-asghair). This instrument is similar to the Arabic sumara; its two pipes sound simultaneously. As with some other wind instruments, the player applies the technique of circular breathing, providing a continuous sound.

Iraqi playing the flute.

Traditional Turkish surna. Conical in bore, this instrument has several fingerholes in front, one at the back, and a few more on the flared bell. A narrowly bored tube, or baslik, is inserted into the instrument. A metal cone carrying a metal lip disc, and the double reed are fitted into the top of the surna.

Straight carnaj: a metal trumpet from Central Asia.

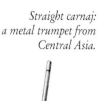

Angel playing the trumpet, miniature from a 14th-century manuscript, Mesopotamia.

Bent carnaj, Central Asia.

Surna. This instrument is known under different names in different parts of the Middle East. It is made from a single piece of wood (usually plum or walnut), including the bell. The surna's length varies from 20 to 60 cm. It has seven fingerholes and its sound is loud and penetrating. The range is usually about an octave but may extend to two octaves. The surna is usually played with the accompaniment of a large double-head drum (davul), in folk, dance, and military music.

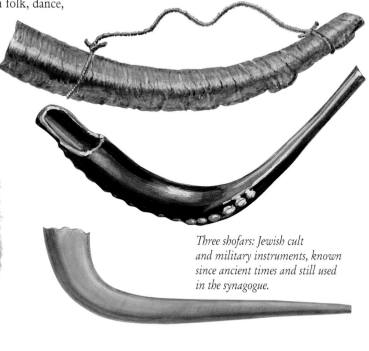

Three shofars: Jewish cult and military instruments, known since ancient times and still used in the synagogue.

Arabic bagpipe.

Shofar. This Jewish instrument is made of a ram's horn, with a mouthpiece at one end. The shofar is decorated with sacred or secular inscriptions. Being primitive in design, it cannot sound many tones but it resounds impressively in the synagogue, creating a solemn atmosphere.

Uzbek sunaj.

Suma oboe, Iraq.

IDIOPHONES

Bronze bells worn on the belt, Siberia, 7th – 9th centuries.

Safail. A struck idiophone found in China, Tajikistan, and Uzbekistan, the safail is a cult instrument also used by wandering musicians. It consists of two pieces of wood bound together, upon which are hung one or two metal rings, with between 10 and 20 smaller rings strung on each of the large rings. The instrument is sounded by shaking or by striking it with the hand or a beater.

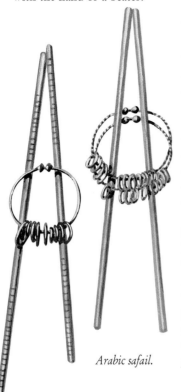

Arabic safail.

Turkish Crescent

This idiophone's prototypes were used by ancient Egyptians, Persians, Arabs, Copts, and Tibetans. It arrived in Europe in the 15th century, and became widely popular in the 16th century, when the so-called "Turkish" music was fashionable. A staff surmounted by a crescent, it was hung with horsetails and numerous bells and chimes that jingled when shaken. The Turkish crescent was used in the British and German armies in the 18th and 19th centuries. In America the Turkish crescent became known as "jingling Johnny." A number of famous composers called for it in their works: Mozart in *The Abduction from the Seraglio* (1782), Haydn in his Symphony No. 100 (*Military*, 1794), and Beethoven in his Symphony No. 9 (1824). In performances of these works the Turkish crescent is now replaced by the triangle for technical reasons. The record goes to Berlioz, who called for as many as four Turkish crescents in his *Symphonie funèbre et triomphale* (1840).

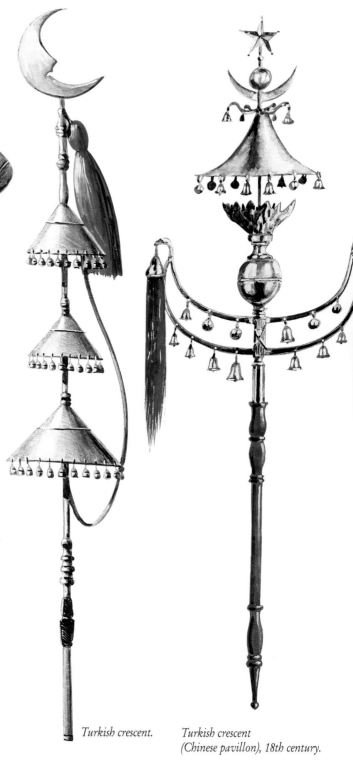

Turkish crescent.

Turkish crescent (Chinese pavillon), 18th century.

Medieval oriental clapper.

Bronze cymbals, Mesopotamia.

Babylonian struck idiophones made of clay.

Cymbals, Central Asia.

Bells used for cult purposes, Palestine.

Assyrian bell.

Bronze cymbals, Assyria, c. 8th century B. C.

Turkish tambourine (tar).

Bronze bell, Assyria, 8th – 7th centuries B. C.

Tambourine with jingles and bells.

MEMBRANOPHONES

Davul. This is the largest of the double-head drums in the Middle East. Its size varies, but most often the diameter is 55 cm and the shell is between 28 and 40 cm deep. The shell is made of wood, and the skin membranes are tied with ropes. The davul is carried on the left shoulder and struck with a curved wooden beater held in the right hand. In the left hand, the player holds a thinner stick to strike the instrument's other head.

Davul, double-head wooden drum, Turkey.

Arabic goblet-shaped drum.

Tensioning the membranes of a double-head drum with hoops and cords.

Richly ornamented goblet-shaped ceramic drum (darabuka), Persia.

Arabic clay darabuka.

Darabuka. A pot-shaped single-head drum, the darabuka is usually made of clay but may also be made of wood or copper. The membrane is glued or tied to the shell. The instrument is held almost horizontally, with the membrane in front. It is usually carried on a strap at thigh level.

Small metal single-head drum (chindaul), Uzbekistan.

Hourglass-shaped single-head wooden drum, Turkey.

Three Arabic drums (darabukke) made of clay.

Arabic naqqara: direct precursor of the European timpani. Made of clay, copper, or wood, these were played in pairs, each pair consisting of a smaller and a larger drum held together by netting. The naqqara are played with two beaters with cloth-covered ends. Though found in the Middle East, they originated in India, where instruments as tall as a man may be seen.

Tambourine, Caucasus region.

Tambourine, Uzbekistan.

Arabic timpani (naqqara).

Daira, Kirghizia.
This instrument is popular in many countries of the Middle East. It differs from the ordinary tambourine in its larger size and in the fine metal rings strung around the inside of the hoop instead of jingles. When the daira is struck or shaken the rings emit a hissing sound.

Square tambourine with a skin membrane.

Naqqara, Central Asia.

Timplipito: another predecessor of European timpani. These are found in Persia, the Caucasus, and Asia Minor. The timplipito are made of two pots of different sizes covered with goatskin or bladder. On the bottom, small holes ensure the membrane's free vibration. The two pots are wrapped in netting and tied together. They are struck with wooden beaters with rounded ends or with the fingers.

Diplipito, a variety of the timplipito, Azerbaijan.

Pair of timplipito timpani.

CHORDOPHONES

In Arabic and Islamic culture, musical instruments, especially chordophones, were related to mystical beliefs about the day and night, the days of the week, the seasons, and the astrological signs. For example, the four strings of the ud symbolized the four seasons, the four phases of the moon, the four alchemical elements, and the four temperaments.

Lyre, Harp and Zither

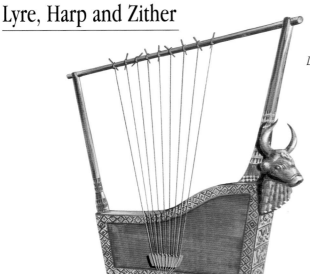

Lyre, Ur, 3000 B. C.

Sumerian 11- string lyre made of silver.

The lyre and the harp were known in Sumer as early as 3000 B. C. Sumerian lyres were asymetrical and the shorter arm of the yoke was held closer to the player. They were quite big in size, standing higher than a seated man.

Assyrian musicians. Relief, 7th century B. C.

Gold harp, Assyria, 2450 B. C.

Bow-shaped harp
of the Ostyaks in Ural.

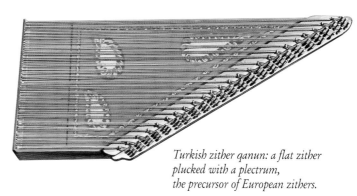

Turkish zither qanun: a flat zither
plucked with a plectrum,
the precursor of European zithers.

Aramaean lyres, Senjirli,
11th century B. C.

Iranian dulcimer (santur).

In Iran and Iraq, the santur is a national instrument. Trapezoidal
in shape, it has quadruple metal strings and a bridge that divides
them in the ratio 2:1 (the two sections giving tones an octave
apart). Some later models are played on a table and have
a damper pedal. The santur traveled from Iran and Iraq to China
and Korea, and later to India where it won great popularity.

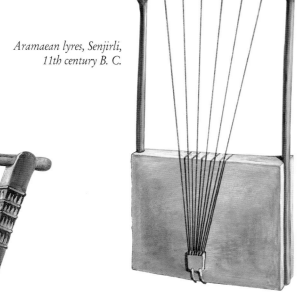

Uzbek dulcimer (chang).

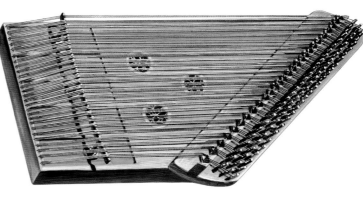

Arabic qanun.

Lute

Ud. This instrument, decorated with oriental lavishness, is the parent of all European lutes. Five double strings once made of silk, today of nylon, run along the short bent neck. Four of the strings are tuned to fourths, while the fifth sounds a tone lower. The rich tone of the ud made it a leading instrument in classical Arabic and Eastern musical ensembles.

Arabic musicologists have studied the characteristics of various instruments of the lute family – the Chinese p'i p'a, the Japanese biwa, the Vietnamese tiba, etc. – and have not only found them related with the ud but have also discovered their paths of influence. On the one hand, this influence arrived through the Persian labourers who took part in the construction of Kaaba; on the other hand, it came with the sailors and merchants whose routes passed through South-East Asia and North Africa. The first musician to have played the ud is believed to be a Saib Hasir in the first century. Although never proven, this legend is important as the ud was the precursor not only of European lutes but also of Arabic plucked instruments.

Because the name "ud" means not only "wood" but also a "flexible stick", many scholars believe that the instrument might have developed from the musical bow. The importance of the ud for Arab musical culture can be compared with the significance of the vina or the koto for the culture of India or Japan. Today the instrument is still widely used in traditional ensembles all over the Middle East.

Tanbur, Tajikistan.

Arabic ud, with a short bent neck and double courses of strings that are plucked with a plectrum.

Tanbur.

Tanbur with four strings and no frets, Kashmir.

Tanbur with five strings and movable frets, Iran.

Young man playing the lute, 14th-century manuscript, Mesopotamia.

Dombra, Uzbekistan.

Saz with a small elegant soundbox and two strings running over a long fretted fingerboard.

Kirghiz komuz.

Kazakh domra.

Eight-string saz, Azerbaijan.

Kirghiz komuz with gut strings.

Dombra is a double lute, used widely in Kazakhstan, Kirghizia, Turkmenistan and Mongolia. The Asian dombra is triangular and has two strings. The dombra is plucked with a plectrum. It was from this instrument that the Russian domra evolved.

Saz

The saz is a long-necked Turkish lute found from Azerbaijan to Albania. The pear-shaped body is hollowed out, and in some versions there are no soundholes. The strings are made of fine dried gut or nylon. Modern examples sold in the East today are fretted for a Pythagorean scale, with additional two frets in the first octave. The popular Greek bouzouki evolved from the saz. In the Islamic religion, the saz has symbolic significance: the instrument's body symbolizes Ali, the fourth caliph, and the fingerboard his sword.

Two-string dutar, Turkmenistan.

Chonguri, Georgia.

Four-string tar with mobile frets, Iran.

Sitar, Iran.

Tar. The body of this instrument is made of wood in a figure-of-eight shape, and is covered with skin. The long neck ends in a pegbox with three or more tuning pegs. The strings are made of metal and are plucked with a plectrum. The tuning of the tar varies across the different regions of the Middle East. Indeed, it may even vary from one village to the next.

Fiddle

Rabab

The rabab or rebab (also rubab) is an Arabic bowed instrument, existing in a variety of shapes and with a belly made of skin instead of a board. There are two main types of this bowed instrument. One is characterized by a small soundbox and a long neck and has two strings. The other has only one string and its neck practically a continuation of the soundbox, being made in one piece with it.

One-string rebab, Syria.

Rubab, Tashkent.

Rebab, Iraq.

Kemancha is a traditional fiddle in Central Asia. It is found from Iran to the former Central Asian Soviet republics. Its body is made of mulberry segments joined together, and the belly is covered with the skin of Caspian fishes. The long neck ends in a metal spike on which the instrument is supported. The three (today four) strings are tuned in fourths. A kemancha variant with four strings and violin tuning has recently become more popular in Central Asia. In Iran, it is successfully replaced by the classical violin.

The Koran bans the use of music in religious services (although the ban is not too strict or implicit), and Arabic music has developed mainly as a secular art form. Music was an integral part of life in the homes of the caliphs, the aristocracy and the connoisseurs, and it was equally valued with poetry. Word and sound were practically inseparable and gradually developed into a rich and sophisticated tradition. The main musical role belonged to the stringed instruments.

The bowed stringed instruments that spread from India quickly became more sophisticated and gained the leading position in the music of the Arabic world. The secular music reached its peak after the 7th century A. D. when Persia became part of the Arab caliphate. A remarkable ruler was Kharun al Rashid, the caliph of Baghdad, mentioned in the 1001 Nights tales. His court attracted many musicians playing mainly stringed instruments such as the rebab, the kemancha, the tar and so on. They composed music on the poetry written by the great caliph. Kharun al Rashid was a capable diplomat and his contacts with Charles the Great became a bridge for the spreading of some plucked and bowed stringed instruments in Europe. At the same time, in the Middle East, and in its Arabic part in particular, the stringed instruments contributed to the development of a musical and performing style characterized by a complicated ornamented phrase in many variations, similar to the ornamental arabesques in the architecture.

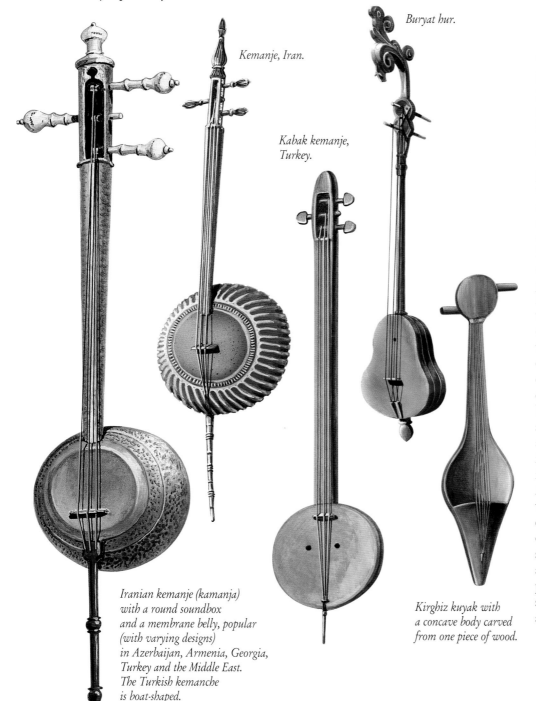

Kemanje, Iran.

Kabak kemanje, Turkey.

Buryat hur.

Iranian kemanje (kamanja) with a round soundbox and a membrane belly, popular (with varying designs) in Azerbaijan, Armenia, Georgia, Turkey and the Middle East. The Turkish kemanche is boat-shaped.

Kirghiz kuyak with a concave body carved from one piece of wood.

EUROPE

IT WAS IN THE EUROPEAN TRADITION that the art of music was first separated from the folklore. Moreover, from the theoretical studies of the ancient Greeks and their application to the present day, Europeans have been working on the evolution of this art, on the perfection of musical instruments and on the exploration of new ways of musical communication.

For almost five hundred years, particularly during the Renaissance and the Enlightenment, Europe has been persistently prioritizing the work of the composer, who is inevitably at the top of the musical hierarchy. Despite this, despite the continuing Euro-centrism in music, and despite the "colonialism" (of the Italian opera, the German symphony art, and the American pop-culture), European culture is highly receptive to a variety of influences. It adapts and incorporates examples of different cultural traditions and in its turn exerts influence on the development of music in other continents and in the world in general. This susceptibility to the flavour of previously alien, non-European cultures has enriched its palette which now ranges from preserved elements of medieval folklore to experiments in electronic music and sound production.

However, the greatest asset of European music is its immense variety: ethnic, regional, national, religious, folk, and even dialect variety. The Old World is the home of a wealth of half-forgotten music, never-played and rediscovered works: a rich resource for the trans-continental culture of the future. It is evident that the beginning of the third millennium A. D. will be an era of active cultural and musical exchange, of rapid integration of culturally less-known parts of the globe.

It has long been known that many of the instruments of the classical symphony orchestra have their origins and prototypes in the East. The development of more "democratic" genres and forms in the late 19th – early 20th century in North and South America reverberated in Europe. What is more, it was Europe that realized what was happening across the ocean and transformed it into a cultural process. The classical musical tradition in its turn was quick to conquer America and was later discovered in Japan. This connection was consolidated in the second half of the 20th century when the East attracted the attention of both artists and the general public with its rich cultural traditions. The gradual disintegration of ideological, political, and religious barriers provided a new opportunity for intercultural communication and influence exchange. This process had its forerunners in a few brilliant minds as early as the beginning of the 20th century. D. H. Lawrence wrote that humanity was like an uprooted giant tree. This thought resounded in the works of the writers James Joyce and André Malraux, the painters Paul Gauguin and Pablo Picasso, and the composers Igor Stravinsky and Karlheinz Stockhausen. Europeans have become increasingly receptive to the culture of non-European peoples.

As a result of this openness and of a wealth of research and theoretical work, Europe is still the only continent to offer a systematic method of tracing its musical development by historical periods, which we have tried to follow in the present chapter through the evolution of musical instruments.

EUROPE — ANTIQUITY

Musical instruments are known to have existed in Europe as long as 25,000 years ago. In the present discussion, however, "antiquity" is used to denote the cultures of ancient Greece and Rome on which modern European culture is based. An introduction to an ode by Pindar, dating back to the 5th century B. C. (published only in 1650), is believed to be the earliest piece of music to have survived in notated form. Ancient Greek civilization is divided into five main periods: the Cretan-Mycenaen period, the Homeric period, the transitional period, the classical period, and the Hellenistic period. In the third of these, from the 8th to the 5th centuries B. C., new musical traditions developed in centers such as Sparta and the island of Lesbos. The school of kithara playing on Lesbos introduced the new art of kitharodia (kithara-accompanied vocal performance), which later served as a model for the aulodia (singing accompanied by the aulos). The choral and solo lyric flourished in the form of the ceremonious ode. In the classical period, drama gave a further impetus to the de-velopment of musical traditions such as the performance of Dithyrambs (hymns in honor of the god Dionysus) by a chorus and soloist.

In antiquity great emphasis was placed on the theory of intervals. The ancient Greeks were familiar not only with the diatonic scale but also with the chromatic and enharmonic forms. They were the first in Europe to attempt a system of musical notation. They also did research in the field of acoustics: in the 6th century B. C. Pythagoras studied intervals acoustically and determined their mathematical proportions.

Though vocal music predominated in Greek antiquity, instruments also had an important role to play. The above-mentioned kitharodia and aulodia were followed by traditions such as the lyrodia and auletic. Practically all groups of instruments were known and used by the ancient Greeks. Of the stringed instruments (or chordophones), the lyre and the kithara were widely used. The aerophone group was represented by the syrinx and the aulos. There was a variety of percussion instruments, although they were less highly regarded than the strings and the winds.

The music of ancient Rome – the empire that ruled the world for centuries – borrowed much from ancient Greece. As the circus, the theater and the games were widely popular, so were the choirs and instrumental ensembles. The performing arts were highly valued and virtuosity was a must for each musician, particularly in playing the aulos. Stringed instruments such as the harp, the lyre, the kithara, wind instruments such as the flute, the syrinx and the tibia, the bagpipe and the organ were borrowed from ancient Greece. Brass tubes, however, were much improved because of their wide use in military campaigns. It might be said that the Roman brass tubes were the earliest ancestors of the modern brass instruments.

AEROPHONES

Bull-roarer

Bull-roarer.   Bull-roarer "forest devil".   Bull-roarer.   Whip.

Panpipe

The panpipe is an ancient musical instrument, dating back to at least 2000 B. C. It was named after the Greek god of woods, fields, and flocks. According to legend, the nymph Syrinx was transformed into a reed by the river god, so that she might escape the advances of Pan. Pan made a flute of the reed and named it after his beloved nymph.
This is why in ancient Greece this instrument was also known as syrinx.
The panpipe consists of a varying number of pipes with simple openings, very occasionally with notches below.
The pipes are joined together with wax or rope, in one or two rows, straight or curved, or sometimes in a circle.
Some panpipes have several channels within a single body.
The pipes vary in length, and when blown they produce tones of different pitches. There are no fingerholes, each tube produces a single tone.

Ancient panpipe.
Reconstruction.

Tibia and Aulos

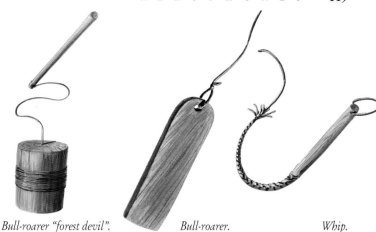

Roman tibia made of bone.

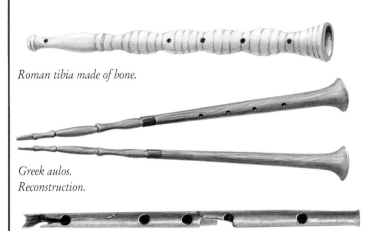

Greek aulos.
Reconstruction.

Wooden aulos from Corinth, fragment.

Musician playing the aulos.
Greek vase, 5th century B. C.

The tibia is a Roman whistle made of bone (tibia means shin-bone). Its sound-making principle is similar to that of the ancient Greek aulos. Aulos were usually played in pairs of two pipes. As varieties of double reed instruments the aulos and tibia are considered to be among the precursors of the oboe, yet it is possible that some of them have been played like flutes. On ancient vases, depictions of aulos players include the strap that was placed around the face to prevent the cheeks from puffing out from the forceful blowing. Aulos music, often associated with the cult of Dionysus, was believed to have strong erotic impact.

Clarinet, Trumpet, Horn

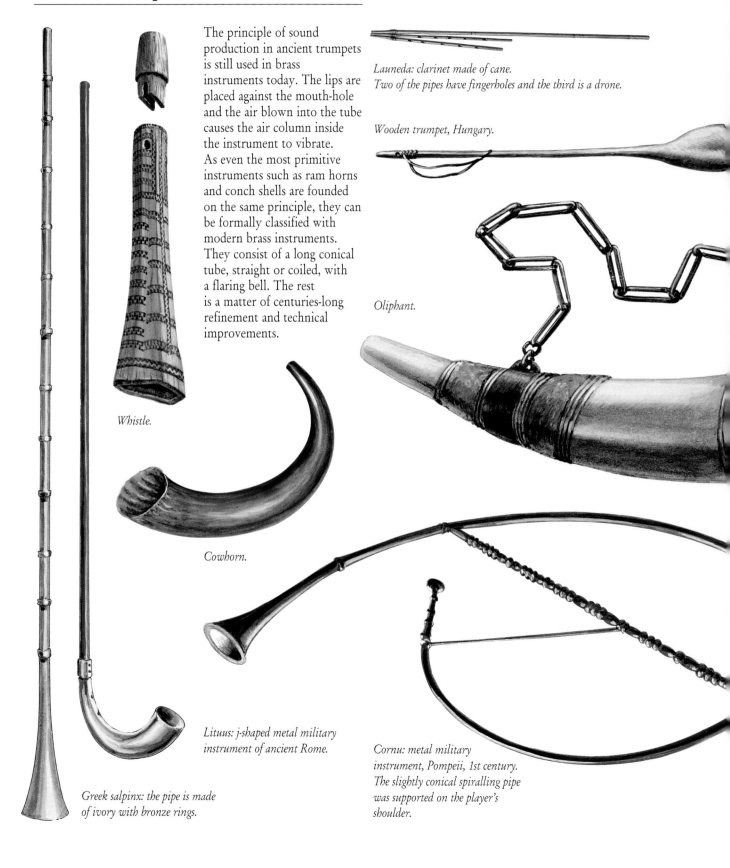

The principle of sound production in ancient trumpets is still used in brass instruments today. The lips are placed against the mouth-hole and the air blown into the tube causes the air column inside the instrument to vibrate. As even the most primitive instruments such as ram horns and conch shells are founded on the same principle, they can be formally classified with modern brass instruments. They consist of a long conical tube, straight or coiled, with a flaring bell. The rest is a matter of centuries-long refinement and technical improvements.

Whistle.

Cowhorn.

Greek salpinx: the pipe is made of ivory with bronze rings.

Lituus: j-shaped metal military instrument of ancient Rome.

Launeda: clarinet made of cane. Two of the pipes have fingerholes and the third is a drone.

Wooden trumpet, Hungary.

Oliphant.

Cornu: metal military instrument, Pompeii, 1st century. The slightly conical spiralling pipe was supported on the player's shoulder.

Lur: a bronze instrument of the Vikings, dating back to the Stone Age. It spread throughout Europe between the 10th and the 5th centuries B. C. In 1797 it was rediscovered and named lur, an old Scandinavian word meaning "a calling horn." Conical in bore, its tube spirals and ends in a wide flare with a flat disc. The shape was probably suggested by the tusk of the mammoth, while the mouthpiece is similar to that of the modern trombone. It was probably used in ceremonies of various sorts.

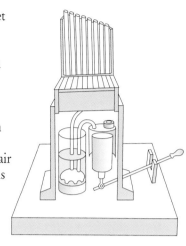

Hydraulis

The water organ has a small set of reed pipes (similar to the aulos) of different shape and construction. The water organ was the first instrument that was capable of playing polyphonic combinations. The most important invention used in this instrument is the mechanical device for feeding air to the pipes regularly by means of a water pump. The hydraulis was used in Greece and Rome, and from there it spread all over the Mediterranean region. In Rome, it was played at royal receptions, theatrical performances, races and games. About 350 A. D., water as a pressure regulator was replaced by bellows and the pneumatic organ appeared: simpler in construction, smaller in size but of inferior and unequal sound quality.

Construction of the hydraulis.

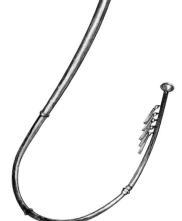

*Scandinavian lur,
5th – 4th centuries B. C.*

*Water organ, Aquincum
(a Roman town near present-day
Budapest), 3rd century.
Reconstruction.*

*Detail of a hydraulis
(also known as Roman organ)
by Ctesibios, Pompeii,
1st century B. C.*

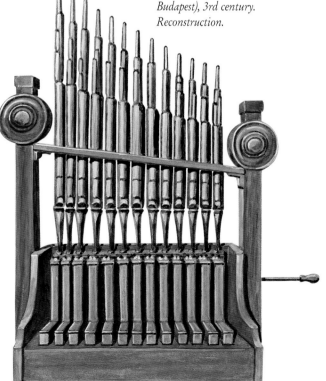

IDIOPHONES

Scraper from the Stone Age.

Bell, ancient Greece.

Goblet-shaped metal drum with engraved symbols (known as the Bernburg drum), 3rd century B. C.

Cymbal

Cymbals are metallophones of indefinite pitch. They were played as cult instruments by the ancient Greeks, Romans, Jews, and Assyrians. They consist of two slightly dished circular plates, usually made of brass and about ten to fifty cm in width. They are either clashed together in pairs or, when suspended, struck with a beater. Smaller antique cymbals are also known as crotales.

Roman cymbals.

Bronze cymbals, Pompeii.

Zilia-massa (metal castanets). This instrument consists of one or more pairs of small cymbals on a frame shaped like a two-pronged fork, or made of steel wire. The sound is of indefinite pitch and is produced by clashing the two rows of crotales together. The instrument is held in the right hand and struck against the left palm, or, for a quick succession of clashes, passed along the fingers of the left hand. Metal castanets were used in ancient Egypt, in Greece and Rome, by the Copts, and in the Orient.

Zilia-massa.

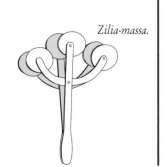

CHORDOPHONES

Lyre

The lyre is a plucked stringed instrument consisting of a rectangular or rounded soundbox and two arms reaching to a crossbar. Strings extend from the crossbar to the lower part of the soundbox. These are played with the fingers or, less often, with a plectrum. The lyres of the ancient cultures are the oldest instruments of this family. Images of lyres exist from the Sumerian culture, c. 2800 B. C. The instrument was used in Egypt, Babylonia, Assyria, and other countries of the Middle East. Nowadays the instrument is associated mainly with ancient Greece, where it was initially identical with the ancient kithara. It was referred to as kithara in Asia Minor and on the islands, while the word lyre was used to the north. Gradually, there developed differences in construction, chiefly in the soundbox: the soundbox of the lyre was rounded and made of tortoise shell, while that of the kithara was flat. At first both instruments had four strings, but their number gradually increased to seven. Pythagoras introduced the diatonically tuned eight-string lyre. The kithara developed further than the lyre, becoming a key element in ancient Greek musical culture while the lyre remained more primitive.

Roman lyre from the time of Octavian Augustus. Reconstruction.

Since ancient times, the lyre has been the symbol of the fundamental deep harmony of figures in the universe. This seven-string instrument expresses the harmony of the celestial spheres, the strings corresponding to the number of planets. The four-string lyre symbolizes the four elements: fire, air, water and earth. The mythology associates it with Erato, Apollo and Aeolus, but chiefly with Orpheus. The legend goes that the music of Orpheus mesmerized not only humans and beasts but even the rocks.

*Ancient Greek lyre,
3rd century B. C.
Reconstruction.*

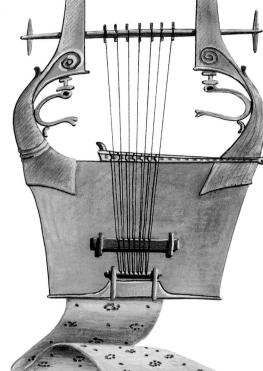

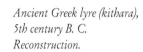

*Ancient Greek lyre (kithara),
5th century B. C.
Reconstruction.*

Musician playing the kithara, amphora, 5th century.

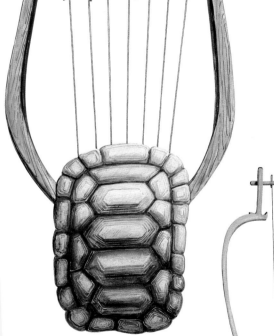

*Ancient Greek lyre
made of tortoise shell.
Reconstruction.*

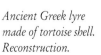

*Ancient Greek lyre with a soundbox
made of skin, 5th century B. C.
Reconstruction.*

EUROPE — FOLK MUSIC

The folk music of Europe found its first "professional" performers in the ancient Greek bards (the aeds) but its significance grew considerably during the Middle Ages, owing to the travelling trouveres and jugglers. With them, the endless circle of music began: from then on, it would pass from person to person, from generation to generation, from one geographical area to another. In the course of that process, the different elements of the art of music were formed, under the influence of the immense variety of instruments. Many of them were the early prototypes of contemporary instruments; others gradually fell out of use and disappeared. At a later stage, particularly during the age of Romanticism in Europe, the folk music incorporated some of the contemporary instruments: the violin, the clarinet, the trumpet, and the accordion.

The folk music of Europe, like that of all other continents, is ancient, rich, and varied. The modern scientific classification of instruments (aerophones, idiophones, membranophones, and chordophones) allows us to follow the evolution of folk music, the relations between the different instrument groups, and the characteristics of the different musical styles in smaller or larger regions of the continent. Many instruments were used to accompany dance, in feasts, or for ritual purposes. The influence of the East transmitted by the Moors in Spain, the crusaders, and the Ottoman invasion in Europe introduced new instruments that were adapted, modified, and perfected. Reed aerophones are found everywhere in Europe, while the great variety of flutes is more typical of Eastern Europe. The zither is most popular in the region of the Alps and in Scandinavia, both as an accompanying and a solo instrument. Fiddles and lutes are used chiefly in the Mediterranean and in Eastern Europe.

A number of folk instruments that preserved their initial design through the ages are now being adapted in accordance with the demands of modern music, which is increasingly interested in unusual timbres.

There is, however, another group of instruments covering the whole range of the scientific classification: the toy instruments and fairground whistles, a specific element of the folk tradition. Their simple construction and their generally loud and penetrating sound bring the world of music closer to children.

The importance of folk music is so significant that there is practically no great composer whose works do not contain reverberations of the folk music and its elements. Until the early 20th century and the emergence of the avant-garde composing techniques, folklore served as a source of ideas, themes, metro-rhythmic structures and harmonic solutions for the rich heritage of musical works. This trend was particularly strong in the 19th century, the time of the national movements in Europe. The virtuosos of the Romantic period incorporated a wealth of folk material in their works, popularizing it in and outside Europe.

AEROPHONES

Ocarina

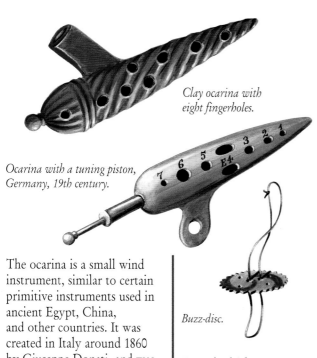

Clay ocarina with eight fingerholes.

Ocarina with a tuning piston, Germany, 19th century.

The ocarina is a small wind instrument, similar to certain primitive instruments used in ancient Egypt, China, and other countries. It was created in Italy around 1860 by Giuseppe Donati, and was introduced into the folk music of many countries.
The ocarina is a diatonic instrument shaped like a goose's head, from which it takes its name ("oca" is the Italian word for "goose"). It is made of terracotta or metal. Larger models may be up to 30 cm long. Some fine examples are made of porcelain and those produced in Meissen are particularly valued by collectors and antique dealers. The ocarina has eight fingerholes in two rows, for the left and right hand respectively. Its range varies from an octave to an octave and a half.

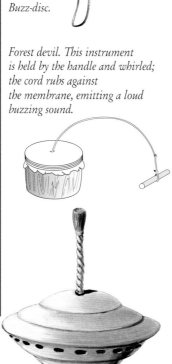

Buzz-disc.

Forest devil. This instrument is held by the handle and whirled; the cord rubs against the membrane, emitting a loud buzzing sound.

Party whistle, which unfolds when blown and makes a penetrating sound.

Metal humming top with holes and a spiral handle for spinning, found everywhere in Europe.

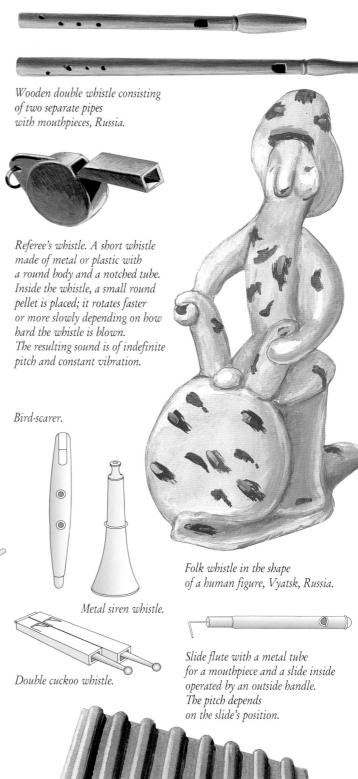

Wooden double whistle consisting of two separate pipes with mouthpieces, Russia.

Referee's whistle. A short whistle made of metal or plastic with a round body and a notched tube. Inside the whistle, a small round pellet is placed; it rotates faster or more slowly depending on how hard the whistle is blown. The resulting sound is of indefinite pitch and constant vibration.

Bird-scarer.

Metal siren whistle.

Double cuckoo whistle.

Folk whistle in the shape of a human figure, Vyatsk, Russia.

Slide flute with a metal tube for a mouthpiece and a slide inside operated by an outside handle. The pitch depends on the slide's position.

Plastic toy panpipe.

Flute

Kaval, Bulgaria.

Flute, Hungary.

Stabule flute, Latvia.

Hungarian flute.

Norwegian recorder.

*Romanian double flute
with two channels,
one of them a drone.*

*Slovak flauta,
with a beautifully
carved ram's head.*

Making of a flute.

Dvoyanka

The dvoyanka is a wooden wind instrument, usually prismatic in shape. It has two parallel ducts and a double mouthpiece. A Slavic instrument, it is most often made in sycamore, ash, or cherry wood, and up to 30 – 40 cm long. In most cases one of the ducts is without fingerholes, with a single side opening, and functions as a drone. The other has fingerholes and plays the melody. The dvoyanka occasionally consists of two separate tubes joined together.

*Dvojnica (dvoyanka): a double
flute of the southern Slavs,
carved from a single piece of wood.*

Russian wooden flute.

Wooden flute with a pitch-adjusting slide.

Panpipe

Panpipes are made of a variety of materials: reed, clay, bone, stone, wood, metal, or, in more recent times, plastic. They are still used in the folk music of Europe, the Far East, South America, and various other regions.

The instrument appears alone or within an ensemble under many different names, such as samponas (Bolivia), nay (Romania), pai hsiao (Japan), and skudchyai (Lithuania). After Mozart used it as Papageno's instrument in his opera *The Magic Flute*, the panpipe also became known as the "Papageno flute." In European musical culture, George Zamfir is well-known as a virtuoso player of the Romanian panpipe.

Wooden panpipe, Moravia.

Romanian panpipe (nay).

Wooden flute with a piston.

Panpipe made from a set of recorders, 15th century.

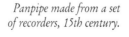

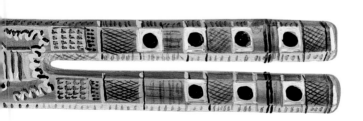

Skudgyay: a Lithuanian panpipe with notched stopped pipes. The pitch is adjusted by placing peas in the pipes.

Clarinet

*Welsh pibcorn clarinet:
a wooden pipe with a mouthpiece
which holds a reed and a bell
made of animal horn.*

*Russian folk instrument
(rozhok).*

Hornpipe, Finland.

*Wooden clarinet
with a horn bell, Scotland.*

Alboca

The alboca is a primitive folk
clarinet used by shepherds
in northern Spain. Made of
cane, elder, or bone, and with
a single reed, some albocas
consist of two pipes joined
together. A cow's horn
is inserted in the upper end,
and the mouthpiece
is covered tightly by the
player's lips. Like the Welsh
pibcorn, the alboca belongs
to the double hornpipe
family. Primitive Russian
clarinets probably developed
from this Spanish instrument,
which in turn probably
originated in the Middle East.
Since the 15th century,
"alboca" has also been the
name of a popular Spanish
dance.

Two Basque albocas.

Cross-section of the alboca.

Basque alboca player.

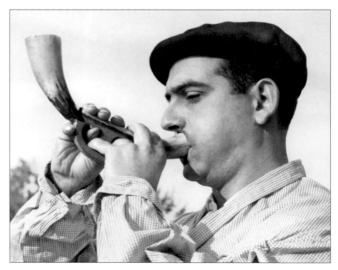

Horn

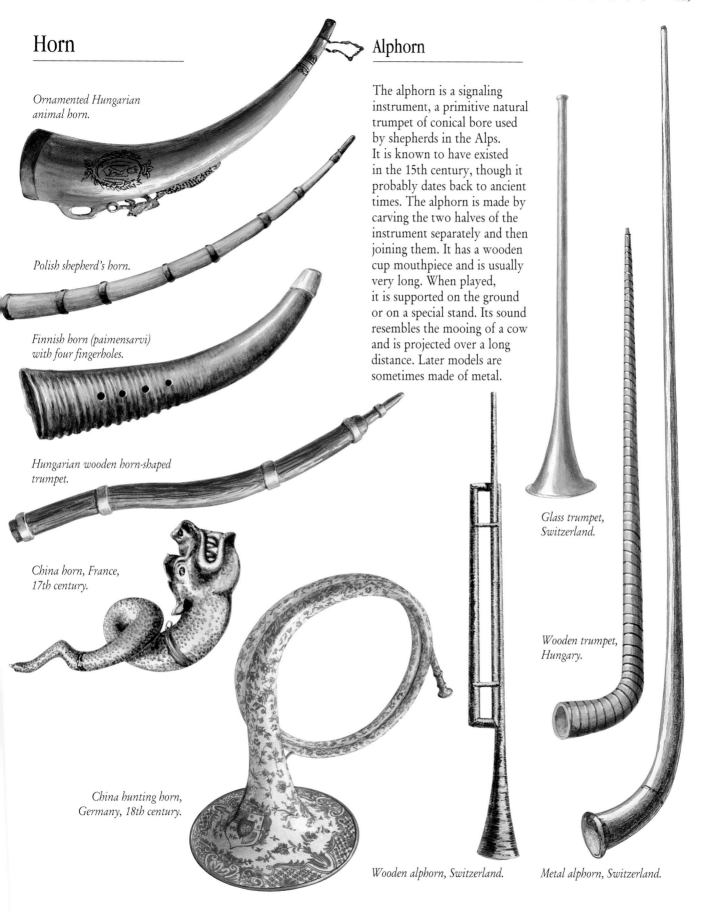

Ornamented Hungarian animal horn.

Polish shepherd's horn.

Finnish horn (paimensarvi) with four fingerholes.

Hungarian wooden horn-shaped trumpet.

China horn, France, 17th century.

China hunting horn, Germany, 18th century.

Wooden alphorn, Switzerland.

Alphorn

The alphorn is a signaling instrument, a primitive natural trumpet of conical bore used by shepherds in the Alps. It is known to have existed in the 15th century, though it probably dates back to ancient times. The alphorn is made by carving the two halves of the instrument separately and then joining them. It has a wooden cup mouthpiece and is usually very long. When played, it is supported on the ground or on a special stand. Its sound resembles the mooing of a cow and is projected over a long distance. Later models are sometimes made of metal.

Glass trumpet, Switzerland.

Wooden trumpet, Hungary.

Metal alphorn, Switzerland.

Bagpipe

The bagpipe is a wind instrument consisting of two or more pipes projecting from a flexible bag (most often made of skin) that acts as an air reservoir. The air is fed either from the mouth or by special bellows. There are at least two pipes: the chanter has fingerholes on it (all but one on the front, the other on the back), while the drone is longer and has no fingerholes. Some bagpipes have two or even three chanters, as well as several drones. Depending on whether the reeds are single or double, slit from the pipe itself or inserted separately, the bagpipe is an idioglot, a heteroglot, or mixed. The wind is fed to the pipes by arm pressure on the bag.

Bagpipe with bellows, Bohemia.

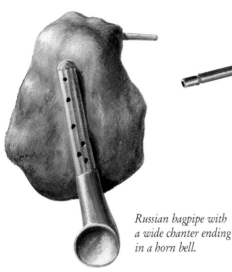

Russian bagpipe with a wide chanter ending in a horn bell.

Moravian bagpiper.

Italian zampogna with two chanters and a drone (all of them double-reed). This instrument is often played in an ensemble with a double-reed shawm.

Bagpipe with a double chanter, Russia.

Bagpipes vary in size and pitch, existing in the keys of C, D, E, A, F, and G. Accordingly, they may be high- or low-pitched. The lowest-pitched bagpipes are built in C and D. The most common are the high-pitched instruments in G. The bagpipe does not have a full chromatic range, particularly in the low register, this is why the high register is better for playing the melody.

The best players are able to compensate for this drawback, playing the missing tones by only half-covering some of the fingerholes. With the exception of bagpipes in C and A, which have a mellower tone, bagpipes sound loud and penetrating in the high register and softer and gentler in the low register. The bagpipe is mainly played in the open air.

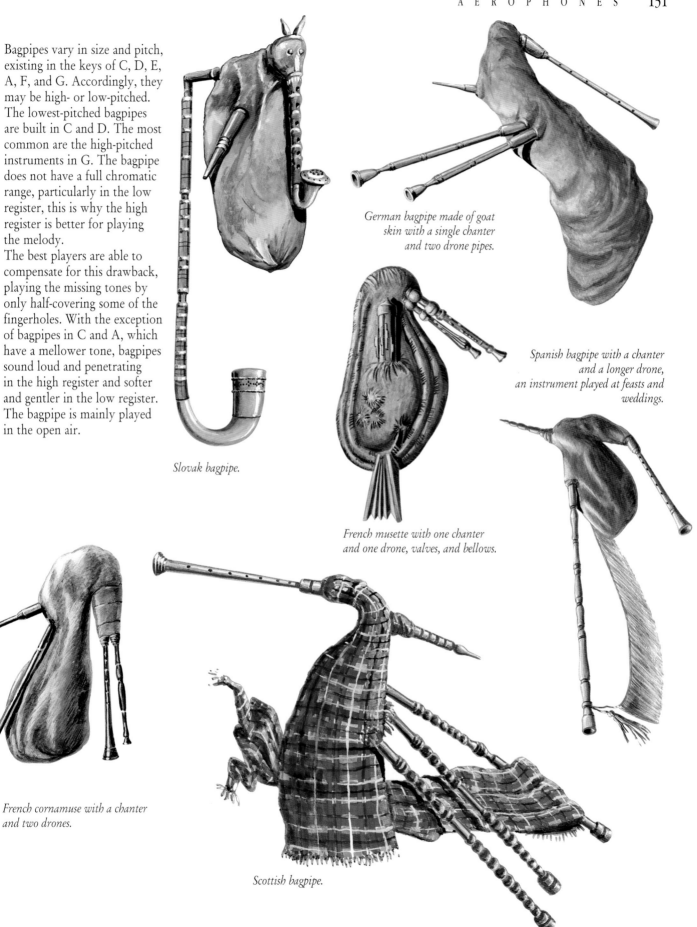

German bagpipe made of goat skin with a single chanter and two drone pipes.

Spanish bagpipe with a chanter and a longer drone, an instrument played at feasts and weddings.

Slovak bagpipe.

French musette with one chanter and one drone, valves, and bellows.

French cornamuse with a chanter and two drones.

Scottish bagpipe.

Concertina

Russian bayan.

Bayan

The bayan is a chromatic Russian concertina, named after
a legendary singer called Bayan or Boyan. It has three rows
of buttons on the right manual, while the left manual
is like that of an accordion. The so-called "selection"
instruments, in which the left manual produces separate notes
instead of chords, are intended for more skilled players.
Both manuals are equipped with a varying number of registers.
The bayan is used in the orchestra, for accompaniment,
and as a solo instrument. It is closely related to the folk form
chastushka (short song with poetic or topical content).

Bandonion

The bandonion, an improved diatonic or chromatic concertina,
was designed by the German teacher Heinrich Band (hence
the instrument's name) in 1846. The two square manuals have
five rows of buttons each. The left manual generates single
tones, the same button producing different tones on the press
and on the draw. Large instruments have 72 buttons for a total
of 144 tones. The player holds the bandonion on his knees.

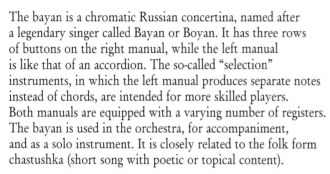

Concertina.

English Concertina

The English concertina with two hexagonal manuals connected
by bellows, was developed by Charles Wheatstone in 1844
and first named "melophone." The name concertina was taken
from the German instrument made by Carl Friedrich Uhlig
in 1834. Unlike the German concertina, the English type
sounds the same note on the press and on the draw.
Simpler models have three rows of buttons, each playing
a different note in G major, D major, and A major. There are
also chromatic models. The concertina exists in several forms:
soprano, alto, tenor, baritone and bass.
It is used both in ensembles and as a solo instrument.

English concertina.

Bandonion.

Russian fisarmonica, Saratov.

IDIOPHONES

Struck, Shaken and Friction Instruments

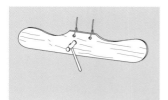

Swiss clapper made of a nut shell.

Wooden semanterions from Orthodox monasteries.

Coins used as a struck idiophone.

Metal spoons used as a struck idiophone.

Wooden clapper used for cult purposes, Switzerland.

Swiss wooden clapper with metal blades.

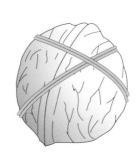

Shaken idiophone: a walnut shell filled with seeds and tied together with a string.

Rattle

The prototypes of the rattle date back to time immemorial. It has been found in Egypt, northeastern Africa, South-East Asia, and in the Americas. In Europe, there are two rattle types: large and small, the former being used for cult and hunting purposes, and the latter as toys or in carnivals.

The rattle consists of a wooden box serving as a resonator, inside which one or several wooden blades are fixed at one end, the free end snapping against the teeth of a wooden cogwheel. The sound is produced by turning the wheel with a handle while the frame is held still, or, as with small rattles, by swinging the frame around. In both cases, the blades snap against the cogwheel, producing a succession of strong-impact sounds.

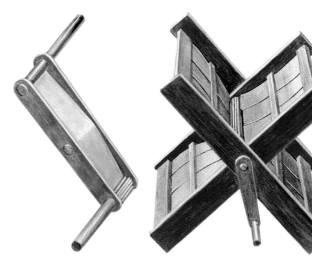

Small Czech rattle.

Large cross-frame rattle, Switzerland.

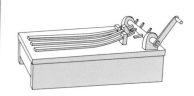

Large rattle in a box, Hungary.

Large frame rattle, Switzerland.

Swiss wooden schlefel.

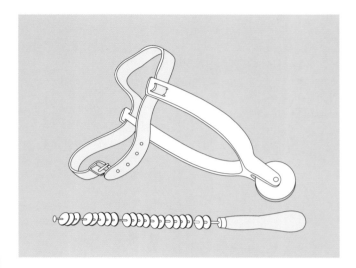

Natural spur and spur with a handle.

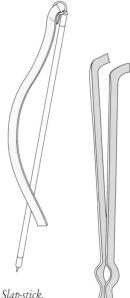

Slap-stick.

*Ordinary tongs used
as a struck idiophone.*

Zilia-massa.

Swiss wooden struck idiophone.

Dance castanets.

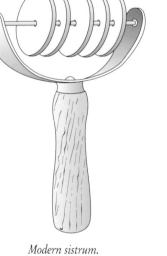

Modern sistrum.

Glass rubbed with a moist finger.

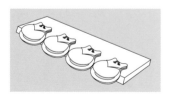

Set of dance castanets.

*The ordinary washboard played with thimbles, became a percussion
instrument. Its use started in the 1880s in spasm bands. In the early
20th century, it was adopted in New Orleans jazz, and in the 1930s,
the groups "Washboard Serenades", "Washboard Rhythm Kings",
"Alabama Washboard Stompers", and "Georgia Washboard Stompers"
gained wide popularity.*

Cymbal and Bell

*Small cymbals,
Balkan Peninsula.*

*Cowbell. A metal idiophone
of a relatively definite pitch,
in its simplest version it is just
a bell with a striker.*

*Bells, used
in ritual dances, Balkans.*

Swiss shepherd's bell.

Cabman's bell.

*Set of mobile bells
with a handle.*

Set of bells affixed to a handle.

*Turkish tambourine without
a membrane, with metal jingles.*

In folk music and later in jazz, pop and rock music, various
sets of bells are used, free-standing or attached to a handle.
Along with the conical bells with beaters, there are round ones
with metal or stone pellets jingling inside. Both varieties
are instruments of indefinite pitch and are used to enrich
the sound effect.

Russian bells.

Set of glasses filled with precisely calculated amounts of water. They are tuned to an octave including all semitones.

Glasses, particularly crystal ones, have long been known for their capacity to produce beautiful tones. Glasses of varying size and thickness, arranged in a box, can be tuned to a full chromatic range by pouring water into them. The sound is produced by rubbing the rim with a moist finger, by striking it gently with beaters, or by striking the glasses against each other, holding them at the stem. Glass playing was very popular in the 18th and 19th centuries, and was resurrected in circuses and bar shows in the 20th century.

Bottlephone: a set of uniform bottles tuned with water and arranged in a row or suspended in two rows from a wooden frame. The tuning is adjusted by changing the amount of water in the bottles. The instrument is played with two wooden mallets or xylophone beaters.

English lithophone consisting of 19 differently tuned stone blocks arranged in a single row on a wooden stand.

Drum made of a barrel with the lid on.

Estonian wooden idiophone (bila): a set of tuned alder plates on a stand.

Jew's Harp

A percussion idiophone of relatively definite pitch known the world over, the jew's harp consists of a metal (rarely, bamboo) frame to which a flexible blade (tongue) is attached on one end, its other end free to vibrate. The player holds the frame in his teeth and plucks the blade with finger or string. The mouth cavity serves as a resonator, and the lips, cheeks and teeth can modify the pitch.

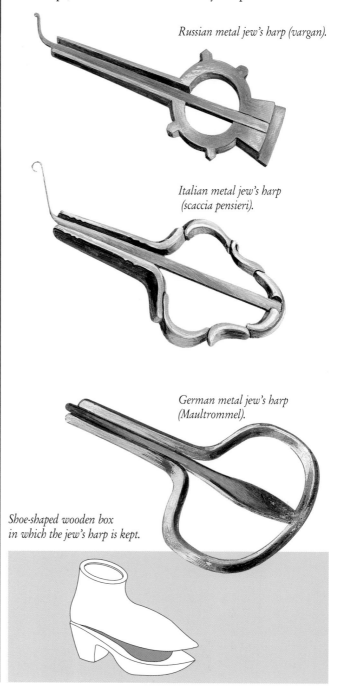

Russian metal jew's harp (vargan).

Italian metal jew's harp (scaccia pensieri).

German metal jew's harp (Maultrommel).

Shoe-shaped wooden box in which the jew's harp is kept.

MEMBRANOPHONES

Mirliton

Mirliton made of paper-covered comb. The sound is produced by making the membrane vibrate by blowing. In this particular case, the membrane is held close to the player's lips and he sings or blows against it. A soft buzzing tone is produced, the pitch varying with the intonation of the singing.

Primitive round mirliton, side-blown, with paper tied at both ends. The two ends of a wooden or cardboard tube are covered with paper. The player blows into an opening on the side of the instrument, causing the paper to vibrate.

Toy mirliton. Blowing into the narrow upper end causes the membrane in the middle to vibrate.

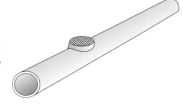

Friction Drum

Friction drum (Lion's roar) with horsehair and tensioning screws, Russia.

Friction drum with horsehair.

Drum

Large double-head wooden drum on a stand, Balkan Peninsula.

Large double-head wooden drum (dauli), Greece.

Folk drum, Greece.

Talamba: a pair of skin-covered wooden timpani, western Balkans.

CHORDOPHONES

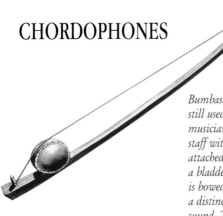

Bumbas: a primitive instrument, still used today by wandering musicians. It consists of a wooden staff with a cogged wooden ring attached at the bottom in which a bladder is set. The single string is bowed or plucked, and produces a distinctive snappy, drum-like sound. The wooden ring adjusts the string's length and, at the same time, acts as a soundbox.

Harp

Angular harp, 18th century, Russia.

Irish harp. Reconstruction.

Zither

Zither is a generic name for a large group of instruments with strings stretched across a soundbox. They vary considerably in shape, construction, number of strings, and tuning, both geographically and in terms of evolution. The strings may be plucked with the fingers or a plectrum, or struck with beaters. With a flat or slightly curved soundbox of rectangular or trapezoidal form and transverse strings, the modern European zither developed from the German Scheitholt, found in Bavaria, Bohemia, Austria, Switzerland, and the northern German provinces. The medieval psaltery existed in a variety of shapes: triangular, square, trapezoidal, wing-shaped (Boehm flugel), rectangular, or slightly trapezoidal (Scheitholt, Aeolian harp).

Scheitholt

A German zither, with melody and drone strings plucked with the fingers and shortened with a small wooden peg. The back of the oblong soundbox may be only partially covered or uncovered.

Aeolian harp

A zither with strings of equal length but different thickness. The wind makes them vibrate, sounding chords. Stronger winds even produce high overtones. Wind-sounded strings have been used since ancient times (an example being King David's kinnor).

Flat French zither, with melody strings running over a fretted fingerboard, and several drone strings.

The zither was widely used in many parts of Europe until the very end of the 19th century, mainly as accompaniment to dances and traditional songs. It is still played in Norway (langleik), Belgium (vlier), Hungary (citara), Sweden (hummel), and elsewhere. The old Alpine Scheitholt is now rare. Johann Strauss, the younger provided a solo for the zither in his *Tales from the Vienna Woods* (1868).

Norwegian zither (langleik), with eight strings and metal frets.

Slovak zither with a violin-like scroll.

German bowed zither, late 19th century.

Zither, Iceland.

Hungarian zither.

Finnish woman playing the kantele.

Finnish zither (kantele) without frets.

Swiss zither (hummel) with melody and drone strings.

Gusli

The gusli is a Russian stringed harp-like zither, very close in shape to the dulcimer. Diatonically tuned strings are stretched over a flat wooden resonator of trapezoidal shape, and the instrument is played with both hands, or with one hand, the other damping the strings' vibration. In the 17th century, a chromatic gusli with metal strings was made.

Russian gusli.

German harp-shaped zither.

Chord zither: a simpler version of the concert zither with no fingerboard under the melody strings and ready chord combinations in the accompanying strings.

Dulcimer

The dulcimer is a stringed instrument played with two beaters. It consists of a fairly large trapezoidal or rectangular soundbox, 1.2 m long and 1.5 m wide, and three or four strings per note. The beaters may vary in shape but "spoons" are the most common. In improved models, a damper is added. Modern dulcimers are placed on four-legged stands.

Dulcimer, 17th century.

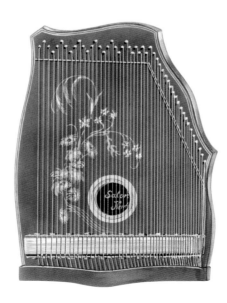

German zither (Hackbrett).

The dulcimer's range is E – e^3, i. e. four full chromatic octaves. Its sound is bright and ringing, and it allows for the playing of complex melodic and rhythmic figures; rapid chords are also characteristic. Music for the dulcimer is notated on one or two staves, in treble and bass clef.
The dulcimer has been known since ancient times, having been used in the kingdom of Assyria. The immediate precursor of the modern European dulcimer was the Swiss hackbrett. Other instruments of the family include the Persian santir, the Russian chang, the Indian santor, and the Korean yangquin. The dulcimer is also found in the Appalachian region of North America, where it was first made by Scottish settlers in the 18th century.

Hungarian cymbalon.

Crwth

The crwth is a bowed lyre used in the western part of the British Isles in the first centuries B. C. Its Celtic name was cruit or crot; in English, it is also found as crowd or crowth. One of the oldest bowed stringed instruments in Europe, its most ancient form had three strings.

Three-string Finnish folk instrument (kantele), carved from a single piece of wood.

Lyre, Sweden.

Estonian lyre.

Modern dulcimer.

The dulcimer has been used by Liszt, Kodály in *Háry János*, and Paderewski, and other composers seeking to give an impression of local color. Stravinsky first introduced it into the chamber orchestra in *Renard* and *Ragtime*. Nowadays the instrument is frequently used by Gypsy orchestras in Hungary, Slovakia, Transylvania, and Romania, some of which feature two dulcimers.

Estonian talharpa.

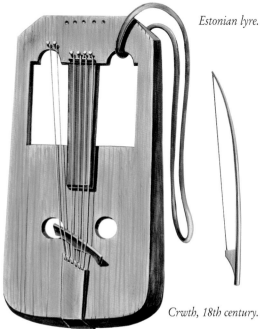

Crwth, 18th century.

Fiddle

Gusla: an instrument found in Serbia, Montenegro, Bosnia and Herzegovina, and Dalmatia.

Lyre, Crete.

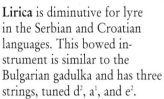

Lirica: found in Serbia and Croatia.

Lirica is diminutive for lyre in the Serbian and Croatian languages. This bowed instrument is similar to the Bulgarian gadulka and has three strings, tuned d^2, a^1, and e^2.

Three-string fiddle.

Gusla

An old folk fiddle of Asian origin, now out of use (it was once popular in the western Balkans). Its curved wooden soundbox passes into a long neck with a single peg. The belly is made of skin with small soundholes. The gusla has no fingerboard; the different tones are produced by touching the single string with the fingertips.

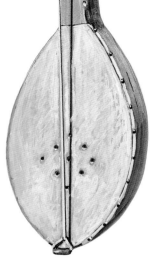

Gusla.

Greek lyre.　　*One-string fiddle.*

Nyckelharpa

The nyckelharpa appeared in the 15th century. In Swedish, its name means "keyed harp." It has seven strings, but unlike the mechanical hurdy-gurdy, in which the strings are made to vibrate by a special disc, the nyckelharpa is bowed like the violin.

Fiddle with pegs (nyckelharpa): a bowed Swedish folk instrument, with a device for shortening the strings operated by the left hand.

Hardingfele is a Norwegian fiddle that developed from the viola d'amore and the folk fiddles. Created for use as accompaniment to the halling folk dances, it has been in use in Norway since the 16th century, and initially had six strings. Grieg used it in some of his instrumental works.

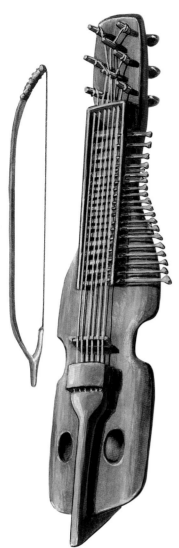

Rebec, France.

Husle, Serbia.

Norwegian violin (hardingfele), with four melody and four off-fingerboard strings.

Polish folk fiddle, with a narrow soundbox and four strings.

Swedish musician playing the nyckelharpa.

Kemanje with three melody strings and three drones, Balkans.

Polish folk double bass with three strings.

Gadulka with three melody strings and seven drones, Bulgaria.

Large three-string violin (husle), a kind of a medieval fiddle, Serbia.

Gadulka

The gadulka is a Bulgarian bowed stringed instrument shaped like a halved pear. The neck may have the shape of a heart, a leaf, or a bird's head. The back, the neck, and the pegbox are made of sycamore, walnut, pear, or some other wood. The body is carved in a single piece. The belly is made of spruce, with two symmetrical oval soundholes. The gadulka has no fingerboard. The strings are traditionally made of lamb gut, though now more often of metal or nylon. In many gadulkas, additional metal strings run under the main strings and sound sympathetically to resonate sounds that are otherwise muffled and indistinct. The bow is made of a supple wood such as willow or dogwood. Unlike the strings of the violin, which are stopped with fingers on the fingerboard, the strings of the gadulka are touched sideways with the nails, producing an airy sound. The bowing technique is also different, in that the instrument is turned in order to change strings, rather than changing the angle of the bow. The range of the gadulka is g – d².

Lute

Balalaika

Russian balalaika, with a characteristic flat triangular soundbox, frets, and three strings. It is currently made in six sizes (piccolo, prime, second, alto, bass and contrabass), which together make up the balalaika orchestra.

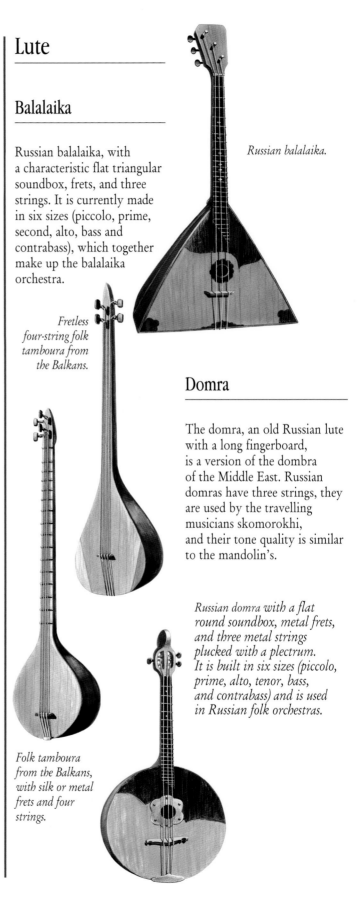

Russian balalaika.

Fretless four-string folk tamboura from the Balkans.

Domra

The domra, an old Russian lute with a long fingerboard, is a version of the dombra of the Middle East. Russian domras have three strings, they are used by the travelling musicians skomorokhi, and their tone quality is similar to the mandolin's.

Russian domra with a flat round soundbox, metal frets, and three metal strings plucked with a plectrum. It is built in six sizes (piccolo, prime, alto, tenor, bass, and contrabass) and is used in Russian folk orchestras.

Folk tamboura from the Balkans, with silk or metal frets and four strings.

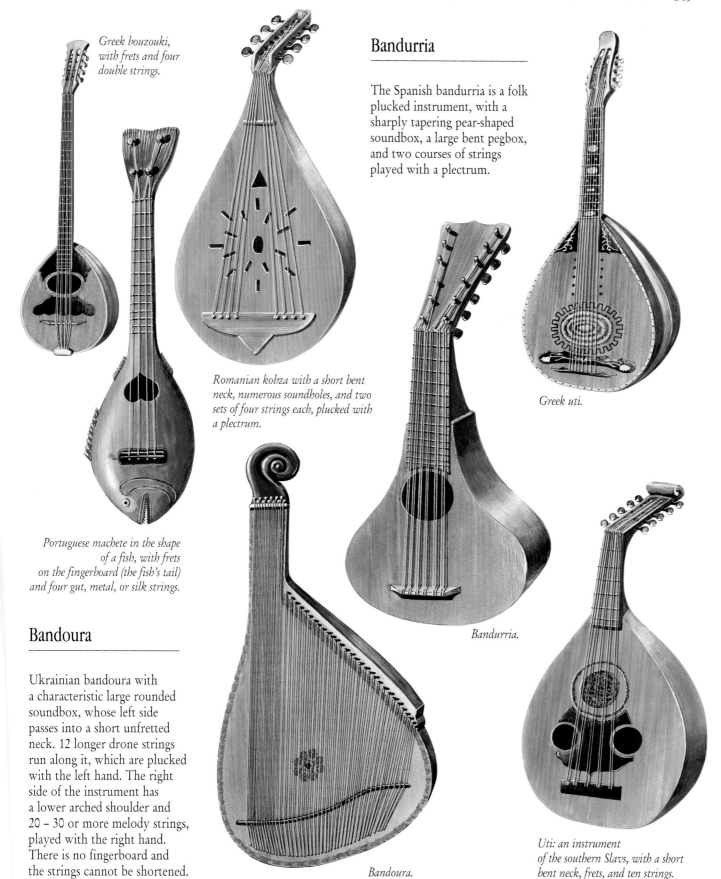

Greek bouzouki, with frets and four double strings.

Bandurria

The Spanish bandurria is a folk plucked instrument, with a sharply tapering pear-shaped soundbox, a large bent pegbox, and two courses of strings played with a plectrum.

Romanian kobza with a short bent neck, numerous soundholes, and two sets of four strings each, plucked with a plectrum.

Greek uti.

Portuguese machete in the shape of a fish, with frets on the fingerboard (the fish's tail) and four gut, metal, or silk strings.

Bandurria.

Bandoura

Ukrainian bandoura with a characteristic large rounded soundbox, whose left side passes into a short unfretted neck. 12 longer drone strings run along it, which are plucked with the left hand. The right side of the instrument has a lower arched shoulder and 20 – 30 or more melody strings, played with the right hand. There is no fingerboard and the strings cannot be shortened.

Bandoura.

Uti: an instrument of the southern Slavs, with a short bent neck, frets, and ten strings.

EUROPE — MIDDLE AGES

In terms of the history of European music, this period covers roughly a thousand years, from 450 to 1450 A. D. A crucial event within the period was the introduction of notation in sacred music. Prior to the 9th century, both sacred and secular music had been transmitted orally from one generation to the next. In the early Middle Ages, priests and monks were the first to write music down, and the only ones capable of reading it. Characters and neumes had been used before the 9th century, but they had been unable to keep pace with the ever-increasing demands of professional music making. Initially, sacred music was monophonic, and it was only with the advent of organum, an early form of polyphony (music for more than one voice or part) that provided an impetus for the development of musical traditions. Monophonic works (for a single voice) nevertheless continued to be composed and performed throughout the period.

Guido d'Arezzo (c. 991 – after 1033) made a fundamental contribution to the development of notation, solving a problem of musical theory and practice that had preoccupied musicians for many years. He introduced the staff notation system that is still in use today. He also invented the solmization of a six-note series, the diatonic hexachord do – la, using the first syllable of each of the first six lines of a religious hymn to arrive at the series ut, re, mi, fa, sol, la. (The ut syllable was later replaced by do.)

In the 12th and 13th centuries the cathedral of Notre Dame in Paris became an important center of music, where the art of organum was brought to perfection. This period is known as Ars Antiqua, as opposed to the Ars Nova of the 14th century. The two leading representatives of the Ars Nova were its creator Philippe de Vitry (1291 – 1361), a French composer and theoretician, and Guillaume de Machaut (c. 1300 – 1377), a composer, poet, and canon of Reims.

From the 11th to the 14th century, a powerful new musical style developed in the new courtly world of the knights. The art of the trouveres, troubadours, and minnesingers first evolved in southern France (Provence), spreading quickly to the north and to the other countries of Western Europe. Their songs were written not in the canonical Latin language, but in the vernacular, which in Provence was known as the "langue d'oc." Such songs were popular with all social strata, and were performed to the accompaniment of harps, lutes, and fiddles.

Although vocal music predominated in the Middle Ages, there was also a wealth of instrumental music, chiefly dance music. It was probably monophonic at first, but by the end of the 12th century polyphonic dance music was also being composed. As mentioned above, the troubadours and the trouveres used lutes and harps for vocal accompaniment. Bowed fiddles were also popular. Wind instruments included the shawm (a double-reed forerunner of the modern oboe) and early trumpets. The percussion family consisted of cymbals, bells, triangles, and many other idiophones. How these instruments were played is unclear, as composers did not generally give specific indications for instrumental performance.

The norms in sacred music were much more clearly defined. We know for certain that sacred vocal music was accompanied by the organ. The organ was of moderate size, the enormous 11th-century instrument in the Winchester Cathedral being an exception rather than the rule. Much more popular was the "portative organ," worn on a strap on the player's shoulder.

AEROPHONES

In medieval Europe, single-pipe, single-reed wind instruments were particularly popular. Because of their similar construction, they had similar names in different countries. One of these instruments was the French chalumeau, which underwent significant development, particularly in its upper section.

Medieval bladder pipe. It consists of a straight or curved tube with fingerholes and an animal bladder for an air reservoir. Reconstruction.

Portative

The portative organ (organetto) is a transportable instrument known as early as the Byzantine period, coming to Western Europe in the late Middle Ages. It had a single manual and stopped flue pipes and was placed on the knees of the player, who played with the right hand while pumping the bellows with the left. The instrument was a favorite with artists, who depicted it as the musical companion of angels.

Oliphant

The oliphant is a medieval horn shaped like an elephant's tusk (hence its name). About 80 medieval instruments preserved to date are made from ivory, three quarters of them by Arabic makers in southern Italy. The oliphants are richly and beautifully decorated. This instrument is mentioned in the *Chanson de Roland*: when the dying hero blew his oliphant it was heard 150 km away!

Portative organ, 15th century.

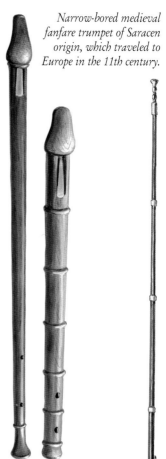

Narrow-bored medieval fanfare trumpet of Saracen origin, which traveled to Europe in the 11th century.

Two flutes with mouthpieces, played with tambourin (tabor) accompaniment.

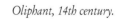

Oliphant, 14th century.

The so-called Roland oliphant, owned by Charlemagne's nephew, 9th – 10th centuries.

Oliphant made of animal horn, Hungary.

IDIOPHONES

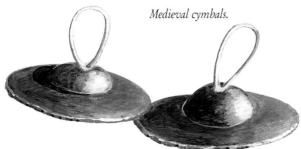

Medieval cymbals.

The medieval cymbals, free standing or suspended, are of very ancient origin. They were widely used by the Turkish military bands and the Janissaries in particular. Cymbals were spread in Europe in the 15th century and became permanent members of European military bands in the 17th century.

Cross-section of a typical medieval bell, used by street musicians and at fairs.

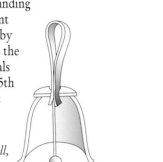

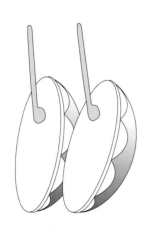

Naqqara: small medieval timpani.

The timpani were first introduced into Europe as early as the 6th century, with the Arab invasion of the Pyrenees. A larger variety of instruments came into use in the 13th century, when the instrument was discovered in the Arab world during the crusades. It became known as nasaires or naquaires, derivatives of the Persian name, naqqara. These instruments were the direct precursors of European screw-tuned timpani. As timpani gradually increased in size, it became customary to tie them on the backs of horses, usually in pairs consisting of two timpani of differing size and pitch. Large timpani arrived in Europe in the second half of the 15th century. At first, the membrane was tensioned by cords, but these were replaced by screws around the 16th century.

MEMBRANOPHONES

Tambourin (Tabor)

The tambourin is closely related to the French tenor drum. It is found in India, Polynesia, Central Asia, Mexico, and elsewhere. The modern tambourin originates from Provence in France, a region inhabited by Basques, and has been in use since the 11th century. It is played at the same time as a small pipe known as galoubet. The tambourin is carried on a string on the player's shoulder and struck with a small beater held in the right hand, while the pipe is played with the left hand. The tambourin is narrower and deeper than the snare drum, and can be single- or double-head. A snare may pass over one of the heads, but models without snares are also used in orchestras. At one time the tambourin was played with a single beater but nowadays a pair is more common. Modern tambourins have membranes tensioned with screws, instead of the original cords and leather rings, and are supported on stands.

Tensioning of the head with a rope-tightened ring.

Medieval tabors.

CHORDOPHONES

Lyre

The oldest European lyres derive from the ancient lyre but differ from it because they were carved from a single piece of wood. During the Middle Ages, the lyre was popular in England, France, Germany and Scandinavia. From the 7th to the end of the 19th century a lyre of Celtic origin known as cruit, crwth, chrotta or rotta was widely used in Brittany, Ireland and Wales. (The interest in this instrument has recently revived.) It was similar to the Greek kithara, with a rounded rectangular soundbox, slightly narrower in its upper part, and strings running over a bridge and between the arms.

German rotta of the early Middle Ages.

Later, a bar with a fingerboard was added between the two arms, with four strings running along it. More unstopped strings ran alongside. The crwth provided a link between plucked and bowed stringed instruments, for as early as the 10th century it was often bowed rather than plucked with the fingers or a plectrum.

Medieval rotta.

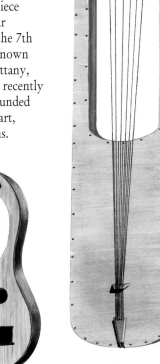

Rotta, 13th century.

Rotta, 7th century.

Monochord

The monochord consisted of a wooden soundbox over which a string was stretched. The bridge could be moved to different positions over a calibrated rule. Pythagoras and other Greek theoreticians used it for acoustic experiments. During the Middle Ages, the monochord was widely used in music teaching, for checking the pitch in singing and for other pedagogical purposes. In time, more strings were added (reaching 14 by the end of the period), the instrument thus becoming a polychord. The clavichord later developed from it.

Welsh crwth.

Monochord.

Monochord, illustration, 1539, Venice.

Harp

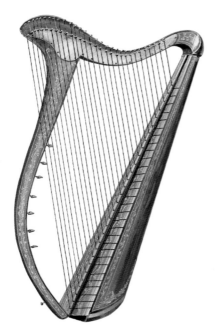

Harp by John Egan, a late replica of a medieval Irish harp, Dublin, 1820. With this instrument, Egan began the revival of the harp-playing tradition in Ireland. The strings are made of gut, and the decoration includes the typical national yellow clover leaves. Seven hand-operated levers are used to adjust the pitch.

Irish harp of the 14th century, the oldest preserved instrument of this type.

Medieval (Gothic) harp.

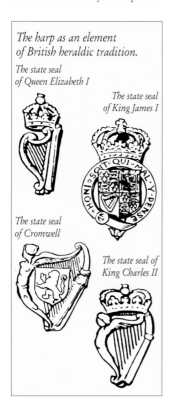

The harp as an element of British heraldic tradition.

The state seal of Queen Elizabeth I

The state seal of King James I

The state seal of Cromwell

The state seal of King Charles II

Zither

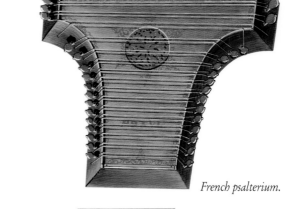

French psalterium.

German lyre-shaped zither. Reconstruction.

A medieval psaltery to be played with a quill plectrum.

Lute

Spanish banduria
of the 15th century with
12 – 14 frets and two courses of strings.

Italian mandolin, 15th century.

Mandola, 15th century.

*Medieval English vihuela:
a fiddle-shaped guitar carved from
a single piece of wood, played
horizontally. At the instrument's
lower end, the strings are attached
to a special carved tailpiece.*

*Medieval vihuela.
Reconstruction.*

Orpheus playing the vihuela. An engraving from Libro de musica,
Valencia, 1535.

Fiddle

The European fiddles marked the next step in the development of the old rebec. They were the direct precursors of the viol and of the related instruments lira da braccio and violin. At first, fiddles were still related to the rebec, although they were played supported on the left shoulder rather than vertically positioned like the older instrument. The number of strings increased from three to four and then to five, tuned a fourth or fifth apart, and unstopped strings (drones) were added. The pegs were first placed vertically, and then laterally, as in the violin. In time, fiddles became increasingly figure-of-eight-shaped, their flat-backed soundboxes resembling that of the guitar.

Medieval viola da gamba. Reconstruction.

Lyre (medieval fiddle). Reconstruction.

Medieval fiddle. Reconstruction.

Rebec

The rebec is a kind of a fiddle whose name probably derives from the Arabic rabab. Shaped like a halved pear, it had a wooden rather than skin top, strings tuned g, d^1, and a^1, and a short, strongly curved bow. The upper part of the body acted as a fingerboard, and the lower (with two symmetrical soundholes) as a resonator, the soundpost between the belly and the bottom improving the tone quality. The rebec quickly gained popularity in Central and Western Europe. Initially, the rebec was played upright; later it was supported on the left shoulder. Used mainly to accompany folk dances, its sound was bright and penetrating. An important change in the construction was the introduction of a flat back and sides (instead of a soundbox carved from one piece). Later, the soundbox became narrower in the middle, forming a characteristic "waist" to facilitate bowing.

Two rebecs with elongated pear-shaped soundboxes, originating from the Arabic rabab. Reconstruction.

Bowed Lyre

The bowed lyre marks the next stage of the development of bowed instruments. Its name derived from the plucked ancient Greek lyre. Flat-backed and figure-of-eight-shaped, the lyre bears a distant resemblance to the modern violin. The first instruments of this kind were created by Italian luthiers of the 12th – 13th centuries. The lyre existed in three sizes: the lira da braccio or "arm lyra," the lira da gamba or "knee lyra," and the lirone, which was supported on the floor. The lirone had 24 strings, and the lira da gamba 12 melody strings and two drones. In size, sound, tone color, and range the lyres are related to the viols, and, distantly, to the modern violin, viola, cello, and double bass.

Hurdy-gurdy

This instrument dates from the early Middle Ages, when it was known as an organistrum and was played by two men, usually an older man with a younger assistant; it was later played by a single musician. It consisted of a resonator with one or two melody strings, tuned in unison; these were stopped with short wooden keys pressed by the fingers of the left hand. Two or four unstopped strings, tuned in unison and called bourdons, sounded drones. The melody strings were sounded by the rosined rim of a wooden wheel turned by a handle at the end of the instrument. The unstopped strings were plucked or bowed. Initially, the hurdy-gurdy was equipped with eight keys in the range of an octave. Besides the melody and the drone, it was capable of providing rhythmic effects. When played by a virtuoso, it created the impression of several instruments sounding together. The hurdy-gurdy was particularly popular from the 10th to the 12th century, and again in the 18th century, when Charles Bâton and Leopold Mozart composed works for it. The French composer Nicolas Chédeville arranged Vivaldi's *The Four Seasons* for hurdy-gurdy, violin, flute, and continuo. By the 18th century, the hurdy-gurdy had a range of two octaves.
In 1972, the Swedish composer Sven-Erik Emanuel composed a concerto for hurdy-gurdy and orchestra. The hurdy-gurdy is used in folk music and, more recently, in jazz.

Hurdy-gurdy by Le Valois, Paris, 1753.

Hurdy-gurdy, Germany, 18th century. A mechanical stringed instrument with an average-sized body, shaped like a viol, lute, guitar or violin, with a wide board instead of a neck. Instead of a bow, a wheel is used to sound the strings. It is partly hidden in the soundbox, and is turned by a handle.

Construction of the hurdy-gurdy. When a key is pressed, the string is stopped at a precise point, giving a definite pitch.

Hurdy-gurdy, Brussels, 1750.

Hurdy-gurdy.

EUROPE – RENAISSANCE AND BAROQUE

The Renaissance covers the period from about 1450 to 1600 in European music history, and includes the work of the Burgundian and Flemish schools as well as that of composers in Italy, Spain, and England. There are different views as to when the period began and ended, relating to the influence of the Burgundian school and the slightly longer duration of the Renaissance in England. The period coincided with the flourishing of painting, sculpture, and architecture in Italy, though in the early part of the period the most important composers came from northern France and from Flanders, an area comprising parts of present-day France, Belgium, Luxembourg, and the Netherlands. Later in the Renaissance, with the rise of secular education, Italy became the center of remarkable developments in music. The Reformation, launched in Germany by Martin Luther (1483 – 1546), not only laid the foundations of Protestantism but also reformed the use of music within the Church, where the Protestant chorale developed on the basis of the old Gregorian chant.

The evolution of music during the Renaissance is primarily related to the development of polyphony. A number of madrigal publications of the time are labeled "for voices or viols." Purely instrumental music (chiefly dance music) was composed for fixed ensembles and also for individual instruments. Songs often appeared in instrumental transcriptions, usually for lute or virginal. The leading instruments of this period included the plucked stringed instruments the lute and the vihuela; the keyboard instruments the harpsichord, the virginal, the clavichord, and the organ; the bowed stringed instruments the rebec and the various viols; and the wind instruments the shawm, the crumhorn, the cornet, and the end-blown flutes.

The lute became a favorite domestic instrument, the vast repertory that exists for it making clear the connection between instrumental music, song, and dance.

Organ music gained prominence in the 16th century with the achievements of the Venetian school; its two main genres were the toccata and the ricercar. Another characteristic form for keyboard instruments was the canzona, which later developed into an ensemble form. The organ also continued to be used in sacred music during the Renaissance. Brass instruments (trumpets, trombones) were used mainly for military and ceremonial purposes and for signaling.

One of the most important musical developments of the Renaissance was the creation of musical drama, which resulted from attempts to revive the performance practices of ancient Greek tragedy. Towards the end of this period, in 1594, Jacopo Peri composed the opera *Dafne* in Florence, and in 1600 two works based on the story of Orpheus and Eurydice were composed in the same city, one by Peri and the other by Giulio Caccini.

Less explicitly at first, the Baroque age (1600 – 1750) started showing certain differences from the predominant tastes and preferences of the Renaissance. An epoch of spectacular musical upsurge and instrument perfection set in. The art of the luthiers reached its peak in the work of the most famous instrument makers, such as Gasparo da Salò, and the Amati, Guarneri, and Stradivari families.

AEROPHONES

Flute

An instrument both ancient and modern, the flute belongs to the woodwind family. Its method of sound generation was probably suggested by natural sounds such as the "song" of a broken reed in the wind. Woodwind instruments are divided into two principal groups, according to the way the air is blown into them: labial (Lat. "labia", lip): the air enters directly through a mouth-hole in the instrument's head (flute); lingual (Lat. "lingua", tongue): the air is blown into the instrument through one or two reeds which start to vibrate and in turn cause the air column inside the instrument to vibrate (clarinet, saxophone, oboe, bassoon).

French transverse flute by Claude Rafi, 16th century.

Three Renaissance transverse flutes: bass, tenor, and alto.

Renaissance descant recorder.

Recorders, 17th century.

Soprano of unusual shape.

Tenor.

Basset with a "swallow" valve.

Recorder

The recorder (or duct flute), an end-blown tubular flute, was popular in many European countries from the early Middle Ages. It is made of wood and ivory, and later of plastic. The construction includes a cylindrically bored tube, a mouthpiece, and seven (later eight) fingerholes, some of them equipped with valves. Its most important part is the rectangular block from which the recorder's German name – Blockflöte – derives. The block aims the breath toward the edge of the "lip", causing the air column in the tube to vibrate. The recorder is a diatonic instrument; chromatic changes are obtained by half-covering the fingerholes or by "fork" fingering. The recorder's popularity reached its peak between the 16th and the 18th century, and it was the leading flute in Renaissance and Baroque music. It was even mentioned in Scene 3 of Shakespeare's *Hamlet*. In the second half of the 18th century, the recorder gave way to the transverse flute but from the beginning of the 20th century it regained its position, largely owing to the efforts of the maker Arnold Dolmetsch.

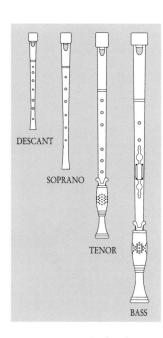

Renaissance recorder family.

DESCANT

SOPRANO

TENOR

BASS

Shawm

Several families of double-reed instruments, precursors
of the modern oboe and bassoon, emerged in the 16th century:
shawm (descant, soprano, and alto), bombard (tenor, baritone,
bass, and contrabass), bassanelli instruments (of the shawm
family, with an s-shaped "crook" made in three sizes: soprano,
alto-tenor, and bass), kortholt (of the shawm family, with a
cylindrical bore and two channels), cornemuse, crumhorn (with
a curved pipe and a pirouette in which the reed is inserted),
Rauschpfeife (the German equivalent of the shawm, also with a
pirouette for the reed), curtal and sordone (very close to the
bassoon prototypes, with a channel that doubles back on itself,
carved in a single body; in the sordone the reed is placed on top
of a metal tube at the instrument's side), racket (a coiled tube in
a wide box with fingerholes, resembling a can), bladderpipe
(a small bagpipe held at the player's mouth), and hornpipe
(Welsh shawm with the upper and lower joints made of horn
and acting as air reservoir and bell). The shawm family as shown
in the *Syntagma musicum* of Michael Praetorius (1571 – 1621)
includes small descant, soprano, alto, tenor (with crook and
pirouette), and bass.

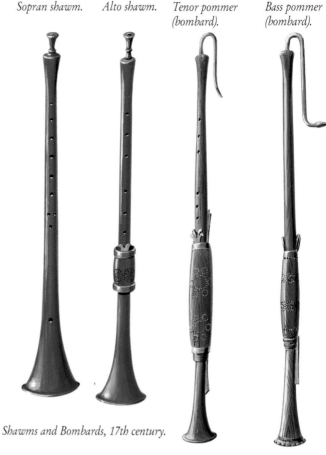

Sopran shawm.   Alto shawm.   Tenor pommer (bombard).   Bass pommer (bombard).

Shawms and Bombards, 17th century.

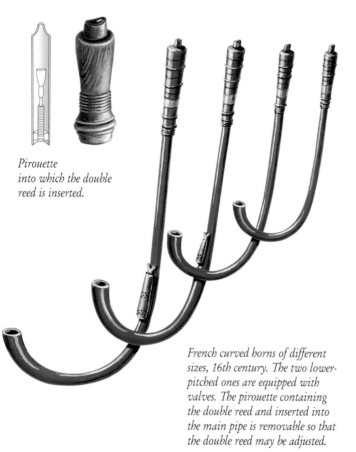

*Pirouette
into which the double
reed is inserted.*

*French curved horns of different
sizes, 16th century. The two lower-
pitched ones are equipped with
valves. The pirouette containing
the double reed and inserted into
the main pipe is removable so that
the double reed may be adjusted.*

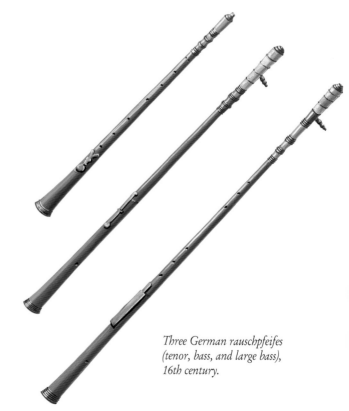

*Three German rauschpfeifes
(tenor, bass, and large bass),
16th century.*

The chalumeau family.

SOPRANO

ALTO

TENOR

BASS

Chalumeau

Believed to have been spread in France in the Middle ages (the French word chalumeau derives from the Latin "calamus" meaning "reed"), chalumeau is a single-reed wind instrument considered to be the precursor of the clarinet. About the 1700, the instrument maker Denner of Nuremberg not only perfected the instrument but created a hybrid between a chalumeau and a recorder – and the clarinet was born. (Even today the clarinet's low register is known as chalumeau.) Yet despite the rise of the clarinet, chalumeaux continued to be used especially in the opera orchestras. In the first quarter of the 18th century more than a hundred works were composed with parts for chalumeau, including operas by Fux, Bononcini, and Gluck, cantatas by Telemann and concertos by Vivaldi.

*Alto cornemuse,
17th century.*

Racket

*Bass racket with double reed,
16th century.*

*Bass racket with double reed
in a pirouette, mid-16th century.*

The tartölt is a form of racket, a wind instrument of the 15th and 16th centuries belonging to the bombard family, with a double reed and a coiled tube enclosed in a dragon-shaped casing. Its tone is soft and pleasant, making it suitable for performance in ensembles with other soft-sounding instruments, such as the viola da gamba. A collection of five instruments, mentioned in an inventory of 1596, is held in Vienna. Ordinary tartölts are shaped more simply as cylindrical boxes.

Bassonor.

*Alto courtaut,
17th century.*

Tartölt, Tyrol, 16th century.

Cornett

Serpent

The serpent is a snake-shaped woodwind instrument. Its tube is in two parts and is covered in leather. The instrument has a cup mouthpiece, a brass crook, and six fingerholes. It was invented in France around 1590 and was used mainly in church music. It has a range of an octave and a half, and a coarse tone, something between the tuba and the bassoon. It later became popular in England, Germany, and other European countries. Around the end of the 18th century it began to be used in military bands, being equipped with valves at about the same time to facilitate playing. The serpent was used to double the trombone part, but in the 19th century gradually fell out of use altogether, being replaced by the ophicleide and the tuba.

Serpent – bass cornett.

Zink

The zink or cornett is a woodwind instrument with a cup mouthpiece and six fingerholes, an early forerunner of the cornet, the trumpet, and the trombone, and the immediate precursor of the serpent. The mouthpiece is made of ivory or hardwood. The zink exists in two forms, white and black. Unlike white zinks, the black instruments are curved, covered in leather, and low-pitched. It is to this cornett that a brass crook was added and the serpent created. In Germany, it was used for signaling purposes until the 18th century, when it finally fell out of use.

Zinks, 16th century.

Black zinks: tenor cornett in C, alto cornett in F.

White zinks: alto cornett in F, sopran cornett in C.

Black zinks: ordinary zink in G, piccolo zink in D.

Trumpet

"Garland trumpet" with freely coiled tube by Antonius Schnitzer, Nuremberg, 1598.

Coiled trumpet by M. Vogt, Elwang, 1750.

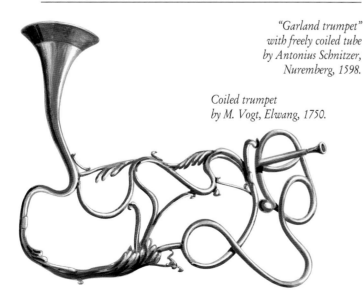

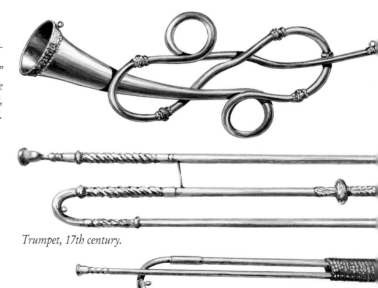

Trumpet, 17th century.

Natural trumpet by Johann Leonhard (1638 – 1707), Nuremberg.

Trombone

The trombone developed from the large horns of the trumpet family. In the Middle Ages, these instruments were known as sackbuts. The trombone first appeared in Europe in the 15th and early 16th centuries. According to Praetorius, by the end of the 16th century the trombone family had four members, the number increasing to five in the 17th century: soprano (descant), alto, tenor, bass, and contrabass. Only the tenor and the bass are still in use today, often combined in a tenor-bass instrument.

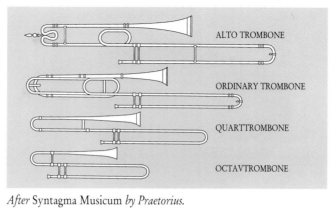

ALTO TROMBONE

ORDINARY TROMBONE

QUARTTROMBONE

OCTAVTROMBONE

After Syntagma Musicum *by Praetorius.*

The trombone acquired its present form in the early 16th century, and was initially made in various sizes – alto, tenor, bass, and contrabass. They are used to double the voices in choral music, but also function as independent instruments. In the 18th century, the number of trombone sizes was reduced to three: alto, tenor, and bass. In time, the alto trombone gradually fell out of use. With the introduction of valves in the 19th century, a valved trombone was also produced. It did not succeed in replacing the slide trombone, which is still used in the brass section of the modern orchestra and as a favoured instrument in jazz ensembles.

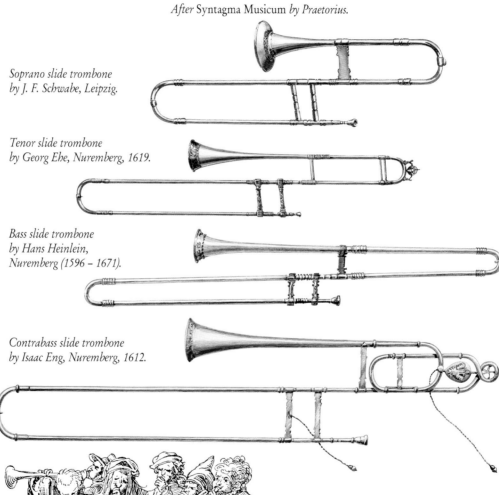

Soprano slide trombone by J. F. Schwabe, Leipzig.

Tenor slide trombone by Georg Ehe, Nuremberg, 1619.

Bass slide trombone by Hans Heinlein, Nuremberg (1596 – 1671).

Contrabass slide trombone by Isaac Eng, Nuremberg, 1612.

Trumpets. Engraving by Albrecht Dürer, 1515. Detail.

Regal

The regal is a small portable organ with one or more registers. It evolved in the mid-15th century, mainly in Germany, and due to its convenience for domestic playing, it continued to be used until the early 17th century. Its keyboard covered a range from E to c^2, but there were also regals with a larger or smaller range. The bellows were operated by an assistant who sat facing the player at the table where the instrument was placed. Claudio Monteverdi used the regal, with its powerful nasal sound, in his opera *Orfeo* (1607). From Monteverdi's time some 30 original regals have been preserved, including the unusual Bible-regal, made for the first time in Nuremberg in the late 16th century.

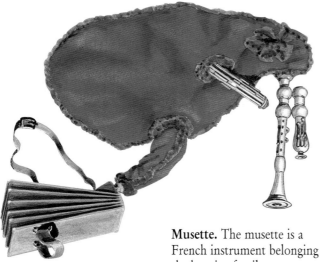

Musette with bellows, France.

Musette. The musette is a French instrument belonging to the bagpipe family.
Its construction is similar to that of the cornemuse. The difference is that the air is blown into the instrument not from the mouth but by arm-operated bellows. It has a single drone and two chanters with between five and seven fingerholes.

German regal, late 16th century. This instrument is lavishly decorated with woodcarvings. The reed pipes are placed behind the manual. The loudness can be regulated by opening or closing the cover. The bellows are operated by an assistant.

Bible regal, late 16th century. The bellows are shaped as a bound Bible, hence the instrument's name. The manual is divided into two foldable parts, and the reed pipes are inside it.

The regal, the portable organ having only reed pipes, has often been confused with other small organs, such as the positif. The appreciation of regal's music has varied throughout the ages. The great organologist and musician of the early 17th century Michael Praetorius describes its sound as "tender and pleasant", but a lot of musicians in the age of Bach, including some of Bach's friends, found the regal's timbre too feeble and dry.

IDIOPHONES

Bell

About the end of the 4th century, bells replaced tubes as the heralds of Christian feasts, as well as in the role of calling the believers to prayer. Although historical evidence in support of this hypothesis is scanty, St. Paulin, a bishop in southern France, is credited with their invention. Bells appeared as an element of Christian services in Rome and Orleans in the 7th century. In the 8th century, Charlemagne introduced them in religious services all over Europe. The bells were cast of a copper and lead alloy to which iron and silver were later added. Pope John XIV established the practice of naming the bells after Christian saints.

In Eastern Europe, bells were used only since the 9th century. In 865 Emperor Vasilius asked doge Orso of Venice to send him 12 bells for the Hagia Sofia church in Constantinople. The doge sent the bells and thus contributed to the introduction of bells into the Eastern Orthodox liturgy. Initially, the monasteries and the churches protested and kept using iron or wooden semanterions. At first, the bells were suspended from a tall wooden structure. Later, belfries were built for them, usually as part of the churches. The first belfry was erected in Rome.

Bell from Antwerp cathedral.

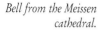

Bell from the Meissen cathedral.

The production of very large bells started only in the 11th century. Of the 30 largest bells in the world, 20 are in Europe. Six of them are in Russia, the largest of them, Tsar Kolokol ("King Bell"), weighing 170 tons and broken in 1733, stands in the Kremlin. The largest bells in Britain are at St. Paul's Cathedral in London, and in the clock tower of the Houses of Parliament (known as Big Ben). Three of the largest bells are in the U.S., the largest of them at the Riverside Church in New York City (18 t).

MEMBRANOPHONES

Drum

Tenor drum, 16th century.

Italian tabor, 17th century.

Provencal drummer.

Basel drum, 1575. The membrane is tensioned with metal clips tied with cords. Its tone is bright and penetrating. First used as a military drum, it was later adopted as a folk instrument. The playing technique developed considerably and a notation system was even devised for it.

The tabor is a double-head drum with a cylindrical shell of up to 25 cm in diameter and a snare on the upper skin or plastic membrane. Some models are equipped with tensioning keys, though their operation requires some skill; besides, the instrument is best kept as light as possible, as the tabor is carried in one hand. If the membrane requires tensioning, it can be moistened and left to dry. The tabor, which first appeared in folk music as a time-beating instrument for the accompaniment of dancing, is usually struck with a beater, though it can also be struck with the fingers. It is often played together with a small galoubet flute. Stravinsky used it for unusual effects in the ballet *Petrushka* (1911).

CHORDOPHONES

The precursors of the European lute date back to 2000 B. C., and come from the Middle and the Far East. The instrument was brought to Europe around the 8th century by the Moors and the Saracens in Spain. During the Middle Ages, it spread all over Europe, and in the 15th century assumed a leading role in domestic music making, both as a solo instrument and in ensembles. Its popularity peaked in the 16th century, and by the second half of the 18th century it had been replaced by the guitar and the piano, only to be revived early in the 20th century for authentic performances of Renaissance and Baroque music.

Lute

This is an instrument with a large pear-shaped body, a curved neck, and a flat soundboard with a richly decorated soundhole carved in a rose or star pattern. The fingerboard is short and wide, most often with frets, and with a pegbox either pointing backwards at roughly a right angle or straight. The number of strings varies from nine to 12, though in the 16th and 17th centuries there were 12 or 13. Some lutes have as many as 24 strings. The strings are generally paired (double courses); some run over the fingerboard, others are unstopped.

Angel playing the lute.
Altar detail, Bartolomeo Montagna, late 15th century.

Italian lute with one single and eight double strings by Vendelio Venere, Padua, c. 1584.

Italian lute with additional bass strings by Vendelin Tieffenbrucker, Padua, c. 1500.

Lute, 16th century.

The tuning of the strings varied considerably. In the 16th century it was either G, c, f, a, d^1, g^1, or A, d, g, b, e^1, a^1. In the 17th century, the tuning was A, d, f, a, d^1, f^1 and (G), F, E, D, C for the bass strings. The lute's sound is gentle and sweet, a perfect accompaniment to the human voice. The modern lute is built with six single strings, tuned like those of the guitar. This instrument, which is in fact a guitar with a lute shape, is known as the guitar-lute.

Small Italian ten-string lute of an original shape and richly decorated, Milan, 16th century.

Theorbo

The theorbo is a bass lute from the second half of the 16th century, with an increased number of bass strings and an additional pegbox either above or beside the usual one. Some instruments have a third pegbox. The additional pegboxes are either a continuation of the first or placed beside it. The neck is relatively long and broad. The melody strings run along the fingerboard to the lower pegbox. The bass strings pass above or beside the fingerboard to the upper pegbox. In European musical practice, the theorbo was used until the mid-18th century in chamber music and ensembles, where it played the continuo part (a chordal accompaniment).

Theorbo, 17th century.

Theorbo, Italy, 17th century.

Theorbo-lute by Tieffenbrucker, 1610, with two pegboxes: one bent back like a lute's, with 12 melody strings, and the other as a slightly curved continuation of the neck, with nine bass strings.

Chitarrone

The chitarrone is another bass lute with a smaller body
and a long neck. The two pegboxes stand one above the other
along the neck; the stopped courses, 11 – 14 in number, run
to the first one, and the five to eight unstopped, off-fingerboard
drone strings run to the second. Despite its name,
this instrument has nothing to do with the guitar. It is found
in Italy after 1580 and is also known as theorbo, theorbo-lute,
or archlute.

Colascione. A lute of Arabic
origin, similar to the tanbur,
popular mainly in Italy from
the 16th to the 18th century,
it had a small body and a long
neck with some 16 – 24 frets
and from two to six metal
or gut strings.

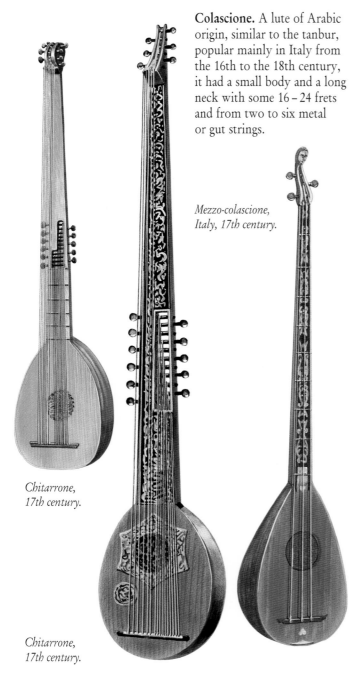

*Mezzo-colascione,
Italy, 17th century.*

*Chitarrone,
17th century.*

*Chitarrone,
17th century.*

Mandora (mandola)

This is a small lute, considered
to be the precursor of the
mandolin. Usually the in-
strument had four or five single
gut strings. It is of Arabic
origin and in Spain it was
referred to as "the moorish
guitar". The mandora was
quite spread in France in
the 16th century and in
Germany was also referred
to as quinterne.

*Mandolin,
17th century.*

*Modern replica
of a 17th-century
bandurria
with six double
strings.*

*Mandora,
17th century.*

The bandurria is a small plucked instrument, particularly used
in popular music in southern Spain. It played the melody,
accompanied by a guitar. The plectrum-sounded tremolo
is very typical of it. The instrument's name dates back to the
14th century but it acquired its present shape only in 1555,
owing to the efforts of the maker Bermudo. The bandurria's
small body is about 7.5 cm deep, and the wide fingerboard
is about 26 cm long. The first of the six double courses of
strings is tuned to a^2, the others are tuned progressively
downwards in fourths.

Cittern

The cittern is a guitar-like instrument known as citole in the Middle Ages, which emerged in the early 16th century, gained popularity in the 16th and 17th centuries, and fell out of use around the beginning of the 19th century. It was pear-shaped and flat-backed, with a soundbox that was deeper in its lower part, frets, and a varying number of metal strings plucked with the fingers or with a plectrum. Easy to handle and play, it was a favorite with amateurs.

German bass cittern of unusual shape, 16th century.

Italian cittern with a soundbox of unusual shape and 11 strings, 17th century.

Cittern by Girolamo de Virchi, Brescia, 1574.

French cittern with flat belly and back, frets and ten strings, 16th – 17th centuries.

Musician playing the cittern, Giacomo Francesco Cipper, 18th century.

Pandora (bandore)

A large bass cittern from England, it had a characteristic round shape with an elaborate contour, frets, five to seven double courses of strings, and a single pegbox.

Penorcon. Shorter than the pandora, with a wider soundbox and neck and no soundhole on the belly, this instrument had frets and nine double courses of strings.

Italian penorcon, 17th century.

Cittern-pandora, 17th century.

Poliphant. A stringed instrument with both stopped and unstopped strings in a special harp-shaped frame with no pegs, it was created by Daniel Farrant around the end of the 16th century and was famous as the instrument played by Queen Elizabeth.

Poliphant by Wendelin Tieffenbrucker, 1590.

Orpharions, 17th century.

Orpharion. A small pandora with slanting frets and eight or nine double courses of strings, it was popular in the 18th century. Orpharion is an Elizabethan stringed instrument designed by the maker John Rose. Typical of it are the wavy-sided body, similar to the bandora's. It is tuned like a lute, and orpharion players use lute tablatures in reading music.

Guitar

Like the lute, the guitar is a stringed instrument with a fingerboard that spread from Spain into Europe in the 17th century. The guitar is played by plucking the strings with the fingers of the right hand, with a plectrum, or with a special pronged thimble. The so-called "classical" guitar has a characteristic figure-of-eight shape, a body length of 48 cm and a total length of 90 – 95 cm. The belly is made of pine, spruce, or redwood, and the ribs of maple, sycamore, mahogany, or rosewood. The strings are of nylon or metal depending on the type of guitar and the repertory for which it is intended. The frets on the fingerboard, once of ivory, are now made of metal.

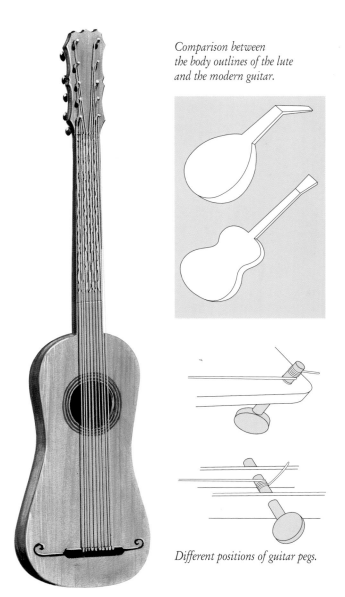

Comparison between the body outlines of the lute and the modern guitar.

Different positions of guitar pegs.

Guitar by Belchior Dias, 1581.

It is not certain whether the origins of the guitar can be found in the European tradition or in the Arabic influence coming through Spain. Among its predecessors are the mandora, the vihuela, and the old viol. In the 15th century the typical Renaissance guitar had a small body and four courses of strings. In the 16th century a fifth course was introduced and became accepted as standard during the Baroque period. A sixth course was added at the end of the 18th century, and later the variant of six single strings was adopted along with other alterations in the guitar's construction. In the work of the 19th-century Spanish instrument maker Antonio de Torres Jurado (1817–1892), the guitar achieved the standard "classical" shape of modern times.

German guitar, 17th century.

Italian battente guitar (i.e. round-backed), early 17th century.

Guitar, c. 1550, Reconstruction.

Until the mid-16th century, the tuning was d, g, b, and e^1, each note being played on two paired strings, similarly to the modern mandolin. Lower-pitched strings were added later: the fifth string (A) by the Spaniard Juan Bermudo in the 16th century and the sixth string (E) in the mid-18th century in Germany.

In the early 17th century, the Italian guitarist Francesco Corbeta popularized the classical guitar in the courts of King Louis XIV of France and King Charles II of England. The guitar became a favourite instrument for domestic playing in French and English high society. In Spain, it has been a widely popular folk instrument from much older times to date.

Musicians with guitar, flute, and lute, Jan Massys, 16th century.

Venetian guitar, early 17th century.

Viol

Soprano viola da gamba, 16th century.

The large viol family, precursors of the modern bowed stringed instruments, emerged around the end of the 15th century. It includes all varieties of viola da gamba, viola da spalla, viola di bordone, viola bastarda, viola d'amore, as well as the later viola pomposa. In their prime in the late 16th century, they had the leading role that now belongs to the instruments of the violin family. For the next century and a half they competed with the newer instruments, finally falling out of use by the second half of the 18th century. The viols differed from the modern bowed instruments both in their appearance and in a number of structural details. The neck sloped backwards, at an angle with the soundbox (as in some older models of today's double bass). The soundholes might have different shapes and lay symmetrically at the two sides of the bridge (with a third circular soundhole sometimes added). The old instruments had much thinner waists and more sloping shoulders, while the lower part of the soundbox was much wider and more rounded. The neck was broader to accommodate the numerous strings, with metal frets (like the guitar's) for stopping, and ended in an elegant scroll shaped like a human or animal head.

Viols had between five and seven strings, sometimes with additional resonating strings below (viola d'amore, viola bastarda). They were tuned in fourths or thirds, while modern bowed stringed instruments are tuned in fifths (with the exception of the double bass whose strings are tuned in pure fourths). They sounded softer than modern bowed instruments. All viols were either held upright, between or on the knees, or supported on a low chair.

The name of the modern viola is somewhat misleading. Though it has the same name as the old viol, it did not develop from it. Around the middle of the 16th century, a distinction was introduced into the nomenclature, the viols being referred to as viola da gamba (supported on the knee), and the viola, a member of the violin family, as viola da braccio (supported on the arm). Around the middle of the 17th century, the latter came to be known simply as viola. The first outstanding Italian violin makers Gasparo da Salò and Giovanni Paolo Maggini also made violas. Violas were larger in size than modern ones until a smaller model, easier to play, was built by Antonio Stradivari. Over the course of the 18th, 19th, and early 20th centuries the viola underwent many transformations, intended to solve the opposing demands of a fuller tone and a convenient size.

Tenor viola da gamba, 17th century.

Bass viola da gamba by Johann Tielke, Hamburg, 1687.

The **soprano viola da gamba** is a high-pitched instrument, which together with its tenor and bass counter parts, forms the backbone of the viol family. The size of a large viola but somewhat deeper, it was tuned a fourth higher than the tenor viola da gamba .

The **tenor viola da gamba** is close in size to the cello, with six strings. A seventh string was added in France in the 17th century. It was popular as a solo instrument, in chamber music, and in the orchestra.

The **bass viola da gamba** is larger in size than the tenor instrument, and tuned a fifth or a fourth lower. Until the mid-18th century, when it was displaced by the cello, the bass viola da gamba was often preferred to it as a solo and ensemble instrument. Bach wrote three sonatas for bass viola da gamba and used it in the six Brandenburg Concertos.

The **double-bass viola da gamba** (violone) is about the size of the modern double bass. The lowest-pitched member of the viol family, it doubles the bass part an octave lower in ensembles.

The **descant viola da gamba**, originating in France from the 16th – 17th century is the size of a violin, with six strings tuned a fourth higher than the soprano viola da gamba. It was played resting on the knee, and was preferred by women players.

The **alto viola da gamba** is a little larger than the descant variety, with a more limited use.

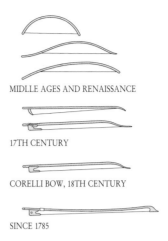

MIDLLE AGES AND RENAISSANCE

17TH CENTURY

CORELLI BOW, 18TH CENTURY

SINCE 1785

Bow

The development and improvement of the bow paralleled the evolution of the violin and the period of the violin and viol families' coexistence. Its initial shape, resembling the hunting bow, was gradually elongated, and by the 15th century it had something like the shape of the modern bow. Around 1700 Archangelo Corelli created the non-elastic bow, and some 50 years later, Giuseppe Tartini made it longer and more flexible. It was only around 1780, however, that the French bow maker François Tourte introduced the modern form of the bow: a band of hair, a mechanism to tighten it by means of a frog and screw, and an inward curve of the stick. Tourte made it of Pernambuco wood (sandalwood from the Pernambuco region of Brazil). Thus improved, the bow allows for more variety in bowing technique and a greater range of tone quality.

Viola bastarda
by Antonio Ciciliano, 16th century.

Tenor viola da gamba, 17th century.   *Alto viola da gamba, 16th century.*

The **viola bastarda** is similar to the tenor viola da gamba but larger in size and having some of the characteristics of the lira da gamba. In the string ensemble it usually played chords, and its part was written with tablature instead of notes. Along with the main models – viola da braccio ("arm viol"), viola da gamba ("leg viol") and violone ("large viol," standing on the floor) – the viol family also included instruments with resonating strings. These were placed below the neck, passing through small holes in the bridge (or beside it), and were not touched by the bow, sounding sympathetically with the bowed strings, giving gentle and pleasant overtones.

Viola d'amore. This arm viola was the most popular instrument with resonating (sympathetic) strings of its time. Built in England in the second half of the 17th century, it reached the peak of its use as a solo instrument in the 18th century. It was the size of a large modern viola but deeper, with six or seven gut strings and at least the same number of sympathetic strings made of steel or brass. The strings were tuned in unison: A, a, d¹, f sharp¹ (f¹), a¹, d².

The viola d'amore is still used today as a solo instrument in chamber music, and in the orchestra. Vivaldi wrote for the instrument, and Bach used it in the *St. John Passion* and the cantatas. Carl Stamitz wrote concertos and sonatas for viola d'amore. Meyerbeer used it in *The Huguenots*, as did Charpentier in *Louise* and Puccini in *Madame Butterfly*. In the 20th century, Hindemith composed solo works for this instrument, Prokofiev used it in his ballet *Romeo and Juliet*, and Janácek used it in the opera *Katya Kabanova*.

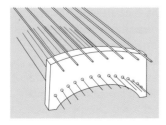

Position of the melody and drone strings over the bridge.

Viola d'amore, 17th century.

Lira da braccio with a soundbox shaped like a violin's, northern Italy, 16th century.

Viola di bordone, 17th century.

Lira da braccio by G. d'Andrea, Verona, 1511.

Lira da gamba with 11 melody and two drone strings, by Antonio Brensio, Bologna, 1592.

The viola di bordone
(baryton) is the bass version of the viola d'amore. It appeared in Germany and spread to Austria and England from the 18th to the mid-19th century. Its body is slightly different in shape, with a cut in the back, and the soundholes are snake-shaped. There are six or seven bowed strings, usually tuned like those of the tenor viola da gamba. The sympathetic strings (from nine to 40, most often between 14 and 18) are tuned diatonically. Because of the large number of sympathetic strings, only some of them are placed below the neck; the rest are to its right, so that they can be plucked with the left thumb. Haydn composed prolifically for the baryton.

The lira da braccio is the main representative of the bowed lyre family. It developed from the medieval fiddle and was known in Europe as early as the 12th to 13th centuries. In widespread use in the 15th to 17th centuries, it acquired its final form in the 16th century. It was supported on the player's left arm, and the shape of its soundbox was similar to that of the violin. It had a wide neck with a fingerboard, a flat pegbox with perpendicular pegs, a varying number of melody strings (most often, five), and two off-fingerboard drone strings, plucked with the left thumb. Because of the similar shape and the tuning in fifths, the lira da braccio is believed to be the main prototype of the modern violin.

Lira da gamba, Italy, 16th century.

The lira da gamba has nine melody strings (and no drones), a short neck with five frets, and a third rosette soundhole. Ordinarily, the lira da gamba (lirone, lirone perfetto, archiviola di lira) had between nine and 16 melody strings and two to four drones, passing through a flat bridge. It was used mainly for playing chords.

In the last quarter of the 16th century, the violin's size, soundbox, proportions, sound characteristics and tone color were finally established.

Violin by Giovanni Ventura, Venice, 1622.

Double bass by Gottfried Tielke, 1662.

Tromba Marina

The tromba marina, popular from the 14th to the 16th century, had one or two strings and a narrow pyramid-shaped body some 2 m tall, and was played by plucking the string with the left hand. One foot of the bridge was free, and rattled loosely on a plate of bone or ebony on the belly when the strings vibrated. Its sound was similar to that of the trumpet, and that, in conjunction with its use as a signaling instrument in the navy, was the reason for its name.

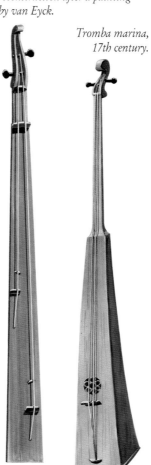

Double tromba marina, reconstruction after a painting by van Eyck.

Tromba marina, 17th century.

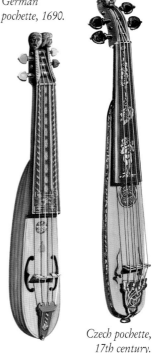

German pochette, 1690.

Czech pochette, 17th century.

Pochette

The pochette is a miniature instrument of the violin family (only 30 – 40 cm long). It was popular as a pocket-sized violin, or dancing master's violin. During dance classes, the master would play the melody or indicate the rhythm with it, and then tuck it away in his pocket in order to demonstrate the more complicated steps. This is why the instrument was called pochette, from the French word for pocket. Having evolved from the rebec, in the 16th to 18th centuries it was produced in a variety of shapes: like an old rebec or like a viol, or even resembling a gondola. From the 18th century onwards it acquired the contours of a violin. The pochette had three or four strings. In Monteverdi's opera *Orfeo* (1607) it was referred to as "violino piccolo alla francese."

LUTHIERS

The spiritual and cultural changes that occurred in Europe during the Renaissance gave rise to new ways of thinking about music, new genres, and new styles of performance. Instruments of the old viol family, with their weak, muted tone, their numerous strings tuned a fourth or a third apart, and their problematic construction, were unable to meet the new demands of musical practice, in particular those of orchestras. Taking as its starting point some of the more successful structural features of older instruments (such as the rebec, the fiddle, the lira da braccio, and the viol), a new instrument, the violin, emerged in northern Italy at the end of the 15th and beginning of the 16th century. Along with the other members of the violin family, this instrument came to be of immense significance for the development of European music. The 17th century is known as the Golden Age of this instrument, when the violin attained its present form and the first significant solo literature was composed for it.

Musical instrument workshop,
French engraving, 18th century.

The name of the first maker of an instrument of the bowed stringed instrument family is unknown. It is clear, however, that the classical violin began to take shape over four centuries ago, owing to the efforts and the skill of a series of remarkable luthiers, who paved the way for the work of the famous European luthier families. The most prominent among them are the Italian schools in Brescia, Cremona, Venice, Milan, Naples, and elsewhere.

The development of these schools is partly due to certain extremely favorable features of the environment in Italy. Instrument makers had easy access to the best types of wood for the different parts of the instruments of the violin family: spruce, sycamore, and maple. In addition, lively trade with the East provided high-quality gums for the varnish and other woods appropriate for instrument making.

The first famous luthier school was in the town of Brescia in northern Italy. It was founded by the talented violin maker Gasparo Bertolotti, known as Gasparo da Salò (1540 – 1609). Another important representative of this school is da Salo's disciple, Giovanni Paolo Maggini (c. 1580 – c. 1632). Maggini is famous for his double basses, which are by no means inferior to the instruments created by the luthiers Stradivari and Guarneri of Cremona.. The Cremona school was founded by

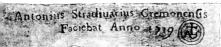

ANDREA AMATI
(before 1511 – before 1580)

and its traditions were continued by his sons Antonio (c. 1540 – ?) and Girolamo (1561 – 1630). However, it reached its peak at the time of Girolamo's son, Nicola Amati (1596 – 1684), from whose workshop came the celebrated Antonio Stradivari (1644 – 1737) and Andrea Guarneri, great-uncle of the famous Giuseppe Guarneri "del Gesù" (1698 – 1744).

ANTONIO STRADIVARI
(1644 – 1737)

is believed to have created about 650 instruments – mainly violins, about 16 violas, 50 cellos, and a number of other stringed instruments such as lutes and guitars. Many of his instruments, unique masterpieces of the luthier art, are known by the names of their owners, e. g. "Sarasate" (1724). Antonio Stradivari's sons Francesco and Omobono took over his craft and brought further fame to the family but never matched their celebrated father.

GIUSEPPE GUARNERI
(1698 – 1744)

continued the luthier dynasty's traditions of the Guarneri family as Antonio Stradivari's rival. The divine inspiration at the core of his exceptional skills finds expression in the way he signed his works: IHS (Jesus Hominum Salvator) and "Joseph Guarnerius del Jesu".

Violin makers in an engraving by Maerten de Vos for the Book of Genesis, 16th century.

Other prominent masters of the Cremona school include Carlo Bergonzi, Francesco Rugeri, Lorenzo Storioni, and Giovanni Battista Ceruti. The Naples school is best represented by the Gagliano family: Alessandro, Gennaro, and Nicola. Prominent representatives of the Milan school are Carlo Giuseppe Testore, Carlo Landolfi, Giovanni Battista Grancino (i), and Giovanni Battista Grancino (ii).

From Italy, the craft spread to other regions of Europe. The most outstanding representative of the Tyrol school is Jacob Stainer (c. 1617 – 1683). Other leading masters are Mathias Klotz of Mittenwald (1653 – 1743); the French makers Nicolas Lupot (1758 – 1824), P.-L. Pique (1758 – 1822), and J.-B. Vuillaume (1798 – 1875), whose instruments are still highly valued; and various makers of the Bohemian school, the English school, and the Polish school (the elder and younger Marzin Goblic). Stringed instruments made as long ago as the late 1500s not only survive as beautiful works of art and testaments to the unsurpassed skill of the Italian luthiers, but are still being played today. Occasional minor repairs are not unusual, while more substantial damage requiring advanced restoration techniques is very rare. When major restoration is necessary, it begins with a careful study of the model: its appearance, its exact dimensions, and all its characteristics. Once the diagnosis has been made, the restorer (also an experienced string instrument maker) opens the instrument to establish what restoration methods should be used.

Damaged varnish is especially difficult to repair. Restorers avoid re-varnishing the entire instrument for fear of impairing the sound quality and thus ruining the instrument's authenticity. As far as possible, the varnish is conserved in the state in which it is found.

In addition to original instruments by Stradivari and Guarneri, the market abounds in copies made "after" the famous luthiers. The industrial production of stringed instruments, particularly of violins, that began in the 1860s has flooded the market with instruments bearing the names of celebrated Italian makers which are somewhat dishonestly used to promote these products.

Clavichord

The clavichord developed directly from the monochord (via the polychord), by the addition of organ-type keys. Metal blades (tangents), attached to the keys, strike the strings and remain held against them as long as the key is held down. Thus, the contact between the player's fingers and the strings provides effective control of the volume and tone color. The timbre itself is slightly metallic, soft but very expressive. The clavichord is best suited for domestic use. The instrument developed around the end of the 14th century, and existed in two versions: fretted and unfretted. In the former, several tangents could be used on the same string, while on the latter there was a separate key for every string. At first the instrument was placed on a table, then on a special stand, and finally legs were added. The clavichord was popular in domestic music making from 1500 to 1750. One of the last important composers of music for the clavichord was Johann Sebastian Bach's second son, Carl Philipp Emanuel.

Small "Bible" clavichord.

The small octave Bible-clavichord is a late version of the Bible-organ for domestic playing. When closed, the instrument is shaped like a book. When open, it turns into a clavichord.

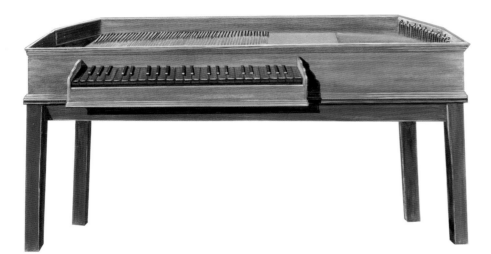

The earliest fretted clavichord, built in 1543 by the Italian maker Domenico da Pesaro.

Young lady playing the harpsichord. Detail. Gonzales Coques, 17th century.

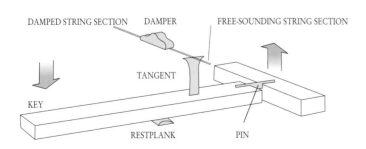

DAMPED STRING SECTION   DAMPER   FREE-SOUNDING STRING SECTION

TANGENT

KEY

RESTPLANK   PIN

Clavichord mechanism.

Harpsichord

The harpsichord appeared at about the same time as the clavichord. Historically and technically, it is unrelated to the monochord and the polychord, having developed from the psaltery and the timpanon. Each key is connected to a sharp plectrum, originally made of quill but later replaced by leather or metal blades. The plectra pluck the strings and their contact is immediately interrupted, causing the sound to decay quickly. The strings vary in length, and the plectra pluck them in the same place, as in the piano mechanism. The range of the harpsichord is $C/F^1 - f^3$. Its sound is louder than that of the clavichord, but more monotonous in terms of tone quality, the volume and tone quality being unaffected by the player's touch. The harpsichord developed continuously from the 16th to the late 18th century as makers made efforts to enrich its tone. The instrument acquired the shape of a bird's wing (the prototype of the grand piano), a soundboard with a rose decoration, and a rest plank over which the strings ran. For each note, the harpsichord has two, three, or even four metal strings (forming a choir) that can be activated with stops or pedals (couplers). There are usually two and occasionally three manuals, with several registers (lute, bassoon, and so on). The strings are tuned in unison or octave. The harpsichord was made in a variety of designs. Some fine examples were richly decorated with paintings and abstract ornamentation. The instrument was first mentioned in Padua in 1397, as "clavicembalo"; the earliest preserved instrument, from Bologna, dates from 1521.

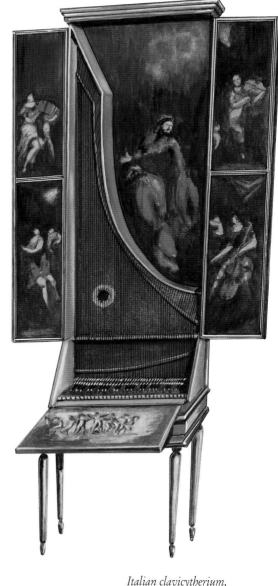

Italian clavicytherium, early 17th century.

A derivative of the harpsichord is the clavicytherium of the 15th century. In this instrument, the frame and the strings are perpendicular to the keyboard, requiring certain changes in the mechanism.

Harpsichord mechanism.

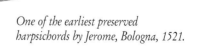

One of the earliest preserved harpsichords by Jerome, Bologna, 1521.

Virginal and Spinet

Virginal and spinet are keyboard instruments with strings
plucked with plectra, similar to the harpsichord but smaller
in size. The virginal is rectangular while spinets can be
triangular, rectangular, pentagonal, hexagonal, and even
heptagonal. There are also examples of oval and trapezoidal
spinets. The virginal was popular as a domestic instrument
in the 16th and 17th centuries in England, and was particularly
favored by women players. The keyboard projected from one
of the long sides. Double virginals with two keyboards were
also produced. The spinet had a single manual.
Both instruments had a single string for each note, running
perpendicular or at an angle to the keys' axes. Very small
virginals and spinets (octavinas) were also made, sounding
an octave higher than the music was notated. In shape they
resembled books, workboxes, or other such objects.

German virginal, 1617.

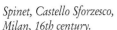

*Spinet, Castello Sforzesco,
Milan, 16th century.*

*Double virginal
by Hans Ruckers the elder, 1581.*

The oldest preserved English virginal, by Gabriel Townsend, 1641.

Portable spinet, 16th century.

The spinet is a version of the early domestic harpsichords that replaced the virginal. It differs from the virginal both in shape and in its acoustic properties.

REPERTORY

The early works for harpsichord were composed for domestic performance. By the end of the 17th century, the repertory had been enriched by Henry Purcell, Louis Couperin, and others. During the 18th century François Couperin wrote over 200 pieces for harpsichord, Domenico Scarlatti about 500 sonatas, J. S. Bach concertos, fantasias, preludes and fugues, the Goldberg Variations, six English Suites, and six French Suites, and Handel six concertos (for organ or harpsichord), 20 suites, four sonatas, and sonatinas. Haydn's keyboard sonatas and Mozart's early keyboard music were amongst the last important works for harpsichord, written when the piano was overtaking it as the leading keyboard instrument. In the 20th century, a number of works were composed and transcriptions made for Wanda Landowska (1879 – 1959), the first great modern international harpsichord soloist.

+ LABORVM + LEVAMEN +

Bowed piano designed by Raimundo Trucado, 1625.

Venetian-style spinet by Anton von Padua, 1550.

The virginal is a stringed instrument with a keyboard. Its name probably derives from the Latin word "virga," meaning "a stick." The virginal has a gentle tone colour and its technical capacities are superior to those of the harpsichord.

EUROPE – BAROQUE AND CLASSICISM

In terms of music history, the Baroque period extends from c. 1600 to c. 1750, or from the time of the first operas to the death of J. S. Bach. Music historians have been using the term "baroque" since the early 20th century to describe the period in which the basso continuo (a figured bass line, indicating the harmonies to be played above the bass) was widely used.

The evolution of polyphony had a pronounced effect on keyboard music, and new genres developed: the fugue, the toccata, and the organ chorale prelude. The leading composers of the period included Monteverdi (who composed the first true opera), Frescobaldi, Vivaldi (who composed numerous concertos), François Couperin, Purcell, and, of course, the two giants, Handel and Bach at the end of the period.

The bowed chordophones flourished during the baroque period, particularly the instruments of the violin family: the violin, the viola, the cello, and the double bass, forming the backbone of the modern symphony orchestra. Instrumental ensembles began to play a lively part in concert activities, as did the solo violin and the clavichord. It was also in this period that the violin became the undisputed leader of instruments, and that the foundations of the enormous violin repertory we enjoy today were laid. The organ also flourished in the 17th and 18th centuries and was widely used in concerts, and new instruments such as the English horn (cor anglais), bassoon, and clarinet joined the aerophone group.

Immediately after the Baroque and before the Classical period, there was a relatively brief pre-Classical period, sometimes referred to as the Rococo period (1740 – 1770). This period is distinguished by a body of particularly elegant keyboard music.

The period of musical classicism, from 1770 to the death of Beethoven in 1827, is sometimes described as the "classic epoque," evoking a direct association with ancient Greek and Roman art. Emotional restraint and structural clarity are general features of the "classical style" as epitomised in certain works by Haydn, Mozart, and Beethoven, but their music also reveals striking dramatic contrasts and lively joking. The most popular instrumental genres of the period included the overture, divertimento, and the variations, as well as the forms associated with the evolving four-movement sonata cycle: instrumental concerto and symphony, which quickly developed alongside the classical symphony orchestra, based on the earlier Mannheim version. Chamber music also flourished with the establishment of the string quartet (two violins, viola, cello) and piano trio (piano, violin, cello) as the major chamber genres. The piano displaced the harpsichord, clavichord, and even the organ as the favoured keyboard instrument, and many of the important classical period composers, including Haydn, Mozart, and Beethoven, were also accomplished pianists.

The basso continuo and preference for polyphonic textures that characterize much Baroque music were displaced by the predominantly homophonic texture of musical classicism, with its simpler, symmetrically structured themes and less involved harmonies. In vocal music, Italian opera types that had conquered Europe during the Baroque continued to prevail, but the major classical period composers succeeded in developing new vocal structures in their operas, oratorios, and masses, taking advantage of the increased potential of the classical symphony orchestra and its instruments.

AEROPHONES

Flute

Transverse flute sword.

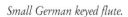

Tuning flute by Delous, Paris, 1772.

Sponge.

South German ceramic transverse flute, 18th century.

Flageolet (flautino). The flageolet is an old woodwind instrument belonging to the end-blown flute family, emerging in the 16th century as a folk instrument. From the 17th to the 19th century, it existed in two major forms, French and English. The former had two fingerholes in front and two on the back, while the latter had all six fingerholes in front. The flageolet is closely related to the recorder, though its pipe is narrower and about 20 cm shorter. In the 18th century, a narrow mouthpiece of ivory or bone was inserted into the top. That led into a funnel-shaped chamber, at the bottom of which a soft sponge was placed. Also known as flautino, this instrument was the precursor of the small transverse flute (piccolo) in the orchestra. Its high soprano voice is characterized by a gentle, pleasant tone color, and it has a range of about two octaves. There are also double and occasionally even triple flageolets.

Small German keyed flute.

German transverse flute made of beechwood, with a single key, by J. Denner, Nuremberg.

Transverse flute walking-stick.

Transverse flute with a removable middle joint.

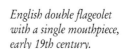

English double flageolet with a single mouthpiece, early 19th century.

French transverse flute made of ivory, with one key, by T. Lot, Paris.

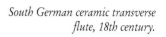

Recorder

From the 16th to the
18th century, the recorder was
produced in different sizes. The
family now has four members:
soprano in C (lowest note c^2),
alto in F (f^1), tenor in C (c^1),
and bass in F (f), the last
of which has a curved metal
mouth pipe inserted into
the upper joint. Music for the
soprano recorder is often
notated an octave lower than
it sounds.

*Czech bass recorder of unusually
narrow bore, 17th century.*

Playing the recorder, Jan Kupecky, 18th century.

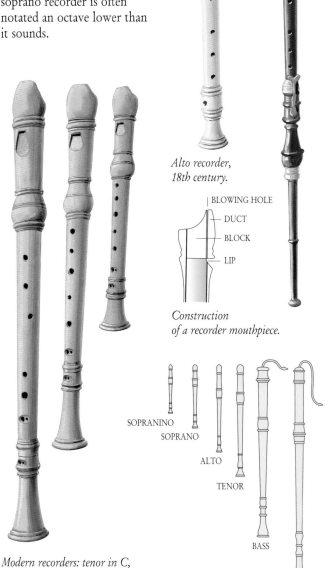

*Alto recorder,
18th century.*

| BLOWING HOLE
|— DUCT
|— BLOCK
|— LIP

*Construction
of a recorder mouthpiece.*

SOPRANINO
SOPRANO
ALTO
TENOR
BASS
CONTRABASS

*Modern recorders: tenor in C,
alto in F, and soprano in C.*

The Baroque recorder family.

REPERTORY

Among Baroque composers of solo and trio sonatas,
the recorder was used by Alessandro Scarlatti, Vivaldi
(seven concertos), Telemann (who wrote a particularly large
number of pieces for the recorder, including eight solo
sonatas, two solo concertos, and various trio sonatas), Handel
(sonatas nos. 2, 4, 7, and 11 of op. 1), Marcello, and Corelli.
A number of modern composers have also written for the
recorder: Hindemith (a trio), Robin Milford (*A Prophet in the
Land)*, one of the first reappearances of the recorder in the
orchestra), Francis Baines (*Quartet for Recorders* and *Fantasia
for Six Recorders*), and Antony Hopkins (a suite).
Even avant-garde composers, such as Luciano Berio in *Gesti*,
made the recorder part of their musical world.

Clarinet

The clarinet derives from the French folk instrument the chalumeau. The first clarinet was built in 1690 by the maker Johann Christoff Denner of Nuremberg. The instrument was further improved up to the 20th century by a series of makers and performers, such as Anton Stadler, Ivan Müller, and Hyacinthe Klosé. The Boehm system clarinet was patented in Paris in 1855 by Louis-Auguste Buffet and the clarinetist Klosé, who was a professor at the Conservatoire.

Descant chalumeau with seven fingerholes in front and one at the back. The single reed is placed in a special chamber at the upper end of the instrument, and begins to vibrate when air is blown into the chamber. The chalumeau family includes the following models: soprano (descant), alto, tenor, and bass.

Clarinet with two keys by Johann Christoff Denner and his son Jacob Denner, early 18th century.

Clarinette d'amour by G. A. Rottenburg, 18th century. This instrument has six keys and the typical bulbous bell. It is made of beechwood, and the upper joint is slightly bent.

Basset horn by F. G. D. Kierst, 18th century.

Small clarinet in E flat, 18th century.

Basset Horn

Bent basset horn with a box in which the air circulates before reaching the bell, 18th century.

Ivory clarinet by Jacob Hans Scherer, 1723.

The basset horn is a tenor version of the clarinet, similar in shape to the bass clarinet. It has the same mouthpiece as the clarinet in B flat, but is slightly longer and angled; alternatively, a metal bell is inserted into its upper part.

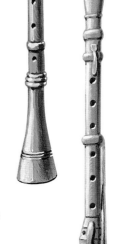

It was created around 1770 but was also used in the 19th and 20th centuries. Many composers, including Mozart, Beethoven, Mendelssohn, Richard Strauss, and Stravinsky, were attracted by its tone quality, which is similar to that of the bass clarinet. Mozart used two basset horns in his Requiem; the instrument also appears in his chamber music, in his operas, and in the Serenade in B minor for 13 wind instruments. Richard Strauss included a basset horn in the orchestra for six of his operas.

Sickle-shaped basset horn, 18th century.

Clarinet with five keys, 18th century.

Oboe

The oboe probably appeared between 1610 and 1640. It evolved from the shawm as a result of the combined efforts of various French makers. The cup-shaped pirouette was removed so that the reed could be held in the mouth, and this had a considerable influence on the instrument's sound. The reed itself was modified, the pipe and the bell became narrower, with a more pronounced conical bore, and the fingerholes became smaller. As a result of all this, sound production was easier, the expressive potential was increased, intonation became more stable, and the tone quality in the upper register improved markedly.

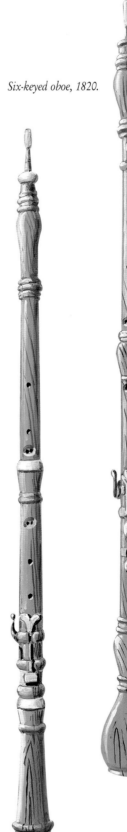

Six-keyed oboe, 1820.

German oboe d'amore (between 1724 and 1738), with a pear-shaped bell and a short brass staple for the reed. This instrument was favored by J. S. Bach.

Two-keyed German oboe, Dresden, 18th century.

Two-keyed oboe.

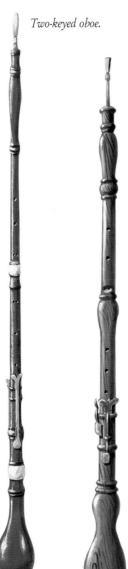

Oboe from the 18th century, the likely precursor of the cor anglais.

Two-keyed oboe resembling a Hotteterre model, c. 1680.

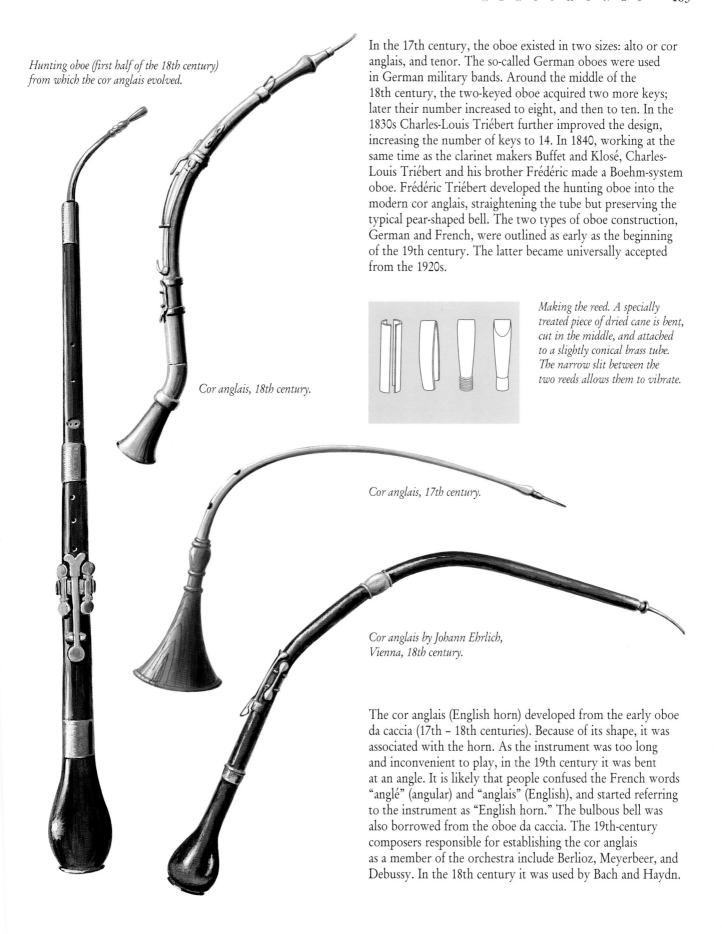

In the 17th century, the oboe existed in two sizes: alto or cor anglais, and tenor. The so-called German oboes were used in German military bands. Around the middle of the 18th century, the two-keyed oboe acquired two more keys; later their number increased to eight, and then to ten. In the 1830s Charles-Louis Triébert further improved the design, increasing the number of keys to 14. In 1840, working at the same time as the clarinet makers Buffet and Klosé, Charles-Louis Triébert and his brother Frédéric made a Boehm-system oboe. Frédéric Triébert developed the hunting oboe into the modern cor anglais, straightening the tube but preserving the typical pear-shaped bell. The two types of oboe construction, German and French, were outlined as early as the beginning of the 19th century. The latter became universally accepted from the 1920s.

Hunting oboe (first half of the 18th century) from which the cor anglais evolved.

Cor anglais, 18th century.

Making the reed. A specially treated piece of dried cane is bent, cut in the middle, and attached to a slightly conical brass tube. The narrow slit between the two reeds allows them to vibrate.

Cor anglais, 17th century.

Cor anglais by Johann Ehrlich, Vienna, 18th century.

The cor anglais (English horn) developed from the early oboe da caccia (17th – 18th centuries). Because of its shape, it was associated with the horn. As the instrument was too long and inconvenient to play, in the 19th century it was bent at an angle. It is likely that people confused the French words "anglé" (angular) and "anglais" (English), and started referring to the instrument as "English horn." The bulbous bell was also borrowed from the oboe da caccia. The 19th-century composers responsible for establishing the cor anglais as a member of the orchestra include Berlioz, Meyerbeer, and Debussy. In the 18th century it was used by Bach and Haydn.

Bassoon

The bassoon's immediate predecessor is the pommer of the 16th century, from the family of double-reed instruments. The stright tubes of some of the low-pitched variants – bombards, bombardons, and large bass pommers – were up to 3 m in length, and the instruments were heavy and quite impractical. In 1530 Afranio degli Albonesi of Ferrara joined two old bombards into a u-shaped instrument, which he called "phagotus." The new shape and the narrower bore made the previously rather coarse sound mellower, and the instrument became easier to play. The greatest difficulty, however, was the cup in which the reed was enclosed, which isolated the reed from the player's lips. In the early 17th century, S. Scheltzer removed the cup, and the bassoon acquired the soft and pleasant sound for which it became known as dulcian (from the Italian word "dolce," meaning sweet, gentle).

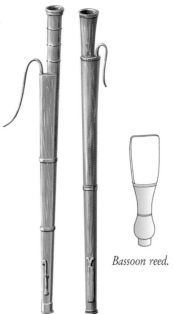

English contrabassoon by Stanesby, London, 1739.

Bassoon reed.

Swiss bassoons with unusual bell shape, used in church music, 18th century.

Musical instrument workshop, engraving by Christoph Weigel, 17th century.

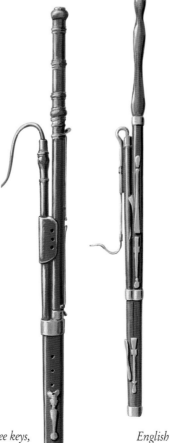

Bassoon with three keys, 17th century.

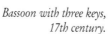

English contrabassoon, 1739.

In the early 16th century Afranio of Ferrara had the excellent idea of dividing the bass pommer into two and joining the two parallel sections. This is how the bassoon was born; the Italian name for it, "fagotto," means a bundle of sticks, in reference to the instrument's appearance. It took a long time to perfect the instrument's mechanism. Theobald Boehm contributed to it, but it was Johann Adam Heckel who brought it to its present design in 1870.

Natural Horn

The natural horn has a narrow cylindrical tube and a flared bell.
The pitch is altered by overblowing, which produces
the tones of the harmonic series. The natural horn was used
in the orchestras of the early 18th century, though its limited
potential restricted its role to merely adding color to the
performance. Composers and conductors did not resort
to it very often.

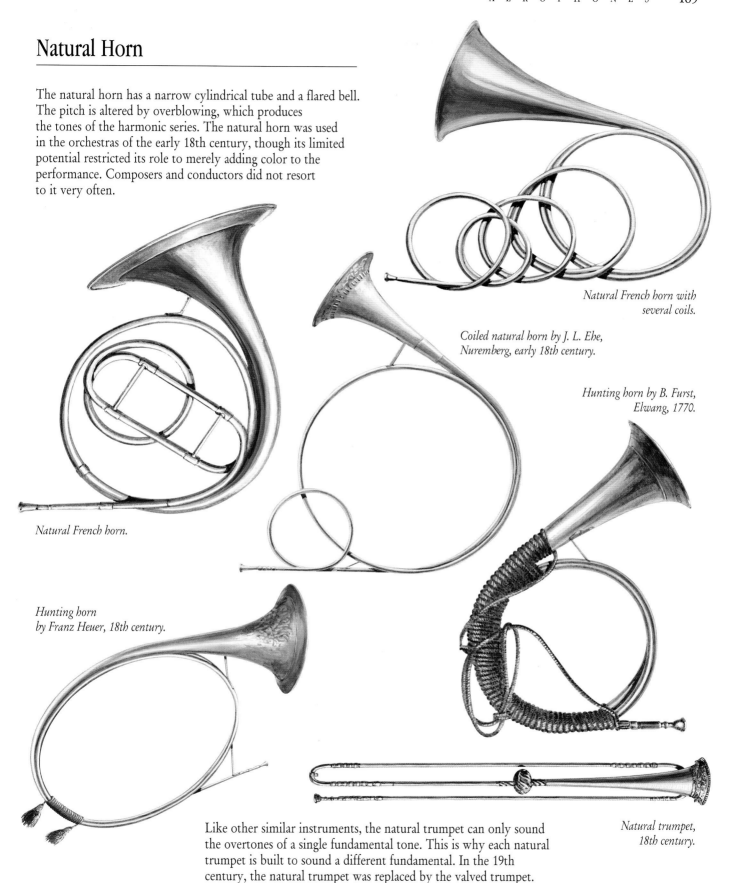

Natural French horn with several coils.

Coiled natural horn by J. L. Ehe, Nuremberg, early 18th century.

Hunting horn by B. Furst, Elwang, 1770.

Natural French horn.

Hunting horn by Franz Heuer, 18th century.

Natural trumpet, 18th century.

Like other similar instruments, the natural trumpet can only sound
the overtones of a single fundamental tone. This is why each natural
trumpet is built to sound a different fundamental. In the 19th
century, the natural trumpet was replaced by the valved trumpet.

Organy

The organ is the largest musical instrument. Its name derives from the Greek word "organon"
and the Latin "organum," both of which mean tool, device, or instrument. That is to say,
the organ is the instrument of instruments. A keyboard instrument, comprising a complex
system of wooden and metal pipes, a pneumatic device (bellows), and a console containing
the keyboards, stops, and pedals, its prototypes date back to ancient times: the Greek panpipe,
the bagpipe, and the mouth organ from the Far East (known in China as sheng).

Organ, 18th century.

SOLI DEO
GLORIA

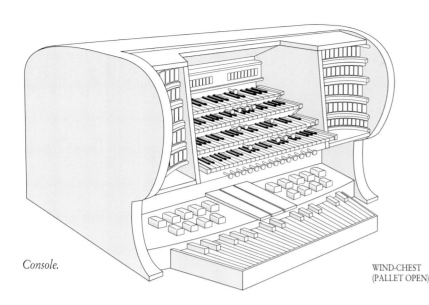

Console.

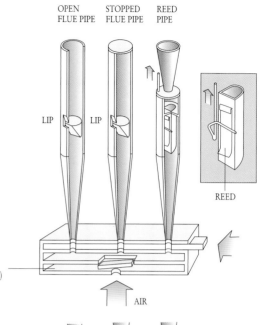

OPEN FLUE PIPE   STOPPED FLUE PIPE   REED PIPE

LIP   LIP

REED

WIND-CHEST (PALLET OPEN)

AIR

WIND-CHEST (PALLET CLOSED)

Organ Mechanism

The organ consists of three main parts: the pipes, the bellows, and the controls. The pipes differ in size, shape, design, and material, and produce different pitches and tone colors. There are three main divisions: great, swell, and pedal. According to their construction, the pipes are divided into two groups: flue pipes (open and stopped), similar to the panpipe, and reeds, with a single vibrating reed, like a clarinet's. All the pipes within a single rank are made of the same material, have the same shape and bore, and produce the same tone color. The number of pipes in a rank corresponds to the number of keys on the manual. For example, an organ with eight ranks, or registers, and two manuals of 60 keys each will have 960 pipes. There are instruments with over 200 registers and up to 12,000 pipes. The pipes are made either of wood or of a tin and lead alloy (the tin producing a ringing sound and the lead a duller one). The registers are labeled on the basis of the pipe length in feet. For example, a C pipe which is 8' (2.5 m) long will have 8' register. The pipe length may vary from 1 cm to over 10 m. The largest ones may have a diameter of over 50 cm, and weigh some 500 kg. Stops marked 8' sound at ordinary pitch, the 4' stop sounds an octave higher, the 16' an octave lower, and the 32' two octaves lower. The pneumatic system includes electrically driven fans, reservoirs, wind-trunks, wind-chests, soundboards, pallets (immediately below the pipes), and trackers connecting the pipes with the keyboard. The controls are on the console, which includes manuals and a pedalboard (for the bass notes). The manuals – from two to seven, depending on the instrument's size – are terraced, and although all manuals and the pedalboard have their own registers, selected by draw-stops, the loudest and fullest "voices" are on the first manual. The so-called couplers allow one manual division to be played from another manual.

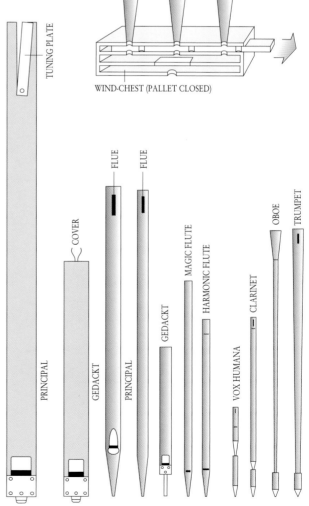

TUNING PLATE

COVER

FLUE   FLUE

PRINCIPAL   GEDACKT   PRINCIPAL   GEDACKT   MAGIC FLUTE   HARMONIC FLUTE   VOX HUMANA   CLARINET   OBOE   TRUMPET

Some organ pipes.

REPERTORY

The organ had a key role in sacred music from the Baroque and Classical periods onwards. In the first half of the 18th century, works for organ were composed by Bach, Handel, and many other composers. Bach, himself a virtuoso organist, used it in the Mass in B Minor, Handel in *Messiah*, Mozart and Haydn in their Latin masses, Beethoven in the Missa solemnis, Brahms in the *German Requiem*, and Berlioz in the *Te Deum*.

Within the operatic repertory, Monteverdi's *Orfeo* features the regal, a small reed organ. The organ is frequently used in opera, and examples may be found in the operas of Meyerbeer (*Robert the Devil, The Huguenots, The Prophet*), Gounod (*Faust, Romeo and Juliet*), Wagner (*Rienzi, Tannhäuser, Lohengrin, The Mastersingers of Nuremberg*), Verdi (*Il trovatore, La forza del destino, Otello*), Ponchielli (*La Gioconda*, Massenet *Manon, Werther*), Moniuszko (*Halka*), and Mascagni (*Cavalleria rusticana*).

In symphonic music, there are several major works for organ composed before the 20th century: Liszt's *A Faust Symphony* (Liszt is believed to have been the first to use the organ in a symphonic poem, in his *The Battle of the Huns*), Saint-Saëns's Symphony No. 3, Mahler's Symphony No. 2 *Resurrection* and Symphony No. 8, and Richard Strauss's symphonic poem *Thus Spoke Zarathustra*.

The 20th century is rich in concertos and other works for organ, including concerto by Jongen and Hindemith, a symphony by Dupré, a concerto by Poulenc with timpani and strings, and a concerto by Charpentier with piano and chamber orchestra.

GEORGE FREDERICK
HANDEL

(1685 – 1759)

Organ by Christian Müller, 1738, Sint-Bavo Church, Haarlem, Holland.

Organ music is notated on two staves, in treble and bass clef, like piano music. When the pedalboard is used, the notation is on three staves. The organ's range is far larger than that of all other orchestral instruments put together, covering nine and a half chromatic octaves from C^2 to g^5.

The organ's dynamic characteristics are unrivalled: it is capable of producing any dynamics, from the softest pianissimo to the loudest fortissimo. Its timbre is rich and complex, capable of imitating the tone color of various instruments of the symphony orchestra as well as that of the human voice (solo and choral).

The organ was introduced into the Catholic service in the 7th century by Pope Vitalius, and has remained an integral part of it. In the 9th century, Pope John VIII ordered the first organ for use in Catholic ceremonies in Rome. In 10th-century England, the organ's pipes were divided into registers. In the 12th century, the number of bellows diminished, and lead pipes were produced along with copper ones. Around the 13th century, springs were installed at the back of the keys to restore them to their initial position. The wide keys were narrowed, and by the end of the 14th century they had been divided into black and white in their present arrangement. By that time, some organs were made with two keyboards (manuals). Each instrument was specifically built for a particular church, and was unique in design and decoration.

Organ concert of sacred music in the Weimar church in 1732. J.G.Walther.

Modern Czech organ, Baroque style.

In the 16th century, the organ's construction was radically improved, and it acquired something like its present design. Small (chamber) instruments became popular: the regal, the positive, and the portative; some of them continued to be used much later. In the early 17th century, the octave included 12 keys, 7 diatonic and 5 chromatic. The organ was equipped with additional bellows and echoes, as well as with registers designed to imitate bowed stringed instruments. In the 18th century, the organ's compass was extended, as were the manuals and the pedalboard. In the 19th century, the hand-operated mechanisms were replaced by pneumatic ones. By that time, there were also electric wind-supply mechanisms. In the 20th century, the organ attained its present form.

Positive

The positive is a small organ with no pedalboard, only a
manual, placed on the floor or on a table. It is used for domestic
music-making as well as in small churches for accompaniment to
the choir. It has only a flute register with stopped pipes for
a more compact size. While the organist plays, the assistant
operates the bellows, manually or through pedals. The positive
is characterized by considerable versatility of sound. Initially it
was placed by the large organ and the player moved between the
two. Later, it was installed permanently in the loft.
In Germany, this instrument was known as "Rückpositiv"
("Rück-" refering to its position at the rear). In England it was
known as "chair organ." About the end of the 18th and the
beginning of the 19th century, the name "choir organ" became
established.

*Positive organ
by G. Silbermann, 1724.*

Positive organ.

*French positive organ
from the time of Louis XIII.
The registers are gilded,
and the bellows are operated
with a leather strap on the right.*

AUTOMATIC AND MECHANICAL MUSICAL INSTRUMENTS

These instruments are designed to play popular works by means of a fully automatic mechanism: a pinned cylinder or perforated paper, creating the sound of one or more musical instruments – strings, percussion, or organ pipes. Mechanical musical instruments are designed to play works, parts of works, or themes, without human intervention. They were first mentioned in the Middle Ages. Mechanical spinets were built around the end of the 16th century. In the 18th century, barrel organs and musical boxes were designed. At about the same time, the first mechanical recording devices were built. From the mid-19th century, some of them used electrical power.

Barrel Organ

This instrument consists of organ pipes, bellows, and a mechanism controlling the wind supply to the pipes. A manually turned handle simultaneously pumps the bellows and turns the barrel, whose projections raise levers to admit air to the pipes. The instrument can be operated manually or by a clockwork mechanism, steam, or electricity.

Fairground organ by Ruth and Sons, using perforated paper, Waldkirch, Germany, 1900.

*Componium:
a kind of orchestrion
with a barrel-driven "composing"
mechanism that could compose
variations on a given theme.
Made by Winkel in Amsterdam, 1821.*

*Barrel organ from the beginning
of the 20th century.*

The orchestrion is a large mechanical barrel organ using pinned cylinders and perforated paper rolls to imitate an orchestra. It was built in Vienna by J. N. Maelzel, who also invented the metronome. Beethoven originally wrote the second part of his battle symphony *Wellington's Victory* (1813) for this instrument. Maelzel later settled in the U. S., where he built a mechanical orchestra of 42 automata, whose repertory included overtures by Mozart and Spontini.

Orchestrion by Fratelli, Hannover, 1920.

Orchestrion.

Mechanical Piano

This instrument existed in many forms, all based on the same principle: broad paper rolls, wooden cylinders, or metal discs, with perforations or pins, activating mallets or mechanical fingers that strike the notes. The pianola belongs to this family of instruments. It is driven by compressed air from pedal-operated bellows. Precisely calculated perforations in a rotating paper roll (a kind of paper "notation") regulate the access of wind to wooden fingers that strike the keys.

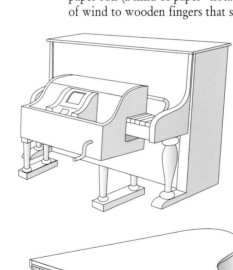

Pianograph: a box placed at the keyboard of an ordinary piano, its mallets striking the keys. The mallets are moved according to the perforations on a paper roll, and the cylinder is turned manually.

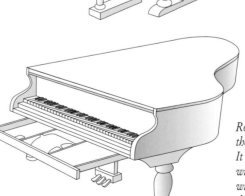

Royal reproducer, reproducing the playing of great pianists. It is a mechanical instrument, with a rotating cylinder covered with perforated paper controlling the dynamics.

Musical Box

The musical box principle evolved in the second half of the 18th century in French-speaking Switzerland, initially for watches and snuffboxes. Notable makers of musical boxes were Nicole Frères of Geneva (1815 – 1903) and others in St. Croix, north of Lausanne. Their musical boxes consisted of a rotating cylinder with pins, plucking metal tongues of different lengths. The tongues were arranged to correspond to a simple tune, with or without accompaniment. Later, the cylinder was replaced by a disc with projections and a similar sound-making principle. Cheaper and easier to change (thus allowing a variety of tunes), the disc displaced the cylinder mechanism by the end of the 19th century.
Disc musical boxes were first built in Leipzig by Paul Lochmann in the 1880s. Before long, the miniature mechanisms – toys, books, watches, tools, mechanical birds, and so on – developed into larger models, named "Symphonium" and "Polyphon." They were made not only in Europe but also in the U. S., for public places such as bars, restaurants, and dance halls. Today historical musical boxes are highly appreciated and priced accordingly, particularly those with working mechanisms and spare discs and cylinders.

The mechanism of a musical box: a rotating cylinder with pins plucking metal tongues.

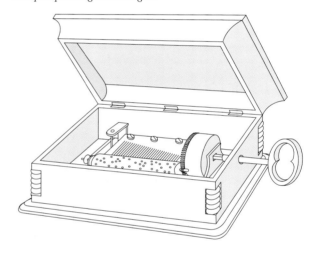

Mechanical Bell and Chime

These have existed since the Middle Ages: a mechanism plays a series of tones on bells, chimes, or hemispheres, by means of a rotating cylinder or disc (or cogwheel). The mechanism may include ropes, levers, and clockwork. It can be seen in the clock towers of many European towns and has been known in northern Europe since the 13th century.

The tune of the famous Big Ben of London (Big Ben is the name of the largest bell, not of the tower) is known as the "Cambridge Chime" or the "Westminster Quarters," and was composed in 1793 by William Crotch on the basis of a motif from Handel's *Messiah*. In Germany and the U.S., the preferred tune is the "Parsifal Quarters," a motif from Wagner's opera *Parsifal*.

Mechanical bells, gradated in size.

IDIOPHONES

Glass Harmonica

A friction idiophone, the glass harmonica is played by rubbing glass bowls. In its earliest form, displayed by the Irishman Richard Pockrich in London in 1744, it contained a set of 20 to 30 "musical glasses." The German composer Christoph Willibald Gluck performed his concerto for this instrument in London in 1746, using 26 glasses. In 1761 Benjamin Franklin replaced the glasses with hemispherical bowls, threaded on a metal axle. The bowls were arranged in a long box and filled to a certain level with a solution of vinegar and water, to keep the rims moist. The axle was rotated by a pedal, and the harmonica was sounded by gently rubbing the rims of the bowls with moist fingertips. Later on, a keyboard was added. In 1799, Ernst Chladni replaced the hemispheres with glass plates.

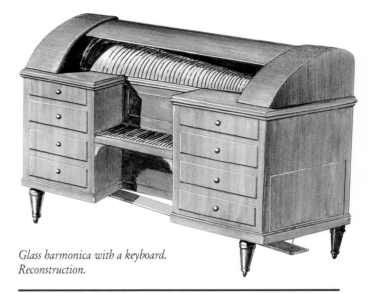

Glass harmonica with a keyboard. Reconstruction.

Glass harmonica, 18th century, by an anonymous German maker. The bowls for the chromatic tones have golden rims.

Nail violin (nail harmonica). A friction idiophone, widely popular in the 18th and 19th centuries, which consisted of 12, 18, or 24 iron nails placed upright in a semicircle around the edge of a wooden soundbox. The sound was produced with a violin bow, the pitch depending on the length of the nails.

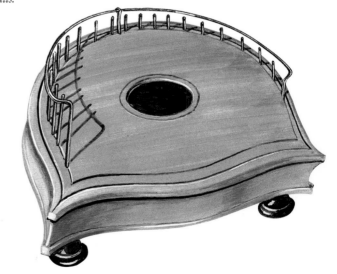

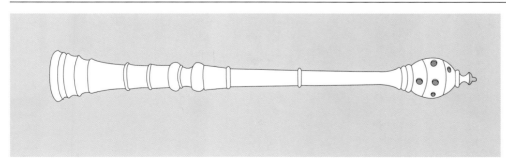

Eunuch flute of the 18th century. The membrane of this mirliton is placed under a removable cap in the upper part of the instrument. It vibrates when the player blows or sings into a side opening. The tube acts as a resonator.

MEMBRANOPHONES

Timpani and Drum

The timpani became a member of the symphony orchestra around the mid-18th century. During the Classical period, two timpani were used, tuned to the tonic and the dominant. Less sophisticated models had a single tensioning screw, some with an additional screw for retuning. Rotary timpani are tuned by rotating the shell. Pedal timpani also exist.

Two french tenor drums, 17th century.

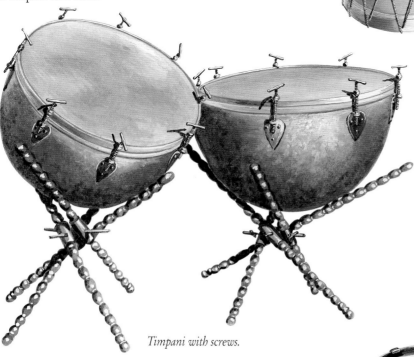

Timpani with screws.

By the time of Handel and Bach, the timpani were included not only in military bands but in all outdoor musical performances. Books of music history often mention Handel's *Music for the Royal Fireworks*. In its first performance in 1749, sixteen timpani and eight tenor drums were used. This is considered a record for the 18th century.

Timpani with screws, 18th century.

Military tambourin.

Military snare drum.

CHORDOPHONES

Harp

The European harp went through a long development process, aimed at overcoming its technical shortcomings. The main problem with this basically diatonic instrument was that of providing for chromatic alterations of pitches (semitones). A variety of solutions were attempted: Welsh harpists shortened the strings manually; Scottish harpists used metal blades to shorten the strings by a semitone; double (Irish) and triple (Welsh) harps were constructed, with an auxiliary row of strings to supply the accidentals. However, they all proved technically and acoustically flawed. Around 1660, in Tyrol, the first hook mechanism was introduced: iron hooks on the neck were turned manually, shortening the strings to raise the pitch by a semitone.

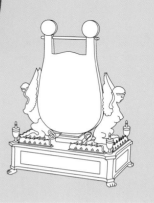

Harp-lute, 19th century.

Harpanette: a vertical psalterium with a wing-shaped soundbox and brass strings, 17th century.

This harp-lyre was made by Carlo Scalti in Italy in the 19th century. It has a shallow soundbox and a wide body similar to that of the ancient Greek kithara. The two courses of strings are stretched to a diagonal bar running to one of the decorated arms. The instrument is more remarkable for its elaborate ornamentation than for its musical qualities.

The specially designed decorated stand, of the Carlo Scalti's harp-lyre.

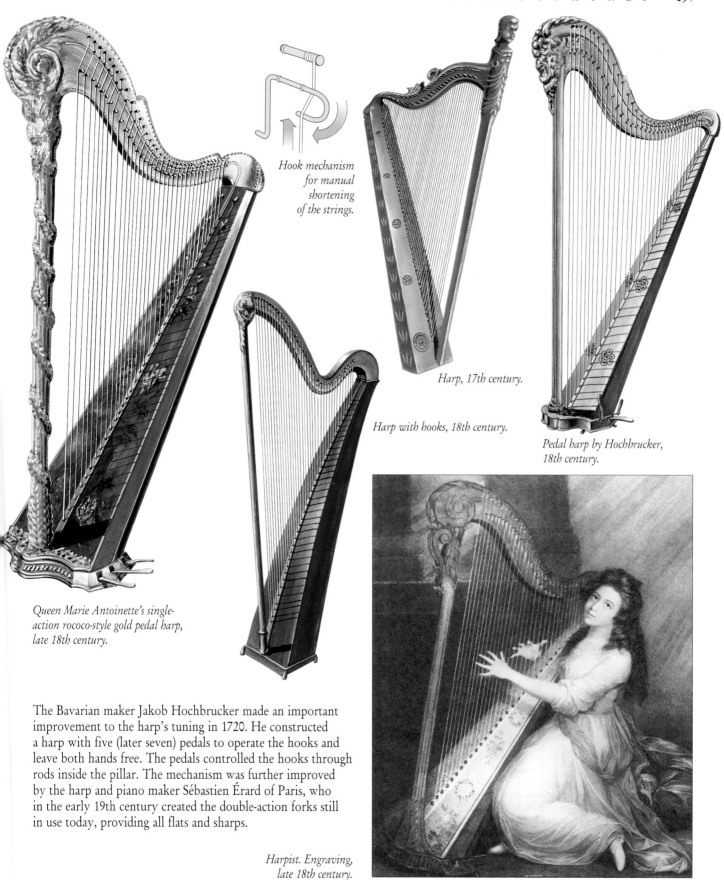

Hook mechanism for manual shortening of the strings.

Harp, 17th century.

Harp with hooks, 18th century.

Pedal harp by Hochbrucker, 18th century.

Queen Marie Antoinette's single-action rococo-style gold pedal harp, late 18th century.

The Bavarian maker Jakob Hochbrucker made an important improvement to the harp's tuning in 1720. He constructed a harp with five (later seven) pedals to operate the hooks and leave both hands free. The pedals controlled the hooks through rods inside the pillar. The mechanism was further improved by the harp and piano maker Sébastien Érard of Paris, who in the early 19th century created the double-action forks still in use today, providing all flats and sharps.

Harpist. Engraving, late 18th century.

Lute

Modern replica of a German lute with 14 frets and six strings, tuned like a guitar. In fact, this is a guitar with a lute soundbox.

Modern replica of a German bass lute.

Italian theorbo, 18th century.

Theorbo. This is a lute, known since the 16th century, gradually fell out of use in the second half of the 18th century, giving way to more modern instruments. The theorbo was often used as an accompaniment to the human voice. It had between 12 and 15 strings, including paired strings tuned in unison and off-fingerboard drones. Because of its specific construction, its length sometimes reached 1.2 m. The theorbo was introduced into the orchestra by Jean-Baptiste Lully in the 17th century.

Chitarrone by B. Dvořák, Prague, late 19th century. The chitarrone is generally considered to be a lute very close if not identical to the theorbo.

German theorbo by Martin Bruner, 1764. The pegbox consists of three terraced segments. The instrument has seven melody and ten (six plus four) drone strings.

Musical lesson using the theorbo, Franz van Mieris, 17th century.

Mandolin

Mandolins (pandurins) are a group of stringed instruments of the large lute family. Their shape is similar to that of the lute, like a halved pear. The rounded back is made of long narrow ribs and the belly is flat with a round soundhole. The neck is short, with six to 24 frets on the fingerboard. The pegbox is flat and relatively large.The mandolin acquired its final shape in the 17th century. A century later it was one of the most popular instruments in Italy. In the 18th century new varieties were added to the family, differing in body and neck shape, and in the number and tuning of strings: the Florentine with five double strings, the Genoese with five to six strings, the Paduan with five strings, and so on. The most popular model, however, was the Neapolitan mandolin, which is still used today. In the 1900s, the mandolin fell out of use, but interest in it was revived at an amateur level at the end of the century. Neapolitan mandolins gradually came to include an increasing number of instruments, such as the piccolo mandolin, tenor mandola, alto mandolin, mandoliola, mandocello, mandolone, bandolobass, and guitar. Among the non-Italian mandolin varieties, the Portuguese and the American are the better known.

Mandolin with a wide fingerboard, a large pegbox, and six double strings, Genoa, 18th century.

Mandola by Vicenti da Verona, 1696.

The most widely used model has four double strings, tuned in fifths, like those of the violin: g/g, d^1/d^1, a^1/a^1, e^2/e^2. The instrument's range is $g–g^3/d^4$. It is played with an almond-shaped plectrum, and its tone is gentler and softer than that of other stringed instruments.

Mandolin (pandurin) with six double strings, Milan, 1773.

Mandolone, Naples, 18th century.

Neapolitan mandolin by J.J. Franck, Dresden, 1789.

REPERTORY

The relatively rich mandolin literature is intended chiefly for amateurs. However, a number of leading composers have also been impressed by this instrument's particular qualities. Vivaldi wrote concertos for one and two mandolins, and Handel also composed for it. Mozart used it in his opera *Don Giovanni*, and Beethoven wrote four short pieces for mandolin and piano. Later, Verdi called for it in *Otello* and Mahler in his Symphony no. 7. In modern times, Schönberg scored for the mandolin in the Serenade op. 24 and in *Moses and Aaron*, Stravinsky in *Agon*, and Webern in *Five Pieces for Orchestra*, op. 10.

Cittern

French bass cittern with melody and off-fingerboard drone strings running to two separate pegboxes, one above the other, 1789.

Lyre-cittern, c. 1700.

Dutch cittern with eight strings by Johannes Theodorus Cuypers, The Hague, 1782.

English keyecittern, 18th century. The keys move small hammers that strike the strings close to the soundhole.

Ceterone, France, late 17th century. This is a big cittern with a second pegbox for up to eight open bass strings.

Guitar

The harp-guitar is a name uniting several plucked stringed instruments, including the harp-lute. It has metal strings and a side projection of the pegbox for the ten unstopped bass strings. Later, a separate arm was added from the soundbox to the pegbox projection, and the bass strings ran over it.

Harp-guitar, 19th century.

Joachim Tielke (1641 – 1719) was a leading luthier, a master of ornamentation. Fifteen of his remarkable guitars are now kept in the world's largest museums. His instruments' bellies, sides, and backs are covered with images of flowers and animals, hunting, and mythological scenes. Tielke used a variety of materials for these decorations: tortoise shell, ivory, silver, ebonite on the fingerboard, and different kinds of wood. He usually made the pegbox of finely carved ivory.

Guitar by Joachim Tielke, Hamburg, 17th century.

The arched guitar is popular in Italy (the region of Calabria), and is known there as chitarra battente. Its belly is arched, and its body is quite deep. Its five double courses of strings are tuned G, c, f, g, d or A, d, g, h, e^1. The arched guitar is played either with a plectrum or with fingers, and an additional sound effect is produced by striking or rubbing the belly with hands. It first appeared in the 17th century, and is still used today along the Adriatic coast as a folk instrument.

Double guitar.

Guitar by T. O. Hulinzky, Prague, 1754.

Viennese guitar, 1692.

Guitar by Ritter, 19th century. A short broad neck and two movable bridges providing the main chords. The 24 metal strings are tuned according to the instructions placed on the belly.

Arched guitar.

Portuguese guitar, 1800.

Viola and Viol

Guitar-shaped viola, France, 1825.

Fiddle-shaped viola, France, 18th century.

Violinists by Pietro Longhi, 18th century.

Bass viol by Joachim Tielke, 1701.

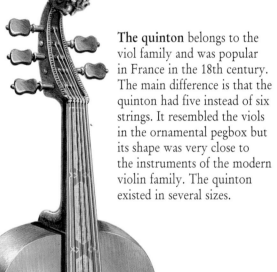

Soprano quinton.

The quinton belongs to the viol family and was popular in France in the 18th century. The main difference is that the quinton had five instead of six strings. It resembled the viols in the ornamental pegbox but its shape was very close to the instruments of the modern violin family. The quinton existed in several sizes.

Tenor quinton.

Viola by Gasparo da Salò, 17th century.

A few later instruments could also be included in the viol family. They are violin-shaped, but their size and number of strings are similar to those of the old medium-tessitura viols.

Viola pomposa by Johann Christian Hoffmann, 1720. With the shape and size of a modern viola, it is tuned an octave lower than the violino pomposo and provided with a strap for supporting on the shoulder.

Viola da spalla by Isepo Marfeoto, Rovigo, 17th century. This instrument is larger than the violin and is supported on the shoulder with a strap.

Viola d'amore by Tomas Ondřej, Prague, 1769.

Violone.

In Italian, violone means "large viol." The name was applied to various instruments in the 17th and 18th centuries; it was usually used to describe the bass or contrabass viola da gamba, but sometimes also the cello and even the double bass.

Modern violone (double bass viol) by Wolfgang Nebel.

Violoncello

Like the violin and the modern viola, the violoncello did not develop from the knee-held viols, which it resembles only in the way it is held. It was created as an instrument with the shape of a violin but approximately the size of the viola da gamba. The earliest violoncellos were built by luthiers of the Brescian school: Gasparo da Salò and Giovanni Paolo Maggini. The instrument's modern proportions were established in the workshops of Guarneri and Rugeri. Antonio Stradivari achieved the best size and proportions, and produced some of the finest examples now preserved in museums and private collections.

Double Bass

The double bass evolved in the 17th century but was slow to gain popularity. Instruments made in the workshops of da Salò, Maggini, Amati, Stradivari, and other leading luthiers are still used in modern symphony orchestras. In 1676 in Rome, the Italian maker Michele Todini published a book in which he claimed to have invented a new bowed instrument, the double bass, by modifying considerably the old contrabass viol. This is how the modern four-string double bass, tuned in fourths and preserving many of the viols' characteristics, developed.

Violoncello by Domenico Galli, Parma, 1691.

Violoncello by Paolo Grancino, Milan, 1690.

One-string double bass by Gasparo da Salò.

Pochette

In the 18th century, the pochette, an instrument that had evolved during the Renaissance, acquired the shape of a modern violin. It existed in several sizes, including a four-string pochette, tuned a fourth higher than the violin (c^1, g^1, d^2, a^2), and a three-string pochette, tuned g^1, d^2, a^2, or even higher, a^1, e^2, b^2. Being used in high society, many of the instruments were richly decorated.

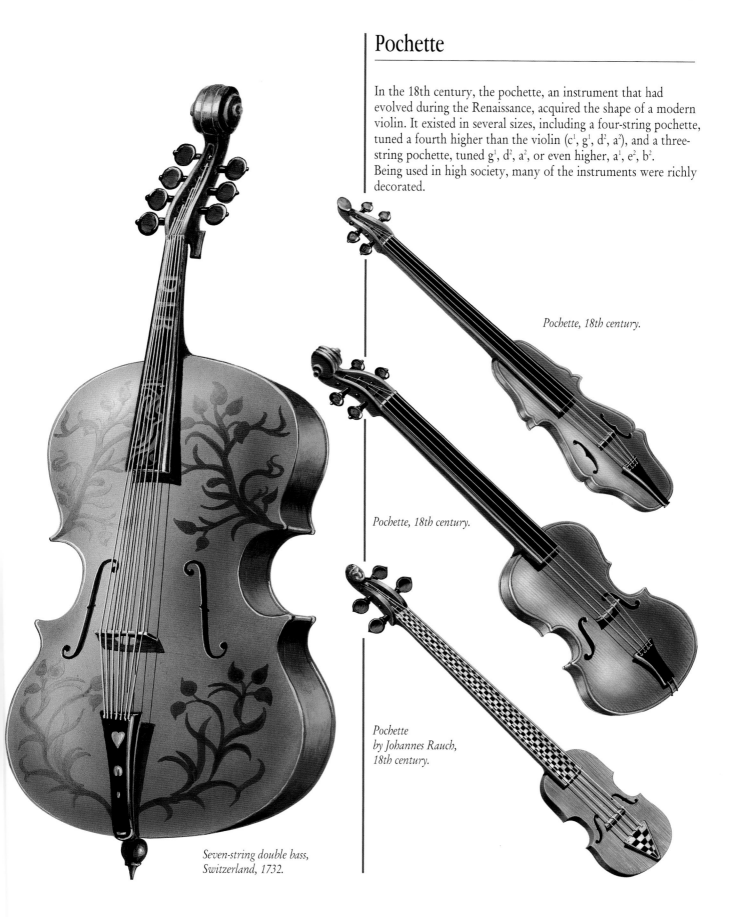

Pochette, 18th century.

Pochette, 18th century.

Pochette by Johannes Rauch, 18th century.

Seven-string double bass, Switzerland, 1732.

Clavichord and Virginal

*Claviharp by J.Ch. Ditty,
Paris, 1821. A chromatic harp
with a key-and-plectrum mechanism.*

*Unfretted clavichord
by Albrecht Hass, Hamburg, 1744.*

*Octave virginal, Germany,
first half of the 18th century.*

The clavichord is a stringed instrument with a keyboard, built in
different sizes. Its metal strings are of equal length. The earliest
examples had a range of four octaves, but by the end of the 18th
century it had reached five octaves, like the harpsichord and the
piano. The clavichord exists in two main versions: fretted
(several tangents used on the same string) and unfretted (with a
separate key for each string). The metal blades or tangents
attached to the keys strike the strings and remain held against
them. The timbre of the clavichord is very expressive but not
too loud, making it convenient for domestic use.
It first became popular in German-speaking countries.

Pedal clavichord by J. D. Gerstenberg, 1760. The strings of the pedal clavichord lie below a clavichord with two manuals. Metal rods connect the pedals with the tangents placed over the strings (unlike those of the manual clavichord). When a pedal is pressed, the respective tangent touches the choir of strings.

Modern clavichord by Hubert, Germany.

Lady playing the virginal, Jan Molenaer, 17th century.

Harpsichord

Harpsichord with three manuals, by A. Frangolini, Florence.

When Johann Sebastian Bach died in Leipzig on 28 July 1750, the inventory of his possessions was found to include enough instruments to furnish an entire orchestra: "a veneered harpsichord (to be kept in the family), a harpsichord, another harpsichord, a small harpsichord, a lute-clavicembalo, another lute-clavicembalo, a Steiner violin, an ordinary violin, a small ordinary violin, a viola, another viola, a small cello, another small cello, a viola da gamba, a lute, a small spinet." Eight of them were keyboard instruments, covering almost the entire range of popular keyboard instruments of the time. (During his lifetime Bach was more famous as an organist and harpsichord player than as a composer.)

The harpsichord enjoyed enormous popularity for three centuries, from 1500 to 1800, and a voluminous repertory was written for it. The instruments were often richly decorated using a technique known as "japanning". The increasing interest in Baroque music in the second half of the 20th century revived harpsichord production. Modern instruments are simpler in design but still serve to restore an authentic sound to music previously played on the piano: recitatives in Mozart's operas, Bach's Brandenburg Concertos, etc. The remarkable art of performer Wanda Landowska (1877-1959) attracted the interest of composers such as De Falla and Poulenc who composed music specially for her.

Two-manual harpsichord, Toulouse, 1679.

In the Baroque orchestra the harpsichord was used to provide harmony and rhythm. The conductor directed the orchestra from a harpsichord placed at its center – hence he was known as "maestro al cembalo." The harpsichord part was notated on a single stave as a figured bass line, the player "realizing" the harmony from the figures provided. This technique anticipates the chord charts of modern jazz.

With the changes in the structure and the sound of the symphony orchestra, by the end of the 18th century the harpsichord had lost its leading role and gradually fell out of use. The rich repertory of works that had been composed for it came to be played on the piano. The 20th century revival of interest in the authentic performance of Baroque music, however, encouraged the production of harpsichords and spinets of modern design but preserving the old colors of the keys. In large concert halls, electric harpsichords are often used, on account of their greater dynamic capacity.

Modern concert harpsichord with a pedalboard, by Sperhacke.

A collapsible harpsichord was created in 1713 by Jean Marius for traveling musicians.

Piano

The piano went through many stages of development before the introduction of a mechanism of hammers connected to keys in the early 18th century by Bartolomeo Cristofori of Florence. Cristofori replaced the tangents and plectra of the clavichord and harpsichord with hammers with leather- and later felt-covered tips, thus providing an immediate connection between the player's fingers and the strings, so that the loudness of a tone depended directly on the force with which the player struck the key. On the new instrument (1709) it was possible to play all tones at various dynamic levels. This quality was emphasized by Cristofori in the new instrument's name: "gravicembalo col piano e forte," or, more simply, pianoforte. Several years later similar instruments were built by the French maker Jacques Marius and by the German Kristof Schrotter. Cristofori's piano was developed further by the famous organ-maker Gottfried Silbermann and his nephew Johann Andreas Silbermann. Johann Andreas Stein improved the mechanics of the instrument, strengthened its construction (specially for Beethoven, who mistreated it mercilessly), and added a second soundboard. These two builders are credited with devising the so-called Viennese or German action.

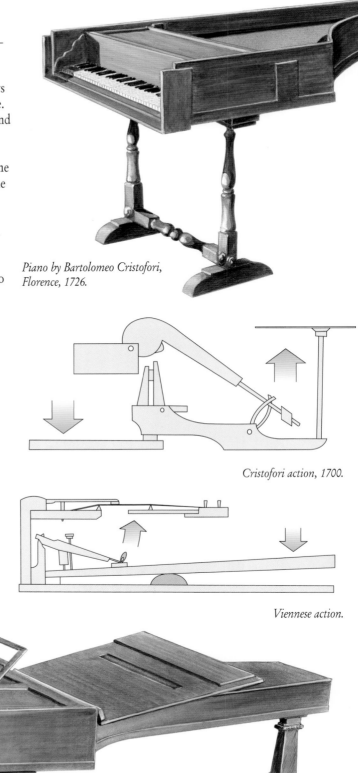

Piano by Bartolomeo Cristofori, Florence, 1726.

Cristofori action, 1700.

Viennese action.

Square piano by Meinke and Peter Meyer, Amsterdam, 1782.

Piano by Streicher, mid-19th century.

Piano by Gottfried Silbermann,
Freiburg, c. 1745, owned
by Frederick the Great.

Viennese action: Around the middle of the 18th century, two schools of piano making were established, south German (first in Augsburg, then in Vienna) and English, with two respective types of action, Viennese and English. In the former the hammers at the back of the keys move in the opposite direction. When a key is struck the hammer goes up to strike the string and then bounces back. This made the keyboard rather heavy and the notes relatively long-sounding and flute-like. The damper mechanism consisted of a box with small padded metal plates attached. The Viennese action flourished in the 18th century, when Vienna was the leading center of piano making, but it is now considered outdated.

Piano by Johann Andreas Stein,
Augsburg, 1773.

Beethoven playing the piano
for Prince Louis Ferdinand. Woodcarving
by Ludwig Pietsch, late 19th century.

In the second half of the 18th century, piano making flourished in England. John Broadwood made the strings thicker, strengthened the frame, and increased the instrument's range to six octaves. However, it was the German Johann Zumpe who founded the piano building industry in Britain. Americus Backers devised the so-called English action, providing a stronger and fuller tone where the Viennese is gentler and drier.

Thus, two main types of piano were established: the softer-sounding "German" and the heavier "English," the former later becoming known as "Viennese" after Streicher workshop opened in the Austro-Hungarian capital in 1794. Until the closure of the workshop in 1896, the Streicher's firm continued to produce fine instruments, favored by the great virtuosos and by composers from Hummel to Beethoven. Haydn, however, preferred Schantz pianos. Other leading makers included Walther, Graf, and later Bösendorfer.

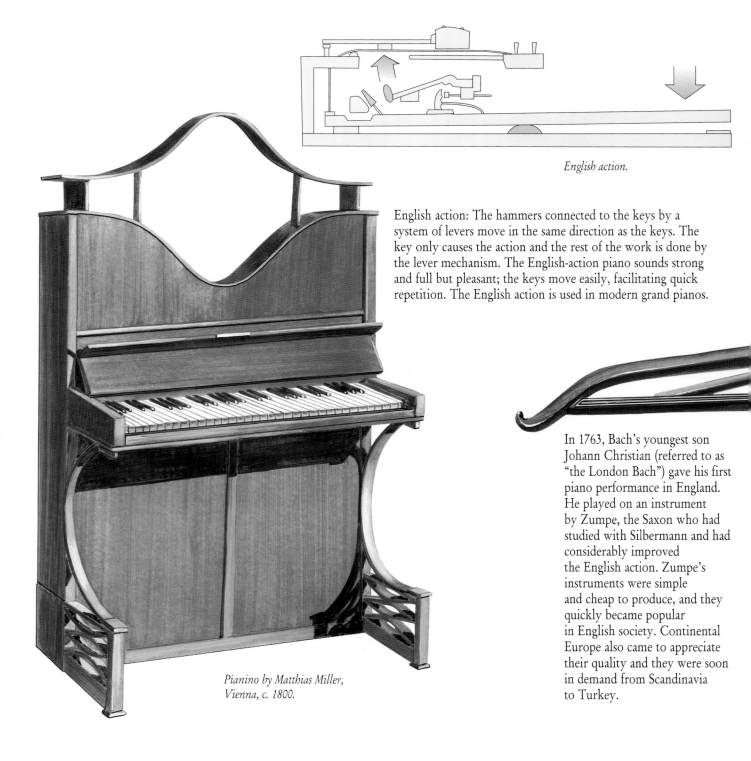

English action.

English action: The hammers connected to the keys by a system of levers move in the same direction as the keys. The key only causes the action and the rest of the work is done by the lever mechanism. The English-action piano sounds strong and full but pleasant; the keys move easily, facilitating quick repetition. The English action is used in modern grand pianos.

Pianino by Matthias Miller,
Vienna, c. 1800.

In 1763, Bach's youngest son Johann Christian (referred to as "the London Bach") gave his first piano performance in England. He played on an instrument by Zumpe, the Saxon who had studied with Silbermann and had considerably improved the English action. Zumpe's instruments were simple and cheap to produce, and they quickly became popular in English society. Continental Europe also came to appreciate their quality and they were soon in demand from Scandinavia to Turkey.

In 1783 the Scotsman John Broadwood patented foot-operated pedals, and in 1788 he introduced the divided bridge for the bass strings. In 1818, Beethoven played on a Broadwood piano. That instrument was later owned by another great composer and pianist, Franz Liszt. Chopin also played on a Broadwood. The Broadwood trademark became so popular that in the second half of the 19th century the factory produced as many as 2,500 pianos a year.

Piano dressing table, c. 1800.

Orphica by J. Donal,
Vienna, c. 1800.
This example has a range of four
octaves and would have been
played on a small table.

Harpsichord concert,
engraving by Pehr Hilleström,
18th century.

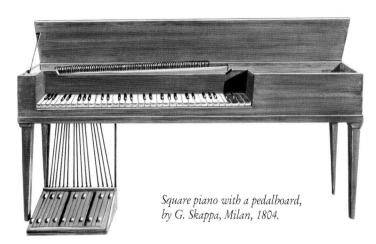

Square piano with a pedalboard,
by G. Skappa, Milan, 1804.

EUROPE — ROMANTICISM

The Romantic period extends from 1820 to 1900 – 1910, thus covering almost the whole of the 19th century. Unlike the words "baroque" and "classical", which are used predominantly by specialists, the term "romantic" is more widely known, not only in relation to music and the other arts, but also in connection with the various national independence movements that developed in Europe in the 19th century. Although of relatively brief duration, the Romantic period in music is marked by rapid and multi-faceted musical development. Moreover, what had formerly been a rather institutionalized approach to music was transcended by movements such as Impressionism and Expressionism, which in their turn were replaced in the first half of the 20th century by neo-Classicism, serialism, the aleatoric movement, and early experiments in electronic music. To a certain extent, this rapid evolution set the standard for the development of music in the latter part of the 20th century.

In music, the age of Romanticism began with the late works of Beethoven and Schubert and ended with composers such as Gustav Mahler and Richard Strauss. The main difference between Classicism and Romanticism was the latter's emphasis on feelings, emotions, and the imagination. These were more highly valued than the balance, the strict proportions, and the sense of unity evoked by Classical works. New musical genres were created and became popular: music drama, the symphonic poem, and the short piano piece. The diatonicism of the Classicism gave way to the chromatic harmonies of Richard Wagner and Richard Strauss. National schools of composition evolved in Germany, Russia, Poland, Bohemia, and elsewhere. The 19th century favored the association of instrumental music with literary and stage works and promoted the concept of the "synthesis of arts."

Opera flourished during the Romantic period: national operatic styles were created, the former Italian domination lessened, and the harshly realistic verismo style developed.

Towards the end of the period, music began to be less Euro-centric and, to an extent, less composer-oriented. Composers began to draw inspiration from a variety of genres and styles, most notably those of folk music and of Eastern music.

Musical instruments acquired their final shape, while their use in the symphony orchestra was no longer restricted to classical orchestral practice.

AEROPHONES

Flute

The period of Romanticism was characterised by an increasing popularity of chamber music which moved from aristocratic salons to concert halls. These developments opened new opportunities for the transverse flute and it was gradually established as a solo instrument. The use of other flute varieties expanded, too.

Giorgi flute, 19th c. Designed in 1880 by the maker Giorgi of Florence, it consists of a thin ebonite tube with wide fingerholes and no keys, or with keys of unusual rectangular shape. This instrument is end-blown, held vertically by the player.

Flageolet

The flageolet is a small instrument of the flute family, similar in shape and sound to the piccolo. It has six fingerholes, four in front and two thumbholes at the back. Although it appeared as early as the 16th century, the flageolet became popular in France and England only in the following centuries. Its various types were still being made in the 19th century, including a keyed French model.

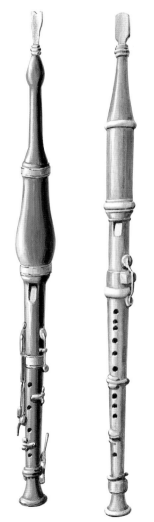

French flageolet with four fingerholes in front and two thumbholes, 19th century.

English flageolet with ten fingerholes, c. 1835.

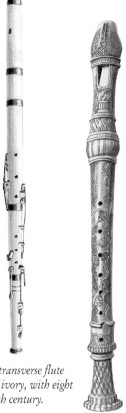

English transverse flute made of ivory, with eight keys, 19th century.

Descant recorder, 19th century.

English alto flute, 19th century.

English bass flute, 19th century.

Contrabass Clarinet

The contrabass clarinet is lower-pitched than the bass clarinet – by a fifth in the E flat version, and by an octave in the B flat version. An important feature of this rare instrument is its beautiful rich sound in the low register, making it a desirable member of the wind or symphony orchestra. In 1930 the famous American maker Selmer produced a model with a metal crook and a flared bell like that of the bass clarinet. Another model in B flat was produced in France and Germany in the late 19th century.
The contrabass clarinet was used by Tchaikovsky, Dvořák, Xenakis, and others.

Bass clarinet, Italy, 19th century.

Contrabass clarinet by F. Besson, Paris, 19th century.

Oboe and Bassoon

Sarrusophone

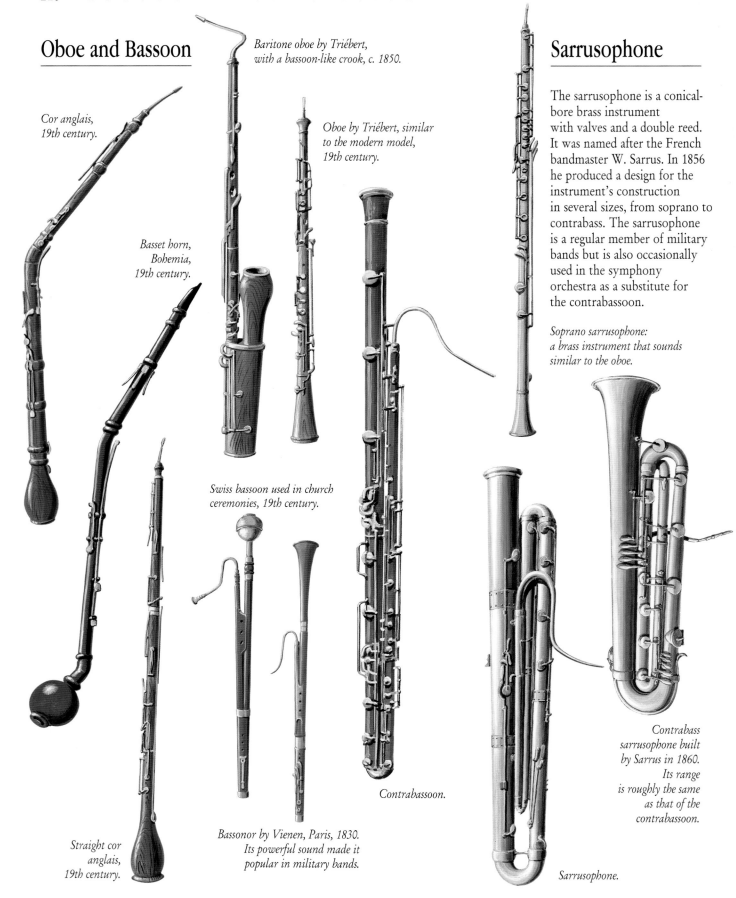

*Cor anglais,
19th century.*

*Baritone oboe by Triébert,
with a bassoon-like crook, c. 1850.*

*Oboe by Triébert, similar
to the modern model,
19th century.*

*Basset horn,
Bohemia,
19th century.*

*Swiss bassoon used in church
ceremonies, 19th century.*

*Straight cor
anglais,
19th century.*

*Bassonor by Vienen, Paris, 1830.
Its powerful sound made it
popular in military bands.*

Contrabassoon.

The sarrusophone is a conical-
bore brass instrument
with valves and a double reed.
It was named after the French
bandmaster W. Sarrus. In 1856
he produced a design for the
instrument's construction
in several sizes, from soprano to
contrabass. The sarrusophone
is a regular member of military
bands but is also occasionally
used in the symphony
orchestra as a substitute for
the contrabassoon.

*Soprano sarrusophone:
a brass instrument that sounds
similar to the oboe.*

*Contrabass
sarrusophone built
by Sarrus in 1860.
Its range
is roughly the same
as that of the
contrabassoon.*

Sarrusophone.

Horn

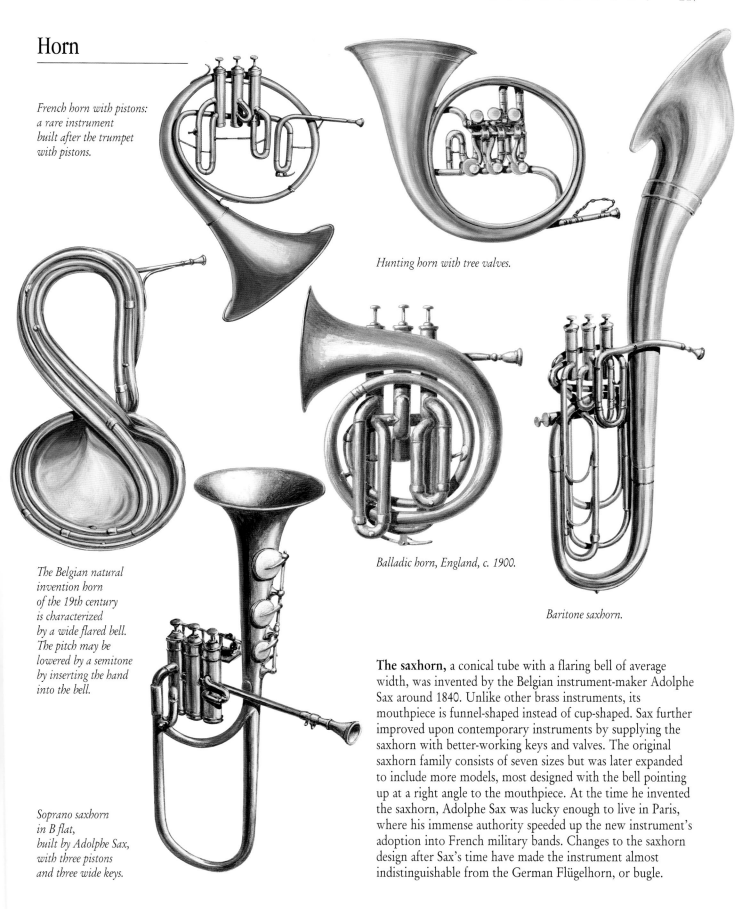

French horn with pistons: a rare instrument built after the trumpet with pistons.

Hunting horn with tree valves.

The Belgian natural invention horn of the 19th century is characterized by a wide flared bell. The pitch may be lowered by a semitone by inserting the hand into the bell.

Balladic horn, England, c. 1900.

Baritone saxhorn.

Soprano saxhorn in B flat, built by Adolphe Sax, with three pistons and three wide keys.

The saxhorn, a conical tube with a flaring bell of average width, was invented by the Belgian instrument-maker Adolphe Sax around 1840. Unlike other brass instruments, its mouthpiece is funnel-shaped instead of cup-shaped. Sax further improved upon contemporary instruments by supplying the saxhorn with better-working keys and valves. The original saxhorn family consists of seven sizes but was later expanded to include more models, most designed with the bell pointing up at a right angle to the mouthpiece. At the time he invented the saxhorn, Adolphe Sax was lucky enough to live in Paris, where his immense authority speeded up the new instrument's adoption into French military bands. Changes to the saxhorn design after Sax's time have made the instrument almost indistinguishable from the German Flügelhorn, or bugle.

Trumpet

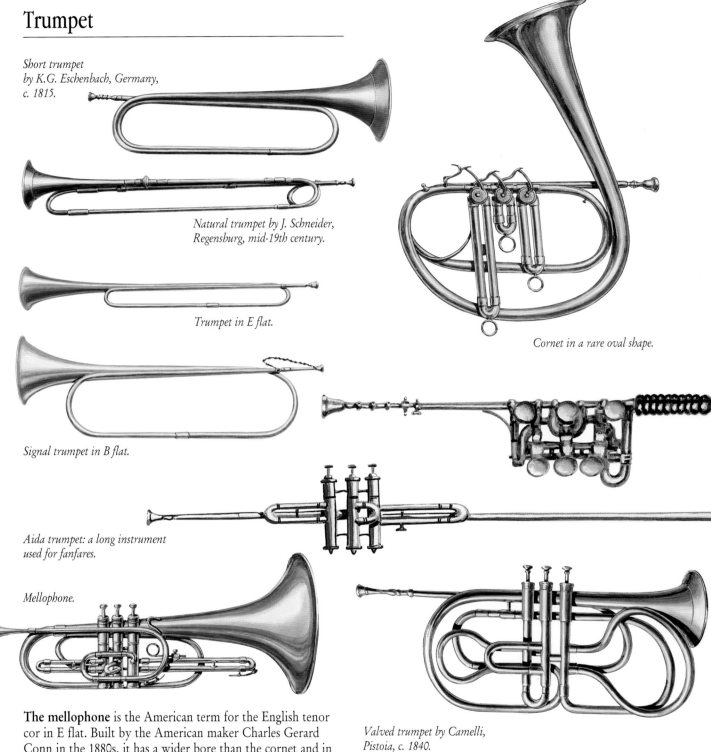

*Short trumpet
by K.G. Eschenbach, Germany,
c. 1815.*

*Natural trumpet by J. Schneider,
Regensburg, mid-19th century.*

Trumpet in E flat.

Signal trumpet in B flat.

Cornet in a rare oval shape.

*Aida trumpet: a long instrument
used for fanfares.*

Mellophone.

The mellophone is the American term for the English tenor cor in E flat. Built by the American maker Charles Gerard Conn in the 1880s, it has a wider bore than the cornet and in some respects (such as the bell size) resembles the French horn. In 1959 the Conn company built a new model with a bell 26 cm wide and 30 cm long. This instrument is much used in concerts, while in jazz it provides an alternative to the solo trumpet. It is also made in France and Germany, though in limited numbers.

*Valved trumpet by Camelli,
Pistoia, c. 1840.*

*English slide trumpet
by Godison, London, 19th century.*

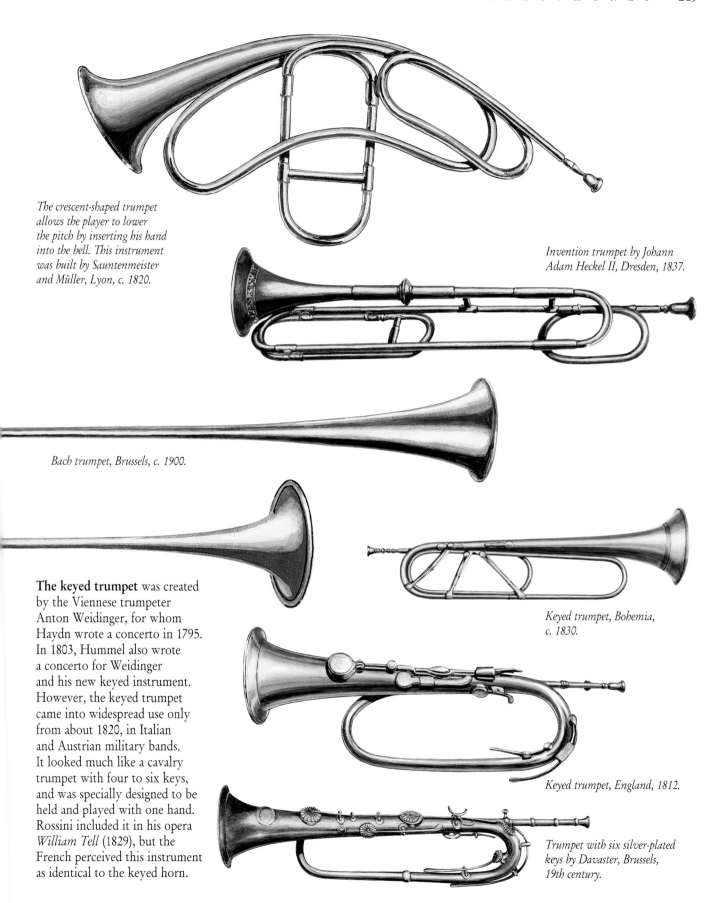

The crescent-shaped trumpet allows the player to lower the pitch by inserting his hand into the bell. This instrument was built by Sautenmeister and Müller, Lyon, c. 1820.

Invention trumpet by Johann Adam Heckel II, Dresden, 1837.

Bach trumpet, Brussels, c. 1900.

The keyed trumpet was created by the Viennese trumpeter Anton Weidinger, for whom Haydn wrote a concerto in 1795. In 1803, Hummel also wrote a concerto for Weidinger and his new keyed instrument. However, the keyed trumpet came into widespread use only from about 1820, in Italian and Austrian military bands. It looked much like a cavalry trumpet with four to six keys, and was specially designed to be held and played with one hand. Rossini included it in his opera *William Tell* (1829), but the French perceived this instrument as identical to the keyed horn.

Keyed trumpet, Bohemia, c. 1830.

Keyed trumpet, England, 1812.

Trumpet with six silver-plated keys by Davaster, Brussels, 19th century.

Rare Instruments

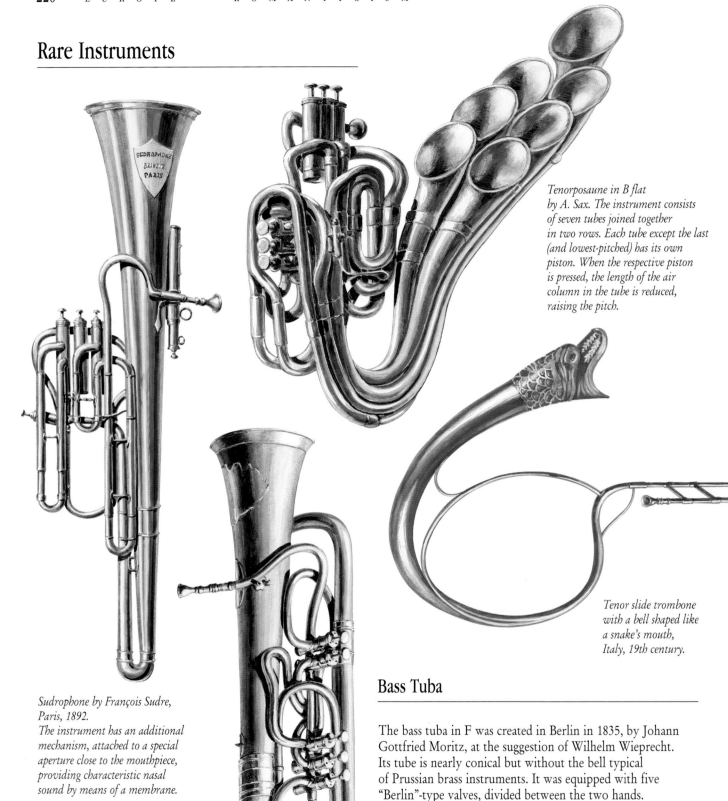

*Tenorposaune in B flat
by A. Sax. The instrument consists
of seven tubes joined together
in two rows. Each tube except the last
(and lowest-pitched) has its own
piston. When the respective piston
is pressed, the length of the air
column in the tube is reduced,
raising the pitch.*

*Tenor slide trombone
with a bell shaped like
a snake's mouth,
Italy, 19th century.*

*Sudrophone by François Sudre,
Paris, 1892.
The instrument has an additional
mechanism, attached to a special
aperture close to the mouthpiece,
providing characteristic nasal
sound by means of a membrane.*

Bass tuba in F.

Bass Tuba

The bass tuba in F was created in Berlin in 1835, by Johann
Gottfried Moritz, at the suggestion of Wilhelm Wieprecht.
Its tube is nearly conical but without the bell typical
of Prussian brass instruments. It was equipped with five
"Berlin"-type valves, divided between the two hands.
The first two were operated by the left hand and were similar
to those of the standard tuba in F. The remaining three
were operated by the right hand. Later models were more
practical, and were built with three or four valves. The bass
tuba in F was used in the German army until World War I.

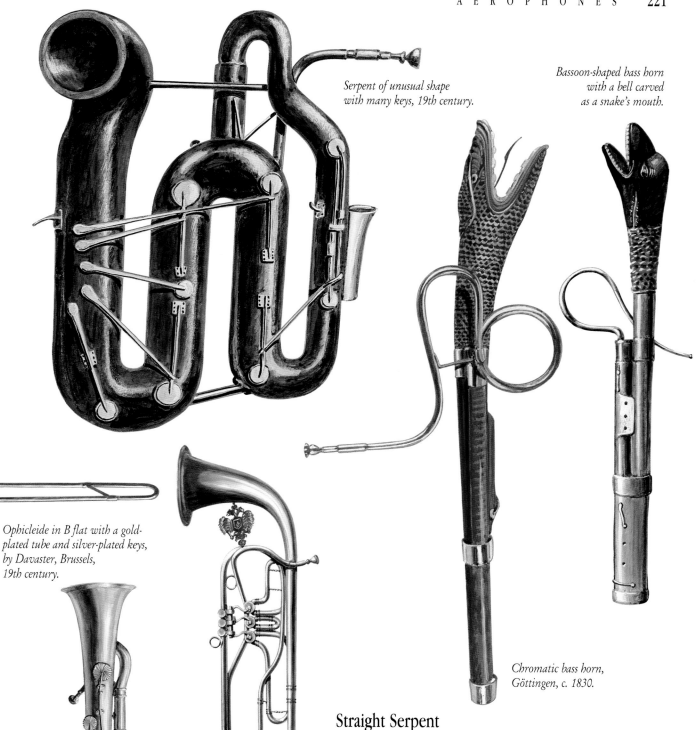

Serpent of unusual shape
with many keys, 19th century.

Bassoon-shaped bass horn
with a bell carved
as a snake's mouth.

Ophicleide in B flat with a gold-
plated tube and silver-plated keys,
by Davaster, Brussels,
19th century.

Military baritone trombone,
shaped like a tuba, bell facing
down, built by Václav František
Červený in 1867 as part
of a full family
from alto to subcontrabass.

Chromatic bass horn,
Göttingen, c. 1830.

Straight Serpent

The upright serpent is a more sophisticated model of serpent
that was made in many countries from 1790 to about 1830.
It was found under different names, but it always had one
feature in common with the bassoon: two bent tubes joined
together. A crook carried the mouthpiece. The upright serpent
had three or four keys and its bell was richly decorated.
A famous representative of the group is the "basson russe,"
or Russian bassoon, with a dragon-shaped bell.

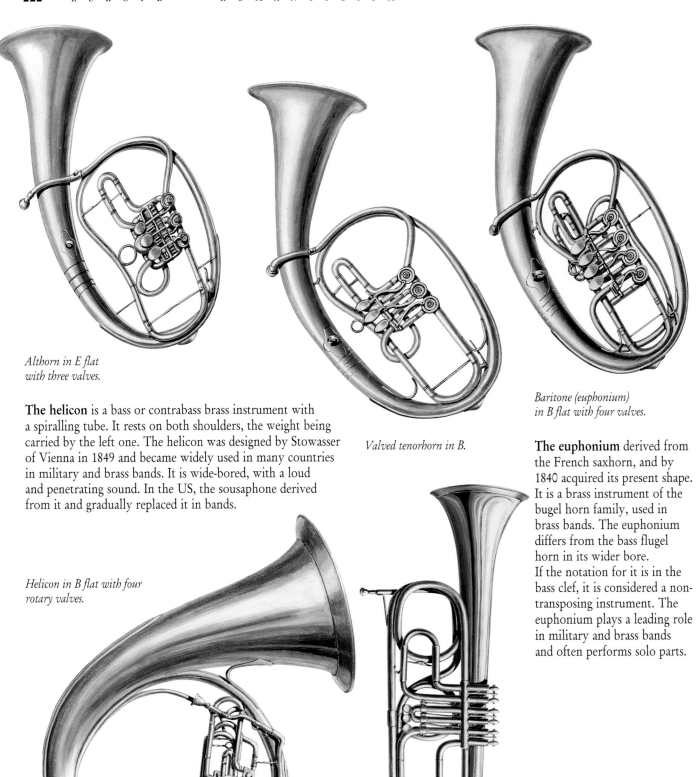

*Althorn in E flat
with three valves.*

The helicon is a bass or contrabass brass instrument with
a spiralling tube. It rests on both shoulders, the weight being
carried by the left one. The helicon was designed by Stowasser
of Vienna in 1849 and became widely used in many countries
in military and brass bands. It is wide-bored, with a loud
and penetrating sound. In the US, the sousaphone derived
from it and gradually replaced it in bands.

Valved tenorhorn in B.

*Baritone (euphonium)
in B flat with four valves.*

The euphonium derived from
the French saxhorn, and by
1840 acquired its present shape.
It is a brass instrument of the
bugel horn family, used in
brass bands. The euphonium
differs from the bass flugel
horn in its wider bore.
If the notation for it is in the
bass clef, it is considered a non-
transposing instrument. The
euphonium plays a leading role
in military and brass bands
and often performs solo parts.

*Helicon in B flat with four
rotary valves.*

Old bass tuba model.

Harmonium

Like the organ, the harmonium is a keyboard wind instrument with foot-operated bellows. It derives from the "orgue expressif" built by Grenié in Paris and Kratzenstein in Copenhagen in the early 19th century. In 1842, Alexandre François Debain patented the harmonium in France, having perfected the instrument and given it a piano design.

The sound is produced by freely vibrating metal reeds on a metal frame under the pressure of the wind from the bellows. There are two systems of wind supply: the German, in which the air is pumped, and the American in which the air is sucked. The bellows are pedal-operated.

Large harmonium for domestic use.

Harmonium by Alexandre François Debain, 1870.

A harmonium usually has a single manual and from six to 20 registers. Improved models have two manuals and occasionally a pedal board. The harmonium is simpler as a mechanism than the organ, less rich in tone color and dynamics, with a compass of C–c⁴.

REPERTORY

The harmonium has been a favorite of many composers, including Saint-Saëns, Franck, Dvořák, Richard Strauss, Smetana, and Mahler. It was used mainly for amateur music making, or in churches where there was no organ, as well as in salon orchestras, opera houses, and, less frequently, in the symphony orchestra.

CHORDOPHONES

Harp

Guitar

Guitar with sympathetic strings stretched at an angle and attached to a second pegbox on the instrument's side. Made by José Porcel, Spain, 1867.

Chromatic harp without pedals, with diatonic strings stretched at an angle from chromatic strings, George Washburn Lyon, 1895.

Guitar with a concave left shoulder for easier playing of the higher notes, 19th century. This shape might have influenced the design of modern electric guitars.

Double-action pedal harp by Sébastien Érard, 19th century.

Guitar with an elongated soundbox for better resonance, 19th century.

Four-string guitar with a small soundbox, shaped like a walking stick, 19th century.

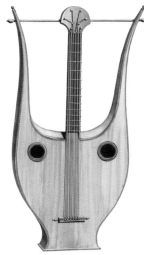

Lyre-guitar shaped like an ancient Greek lyre, 19th century.

Arpeggione

The arpeggione is a bowed stringed instrument also known as the guitare d'amour. It developed from the six-string bass viol, but has a guitar-like sound and metal frets, and is bowed like the cello. It was invented in 1823 by the Viennese maker J. G. Staufer, for whom Schubert composed the Sonata in A minor D (1824) for arpeggione and piano, still known as the Arpeggione Sonata though usually played on a cello. The arpeggione's strings were tuned E, A, d, g, b, e¹.

Lyre-shaped guitar with six double strings attached to screws on the pegbox, England, 19th century.

Three-string Double Bass

The three-string double bass was a standard, frequently used instrument in the 19th and early 20th century, particularly in England and France. The strings were tuned either A, d, g or G, d, g. It was favored by two famous 19th-century soloists, Domenico Dragonetti and Giovanni Bottesini. Bottesini used a bow of his own design, which was later widely adopted as the "French bow." Richard Strauss preferred the three-string double bass to some four-string models, because of the full sound of the low strings.

Arpeggione, 19th century.

Three-string double bass of Giovanni Bottesini, 1821–1889.

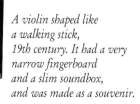

A violin shaped like a walking stick, 19th century. It had a very narrow fingerboard and a slim soundbox, and was made as a souvenir.

Octobass by Jean-Baptiste Vuillaume, Paris, 1850. The strings are shortened by mechanical "fingers," which press them onto the frets on the fingerboard. These "fingers" are operated by eight levers behind the fingerboard, controlled by the left hand, and by seven pedals. This instrument is much taller than an average man.

Piano

*Pyramid-shaped piano
by Kaspar Schlimbach,
Königshofen, c. 1825.*

The upright piano was an essential element of European living rooms throughout the 19th century. Its popularity spread across the ocean, and Americans first bought and later began producing these instruments. By 1863 Steinway had established the modern prototype, which has changed little since.

*Lyra piano
by Johann Christian Schleip, Berlin.*

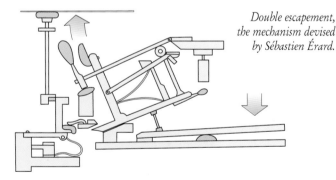

*Double escapement,
the mechanism devised
by Sébastien Érard.*

*"Giraffe" piano
by Hoef, Amsterdam, c. 1810.*

Sébastien Érard was a Frenchman who left France after the revolution and settled in London in 1792. He opened a piano workshop, the first great success of which was the refinement of the "English action" in 1796–97. In the first quarter of the 19th century, Érard introduced the so-called double escapement, enabling the hammer to fall and be ready for a new strike while the key is still down. This mechanism improved the English action and made the Viennese action outdated. Further improvements followed: an iron frame to improve the resonance and strengthen the construction, thicker strings, and felt tips on the hammers. The instrument increased in size, the grand piano reaching over 3.5 m.

Pianino by Pierre Érard, Paris, 1834.

The instruments produced by Clementi and Broadwood in London, Bösendorfer in Vienna, Blüthner in Leipzig, Bechstein in Berlin, and Steinway in New York are credited with the promotion and popularization of piano music in the 19th and the 20th century.

Grand piano shaped like a tea-table, 1840.

Square piano by L. Sauer, Prague, 19th century.

Piano with six rows of keys, produced by Goetze in the second half of the 19th century. This type of keyboard was invented by the Hungarian Paul von Janko in 1882. Each key had three terraced striking surfaces. For example, if the keys C, D, E, F sharp, G sharp and B flat in rows I, III, and V were alternated with the keys C sharp, D sharp, F, G, A and B in rows II, IV, and VI, these surfaces formed a chromatic keyboard. This keyboard provided for consistency of playing technique across the various keys and assisted the performance of otherwise difficult chords. It was soon abandoned, however, as it was not convenient to use and the pressure on the keys was uneven.

Along with its other specifics, the age of Romanticism brought to the foreground the piano, the music for it, and the popularity of virtuoso pianists. In terms of genres, piano music was enriched with miniatures: impromptus, nocturnes, waltzes, mazurkas, songs without lyrics, as well as with larger genres such as the ballad, the fantasia, the polonaise, and the scherzo. Along with the development of the so-called "nationalism" in music (particularly in the opera repertory), the folklore was widely used as a source, adding much colour to the age's musical heritage. Here we should mention the names of Schumann, Felix Mendelssohn, Brahms, and the two brilliant pianists Frederic Chopin and Franz Liszt. Like Paganini with his violin, Liszt became the emblematic piano virtuoso of his age, and the last great master of improvisation of the 19th century. The Polish-born Chopin was the most sophisticated lyrical composer of his time, and his major works are still a must in pianists' repertory. Piano music and piano making were closely related; during that age, the upright piano and the grand piano acquired their completed present design, and the two leading makers became firmly established on the market.

EUROPE – TWENTIETH CENTURY

From the beginning of the twentieth century a variety of musical styles evolved. Composers began to use different musical languages, rather than merely different "dialects" of the same language, drawing from the rich and varied musical traditions of all continents, ages, and cultures. The first decades of the century were dominated by neo-Classicism and serial music. After World War II, serial technique, first introduced by the Viennese composer Arnold Schönberg in the early 1920s, came to be applied to rhythm and dynamics as well as pitch. Some composers, however, rejected what they saw as a mathematical method and sought freer approaches, and the aleatoric style and the principle of minimalism evolved. An emphasis on tonality and the modern interpretation of romantic attitudes resulted in the development of neo-Romanticism. The most significant step forward, however, was made in the second half of the century, with the advent of electronic music and electro-acoustic works. Traditional instruments provided opportunities for experimentation with new timbres, techniques, and effects. The creation of the synthesizer and the potential of computers attracted both composers and performers seeking to perfect their art. Later, they left their studios in favor of live concerts and direct contact with the audience.

The ultimate dream of Romantic artists for a "synthesis of arts" was finally fulfilled with the participation of the media, the resulting syncretic art form containing elements of drama, opera, dance, lighting, and all kinds of sounds (multimedia or performance art).

Other important characteristics of 20th century music were the popularity of non-classical genres, the industrialization of mass culture, and the introduction of new recording media. Before World War II, as a result of the dancing craze, popular music, jazz, and blues gained wide popularity. After the war, the many varieties of rock music dominated, giving way around the end of the century to popular music dominated by electronic sound.

Technical innovations are irresistible, particularly to younger people. As in the other arts, the strictly hierarchical system of values disintegrates, as integration processes free of aesthetic purism take place. Open to "exotic" musical traditions from throughout the world, our "globalized" Europe has become the focal point of musical culture since the 1970s.

A wealth of musical instruments is now in use. Traditional instruments continue their evolution, and electronic versions of these are developed alongside an endless variety of music-making devices.

AEROPHONES

Saxophone

The youngest of the woodwind family, this single-reed instrument has always been made of metal alloy – copper, nickel, and zinc, or copper and zinc (brass) – and is nickel-, silver-, or gold-plated. Patented in Paris in 1846 by the Belgian Adolphe Sax (1814–1894), the saxophone combines the characteristics of the oboe and the clarinet, and, in a sense, of woodwind and brass instruments. Its keywork is similar to that of the oboe, and the mouthpiece and reed to that of the clarinet. The alto, tenor, and baritone models are bent in an s-shape, on account of the length of the tube; only the sopranino and the soprano saxophone have straight conical tubes. Nowadays only four saxophone types are used: soprano, alto, tenor, and baritone. Adolphe Sax developed the instrument in two versions, one for a brass band and one for a symphony orchestra. The instrument was first introduced into French military bands in 1854, after which it quickly gained a position in the brass bands of many European countries as well as in the U.S. In the symphony orchestra, the saxophone was used for the first time by Bizet in his music for *L'arlésienne* (1872).

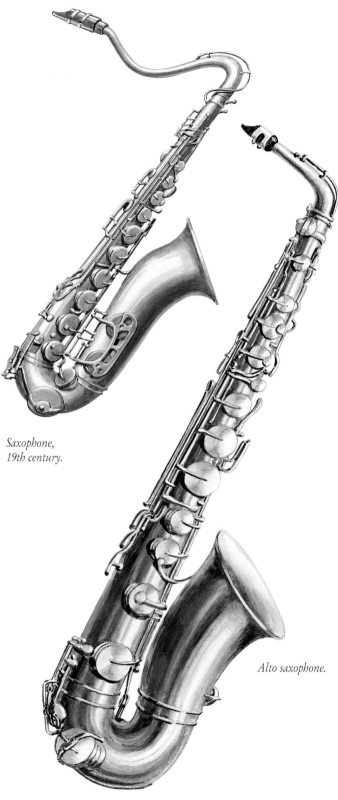

*Saxophone,
19th century.*

Alto saxophone.

*Jazz saxophonist Louis Jordan
playing a saxophone.*

In terms of its timbre, the saxophone stands between the woodwind and brass groups, with a full and powerful tone. Its different registers are more balanced than those of the clarinet, and it has great technical potential. Saxophones are built in the following keys: soprano in B flat, alto in E flat, tenor in B flat, and baritone in E flat. All are notated in the treble clef, with a written range of b flat – f³. They are all downward transposing instruments.

Sopranino in E flat. Built but rarely used. Ravel scored for it in *Boléro* but today the part is most often played by a soprano saxophone.
Soprano in B flat. Highly popular in the 1920s thanks to the legendary jazz clarinettist Sidney Bechet who played it. Outside jazz this instrument is found only in saxophone quartets.
Alto in E flat. The first instrument of the family to be included in the symphony orchestra. Ambroise Thomas scored for it in *Hamlet* (1868).
Tenor in B flat. The most popular instrument in modern jazz, later replacing the alto saxophone in the symphony orchestra. A variant in C is widely used in the U. S.
Baritone in E flat. A permanent member of the big band saxophone section, as a solo instrument it became popular in jazz thanks to Gerry Mulligan (1927 – 1996). Karlheinz Stockhausen scored for it in *Carré* (1960).
Bass in B flat. Rarely used except in full saxophone ensembles.
Contrabass in E flat. A very rare instrument, built only upon request.
Sub-contrabass saxophone in B. Designed in 1904 by the maker Conn.

Soprano saxophone.

Tenor saxophone.

Baritone saxophone.

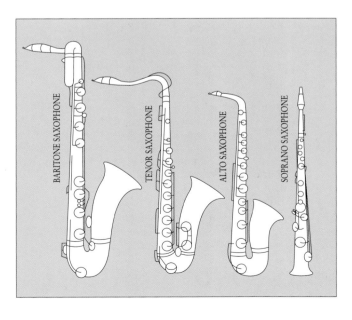

BARITONE SAXOPHONE   TENOR SAXOPHONE   ALTO SAXOPHONE   SOPRANO SAXOPHONE

Many composers used the saxophone in the orchestra: Meyerbeer, Massenet, Bizet, Richard Strauss, Ravel, Prokofiev, Shostakovich, and others. However, the solo repertory is relatively poor: a Concerto for alto-saxophone by Glazunov, Ibert's Concertino da camera, Debussy's Rhapsody for saxophone and piano, a Fantasia for saxophone and piano by Villa-Lobos, and some other compositions. It was in jazz that the saxophone gained immense recognition, from 1915 on. In the swing age in the 1930s, the saxophones formed a special section of three to six. Jazz saxophone soloists who developed the instrument's technique and expressive capacities include Sidney Bechet, Coleman Hawkins, Charlie Parker, John Coltrane, Gerry Mulligan, and many others.

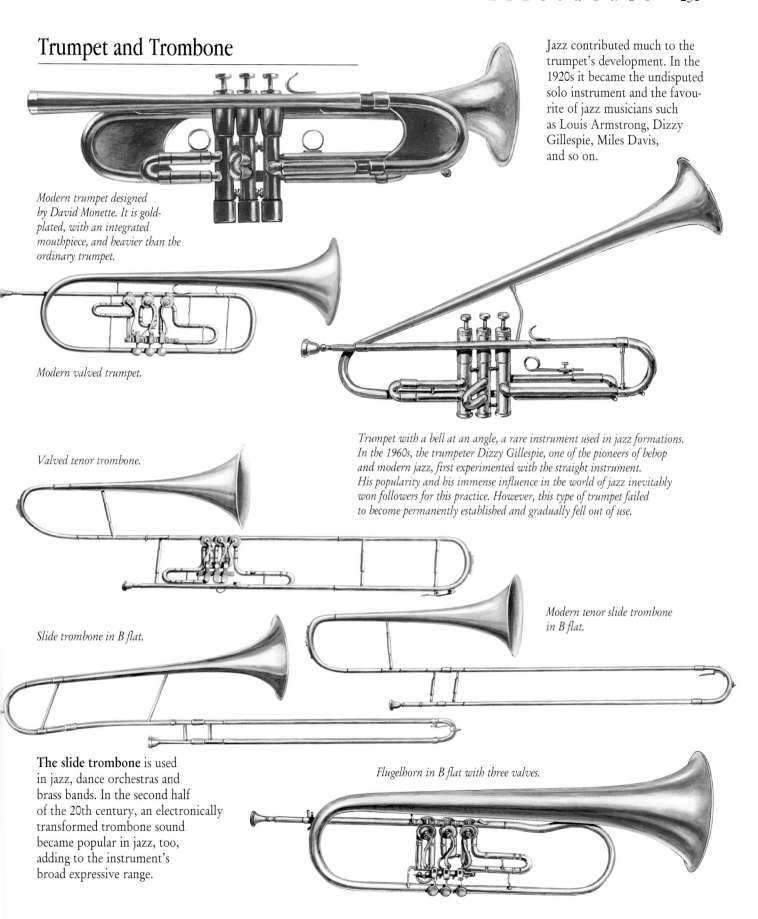

Trumpet and Trombone

Jazz contributed much to the trumpet's development. In the 1920s it became the undisputed solo instrument and the favourite of jazz musicians such as Louis Armstrong, Dizzy Gillespie, Miles Davis, and so on.

Modern trumpet designed by David Monette. It is gold-plated, with an integrated mouthpiece, and heavier than the ordinary trumpet.

Modern valved trumpet.

Trumpet with a bell at an angle, a rare instrument used in jazz formations. In the 1960s, the trumpeter Dizzy Gillespie, one of the pioneers of bebop and modern jazz, first experimented with the straight instrument. His popularity and his immense influence in the world of jazz inevitably won followers for this practice. However, this type of trumpet failed to become permanently established and gradually fell out of use.

Valved tenor trombone.

Slide trombone in B flat.

Modern tenor slide trombone in B flat.

The slide trombone is used in jazz, dance orchestras and brass bands. In the second half of the 20th century, an electronically transformed trombone sound became popular in jazz, too, adding to the instrument's broad expressive range.

Flugelhorn in B flat with three valves.

Mouth Organ (Harmonica)

This instrument is closely related to the mouth organ of the Far East. Designed in 1821 by Friedrich Buschmann of Berlin, it became widely popular as a product of Hohner's workshop. A keyless multiphonic wind instrument, the mouth organ's sound is generated by thin brass reeds, set into vibration by air blown through the holes. The reeds are riveted on either side of a metal plate with square openings. A single opening provides two notes – one on the "blow" and one on the "draw." The player can blow into more than one hole at a time, producing combinations of a number of tones while blocking the unwanted holes with the tongue.

In addition to the popular mouth organ, a number of models exist, including the Richter, Knitlinger, and Viennese (Viennese tremolo harmonica, Viennese octave harmonica, double Viennese harmonica). Bass, chord, and bass-chord harmonicas are also built, and are used for accompaniment. Other important models are the chromatic harmonica (educator, chromonic) and the keyboard harmonica (melodica, melodeon).

Mouth organ with bells.

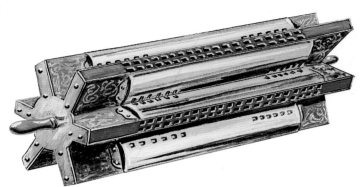

Hexagonal mouth organ: six mouth organs, each in a different key, joined together.

Chromatic mouth organ with a slide.

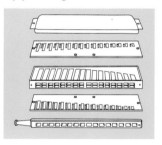

Construction of the mouth organ.

Modern keyboard melodica.

The harmonica is a popular instrument, used often in blues, jazz, and folk music. A number of composers have written for this instrument as a soloist with orchestra, including Milhaud (Suite for Harmonica and Orchestra), Vaughan Williams (Romance for Harmonica and Orchestra), and Villa-Lobos (Concerto for Harmonica and Orchestra).

Trumpet mouth organ.

Chromatic mouth organ.

Modern side-blown soprano melodica.

Chord harmonica.

Curved mouth organ with two consoles.

Concertina and Melodeon

The melodeon is a wind instrument similar to the accordion, and sounded with free reeds. These are made to vibrate by a mass of air set in motion by the pulling or compressing of bellows. Improved versions sound the same note on the "press" and on the "draw". The air mass is controlled by buttons: the melody is played on the right manual, and the left manual provides the accompaniment.

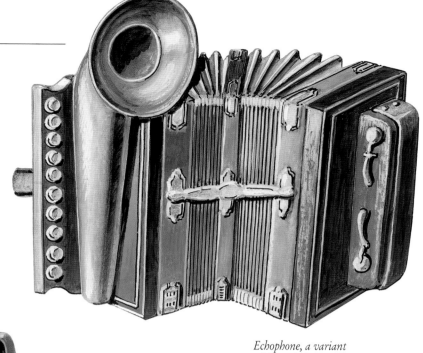

German melodeon.

Echophone, a variant of the melodeon, with a special trumpet-like amplifyer, Germany.

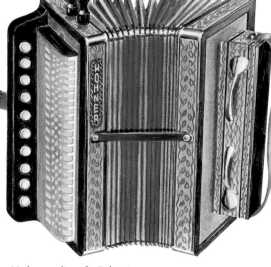

Modern replica of a Bohemian concertina by Hohner.

Viennese melodeon.

Viennese style melodeon by Hohner, with ten buttons for the right hand and four for the left.

Accordion

The accordion is a free-reed instrument with hand-operated bellows and two manuals, the left one with buttons and the right one with piano-style keys. The name derives from the German word "Akkord" (meaning "chord"), and was first used in Vienna by Cyrillus Demian. He and his sons patented the accordion in 1829.

The modern accordion consists of two panels connected with the bellows. Unlike the concertina (a similar instrument), the right-hand panel accommodates the melody keys (descant), while the left-hand panel plays the bass part. The steel reeds, riveted on wooden plates with slots underneath, are arranged in rows, each of them a choir of uniformly tuned reeds (four, sometimes five). Depending on the size of the instrument, it may have from 22 to 45 piano-style keys. The bass panel contains a varying number of buttons, again depending on the accordion's size: 8, 12, 24, 32, 36, 48, 60, 72, 80, 96, or 120. They are arranged in parallel vertical rows, each providing a certain type of bass. Accordions have registers on the right manual, and larger instruments may also have registers on the left manual.

Accordion by Hohner.

French concert accordion.

The accordion is carried on two straps on the player's chest. The air can be let out of the bellows through a special button on the left panel. When the instrument is idle, the bellows are compressed and the two manuals are held together with straps. The accordion is widely used by both amateurs and professionals, both as a solo instrument and in ensembles, as well as in folk music. It has occasionally been called for by major composers. Tchaikovsky included it in an orchestral suite of 1883, Berg in his opera *Wozzeck* (1925), and Prokofiev in a cantata of 1936. It was also used by Paul Hindemith, Charles Ives, Virgil Thomson, and various other composers.

Modern accordion.

IDIOPHONES

Struck, Shaken and Friction Instruments

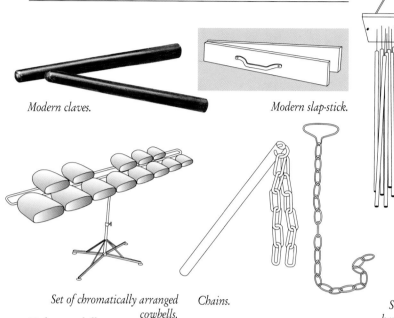

Modern claves.

Modern slap-stick.

Set of chromatically arranged cowbells.

Modern cowbell.

Chains.

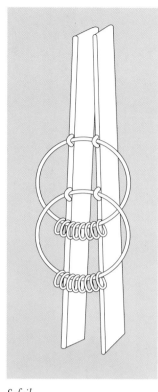

Suspended glass plates or rods: hanging from frames of various designs, they produce graceful tones when struck.

Safail.

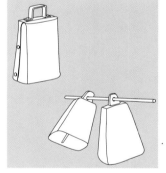
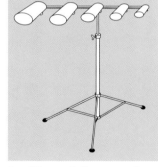

Set of strung cowbells.

Set of five cowbells on a stand.

Set of crotales arranged in two rows on a stand in the manner of a keyboard.

Modern bells on a frame with a pedal-operated damper.

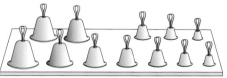

Chromatically arranged bells.

Set of bells of different sizes.

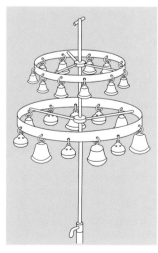

Chinese pavillon with a stand, sounded by shaking.

Bass metallophone built by John Levis, U. S.

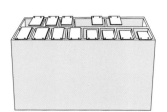

Four-row xylophone with spoon-shaped beaters.

This wooden drum is held in the middle and the sound is produced by striking with the beater. The sound has different pitch depending on the side the drum is struck.

Modern woodblock.

Modern xylophone with small resonator tubes.

Musical saw: a friction instrument, narrower at one end and with a handle at the other. The seated player grips the handle between his knees, bows with his right hand, and bends the blade with his left, thereby controlling the pitch.

Glass trombone by the Baschet brothers of Paris: a dozen crystal rods of different sizes on a metal structure that modulates the sound. The instrument is played by rubbing with moist fingertips, and a curved metal disc acts as an amplifier.

Bass xylophone with larger bars and resonators.

Four woodblocks on a stand. Between 2 and 7 blocks of different sizes are clamped to a stand, tuned in a scale, and struck with rubber- or felt-tipped beaters, or with drum beaters. The long slot carved along the side of each block determines to a great extent the instrument's timbre. Sometimes two slots are carved on the opposite vertical sides, allowing the instrument to play two tones about a minor third apart. Woodblocks are placed on stands, often in sets, and played with drum, xylophone, or marimba beaters.

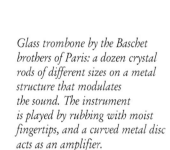

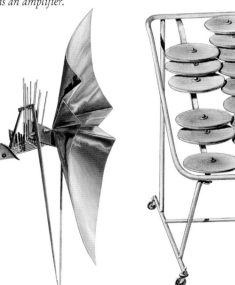

Modern lithophone: 15 chromatically tuned round stone plates, pierced at the center, with rubber-covered metal sleeves inserted in the openings. The plates are arranged in two rows, corresponding to the black and white piano keys, on a wheeled metal frame. The instrument is sounded by striking the stones with hard beaters.

Modern crotales.

Extremely popular in jazz and rock music are the pedal cymbals (hi-hat, charleston), designed by Vic Berton and constructed by Kaiser Marshal in the later 1920s. The hi-hat is not a separate instrument but a mechanism attached to a tripod. A pair of cymbals (with a diameter of about 35 cm) is mounted horizontally one above the other, their concave sides facing each other. The lower cymbal is fixed on the stand and the upper one attached to a pedal. When the pedal is pressed, the upper cymbal clashes down onto the lower one. There are three possible positions of the upper disc: open, half open, and closed. Chick Webb and Philly Joe Jones were the first drummers to introduce the hi-hat into the orchestra. It was widely used in large orchestras in the second half of the 1930s, and in modern jazz it is indispensable and is given a leading rhythmic role.

Ordinary anvil.

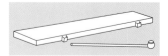

Shallow rectangular anvil.

Pedal-operated cymbal (charleston).

Studded cymbal.

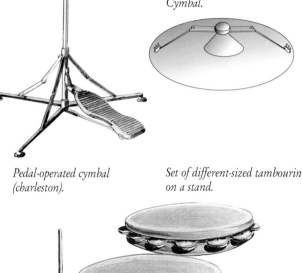

Cymbal.

Set of different-sized tambourines on a stand.

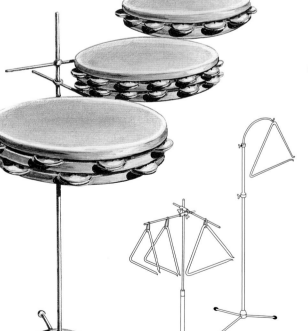

Triangles on stands.

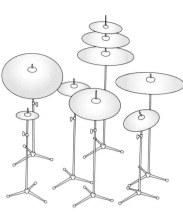

Different-sized cymbals on stands.

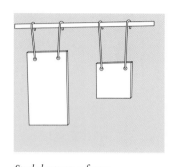

Steel sheets on a frame.

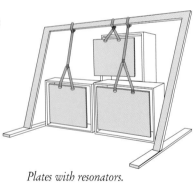

Plates with resonators.

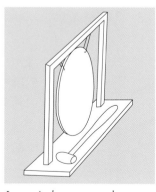

Improvised gong: a wooden or metal disc suspended from a frame and struck with a beater.

MEMBRANOPHONES

Drum and Timpani

Snare drum viewed from the back (the snare can be seen), and two beaters.

Side drums of different sizes.

Double-head bass drum.

Concert snare drum.

Snare drum with beater.

Double-head bass drum on a rotating stand.

Modern tenor drum with screws.

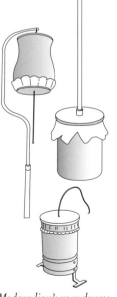

Modern lion's roar drums.

Modern rotary timpani.

Modern pedal timpani.

The single or double-head bass drum has a diameter of 50 – 60 cm and a powerful low sound. A special damper consisting of two felt pads can be pressed to the head, making the sound sharper and drier. The player holds the bass drum vertically and strikes the rhythm with a felt- or rubber-tipped beater. The beater is connected with a pedal operated by the right foot, leaving the drummer's hands free to play the other instruments of the percussion kit.

Modern screw-tensioned tenor drum on a stand.

Modern screw-tensioned tenor drum on a stand.

Double-head bass drum with foot pedal.

Billy Cobham is a drummer and percussionist who contributed much to the development of modern jazz, particularly in the 1970s. He was the leader of several successful jazz groups.

Tom-tom

Double-head tom-toms. Made of plywood, cylindrical in shape, and equipped with tensioning rings, double-head tom-toms come in soprano, alto, tenor, baritone, bass, and contrabass sizes. The two beaters have wooden- or felt-covered ends. The jazz drum kit usually includes two tom-toms: a small one attached to the bass drum, and a large one standing on its own metal legs. Three or four tom-toms may be placed on a common stand. Double-head tom-toms are instruments of indefinite pitch.

Single-head tom-toms. The skin membrane of the single-head tom-tom is stretched across the plywood shell and tuned with tensioning screws, making it an instrument of relatively definite pitch.

Wooden tom-toms.

Three double-head tom-toms.

Drum Kit

Differently from the way they are used in classical orchestras and bands, the percussion instruments in the dance orchestra and the jazz or rock band are combined in a drum kit played by a single musician. The drum kit usually includes a bass drum, a side drum, tom-toms, a hi-hat, and suspended cymbals on a stand. Other percussion instruments may be added to the set as required by the music performed.

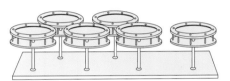

Modern chromatic tom-toms on a stand.

Side drum sticks.

Wire brushes.

Timpani sticks.

The drum kit is played with a variety of beaters, brushes, and hand strokes. The hi-hat and the bass drum are operated with a foot pedal. This rational distribution of functions offers an excellent opportunity for the player to display his virtuosity. Bands may invite a second drummer to play a set of various percussion instruments that are not included in the standard kit. Alternatively, such instruments may be played by musicians from the orchestra who are not currently engaged.

The increasing importance of rhythm has assured the percussion section of a central place in the jazz band. While its main function is that of providing background rhythm, jazz has also promoted percussion solos. The cymbals in use in the jazz world are of Turkish origin. For over 350 years, the best maker of Turkish cymbals has been the Armenian family that founded the Avedis Zildjian company, which moved to the U. S. in 1929.

Conga and Tumba

These are single-head drums with tapering wooden shells about 70-90 cm long, and skin membranes around 30 cm in diameter. They are more often played with hands than with beaters, and produce a timbre similar to that of the timpani. The player may grip a conga or tumba between the knees or use a set of two or three of these instruments. They are very popular in Latin American dance music where they sustain the main beat in dances such as the rumba. Apart from their use in jazz and in steel bands, congas and tumbas are sometimes present in the percussion section of the symphony orchestra.

Modern tumba.

Modern conga.

Mambo-drum

A double drum with a long rectangular body and two skin membranes of different sizes stretched over it with nails, each of them producing a different pitch. The instrument is placed on legs and is usually played with hands.

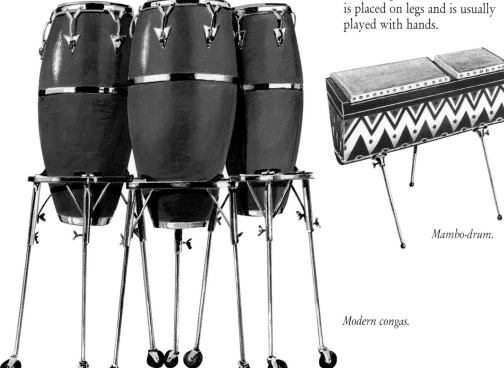

Mambo-drum.

Modern congas.

Bu-bam

The bu-bam is a recent North American instrument of relatively definite pitch. Made of bamboo, tall and slender, the bu-bam is played in sets of five to eight instruments of different sizes, suspended from a stand or arranged chromatically in two rows. An improved version also includes a bamboo or wooden resonator, cylindrical or prismatic in shape. The tensioning and consequently the pitch of the instrument are adjusted with hoops above the resonator. The bu-bam is played with the fingers or beaters, and the sound is amplified through an electro-acoustic system.

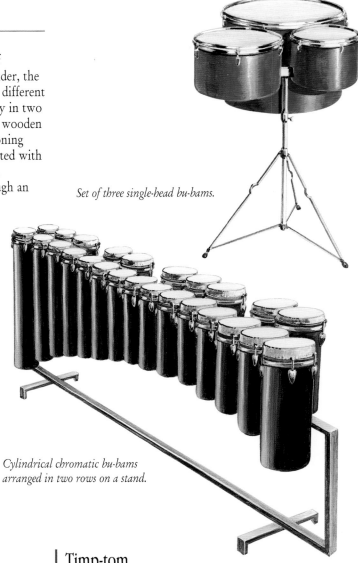

Set of three single-head bu-bams.

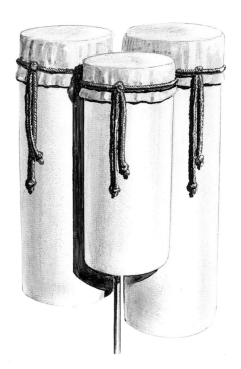

Cylindrical chromatic bu-bams arranged in two rows on a stand.

Bu-bam on a stand, a set of three.

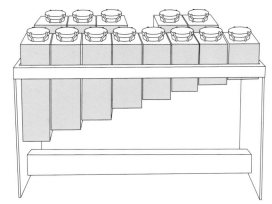

More sophisticated bu-bams with prismatic resonators.

Timp-tom

American single-head drums with a shallow shell made of wood or cardboard. The membrane can be tuned by means of screws. The timp-toms are played in sets.

Single-head timp-tom.

Bongos

Double-head drums of indefinite pitch, these came to Europe from Latin America, and are probably of Indian origin. The shells of modern bongos (bongo drums) are made of plywood or metal, and the membrane is stretched with a ring pulled down by screws. The bongos are played with the fingers, the hands, or beaters. Sets of two, three, or four bongos of different sizes are used.

Set of two bongos.

Set of two bongos on a stand.

Latin American (Cuban) Timpani

Taken to Latin America by African slaves, these instruments are related to the bongos and the single-head tom-toms. Modern Cuban timpani consist of a pair of fairly shallow plywood shells shaped like small tom-toms, with a screw-tensioned head. They are played in pairs of the same depth but of different diameter, placed on a high stand. A cowbell may be suspended between the two timpani. The beaters are straight, without a head.

Three sets of Latin American timpani.

Cuban timpani with cow-bell.

Latin American timpani.

CHORDOPHONES

Guitar

The classical guitar has six strings tuned E, A, d, g, b, e^1. Its range is E – a^2 (e^3), guitar music sounding an octave lower than notated. The guitar's sound is gentle but very beautiful. The playing technique allows for exceptional subtlety, agility, and brilliance. The popularity of this instrument, particularly suited for domestic use, declined in the mid-19th century, only to be reestablished in the 20th century. The guitar's revival may be partly attributed to the remarkable abilities of the guitarists Francisco Tárrega (1852 – 1909) and Andrés Segovia (1893 – 1987), and to a number of fine works for guitar by European composers. Folk music, blues, jazz, and rock music of the second half of the 20th century also contributed to the widespread popularity of the instrument.

Domestic music making in Europe prompted the creation of both a rich solo guitar repertory and of works for duos, trios, and quartets. In a guitar quartet, alongside the ordinary "prima" guitar, there is a "terza" guitar tuned a minor third higher, a "quarte" tuned a perfect fourth higher, and a "quinte" tuned a perfect fifth higher.

Modern guitar.

Folk Guitar

Larger or smaller in size, the folk guitar has an accompanying function and brings variety to the repertory. The folk guitar is very convenient for domestic performance as well as for composing.

Folk guitar.

Side view of the soundbox of an acoustic guitar.

Jumbo guitar with an extra large soundbox and a powerful acoustic effect.

Modern capotasto.

Different plectra for playing the guitar.

Cross-section of fingerboards.

Twelve-string Guitar

The 12-string guitar is often used for accompanying vocal solos. It is shaped like the modern folk guitar.

Jazz guitar.

Twelve-string guitar.

Jazz Guitar

The jazz guitar is a Gibson acoustic guitar of the 1930s with s-holes. With its wide soundbox and a proportional fingerboard, it belongs to the highest class of acoustic guitars, equally suitable for solos and accompaniment.

REPERTORY

Although an instrument with a softer sound, the guitar is used in the opera and the symphony orchestra. Rossini called for it in *The Barber of Seville*, Weber in *Oberon*, Berlioz in *La Damnation de Faust*, Verdi in *Otello* and *Falstaff*. Gustav Mahler included it in his Symphony no. 7. It should be noted that Schubert, Paganini and Weber themselves played the guitar and used it in chamber music. From the 1920s, the instrument found a place in the works of composers such as Webern, Schönberg, Henze, and Maxwell Davies. The tradition of the composer-guitarist was continued by Tárrega ("Chopin of the guitar"), Leo Brouwer, and many others. Major guitar pieces include works by Villa-Lobos (Suite popular brasiliera), Joaquin Rodrigo (Concerto de Aranjues), Benjamin Britten, William Bolcom, and Andre Previn.

Mandolin

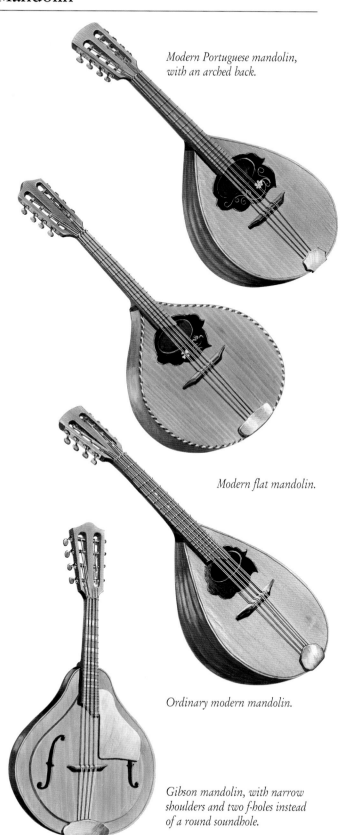

Modern Portuguese mandolin, with an arched back.

Modern flat mandolin.

Ordinary modern mandolin.

Gibson mandolin, with narrow shoulders and two f-holes instead of a round soundhole.

Piano

Bösendorfer, Vienna, 1978–1995.

Electric harpsichord. Microphones above the strings are connected to loudspeakers.

Grand piano by Morley, London, 1934. The whole front assembly is detachable from the sound board and frame to make the piano easier to move.

With the establishment of the piano as a leading instrument in the music of the 20th century, an increasing number of piano-makers become involved in its technical improvement. Along with the traditionally shaped pianos, models with exotic designs appear. Piano-makers endeavour to combine the acoustic qualities of the instrument with the possibilities of electronics and digital sound processing, thus broadening its creative potential and facilitating both composers and performers.

There is also continuing interest in hand-made pianos produced during the first half of the 20th century. It is important to note that due to the enormous number of moving and interacting parts and its complicated mechanism, the piano is more sensitive than the violin to incompetent maintenance and to such factors as excessive temperature, moisture, or dust.

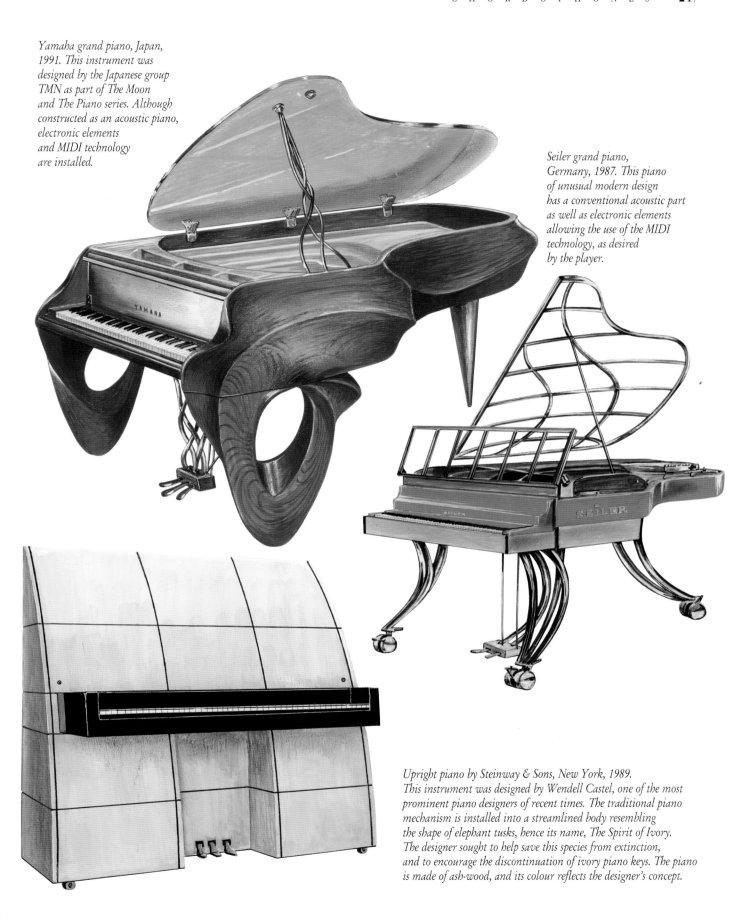

Yamaha grand piano, Japan, 1991. This instrument was designed by the Japanese group TMN as part of The Moon and The Piano series. Although constructed as an acoustic piano, electronic elements and MIDI technology are installed.

Seiler grand piano, Germany, 1987. This piano of unusual modern design has a conventional acoustic part as well as electronic elements allowing the use of the MIDI technology, as desired by the player.

Upright piano by Steinway & Sons, New York, 1989. This instrument was designed by Wendell Castel, one of the most prominent piano designers of recent times. The traditional piano mechanism is installed into a streamlined body resembling the shape of elephant tusks, hence its name, The Spirit of Ivory. The designer sought to help save this species from extinction, and to encourage the discontinuation of ivory piano keys. The piano is made of ash-wood, and its colour reflects the designer's concept.

ELECTRONIC INSTRUMENTS

Electronic instruments and devices using electric oscillation to create musical tones can be divided into four large groups. The first contains machines that imitate the sound of existing musical instruments (such as the machines built by Hammond, Debeux, Martin, and others). The second group consists of instruments intended to eliminate the drawbacks of existing musical instruments (particularly to make them louder) by building an electro-acoustic transducer into the resonator and adding an amplifier (as in the electric guitar, electric violin, and electric saxophone). Instruments designed to generate new sounds, the timbre of which differs from that of traditional acoustic instruments, form the third group. In these the composer or player can easily modify the spectrum and dynamics of the electrical signal. The development and perfection of the instruments of this group attracted the attention of a number of modern composers, and led to the establishment of a whole new branch of modern music, namely electronic music. The fourth group of electronic instruments comprises the devices used for the transformation of pre-existing, prerecorded (magnetically or otherwise) sounds. These were used in "musique concrète" and in experimental music, and in the 1990s were adopted on a mass scale in popular music.

Lev Termen's theremin.

Ondes Martenot, 1928.

Russolo and Piatti in their studio in Milan with the avant-garde instrument INTONARUMORI.

Between the two world wars, the idea of a new electronic sound, new music, and new aesthetics in general gained momentum the world over. In Russia, the scientist Lev Termen created the instrument theremin, or termenvoks, which became immensely popular in the U. S. It consisted of an oscillator controlled by movement of the hands instead of a keyboard.

The ondes martenot (Martenot waves) was patented by the Frenchman Maurice Martenot in 1928 and was probably the best-designed electronic musical instrument since Thaddeus Cahill's telharmonium which produced alternating electric wave forms and was completed in 1906. Like the theremin, it used oscillating valves, but the tone could be controlled more easily with the left hand. Timbres and effects were controlled with keys and buttons. Martenot built this instrument in 1928, and a number of prominent contemporary composers such as Honegger, Boulez, and Messiaen used it in their works.

In 1935 the American Laurens Hammond devised an electronic organ, using an electric device similar to the ondes martenot.

A similar electronic instrument, known as the trautonium, was built in 1930 by the German Friedrich Trautwein.

Electronic Studios

The increasing popularity of electronic instruments and electronic music in Europe, America, and Japan and the search for new sounds resulted in the foundation and equipment of experimental studios in Tokyo, Warsaw, Munich, Brussels, Eindhoven, Toronto, London, Ann Arbor (Michigan), San Francisco, and Urbana (Illinois) from the 1950s on. These centres were quick to attract groups of talented composers, musicians, engineers, and musicologists, who contributed further to the popularization of electronic instruments and of the application of computer programming in the composition of music.

The most famous studios include:
Columbia-Princeton Electronic Music Center, founded in New York in 1951 by Vladimir Ussachevsky and Otto Luening. This is where the first large synthesizer, the Mark II RCA Music Synthesizer, was installed. The studio's popularity, in part due to the advanced technology that allowed for the realization of new ideas, attracted composers such as Milton Babbitt, Mario Davidovsky, Bulent Arel, and other pioneers of electronic music.

Studio for Electronic Music, Cologne, established in 1951 by Herbert Eimert, but better known as Stockhausen's studio. This is the first studio in which music was created entirely by electronic means. Stockhausen was one of the first composers to work there, and his works *Electronic Study I* (1953) and *Electronic Study II* (1954) are the first examples of the synthesis of "musique concrète" and electronic music.

Studio di fonologia, Milan, established in 1953. This center was the most active in working with composers. The most prominent among them include Luciano Berio, Luigi Nono, Bruno Maderna, and Henri Pousseur. This is where John Cage wrote his *Fontana Mix* (1958).

Institut de recherche et de coordination acoustic/musique (IRCAM), Paris. Founded in 1969 (opened 1977) with the aim of being one of the best centers for the production of electronic music, it was supported by the French government and flourished under the direction of the prominent composer and conductor Pierre Boulez. In fact, it became active in several directions: composition, research into the transformation of "live sound," and the psychology of sound perception. A circle of outstanding composers formed around Boulez and the studio: Luciano Berio, Harrison Birtwistle, Trevor Wishart, George Benjamin, Jonathan Harvey, and the jazz composer George Lewis.

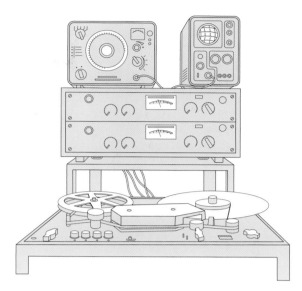

Equipment for composing and reproducing electronic music in a studio, consisting of a two-track stereo recorder, a sound generator, and an oscillograph.

Spherophone: a radioelectronic instrument developed by Jorg Mager in 1928.

The composer Karlheinz Stockhausen in his electronic studio.

Hawaiian Guitar

Having developed from the Portuguese guitar, it is also known as a steel guitar. Its body is carved of thicker wood and its sides are deeper, but the shape remains unchanged. The Hawaiian guitar is placed across the musician's knees, metal rings are worn on the right hand, and the left hand holds a comb-like device for a glissando effect. In the electric Hawaiian guitar, the soundbox is replaced by a trapezoidal board and the sound amplified by an electro-acoustic system. Typical effects are the vibrato and the glissando. This instrument is increasingly used in American country music.

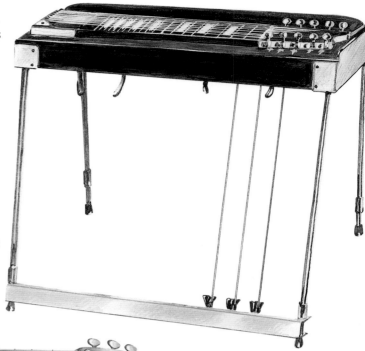

Electric Hawaiian guitar with pedals, for concert purposes. This model is not placed on the knees; the musician plays it standing.

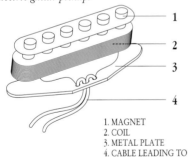

Traditional electric Hawaiian guitar.

Electric guitar pickup.

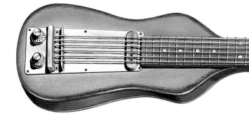

1
2
3
4

1. MAGNET
2. COIL
3. METAL PLATE
4. CABLE LEADING TO THE AMPLIFIER

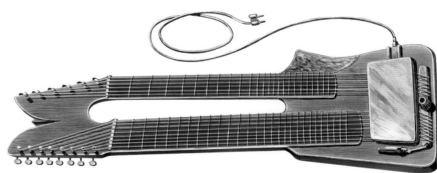

Electric Hawaiian guitar with two fingerboards, 1950s.

Modern electric Hawaiian guitar by Fender, 1953. Fender became a leading producer not only of electric guitars but also of electric Hawaiian guitars of excellent design.

Bottleneck for a Hawaiian guitar.

Electric Guitar

Although the first jazz models of the Gibson guitar appeared in 1924 (instead of a soundhole they had two f-holes like a violin and a solid block inside), it reached its culmination in 1934 with the Super 400 model. Pioneers such as Les Paul experimented with various constructions and amplifiers, but their achievements were largely unrecognized. In 1936, Gibson put their first fully equipped electric guitar on the market. The legendary guitarist Andrés Segovia was firmly opposed to the new instrument, but that did not prevent many jazz, blues, and swing virtuosos from admiring it and exploiting its potential to the full. The Gibson guitars produce what is essentially an acoustic sound converted by pickups.

Double electric guitar EDS by Gibson, 1961. There are six strings running over one fingerboard and twelve over the other. This instrument was used by the rock band Led Zeppelin's soloist Jimmy Page.

Acoustic-electric guitar of the mid-1950s, built by Epiphone before the company was taken over by Gibson. After the merger, Gibson preserved Epiphone's specific design but modernized the electric system to a considerable extent.

SG electric guitar by Gibson-Les-Paul, c. 1962, a beautifully designed instrument with a solid body and excellent proportions.

Gibson acoustic-electric guitar of the 1950s, a popular model.

Semi-acoustic guitar by Gibson-Les-Paul, an extremely popular design among pop and rock musicians from the 1960s to the present day.

"Slow Hand" Eric Clapton, one of the best modern guitar soloists, a composer and a member of leading rock groups such as Yardbirds, Cream, and Blind Faith.

Post-war stagnation delayed the popularization and refinement of the electric guitar until in 1950 the Leo Fender Musical Instrument Company of California launched a solid-body instrument. It is a standard-type guitar with no soundbox, and six strings of steel or nickel alloy. The strings pass through electromagnetic pickups converting the acoustic vibrations into electrical energy. A year later Fender revolutionized the traditional double bass, producing an electric bass guitar. The new instrument would soon fit perfectly into the musical environment, with the appearance of rock and roll in the mid 1950s.

Because of Leo Fender's innovations, the accessibility of his instruments, and their simplified and elegant design, he became known as the Henry Ford of the electric guitar.

Fender-Telecaster guitar, 1968. George Harrison played this guitar shortly before The Beatles separated.

1. HEADSTOCK
2. TUNERS
3. FINGERBOARD
4. FRETS
5. STRAP SCREW
6. SOLID WOODEN BODY
7. PICK GUARD
8. PICKUPS
9. CONTROL KNOBS
10. TREMOLO ARM
11. BRIDGE
12. OUTPUT SOCKET TO AMPLIFIER
13. PICKUP SELECTOR

Rickenbaker guitar, 1964. These are the guitars that brought The Beatles to world fame. The guitar in this illustration was John Lennon's, while George Harrison used a 12-string model. The Birds also used Rickenbaker 12-string guitars in the 1960s.

Modern electric guitar by Ibanez in the fashionable colors of the 1980s, imitating the classical shape and the solid body typical of Fender models.

The Fender-Stratocaster, known as the Strate: the most popular electric guitar in rock music from the 1960s to the present day. The instrument in this illustration was one of Jimi Hendrix's guitars. Although he was a left-hander, he used a guitar for right-handers, turning it over and having the string order reversed. The Strate design is one of the most frequently copied in the production of electric guitars.

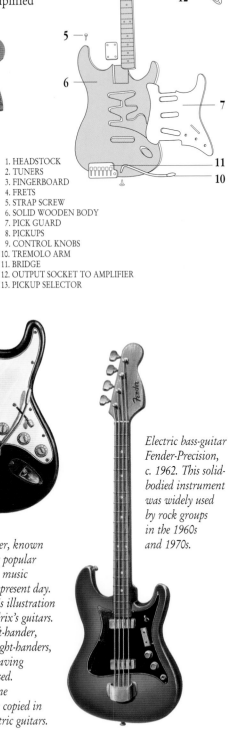

Electric bass-guitar Fender-Precision, c. 1962. This solid-bodied instrument was widely used by rock groups in the 1960s and 1970s.

It is paradoxical that the quality of industrial electric guitars on the market began to decline in the 1960s, exactly at the time of the invasion of British rock and roll. Many young makers then set about studying the older models, replicating, modifying, and perfecting them. In the 1970s and 1980s there was increasing interest in high-quality electric guitars, and small shops selling handmade instruments proliferated in the United States, Canada, and Britain.

Electric violin by Fender, c. 1958. One of the company's first attempts to create an electric violin, it has a recognizable Fender design: a massive body and characteristic headstock shape.

B.C. Rich electric guitar with a solid body of original design. Such shapes were favored by heavy-metal groups of the 1970s.

Arrow-shaped electric guitar by Jackson. Such guitars have been used since the early 1960s, though the one illustrated is a modernized design of the 1980s.

Small amplifier for an electric guitar, with a loudspeaker.

Electric bass guitar by Ned Steinberger, late 1980s. This is one of a new generation of electric guitars without a headstock; the tuners are down on the body. The same system is used for the production of six-string guitars. They are made of epoxy resins with carbon fibers, and have a built-in preamplifier.

Modern electric bass guitar by Warwick-Corvet-Proline of a fashionable design, late 1980s.

Wah-wah pedal, which is connected between the electric guitar and the amplifier. Particularly popular in the 1960s, it was used by Jimi Hendrix, Eric Clapton (with the group Cream), and others. A version providing a bow-wow effect is also produced.

Electric Piano and Organ

The electric piano is an instrument of the electro-acoustic category. The vibrations generated in the strings or tines are sensed by pickups like those of an electric guitar and heard as sound through a loudspeaker. This instrument has no use for traditional soundboard and technologically belongs with true electronic instruments.

The electric piano family includes at least two types. An early version of the first, string-based family of electronic instrument is known as the "Neo-Bechstein" (Bechstein-Siemens, 1931). With the shape of a grand piano, it uses magnetic pickups and, unlike its acoustic equivalent, a single string for each note. As in a normal grand piano, the right pedal raises the dampers. The left pedal functions as an independent volume control through the amplification system. Thus, a note can be sustained, perfectly equalized, and even swelled (crescendo then diminuendo) while sustained.

Hammond organ with two manuals and a pedal. Each manual has nine registers, three couplers and nine overtone regulators.

Tubon: a portable electric keyboard instrument.

Electric grand piano by Bechstein-Siemens-Sernst ("Neo-Bechstein").

Electronic organ by the Dutch maker F. Vrieken.

Single-manual electronic piano.

The other type is the classical Fender-Rhodes form, invented by Harold Rhodes in the U. S. in the 1960s. Here the strings are replaced by small steel tines, one for each tone. The instrument resembles a mini-piano and is now one of the favourites among electric pianos. The Japanese company Yamaha has also mastered the production of electric pianos and is now a world leader in this field. The electric piano family contains a number of other variants, including the clavinet.

Synthesizer

The synthesizer, an electronic musical instrument, is an involved complex of numerous functional units. These are controlled by an electronic signal-generating device operated through a keyboard. The instrument can imitate the timbre of various instruments, can produce innumerable sound combinations, and has an immense potential to generate specific timbres, sounds, and effects, which do not always conform to the traditional idea of a musical tone.

Master keyboard.

Synthesizer.

CD (audio-compact disc or audio-visual CD – ROM), a modern musical medium of composing software.

The first synthesizer, RCA Mark II, was created at the Sarnoff Research Center, New Jersey, in 1955, and was installed at the Columbia-Princeton Electronic Studio. The valves were soon replaced by transistors, and the large and heavy instrument by smaller portable models.

In the mid-1960s, Robert Moog and Donald Buchla developed the first commercial synthesizers. Professor Moog designed the stereophonic synthesizer and made a company to market the new instrument. Its early models were monophonic (Minimoog), with output sockets for an amplifier and an acoustic system. The Minimoog was used widely in concerts but was relatively limited. Later, a polyphonic successor was developed (Polymoog) for studio purposes, recording, and film music. Differently from the Minimoog, the volume of the Polymoog depends on the power of the attack, as it does in the piano.

Polymoog models include:
Vocoder: a synthesizer that manipulates the parameters of the generated sound by means of the player's voice characteristics.
Melotrone: an instrument sensitive to the slightest vibration that generates noise effects and the sound of woodwind, brass, and even stringed instruments; it uses recorded wave forms generated by authentic acoustic sources.
Complex synthesizers are capable of imitating the sound of any instrument and even of a choir. As a rule, they contain a rhythmic backing block. Playing the synthesizer is quite different from playing any other electro-acoustic instrument. The composer or player needs to possess extensive knowledge of the possible sound combinations as well.

MIDI technologies.
The optimization of the interface between separate synthesizer units and of the remote control of their parameters and characteristics, became possible only with the introduction of the MIDI world standard (MIDI stands for Musical Instrument Digital Interface). This is a digital interface for musical instruments, which unified the technologies of multi-channel data transfer, including tones/frequencies, duration, spectral and dynamic characteristics, the parameters of electronic effects, and even the control of light effects.

SYMPHONY ORCHESTRA

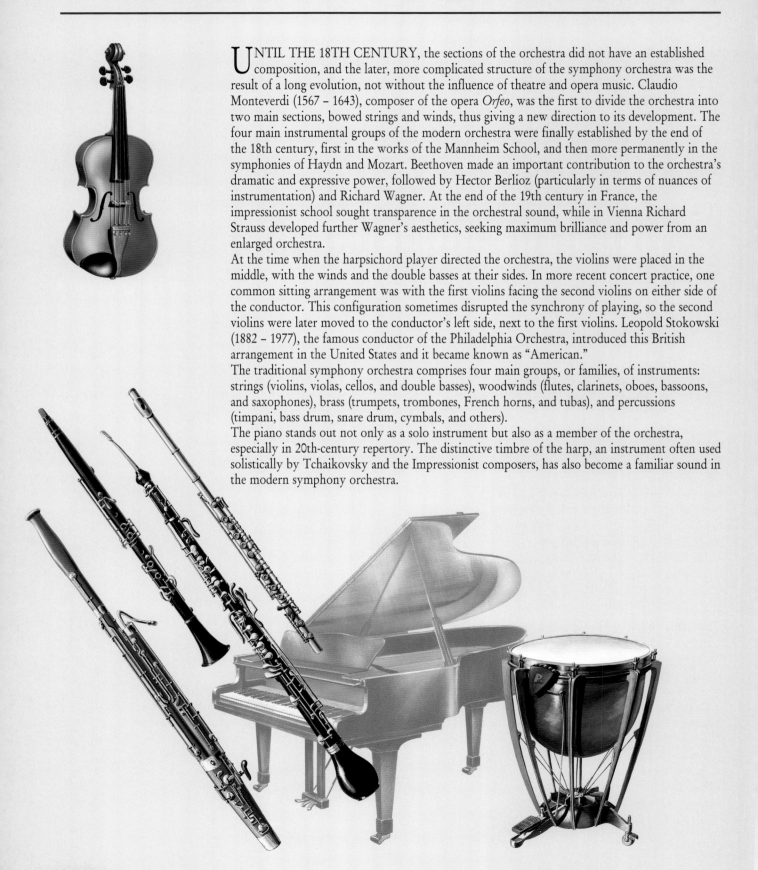

UNTIL THE 18TH CENTURY, the sections of the orchestra did not have an established composition, and the later, more complicated structure of the symphony orchestra was the result of a long evolution, not without the influence of theatre and opera music. Claudio Monteverdi (1567 – 1643), composer of the opera *Orfeo*, was the first to divide the orchestra into two main sections, bowed strings and winds, thus giving a new direction to its development. The four main instrumental groups of the modern orchestra were finally established by the end of the 18th century, first in the works of the Mannheim School, and then more permanently in the symphonies of Haydn and Mozart. Beethoven made an important contribution to the orchestra's dramatic and expressive power, followed by Hector Berlioz (particularly in terms of nuances of instrumentation) and Richard Wagner. At the end of the 19th century in France, the impressionist school sought transparence in the orchestral sound, while in Vienna Richard Strauss developed further Wagner's aesthetics, seeking maximum brilliance and power from an enlarged orchestra.

At the time when the harpsichord player directed the orchestra, the violins were placed in the middle, with the winds and the double basses at their sides. In more recent concert practice, one common sitting arrangement was with the first violins facing the second violins on either side of the conductor. This configuration sometimes disrupted the synchrony of playing, so the second violins were later moved to the conductor's left side, next to the first violins. Leopold Stokowski (1882 – 1977), the famous conductor of the Philadelphia Orchestra, introduced this British arrangement in the United States and it became known as "American."

The traditional symphony orchestra comprises four main groups, or families, of instruments: strings (violins, violas, cellos, and double basses), woodwinds (flutes, clarinets, oboes, bassoons, and saxophones), brass (trumpets, trombones, French horns, and tubas), and percussions (timpani, bass drum, snare drum, cymbals, and others).

The piano stands out not only as a solo instrument but also as a member of the orchestra, especially in 20th-century repertory. The distinctive timbre of the harp, an instrument often used solistically by Tchaikovsky and the Impressionist composers, has also become a familiar sound in the modern symphony orchestra.

WOODWIND INSTRUMENTS

Flute

IT.: FLAUTO, FR.: FLÛTE, GER.: FLÖTE, SP.: FLAUTA, RU.: FLEYTA

Historically, the modern transverse (side-blown) flute was preceded by the end-blown flute, which was used particularly in the Renaissance period. The transverse flute became immensely popular first in military bands, and later in opera and chamber orchestras in Germany. The inventor and flautist Theobald Boehm of Munich (1784 – 1881) redesigned the instrument in 1848, two years after Adolphe Sax patented the saxophone. Later, Boehm's improvements were applied to other instruments of the same family: the clarinet, the oboe, the saxophone, and, to a lesser degree, the bassoon.

End-blown flute (recorder).

The flute is a cylindrical tube consisting of three joints, detachable for easier carrying. The upper or head joint contains the mouth hole, with a curved lip-plate across which the air is blown. The head joint is closed by a removable stopper, which is used for tuning the instrument.

On the middle or body joint are the soundholes, covered by lever-connected keys. On the lower or foot joint there are an additional two or three (of a total of 16 – 18) keys, operated by the little finger of the right hand. The right thumb supports the instrument, which is held sideways to the player's right. The modern flute is made of alloys, either nickel and silver (German silver), or other silver and gold alloys.

There are also fine models in stainless steel.

The flute's normal range is $c^1 - c^4$, though it can go up to d^4 or e^4. Of all the wind instruments it is the most agile and the most technically advanced. In the lower register its tone is full and rich, in the middle register it is gentle and clear, and in the high register bright and penetrating.

Transverse flutes.

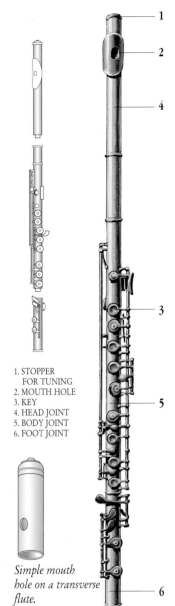

1. STOPPER FOR TUNING
2. MOUTH HOLE
3. KEY
4. HEAD JOINT
5. BODY JOINT
6. FOOT JOINT

Simple mouth hole on a transverse flute.

SYMPHONY ORCHESTRA

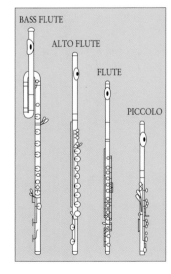

BASS FLUTE

ALTO FLUTE

FLUTE

PICCOLO

Alto flute.

Bass flutes.

Alto Flute

IT.: FLAUTO CONTRALTO, FR.: FLÛTE ALTO,
GER.: ALTFLÖTE, SP.: FLAUTA CONTRALTO,
RU.: ALTOVAYA FLEYTA

Used for the first time by Rimsky-Korsakov in his opera *Mlada* of 1892 and again in his opera *The Legend of the Invisible City of Kitezh* of 1907, the alto flute then appeared in three major orchestral works: Ravel's *Daphnis and Chloe* (1912), Stravinsky's *The Rite of Spring* (1913), and Gustav Holst's *The Planets* (1916). The alto flute has the same written range as the flute, though models pitched in G sound a perfect fourth lower than the flute and models in F a perfect fifth lower.

Bass Flute

IT.: FLAUTO BASSO, FR.: FLÛTE BASSE,
GER.: BASSFLÖTE, SP.: BAJÓN,
RU.: BASOVAYA FLEYTA

The lowest-pitched flute created by the flautist Albizzi of Milan in 1910. The bass flute is pitched in C and has a range of c – g^2.

Piccolo

IT.: OTTAVINO, FR.: PETITE FLÛTE, GER.: PIKKOLOFLÖTE,
SP.: FLAUTÍN, RU.: MALAYA FLEYTA

The piccolo is the highest-pitched instrument in the symphony orchestra. Half the size of the flute, it has the same construction and keys.

The piccolo was used in the orchestra as early as the time of Handel, but it was only in the 18th century that it became an established member of the opera orchestra. Gluck used it in his opera *Iphigénie en Tauride*, Haydn in his oratorio *The Seasons*, Mozart in his operas, and Beethoven in his Fifth, Sixth, and Ninth Symphonies. Its range is d^2– d^5, notated an octave lower. Less rich in overtones than the flute, its sound is very bright and easily recognizable within the orchestra. Many musicians prefer piccolos made of wood to those of silver, for their softer tone color.

REPERTORY

Widely used in orchestral, solo, and chamber music, the flute has a vast repertory. Bach composed numerous works for it, including six sonatas and a concerto in D minor. Vivaldi, Telemann, Cimarosa, Handel, and Haydn also wrote for the flute. In the Classical period in Vienna the repertory was further enriched by two concertos by Mozart, K.313 and K.314, and also by a number of chamber works. The flute was particularly important for the so-called French Impressionist composers: Debussy (*Prélude à l'après-midi d'un faune*, *Syrinx*, Sonata for Flute, Viola, and Harp), Ravel (*Shéhérazade*), Ibert, Poulenc, and others. In more recent times, the flute has again become a favorite, appearing in sonatas by Hindemith, Prokofiev, Milhaud, Frank Martin, and Henze, as well as in a solo piece by the avant-garde composer John Cage. The flute is a permanent member of the symphony orchestra, usually in a combination of two large flutes and one piccolo.

CLAUDE DEBUSSY
(1862–1918)

Enrico Caruso, one of the world's greatest tenors, owes his fame partly to the phonograph and the flute. During his military service around 1890, Caruso used to play the flute, believing that he would have a career as a flautist. One day, a traveling salesman visited his regiment with a new sound-recording device, the phonograph. The salesman invited the young soldier to play something on his flute. Caruso recalled: "I thought I was playing with great artistry ... The phonograph played my performance back exactly and I realized for the first time that it was not my calling to become a flautist – that I was, in fact, playing abominably ..."

Clarinet

IT.: CLARINETTO, CLARINO, FR.: CLARINETTE, GER.: KLARINETTE, SP.: CLARINETE, RU.: KLARNET

The clarinet is a single-reed woodwind instrument that was perfected and installed in the symphony orchestra in the late 18th century, relatively late in comparison with the flute and the oboe.
Made of ebony, coco wood, ebonite, plastic, or metal, it consists of five parts connected by cork rings: a mouthpiece with a reed secured by a two-screw ligature, a barrel for fine tuning, an upper and a lower joint with 23 – 26 soundholes (17 with ring keys), and a bell.

Early clarinet.

With its wide and flexible range and its noble, gentle, warm, and bright tone color, the clarinet is the most expressive voice in the orchestra. It exists in B flat and in A, and while its normal range is e – a^3, it can reach up to c^4. Among the woodwind instruments the clarinet has the greatest difference of sound between its various registers. The low register, known as the chalumeau, is full, soft, and veiled. The middle register is weaker and less expressive. The high "clarion" register is bright and silvery.

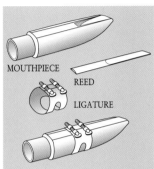

MOUTHPIECE

REED

LIGATURE

Mouthpiece.

Modern clarinets.

S Y M P H O N Y   O R C H E S T R A

1. MOUTHPIECE TAPERS
2. LIGATURE HOLDS SINGLE REED
3. BARREL JOINT
4. KEYS FOR LEFT HAND
   ON UPPER JOINT
5. KEYS FOR LITTLE FINGER
   OF LEFT HAND
6. KEYS FOR RIGHT HAND
   ON LOWER JOINT
7. KEYS FOR LITTLE FINGER
   OF RIGHT HAND
8. FLARED BELL

The symphony orchestra includes at least two clarinets (tuned in either B flat or A), as well as a smaller, higher-pitched clarinet in E flat and a low pitched bass clarinet.

REPERTORY

The clarinet was established as a permanent member of the orchestra by the works of Beethoven. Composers who recognized the qualities of this instrument included Mozart (Clarinet Concerto, K.622; Clarinet Quintet, K. 581), Weber (two concertos), Stamitz (Clarinet Concerto), Beethoven (Trio, op. 11), and Brahms (Trio for Clarinet, Cello, and Piano, op. 114; Quintet for Clarinet and Strings, op. 115; Sonatas for Clarinet and Piano, op. 120). The 20th century is even richer in clarinet works and in clarinet orchestral solos. Hindemith (Sonata for Clarinet and Piano), Stravinsky (Ebony Concerto, Three Pieces for clarinet solo), Bartók (Contrasts), and Copland (Clarinet Concerto) are only a few of the 20th-century composers who produced music for this instrument.

IGOR STRAVINSKY

(1882 – 1971)

Benny Goodman was the first clarinetist in the world to combine jazz and classical music in a single brilliant career. It was especially for him that Aaron Copland composed his Clarinet Concerto, first performed in 1950.

Clarinet in A flat.
Clarinet in B flat.
Clarinet in E flat.

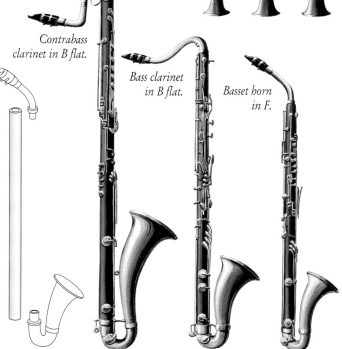

Contrabass clarinet in B flat.

Bass clarinet in B flat.

Basset horn in F.

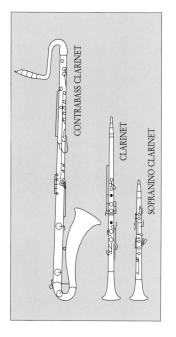

When the 8-year-old Mozart arrived in London in 1764, he was asked by the German composer Carl Friedrich Abel to adapt one of his symphonies. Mozart did so, rewriting the oboe part for clarinet. His autograph manuscript of Abel's work confused music scholars for two centuries. Indeed, the confusion was perpetuated by Köchel's catalogue of Mozart's works, in which Abel's work is listed as Mozart's Symphony No. 3 (K.18).

Oboe

IT.: OBOE, FR.: HAUTBOIS, GER.: OBOE, SP.: OBOE, RU.: GOBOY

The oboe is a double-reed woodwind instrument. The oboe reed is made of a strip of cane, which is folded at mid-point; its ends are then tightly bound to a corked staple, the fold is cut, and the blades shaved thin. The two reeds cause the air column in the instrument to vibrate.

Early oboe.

The oboe has a slightly conical tube with a narrow bell, and is made of grenadilla (African blackwood), ebony, or plastic. It consists of four parts: reeds, upper joint, lower joint, and bell. The instrument is as long as the clarinet but looks smaller because of its slender tube and because the player's hands come about 5 cm closer to the face. On the upper and the lower joints there are 25 soundholes covered with keys.

The precursors of the oboe date back to ancient times, but the improved instrument was introduced into the concert orchestra only in the mid-17th century. The Boehm system, applied to the oboe by Louis-Auguste Buffet, was patented in Paris at the same time as the Boehm system for the clarinet (1844). The oboe's range is b flat¹–a³. It produces a gentle sound with a distinctive nasal tone. The middle and high registers are richer and more flexible than the low register, though their dynamic potential does not compare with that of the flute or clarinet.

Double reed.

Modern oboe.

1. DOUBLE REED
2. UPPER JOINT
3. RODS CONNECT THE KEYS
4. KEY
5. LOWER JOINT
6. FLARED BELL

The oboe has been a permanent member of the orchestra since the time of Bach, Handel, Vivaldi, and Scarlatti. It also has a role in solo and chamber music. A valuable though limited repertory for this instrument was created in the Romantic period and in the 20th century.

Oboe d'amore

IT.: OBOE D'AMORE, FR.: HAUTBOIS D'AMOUR,
GER.: OBOE D'AMORE, RU.: GOBOY D'AMUR

Somewhat larger than the
ordinary oboe and smaller than
the cor anglais, with a bulbous
bell, the oboe d'amore
is a downward transposing
instrument in A. It has the
same written range as the oboe
but sounds a minor third lower.
The oboe d'amore appeared at
the same time as the cor anglais.
After the time of Bach,
who used it extensively in his
concertos and cantatas, it
disappeared from the orchestra,
reappearing from the end
of the 19th century in the works
of Debussy, Ravel, Richard
Strauss, Stockhausen,
and others.
Less popular and more rarely
used oboes include the piccolo
oboe and the baritone oboe.
Similar to the baritone oboe
is the heckelphone (named after
the Heckel family of woodwind
instrument makers, who
invented it in 1904).

*Heinz Holliger, oboist and
composer, renowned for his
innovative experiments with
sounds and effects on the oboe.*

*Oboe d'amore
(mezzo-soprano oboe).*

Modern baritone oboe.

HECKELPHONE · BARITONE OBOE · ALTO OBOE · MEZZO-SOPRANO OBOE · OBOE

Heckelphone.

REPERTORY

Although composers used the cor anglais as early
as in Bach's time, it was only later that it was entrusted
with solos in the orchestra. Its rich dreamy tone color
makes it particularly convenient for slow long solos
in pastoral style. Rossini used it in his overture to *William
Tell*, Berlioz in the overture to *Le carnaval romain*, Wagner
in *Tristan und Isolde*, and Dvořák in his symphony *From the
New World*. Beethoven scored for the cor anglais in his
chamber works; Mozart appreciated it, too, while in
modern times it appears in works by Sibelius, Stockhausen
and other composers.

Cor anglais

IT.: CORNO INGLESE, FR.: COR ANGLAIS,
GER.: ENGLISCHHORN, SP.: CORNO INGLÉS,
RU.: ANGLIISKI ROZHOK

The cor anglais is an alto
oboe with a bulbous bell
and a double reed attached
to a metal mouth pipe.
The cor anglais is pitched
in F, with the same written
range as the oboe,
but sounding a perfect fifth
lower. The registers are
similar to those of the oboe,
but the sound is deeper
and more melancholic. In the
orchestra, the cor anglais
sometimes plays
the third oboe part.

Cor anglais (alto oboe).

Bassoon

IT.: FAGOTTO, FR.: BASSON, GER.: FAGOTT, SP.: FAGOT, BAJÓN, RU.: FAGOT

The tallest of the woodwind instruments, the bassoon is 134 cm high, with a conical bore, and is played with a double reed. It is made of maple, sycamore, or ash, and consists of five parts: crook, wing or tenor joint, boot or butt (the u-bend), long or bass joint, and bell. For the player's convenience, the instrument is worn on a sling round the neck.

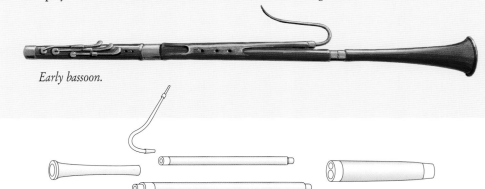

Early bassoon.

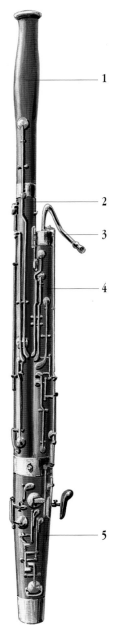

1. BELL
2. LONG JOINT
3. CROOK
4. WING JOINT
5. BUTT

Modern bassoon.

The bassoon family includes two more rarely used models: the fagottino or octave bassoon, pitched an octave higher, and the tenoroon or basson quinte, pitched a fifth higher.

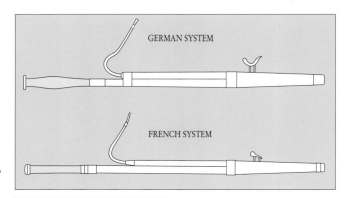

GERMAN SYSTEM

FRENCH SYSTEM

Two main bassoon systems now exist: the German system, named after the renowned maker Johann Adam Heckel, who did much to perfect the instrument, and the system designed by Buffet-Crampon of Paris. The Heckel-system bassoon is made in maple, with some of its parts lined with ebonite to resist moisture. Most German instruments have an ivory ring at the top.
The French-system bassoon is made in rosewood, without the white ivory ring. It was popular in France and to an extent in Britain, as well as in Italy and Spain until the 1930s. In the U. S. the German system is preferred, though the French is also used, as in the Boston Symphony Orchestra.

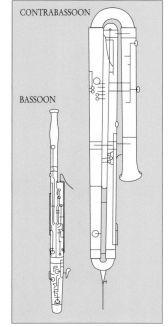

CONTRABASSOON

BASSOON

Reed.

The bassoon is a non-transposing instrument with a range of B flat^1 – e^2. It is expressive and rich in overtones across its entire range. The middle register is the sweetest of all, and hence the best suited to a cantabile style. The instrument has excellent technical qualities, and its staccato articulation is unrivalled.

The bassoon became a regular member of the orchestra relatively early, though Beethoven was the first to write a solo part for it. Central to the bassoon repertory are the concertos by Mozart (K.191) and Weber (op. 75). Glinka, Saint-Saëns, Hindemith, Poulenc, Elgar, and others wrote chamber pieces for the instrument.

Contrabassoon (Double Bassoon)

IT.: CONTROFAGOTTO, FR.: CONTREBASSON, GER.: KONTRAFAGOTT, SP.: CONTRAFAGOT, RU.: KONTRAFAGOT

Twice the length of the bassoon, the contrabassoon's long tube consists of four joints, with three u-bends, and stands on a metal spike like the cello and the double bass.

Early contrabassoon.

The instrument's modern design dates from 1910, when it was perfected by the Heckel firm. The conical maple tube has a total length of 550 cm or more, and for the player's convenience is constructed in four parallel sections connected by u-bends. The funnel-shaped bell is made of metal. Although contrabassoons are produced in the U. S., Britain, and France, the German Heckel model is still the most popular throughout the world.

Music for the contrabassoon sounds an octave lower than written, the instrument's range covering A^2 – g. It has a distinctive full-bodied, rumbling sound. In the orchestra it is usually played by the third bassoonist; as a change of instruments is impractical, it is advisable to have a separate player for the contrabassoon.

Reed.

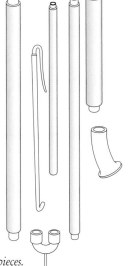

A contrabassoon taken to pieces.

Modern contrabassoon.

Handel was the first to write for the contrabassoon. It also appeared in Haydn's oratorios *The Creation* and *The Seasons*, in Beethoven's Fifth and Ninth Symphonies, and in his opera *Fidelio*. Richard Strauss created his longest orchestral solo for the contrabassoon in the opera *Salome*.

SYMPHONY ORCHESTRA

BRASS INSTRUMENTS

Horn (French horn)

IT.: CORNO, FR.: COR, GER.: HORN, WALDHORN, SP.: TROMPA, RU.: VALTORNA

A brass instrument with a long, coiled, cylindrical tube, widening around the middle into a cone and ending in a wide bell, its total length of tubing can reach 3.65 m. The mouthpiece is cone-shaped. The horn is the only brass instrument played with the fingers of the left hand.

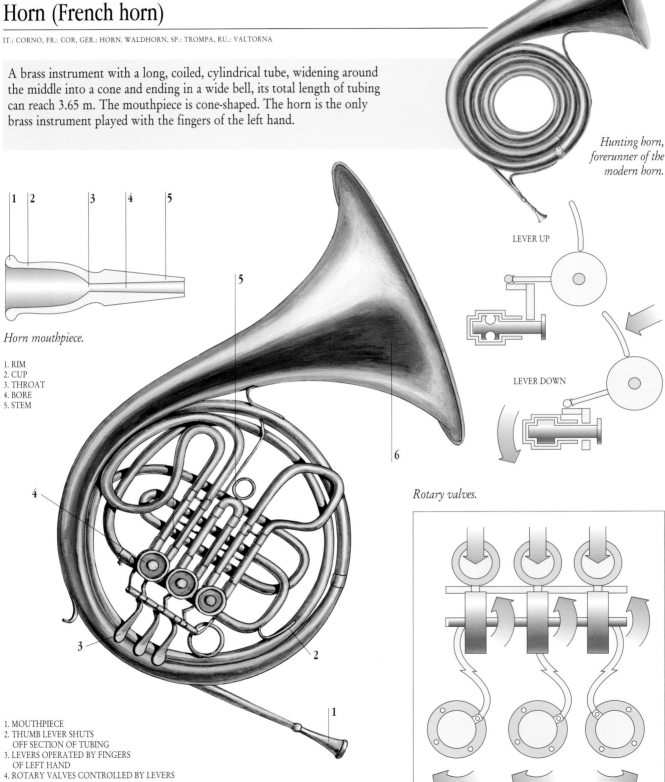

Hunting horn, forerunner of the modern horn.

LEVER UP

LEVER DOWN

Horn mouthpiece.

1. RIM
2. CUP
3. THROAT
4. BORE
5. STEM

Rotary valves.

1. MOUTHPIECE
2. THUMB LEVER SHUTS
   OFF SECTION OF TUBING
3. LEVERS OPERATED BY FINGERS
   OF LEFT HAND
4. ROTARY VALVES CONTROLLED BY LEVERS
5. SLIDE PULL
6. WIDE FLARED BELL

The origins of the instrument are to be found in the hunting horn. Only in the 19th century, with the introduction of valves, did the natural horn develop into a chromatic instrument. For the purposes of the modern symphony orchestra the horn is built in F, with a range of B flat^1 – f^2. Music for the horn is notated in the treble and the bass clef. In the double horn, which is equipped with a fourth valve, the pitch can be changed from F to B flat, which facilitates the higher notes.

The horn has a broad expressive range and can sound heroic or sad with equal ease. This range is further increased by inserting a mute or the right hand inside the bell ("hand-muting"). In terms of both function and sound, the horn stands between the woodwind and brass instruments and actually links them.

This is why in orchestral scores the horn parts are found above the trumpet line, even though the horn is lower-pitched.

REPERTORY

The hunting horn – the direct precursor of the orchestral horn – was used in the orchestra for the first time by Cavalli in his opera *The Marriage of Thetis and Peleus* (1639), while the chromatic or valved horn made its orchestral debut in Halévy's opera *La juive* (1835). In his Brandenburg Concerto no. 1 Bach initially wrote a part for a hunting horn, but later entrusted it to a natural horn. Mozart composed four concertos for horn and orchestra and Haydn only one, while Schumann's *Konzertstück* is for four horns and orchestra. Richard Strauss's two horn concertos are also important solo works for the instrument. In the field of chamber music there are works by Mozart (Quintet for Horn and Strings, K. 407), Beethoven (Sonata for Horn and Piano, op. 17), and Brahms (Trio for Violin, Horn, and Piano, op. 40). Dukas, Skryabin, Poulenc, Glazunov, and other composers have also contributed to the repertory. Although the valved horn was perfected by the middle of the 19th century, a number of composers, such as Weber, continued to exploit the distinctive sound qualities of the natural horn. Even Wagner used natural horns alongside valved horns for a while.

In more recent times, virtuoso players have prompted leading composers to create music for the modern valved instrument. Tippett and Hindemith wrote sonatas for horns, and Britten a Serenade for Tenor, Horn, and Strings (1943). Recent concertos for horn and orchestra include those by Thea Musgrave (1971) and Anthony Powers (1991).

RICHARD WAGNER
(1813–1883)

In fact, the horn comprises two instruments in one. A lever controlled with the left thumb connects two sections of tubing, the one producing deep and full tones, and the other bright and penetrating ones. Thus, the horn has been described as the most refined and poetic voice in the symphony orchestra, as well as being the hardest to master.

The orchestra may include two, four, or more horns.

Trumpet

IT.: TROMBA, FR.: TROMPETTE, GER.: TROMPETE, SP.: TROMPETA, RU.: TRUBA

The trumpet is a brass wind instrument with an oval shape, a cup mouthpiece at the one end, and a flared bell at the other. Like the French horn, it is equipped with three valves that lower the pitch of the instrument and make its range fully chromatic.

The valves are operated by the index finger, middle finger, and fourth finger of the right hand, while the left hand supports the instrument. Each valve has openings that allow the air to pass through an additional loop of tubing, thereby lowering the pitch.

The idea of adding more tubing and a second valve first emerged at the beginning of the 19th century, as the invention of the Germans Stölzel and Blühmel. Later, a third valve was added by Müller.

Early valved trumpet.

1. CUP-SHAPED MOUTHPIECE
2. PISTON VALVES
3. TUNING SLIDE CHANGES PITCH
4. WATER KEY
5. BELL

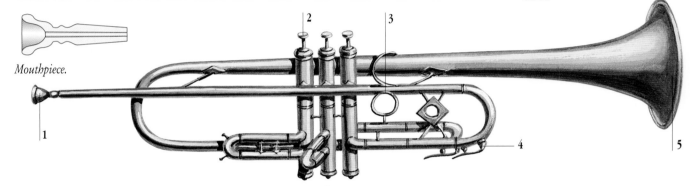

Mouthpiece.

Modern trumpet.

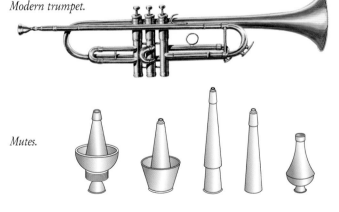

Mutes.

The trumpet is the highest-pitched brass instrument. Pitched in B flat or C, it has a written range of f – c³/e³, the B flat model sounding a major second lower than written. The sound of the trumpet is bright and penetrating, slightly muffled in the lower register, and brilliant in the upper register. Like the other brass instruments, the trumpet is equipped with a set of mutes. Made of wood, light metal, papier-mâché, or plastic, a mute can be placed in the bell of the instrument to modify or subdue its timbre. Mute styles include straight, cup, and Harmon.

REPERTORY

The trumpet appeared in the orchestra for the first time in Monteverdi's opera *Orfeo* (1607), and was then widely used in the Baroque period, particularly in the works of Bach and Handel. Initially, the trumpet was as valued as the stringed instruments, but lost its leading position during the Classical period only to be revived in the early 19th century.

Many composers were attracted by the versatility and great technical potential of the trumpet, and this resulted in the composition of concertos for one or more trumpets by Torelli, Vivaldi, Telemann, Haydn, and Hummel, and chamber music with trumpet and piano by Saint-Saëns, Hindemith, Poulenc, Henze, and Shostakovich.

Piccolo Trumpet (Bach Trumpet)

IT.: TROMBA PICCOLA, TROMBETTA, FR.: PETITE TROMPETTE,
GER.: BACH-TROMPETE, PIKKOLOTROMPETE, SP.: CLARÍN, RU.: TRUBA PIKKOLO

A higher-pitched valved trumpet built in D, this modern
valved instrument is often used for the high trumpet parts in
the works of Handel and Bach. The highest passages, originally
written for the trumpet's precursor, the clarino, are played on
natural trumpets. The piccolo trumpet is also built in E flat, F,
A, and B flat. All sizes have the same written range as the
ordinary trumpet in C, but sound higher: the instrument in D
a major second higher, the one in E flat a minor third higher,
the one in F a perfect fourth higher, the one in A a major sixth
higher, and the one in B flat a minor seventh higher.

Bass Trumpet

IT.: TROMBA BASSA, FR.: TROMPETTE BASSE, GER.: BASSTROMPETE,
SP.: TROMPETA BAJO, RU.: BASOVAYA TRUBA

Built in C or B flat, its written range is the same as that of the
standard trumpet in C, but it sounds respectively an octave
or a major ninth lower. The bass trumpet was used for the first
time by Wagner in his operatic cycle *The Ring of the Nibelung*,
and later by Stravinsky (*The Rite of Spring*), Richard Strauss
(*Elektra*), Glazunov, and other composers.

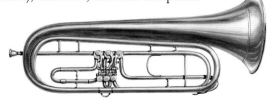

Aida Trumpet

IT.: TROMBA D'AIDA, FR.: TROMPETTE D'AIDA, GER.: AIDA-TROMPETE,
SP.: TROMPETA DE AIDA, RU.: египетская труба

Built to be played on stage in Act II Verdi's opera *Aida* (1871),
it has a single valve that lowers its tuning from B flat to A flat.
Today's improved models have three valves.

Cornet

IT.: CORNETTA, FR.: CORNET À PISTON, GER.: KORNETT, SP.: CORNETA,
RU.: KORNET-A-PISTON

A brass wind instrument, slightly longer than the trumpet,
with a wider conical bore and a larger mouthpiece, making the
sound mellower and more melodious. The cornet is usually
built in B flat, though there is also a smaller soprano model
in E flat. The written range is the same as that of the trumpet
in C, though the B flat model sounds a tone lower. The cornet
is used in brass and military bands but can also be found
in opera and symphonic music.

Alto Trumpet

IT.: TROMBA CONTRALTA, FR.: TROMPETTE ALTO, GER.: ALTTROMPETE,
SP.: TROMPETA CONRALTO, RU.: ALTOVAYA TRUBA

A transposing instrument built in F, the alto trumpet has the
written range of the standard trumpet but sounds a perfect fifth
lower. It was developed at the express request of Rimsky-
Korsakov, who used it in most of his operas.

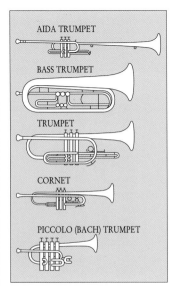

AIDA TRUMPET

BASS TRUMPET

TRUMPET

CORNET

PICCOLO (BACH) TRUMPET

SYMPHONY ORCHESTRA

Trombone

IT.: TROMBONE, FR.: TROMBONE, GER.: POSAUNE, SP.: TROMBÓN, RU.: TROMBON

The trombone was the first chromatic brass instrument ever made. It is s-shaped and consists of a main tube with a bell at one end and a mouthpiece at the other, and a u-shaped extendable slide inserted into the main tube. The instrument is held in the left hand, while the right hand moves the slide through seven different positions, producing all of the chromatic tones within the trombone's range of E – c²/f².

Early trombone.

1. MOUTHPIECE
2. COUNTERWEIGHT BALANCES INSTRUMENT
3. TUNING SLIDE BOW
4. BRACE FOR LEFT HAND
5. SLIDE BRACE FOR RIGHT HAND
6. OUTER TUBE OF SLIDE
7. WATER KEY
8. BUMPER KNOB PROTECTS TUBING

The seven positions of the slide.

Mouthpiece.

Within the symphony orchestra, the slide trombone is preferred to the valved trombone because of its clear, penetrating, noble sound. In order to extend the instrument's range (down to C), a tenor-bass trombone is used. As in the case of the trumpet, a mute can be inserted into the bell for special effects or a more muffled sound. The modern symphony orchestra most often includes three slide trombones, two tenor and one bass, though a fourth trombone is sometimes included.

PISTON UP

PISTONS

PISTON DOWN

Valved trombone.

TENOR TROMBONE

BASS TROMBONE

An improved tenor trombone includes a quart valve (also known as the Sax valve after its inventor Adolphe Sax). This valve is used to retune the instrument from B flat to F, practically transforming it from a tenor to a bass trombone and greatly expanding its technical potential.

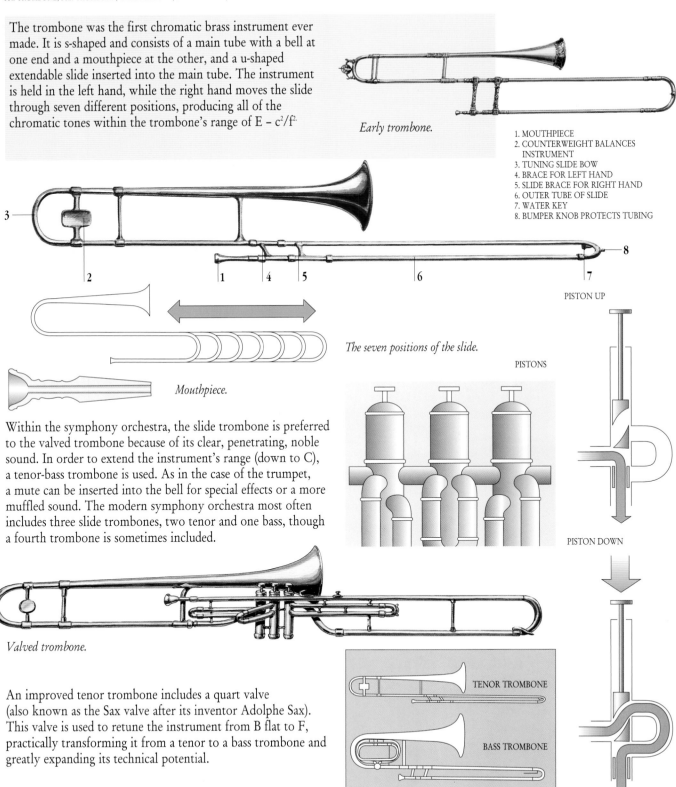

REPERTORY

The repertory for solo trombone, while not very extensive, includes notable works such as a concerto by Rimsky-Korsakov, a cavatina by Saint-Saëns, Sonata for Trombone and Orchestra by Hindemith, *Concerto d'hiver* by Milhaud, Symphony for Trombone and Orchestra by Bloch.

RIMSKY – KORSAKOV

(1844–1908)

Albert Mangelsdorff,
a musician who most fully exploited the trombone's technical
and expressive qualities during the second half of the 20th century.
A world-famous jazz performer, he was a universal musician, participating
in a variety of ensembles, and composing with a natural feeling
for the modern cross-culture style.

Bass Trombone

IT.: TROMBONE BASSO, FR.: TROMBONE BASSE, GER.: BASSPOSAUNE, SP.: TROMBÓN BAJO,
RU.: BASOVY TROMBON

Slightly larger than the tenor slide trombone, the bass instrument is less technically agile but produces a louder and fuller tone. The limits of its range are a fourth lower than those of the tenor trombone.

Bass trombone.

The trombone was included in the orchestra for the first time by Monteverdi in his opera *Orfeo* (1607). Beethoven was the first to introduce it into symphonic music, and the instrument was soon an indispensable member of the symphony orchestra.

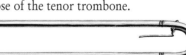

Tuba

IT.: TUBA, FR.: TUBA, GER.: TUBA, SP.: TUBA, RU.: TUBA

The tuba is the lowest-pitched and the largest instrument of the brass group, with a wide bore, a cup mouthpiece, and a total tubing length of up to 14 m. The instrument is held with the bell pointing upwards. Designed and built by Wilhelm Wieprecht and Johann Gottfried Moritz, the tuba was first patented in 1835.
Initially, it had three valves, but a fourth one was added later to lower the instrument's pitch by a perfect fourth.
The tuba was later furnished with a fifth and even a sixth valve.

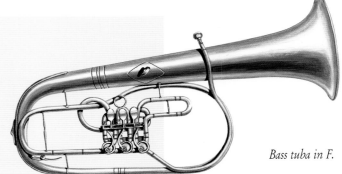

Bass tuba in F.

The tuba plays the bass part in the opera and symphony orchestra. The existing sizes are tenor tuba in B flat, bass tuba in F and E flat, and contrabass tuba in C and B flat. In today's symphony orchestra, a contrabass tuba with five or six valves is used, with a range of $C^1 - c^1/f^1$.

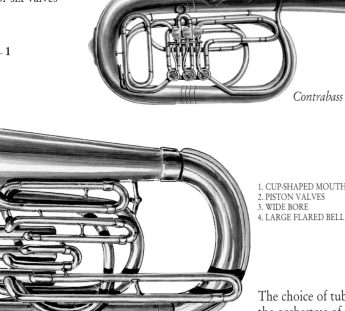

Contrabass tuba in B flat.

1. CUP-SHAPED MOUTHPIECE
2. PISTON VALVES
3. WIDE BORE
4. LARGE FLARED BELL

Orchestral contrabass tuba with three pistons.

Orchestral contrabass tuba with four rotary valves.

The choice of tube size by the orchestras of the U. S., Britain, and continental Europe is surprisingly stable. American and German orchestras use contrabass tubas in C, while in Britain the bass tuba in E flat is now preferred to the instrument in F that was standard at the end of the 19th century. French orchestras use a small tuba in C. After World War II, the tuba enjoyed a renaissance in jazz and avant-garde music.

The so-called "Wagner tuba" was developed at Wagner's request, for use in his *Ring* cycle. Usually equipped with four valves, it is played with the left hand and has a funnel-shaped mouthpiece like that of the horn. It can be played by any horn player, and usually appears in a quartet: two tenor tubas in B flat and two bass tubas in F. The Wagner tuba produces a soft sound, integrating the characteristics of the horn, the trombone, and the tuba. It exists in two sizes: tenor in B flat and bass in F. The written range is F – g², sounding a major second lower in B flat and a perfect fifth lower in F. Composers who have scored for the Wagner tuba include Bruckner, Strauss, and Stravinsky.

Bob Stuart,
the American musician who revolutionized the image of the tuba, traditionally regarded as a heavy and rather clumsy instrument. His brilliant jazz improvisations established it as a solo instrument in its own right, as it indeed appears in works by Vaughan Williams, Gordon Jacob, Edward Gregson, and Derek Bourgeois.

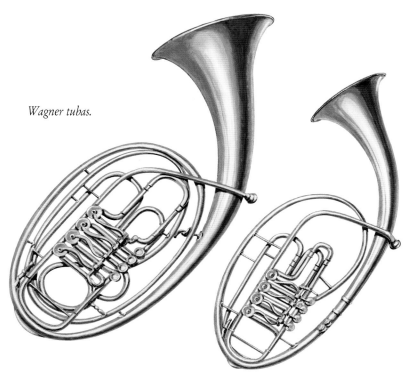

Wagner tubas.

From the second half of the 19th century, the tuba became a regular member of the symphony orchestra. In larger orchestras two tubas can be used, as in Berlioz's *Symphonie fantastique* and Richard Strauss's *Thus Spoke Zarathustra*. The solo repertory is not particularly extensive. Among the more popular works are a concerto by Vaughan Williams, a sonata for tuba and piano by Hindemith, and a suite by Gordon Jacobs. In the jazz world, the tuba acquired the status of a solo instrument only in the last quarter of the 20th century.

STRING INSTRUMENTS

Violin

IT.: VIOLINO, FR.: VIOLON, GER.: VIOLINE, GEIGE, SP.: VIOLÍN, RU.: SKRIPKA.

The violin is the leading bowed instrument of the modern string family, as well as in classical music of all periods. Its special timbral and expressive qualities are unequalled in the performance of solo, chamber, and symphonic music, as well as in the folk music of many cultures.

Before the era of musical Romanticism, conductors were often violinists, who would lead the orchestra with violins in their hands, occasionally interrupting their conducting to play (or in some cases, vice versa). Later, conducting became a profession in itself. Even now, however, the so-called leader of the symphony orchestra is the concertmaster, or principal first violinist. The violin has the same leading role in chamber ensembles such as the string quartets and trio. Genres such as the solo sonata and the solo concerto first emerged as works for violin, and many of the masterpieces of the musical literature were composed with a solo violin at the forefront.

The unrivalled expressive potential of the violin reached its height in the work of the famous luthiers of the past three centuries, and the composers and virtuoso performers of the past two centuries. Its powerful tone, rich nuancing, and timbral variety, as well as its capacity to perform complex melodies, allow the violin to express, like the human voice, the subtlest shades of emotion. In that sense, the violin has retained its position of superiority among musical instruments from the Baroque period (17th – 18th centuries) to the present day. From the beginning of the 20th century, it has also appeared as a solo instrument in jazz and even in rock music.

Lira da braccio, early 16th century.

A number of the essential features of the violin show that one of its closest predecessors was the lira da braccio. Both are supported on the left shoulder, and the shape and structure of the body, as well as the number and tuning of the strings, are similar. The total length of the violin is 60 cm, the body taking up 35.5 – 36 cm. It has four strings, tuned in perfect fifths: g, d^1, a^1, and e^2, but in the various folk traditions, the tuning may differ according to the performer's technique and abilities. The range of the violin is g – g^4, though this may be extended by retuning the strings (scordatura). Violin music is notated in the treble clef.

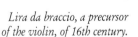

Lira da braccio, a precursor of the violin, of 16th century.

Kennedy (formerly Nigel Kennedy), one of the first musicians in the world to renounce stylistic purism and the reserve with which performers had traditionally behaved on stage. He is not only a virtuoso violinist, equally at home with standard classical literature, jazz, and popular music, but also an excellent viola player.

Modern violin.

The violin is held
placed between the collarbone
and the chin, although in the
Anglo-Saxon tradition fiddling
is also popular, with the violin
supported on the waist.
The different kinds of bowing
are indicated as follows:
Π for a "down-bow"
and V for an "up-bow."

*Below, a solid-bodied violin
of 1910 by an English maker,
intended for quiet practicing.*

The violin is a complex
acoustic system consisting
of two sound-producing
elements: vibrating strings
and a resonating soundbox.
By amplifying the basic
vibration frequencies of the
strings and their overtones, the
soundbox actually determines
the general sounding qualities
of the instrument. The effect
of the varnish, from golden
to reddish-brown in color
improves its acoustic
characteristics.

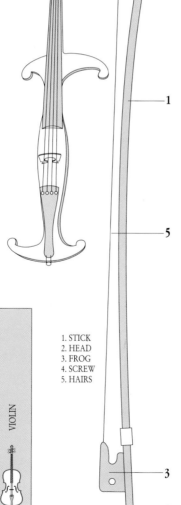

1. STICK
2. HEAD
3. FROG
4. SCREW
5. HAIRS

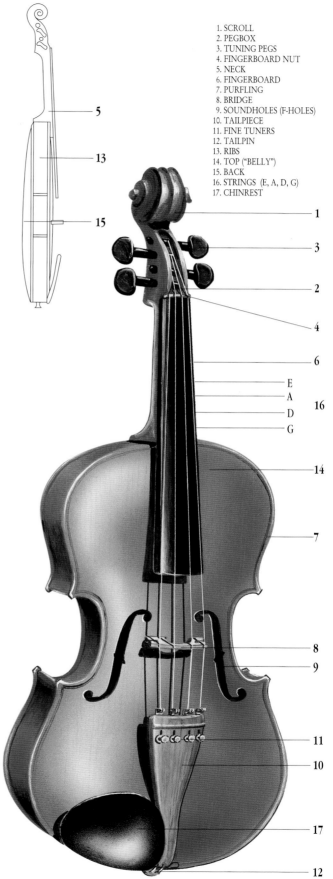

1. SCROLL
2. PEGBOX
3. TUNING PEGS
4. FINGERBOARD NUT
5. NECK
6. FINGERBOARD
7. PURFLING
8. BRIDGE
9. SOUNDHOLES (F-HOLES)
10. TAILPIECE
11. FINE TUNERS
12. TAILPIN
13. RIBS
14. TOP ("BELLY")
15. BACK
16. STRINGS (E, A, D, G)
17. CHINREST

DOUBLE BASS
CELLO
VIOLA
VIOLIN

Construction

The main parts of the body (soundbox) are the top or "belly," the back, and the ribs made of well-seasoned spruce. Inside the soundbox, narrow strips line the ribs, and six blocks are glued to the corners, the top, and the bottom.

A piece of spruce called the bass-bar is glued lengthwise to the inside of the belly, strengthening it and helping distribute the vibrations across it. The soundpost, a round stick also made of spruce, is placed inside the soundbox beneath the right foot of the bridge to transmit vibrations to the back and improve the resonating qualities of the soundbox.

The bow, held by a "frog" in the right hand, consists of a curved wooden stick and a band of horsehair that sounds the strings when drawn across them.

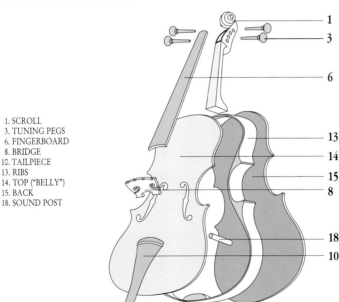

1. SCROLL
3. TUNING PEGS
6. FINGERBOARD
8. BRIDGE
10. TAILPIECE
13. RIBS
14. TOP ("BELLY")
15. BACK
18. SOUND POST

Restoration

In the second half of the 20th century, the antiques business showed an increasing interest in violins made by the great European luthiers. This focused attention on the profession of the restoration expert. On the basis of an instrument's appearance, its sound qualities, and various other details, the restorer is able to determine its age, school, perhaps even its maker. Some of the best-known violins, named after their present or former owners (usually virtuoso violinists) have well-documented biographies establishing their authenticity. Traditionally, a maker puts a label giving his name and the place and date of manufacture inside the instrument, on the inside of the back where it can be seen through the left f-hole.

There are in existence, however, both anonymous historical instruments, lacking a label of this sort, as well as new instruments bearing forged labels to increase their commercial value. Also, the best modern makers are able to create exact copies of old Italian masterpieces, and sometimes these appear on the market as newly-discovered rarities by early Italian luthiers. Authentic modern instruments may have a label indicating that the construction has been based on a model by an old master. This approach has been widely adopted and is not regarded as forgery.

In the modern symphony orchestra there are two violin sections, each playing separate parts. The first violin section, with the leader (concertmaster) sitting directly to the left of the conductor, has 16 – 20 players, while the second violins number 14 – 18.

REPERTORY

The first works in which the violin is used as a solo instrument appeared in Italy and Germany in the late 17th and early 18th centuries, during the Baroque period. Solo sonatas by Biber, trio sonatas by Corelli and Vitali, the numerous solo concertos and concertos for two, three, and four violins by Vivaldi, and the sonatas by Veracini, Geminiani, Locatelli, and Tartini (including the famous *Devil's Trill*) all anticipate the rich repertory of violin works that was to come.

At about the same time, Bach composed two violin concertos and a set of three sonatas and three partitas for solo violin. Handel composed sonatas for one and two violins, as did Telemann and various other composers. The Classical period is particularly rich in works written for this instrument, including Haydn's three concertos, Mozart's seven concertos and 34 sonatinas, Beethoven's Violin Concerto, Triple Concerto, 10 sonatas (including op. 47, the *Kreutzer Sonata*) and two romances. Among the important 19th- and 20-century violin concertos are those by Mendelssohn, Saint-Saëns, Brahms, Bruch, Wieniawski, Tchaikovsky, Dvořák, Elgar, Sibelius, Szymanowski, Bartok, Stravinsky, Berg, Prokofiev, Shostakovich, Hindemith, and Penderecki.

NICOLÒ PAGANINI

(1782 – 1840)

The famous virtuoso Nicolò Paganini produced no fewer than seven concertos for violin and orchestra and 24 caprices for solo violin. The Caprice no. 24 in A minor has been used as a variation theme by a number of composers, including Brahms, Rakhmaninov, and Lutoslawski. Benny Goodman recorded his own version of this theme with his swing orchestra.

Pablo Sarasate
was the first violinist to make a phonographic record, in Odessa, Russia, in 1879. The phonograph had been invented only two years earlier by Thomas Edison. The recording is kept at the Glinka Museum in Moscow. Later, Sarasate also made gramophone recordings under much better technical conditions.

The following violinists are among the virtuosos of the 20th century who made their art famous around the world:

Fritz Kreisler (1875 – 1962), the link between the last great violinists of the Romantic age and modern times, and the first to perform Elgar's Violin Concerto.

Jascha Heifetz (1901 – 1987), a virtuoso for whom works were especially composed, such as Walton's Violin Concerto.

David Oistrakh (1908 – 1974), the most famous post-war Russian violinist. Prokofiev and Shostakovich composed works for him.

Yehudi Menuhin (1916 – 1999), the violinist of the century who taught countless young musicians in the school he founded in 1963, Bârtok composed a sonata for him.

Isaac Stern (1920 – 2001) was both an outstanding soloist and active chamber musician. Peter Maxwell Davies dedicated his violin concerto to Stern.

Itzhak Perlman (b. 1945) began his brilliant solo career with a concert in Carnegie Hall in 1963.

Viola

IT.: ALTO, VIOLA, FR.: ALTO, VIOLA, GER.: VIOLA, BRATSCHE, SP.: ALTO, VIOLA, RU.: AL'T

A bowed stringed instrument of the violin family, slightly larger than the violin but held and played in the same way. The size of the viola is not completely standardized, but its body is usually 6.5 cm longer than that of the violin. For the sake of uniformity of violin and viola technique, the practice of using a violin bow has recently been introduced among violists, but there are also violinists who prefer using the slightly heavier viola bow.

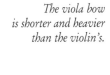

The viola bow is shorter and heavier than the violin's.

Early guitar-shaped viola.

The viola poses considerable challenges to luthiers. Its body length varies according to the preferences of individual players, and the proportions of the instrument vary as a result. Violas may be anything between 38 and 44 cm, though most are about 42 cm long.

Old fiddle-shaped viola.

The viola's four strings are tuned in perfect fifths: c, g, d^1, a^1. Its music is notated in the alto clef but for higher parts it moves into the treble clef. The viola is tuned a fifth lower than the violin and its range is c – a^3. Its sound is fuller and more mellow than the violin's.

Modern viola.

Early viol bridge.   *Modern viola bridge.*

Early viols and modern violas differ in their shapes and bridges.

REPERTORY

For a long time, the viola was considered an instrument of secondary importance in the orchestra. Berlioz devoted more attention to it, writing a symphony for viola and orchestra, *Harold in Italy*, for Paganini in 1834 (Paganini never performed it). Mozart also contributed to the viola repertory with his *Sinfonia concertante*, K. 364, for violin, viola, and orchestra. Debussy, Hindemith, Bartók, Martin, Walton, and the more recent composers Schnittke and Cancelli also added to the relatively small viola repertory, inspired by various virtuoso players.

BÉLA BARTÓK
(1881 – 1945)

*Yuri Bashmet,
the charismatic violist who raised this instrument's
prestige to an unprecedented level.*

The timbre of the viola also gives rise to a number of problems, in that its A string should not sound like that of the violin, nor its C string like the corresponding register on the cello.

The best viola players tend to be former violinists. As violas are not produced in smaller sizes, children learn to play on suitably sized violins, and only move on to the viola at a later age.

Within the orchestra, the violas are usually placed between the high-pitched violins and the lower-pitched cellos and double basses. The viola is mainly used to provide the middle part of the string texture, though it often functions as a solo voice. The viola section of the modern symphony orchestra consists of 10 to 12 players.

SYMPHONY ORCHESTRA

Violoncello

IT.: VIOLONCELLO, FR.: VIOLONCELLE, GER.: VIOLONCELLO, SP.: VIOLONCELO, RU.: VIOLONCHEL'

The cello is the commonly-used name for the violoncello, a low-pitched bowed stringed instrument of the violin family. Its shape and proportions are similar to those of the violin, its body about twice the violin's length, its sides about four times as deep, with a relatively longer neck. Its total length is 1.55 – 1.56 m, the body accounting for 0.76 m.
While adult players use full-size cellos, smaller cellos also exist, including half, three-quarters, and seven-eighths sizes. The instrument is held at an angle against the chest, between the knees of the player, who is always seated. In earlier centuries it was gripped almost vertically between the knees or even played standing (in church processions), but by the mid-19th century the requirements of the playing technique in the higher register necessitated a more stable support, and a metal endpin was introduced that supported it from the floor. The bow of the cello is similar to that of the violin, but somewhat shorter and heavier.

Early cello.

Mstislav Rostropovich,
playing in front of the Berlin Wall. Rostropovich, the first cellist to perform works written especially for him by Britten, Shostakovich, and Prokofiev, has carried through into the 21st century the noble image of the cello established by the great Pablo Casals. One of his instruments, an old Italian cello by Stradivari, has been the object of endless curiosity since the time of Napoleon, who unwittingly scratched it with his spur in a half-serious attempt to play it.

Owing to its wide range and extreme versatility, the cello is second only to the violin as a solo instrument within the violin family. In the orchestra and in chamber ensembles it functions both as the bass part and as a melodic instrument. The cello's sound is warm, intimate, and expressive, resembling the human voice, making it a favorite with Romantic composers.
Widely used as a solo and a chamber instrument, there are numerous works for the cello. Solo works for cello written in the 20th century probably outnumber those for the violin, leading to the suspicion that the cello repertory has not been fully studied or performed. At the same time, modern luthiers build excellent replicas of older instruments, turning attention to early cello works as well.
The cello is tuned an octave below the viola, in fifths: C, G, d, a. Music for the cello is notated in the bass clef, moving to tenor and treble clef for the higher tones. The instrument's range is C – e^3, but higher tones are also used in modern works for solo cello.

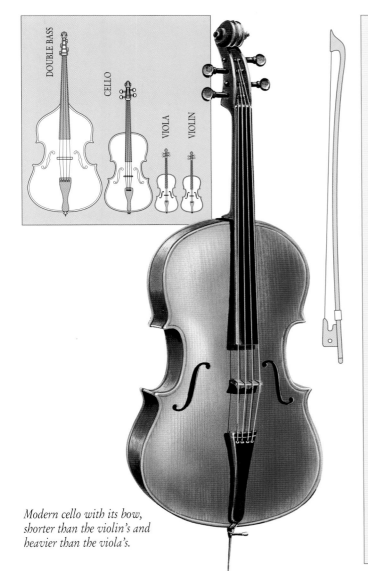

Modern cello with its bow, shorter than the violin's and heavier than the viola's.

REPERTORY

The first solo works for cello were written in the 1680's by Domenico Gabrielli, an early cellist-composer. The cello repertory was further enriched by Locatelli, Vivaldi, and many other composers with sonatas and concertos. Bach's six suites for cello alone have a special place in the repertory, and are extremely popular with virtuosos. Cello music was also composed by Haydn, Boccherini, and Bernhard Heinrich Romberg. Beethoven, too, recognized the instrument's potential in his five sonatas and three variation sets, and entrusted it with the main theme in his Symphony no. 3. Romantic composers devoted a great deal of attention to the cello, as evidenced by the concertos of Saint-Saëns, Schumann, Dvořák, and Lalo, the sonatas of Mendelssohn, Chopin, Rakhmaninov, Brahms, and Grieg, and Tchaikovsky's Variations on a Rococo Theme.

In the 20th century, the cello repertory was further enriched by solo works by Honegger, Hindemith, Debussy, Kodály, Webern, Prokofiev, Shostakovich, Xenakis, Britten, and Penderecki.

JOHANN SEBASTIAN BACH
(1685–1750)

For a long time, the cello had a limited use within the Baroque orchestra, playing only the basso continuo with the double bass, the bassoon, and the harpsichord. By the end of the 18th century, after a prolonged controversy, particularly in France, it took the place of the old tenor viola da gamba. The cello won recognition first in the trio sonata, then in the string quartet, and finally in the symphony orchestra, where the cello section usually has 10-12 players.

Double bass

IT.: CONTRABBASSO, FR.: CONTREBASSE, GER.: KONTRABASS, SP.: CONTRABAJO, RU.: KONTRABAS

The double bass is the largest and the lowest-pitched bowed stringed instrument of the violin family. Its total length (without the endpin) is 1.80 – 1.90 m. The size varies depending on the instrument's use and on the player's preferences, but generally an orchestral bass is larger than the solo instrument. Similarly to the cello, the double bass is held almost vertically and slanting back slightly, with the player standing or seated on a high stool. The metal endpin holding the instrument off the floor is shorter than that of the cello. In its shape and its tuning in fourths, the double bass resembles the old knee-held viols, particularly the bass viola da gamba, known as violone in Italy, the country of its origin.

Two types of bows are used, each with its own technique: French and German.

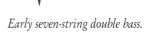

The German bow is shorter and stouter, with a relatively wider and higher frog, and is held with the palm facing upwards. It is known by the name of Franz Simandl of Vienna, who introduced this type of bow in 1874. In form and playing method, the German bass bow is similar to the old-fashioned viola da gamba bows. Simandl's technique produces a stronger and fuller sound but allows for less flexibility.
It is therefore suitable for orchestral performances.

The French bow, introduced by François Tourte the younger, is lighter and has a lower frog. It is held with the palm facing downwards, like the cello bow, to which it is very similar.
The player's hand is therefore more mobile and finer nuances can be produced. This type is largely used in France, Britain, and the U. S.

Modern double bass.

Early seven-string double bass.

The double bass is tuned in perfect fourths to E^1, A^1, D, and G, and its music is notated an octave higher than it sounds. Five-stringed double basses with an additional C^1-string are also used. If there is no such instrument in the orchestra, the low E^1-string is tuned down to C^1 (scordatura).

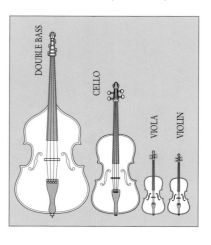

Construction

Because the double bass is so large, it has to be constructed somewhat differently from the other members of the violin family. Massive rings strengthen the body from the inside, and four spruce sticks are glued below the lower part of the belly. As the long, thick strings are very taut, the pegs are turned with the help of small metal cogwheels.

Double basses with sloping shoulders, typical of Germany in the 18th century, bear a resemblance to the old violas da gamba. Those with more curved, rounded shoulders look more like the other instruments of the violin family. The latter were popular in Italy and are widely used today.

REPERTORY

The double bass repertory is not very extensive, though its role in the orchestra developed through the works of Beethoven (the Scherzo of his Symphony No. 5, the recitative in the fourth movement of his Symphony No. 9), Verdi (*Don Carlos*, *Otello*), Saint-Saëns (*Carnival of the Animals*). It also appeared in quintets by Dvořák and Schubert (the *Trout Quintet*). As a solo instrument it was used by Mozart (Aria for bass and double bass), Carl Ditters von Dittersdorf, Domenico Dragonetti, Giovanni Bottesini, Franz Simandl, and Sergey Koussevitsky (concertos for double bass with orchestra).

GIUSEPPE VERDI
(1813 – 1901)

Niels-Henning Ørsted Pedersen was the uncontested leader among double bass players in late 20th-century jazz.

In the Baroque orchestra the double bass was part of the basso continuo.
In the Classical and modern symphony orchestra, it plays the sub-bass part of the bowed stringed group, usually an octave below the cellos. The double bass section of the modern symphony orchestra includes from six to ten players.

SYMPHONY ORCHESTRA

Harp

IT.: ARPA, FR.: HARPE, GER.: HARFE, SP.: ARPA, RU.: ARFA

The modern pedal harp is the descendant of the oldest stringed instrument from the earliest period of human civilization. The harp made its debut in the symphony orchestra in 1830 in Berlioz's *Symphonie fantastique*. The composer had intended to include six harps in the orchestra, but in the end used only two.

The harp is roughly triangular, 1.75 – 1.90 m in height, and unlike other finger-plucked stringed instruments, has no fingerboard. Its construction includes a pillar (column), an s-shaped neck, and a sloping soundboard. The strings are parallel to the pillar, and number 46 or 47. For the player's convenience, all C strings are colored red, and F strings blue. The strings for the high and middle registers are made of gut and those for the low register of steel or silk sheathed with brass; this is why the 11 – 12 lowest (bass) strings are referred to as "metal."

The seven pedals are installed at the base of the harp, where the pillar meets the soundboard. The harp mechanism is extremely complicated, consisting of some 1,415 pieces.

The harp stands on the floor between the player's knees and is tilted back to rest on the right shoulder. The right hand normally plays in the treble range and the left in the bass, though both hands may be used over the instrument's entire range.

The harp is essentially a diatonic instrument. Chromatic changes may be made with the pedals, but time must be allowed for their operation. There is a pedal for each note of the scale, each pedal having three positions, tuning the strings to flat, natural, and sharp respectively. The harp's range is C^1–g^4 and its music is notated on two staves, like that of the piano. There is no marked difference of sound quality when the harp changes registers.

Early harp.

Since ancient times, a gentle but rapid sliding of the fingers over the strings, known as glissando, has been a popular effect on many types of harp. On the modern pedal harp, glissandos can be executed in any key or scale type simply by repositioning the pedals. By contrast, a scale in glissando is possible on the piano only in C Major (by sliding over the white keys).

Nowadays the harp has a wide application as a solo, ensemble and orchestra instrument. It is a frequent member of the symphony orchestra although its presence is not a must. Usually one harp (less often two) is used as an instrument with quiet, tender and delicate sound. In the symphony orchestra the harp takes one of the most poetic and colorful parts.

1. PILLAR (COLUMN)
2. BASE
3. NECK
4. TUNING PINS
5. DISCS
6. STRINGS
7. SOUNDBOARD
8. PEDALS
9. FEET

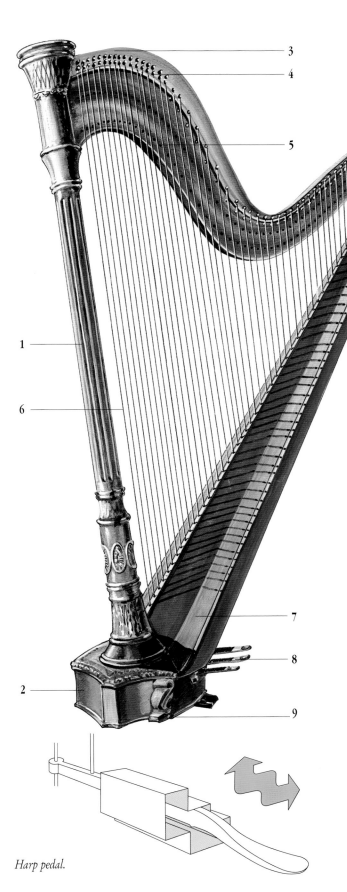

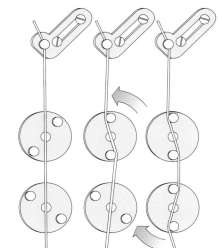

Movement of the discs activated by the pedals.

REPERTORY

The harp became a regular member of the orchestra in the 19th century. One of its first orchestral solos was in the Act I Fountain Scene of Donizetti's opera *Lucia di Lammermoor* (1834). Important works for it include concertos by Handel, Mozart (Concerto for Flute and Harp, K. 299), and Saint-Saëns (Concert Piece for Harp and Orchestra, op. 154, Fantasie, op. 95), Fauré (Impromptu, op. 86), Debussy's Sonata for Flute, Viola, and Harp. Among other authors of notable works should be mentioned Maurice Ravel (*Introduction and Allegro* for Harp, String Quartet, Flute and Clarinet), Hindemith (Harp Sonata), Britten, Bax (Quintet for Harp and String), Krenek, Ginastera, Gliere, and Villa-Lobos (Concerto for Harp and orchestra), Lutoslawski, Henze (Double Concerto for Harp, Oboe and Strings), and Schnittke. Among the avant-garde compositions ranks *Sequenza II* by Luciano Berio.

MAURICE RAVEL

(1875 – 1937)

Harp pedal.

Piano, Grand Piano

IT.: PIANOFORTE, PIANO A CODA, FR.: PIANO DROIT, PIANO À QUEUE, GER.: PIANINO, KLAVIER, FLÜGEL,
SP.: PIANO VERTICAL, PIANO DE COLA, RU.: PIANINO, FORTEP'YANO, ROYAL'

The grand piano is the largest portable musical instrument. The most significant difference between the grand piano and the upright piano is that the iron frame is horizontal in the former and vertical in the latter. Both the grand and the upright are keyboard instruments with a mechanism that sets the strings into vibration using felt-tipped hammers.
Because it is a chordal instrument with an extended range, capable of sounding many tones simultaneously, it is possible to "reduce" even the most complex orchestral scores on the piano.

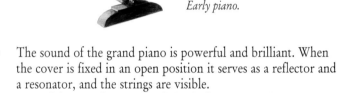

Early piano.

The piano's exceptional technical potential, rich sound, and wide range make it indispensable in all musical activities: composing, conducting, performing, and teaching. The accumulation of an extensive piano repertory began in the 19th century and continued throughout the 20th as a result of the piano's wide use as a solo instrument, in symphony, opera, and chamber orchestras, in dance music, in popular music and jazz, and occasionally in folk music. Hector Berlioz was the first to include the piano in the symphony orchestra and it soon became a permanent member.

The main representative of the piano family – the grand piano – is the most frequently used in concert practice and often in the symphony orchestra as well. Its wing-like shape is related to the length of the strings that are stretched on the iron frame. The shortest strings produce the highest notes, and the longest ones the lowest notes. A key may sound up to three strings producing the same note; in the lower octaves the strings are two per note, and the lowest notes are sounded by single strings. Depending on their use, the grand pianos are produced in various versions: concert, study, salon, and so on. The largest ones may be up to 3 m long, and the smallest ones are about 1.1 – 1.2 m long.

The sound of the grand piano is powerful and brilliant. When the cover is fixed in an open position it serves as a reflector and a resonator, and the strings are visible.

One of the upright piano varieties is the concert piano. Its sound is more powerful than the ordinary instrument's, and its range is like the concert grand piano's.

There are two kinds of piano string: steel for the high register and steel sheathed with copper wire for the low register. The length of the bass strings means that they have to be strung at an angle across the treble strings. The total number of strings is 225 – 230.

Though mostly used as a solo instrument and for accompaning other instruments, since the beginning of the 20th century the piano is a frequent member of the symphony orchestra.

To the two pedals, of which the left one mutes the sound and the right one makes it sound longer (or may interrupt it gradually or abruptly: when the pedal is pressed, all dampers are released, and when the pedal is released, all dampers interrupt the strings' vibration), a third one was added. It was perfected by Henry Steinway, and its function is to prolong some notes and eliminate others. The piano pedals were first introduced by Stein in 1789.

By comparison with the clavichord and the harpsichord, the piano is a much richer instrument in terms of both tone color and dynamics. Piano music is notated on two staves, in treble and bass clef. The instrument's range includes a total of 88 tones, A^2-c^5.

Glenn Gould playing, 1959.
The 20th century was marked by the interpretational talent of virtuoso pianists such as Vladimir Horowitz (1904 – 1989), Glenn Gould (1932 – 1982), Sviatoslav Richter (1915 – 1997), Artur Rubinstein (1886 – 1982) and many others, each of them having made a unique contribution to piano art.

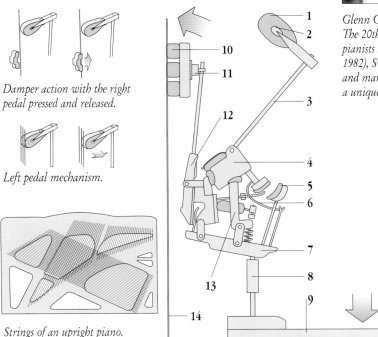

Damper action with the right pedal pressed and released.

Left pedal mechanism.

Strings of an upright piano.

1. HAMMER FELT
2. HAMMER CORE
3. HAMMER SHANK
4. BUTT OF HAMMER
5. CHECK
6. TAPE
7. SUPPORT
8. PILOT
9. KEY
10. DAMPER PADS
11. DAMPER HEAD
12. DAMPER HOLDER
13. ESCAPEMENT
14. STRING

Upright piano action.

The range of the piano expanded as the instrument developed. Bartolomeo Cristofori's early 18th-century model covered four octaves ($C-c^3$). In the second half of the century (the time of Mozart) another octave was added (F^1-f^3). In the early 19th century (the time of Beethoven) the range was five and a half octaves (F^1-c^4), and in the second quarter of the century (the time of Chopin) it was six and a half octaves (C^1-f^4). In the second half of the 19th century the piano was close to its present range, covering seven octaves (A^2-a^4), which were extended to seven octaves and a third (A^2-c^5) in 1860.

In modern music, a so-called "prepared" piano is sometimes used, with paper or sonorous objects placed on the strings, or with tacks driven into the hammers to produce specific sound effects.

Modern piano.

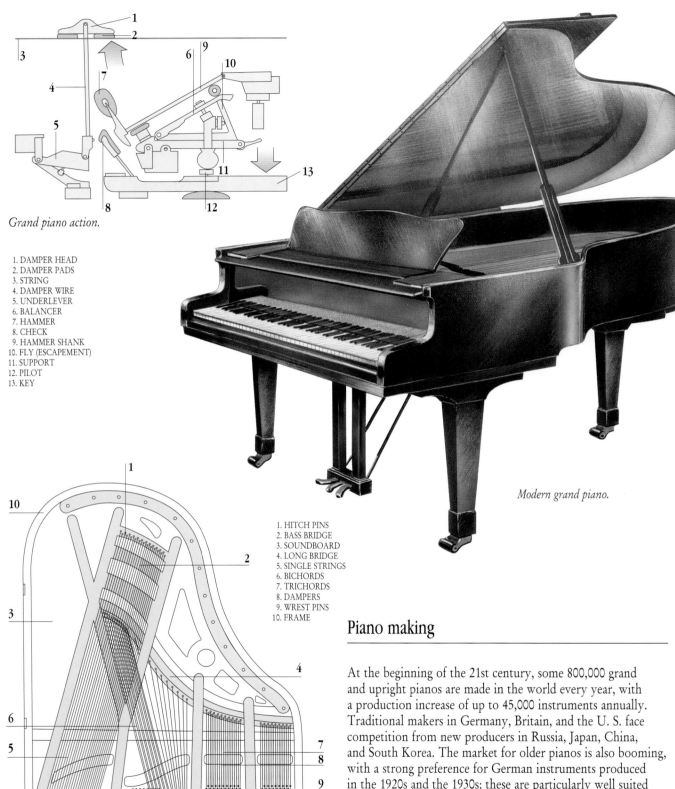

Grand piano action.

1. DAMPER HEAD
2. DAMPER PADS
3. STRING
4. DAMPER WIRE
5. UNDERLEVER
6. BALANCER
7. HAMMER
8. CHECK
9. HAMMER SHANK
10. FLY (ESCAPEMENT)
11. SUPPORT
12. PILOT
13. KEY

1. HITCH PINS
2. BASS BRIDGE
3. SOUNDBOARD
4. LONG BRIDGE
5. SINGLE STRINGS
6. BICHORDS
7. TRICHORDS
8. DAMPERS
9. WREST PINS
10. FRAME

Modern grand piano.

Piano making

At the beginning of the 21st century, some 800,000 grand and upright pianos are made in the world every year, with a production increase of up to 45,000 instruments annually. Traditional makers in Germany, Britain, and the U. S. face competition from new producers in Russia, Japan, China, and South Korea. The market for older pianos is also booming, with a strong preference for German instruments produced in the 1920s and the 1930s; these are particularly well suited to domestic use.

Among the makers with a well-deserved international reputation are Bechstein, Bösendorfer, Blüthner, Steinway, and Yamaha.

REPERTORY

The piano repertory is certainly the largest of all instrumental repertories. Within this immense body of works, ranging from song accompaniments to concertos with orchestra, the following composers and works stand out:

Clementi: One hundred piano etudes, *Gradus ad Parnassum*.

Haydn: numerous concertos and sonatas.

Mozart: 27 concertos, 18 sonatas, many other solo pieces.

Beethoven: five concertos, 32 sonatas (including the *Pathétique*, the *Moonlight*, the *Waldstein*, the *Appassionata*, and *Les Adieux*), the *Diabelli Variations*, many other pieces.

Hummel: eight concertos and some 80 solo pieces.

Schubert: sonatas, *Moments musicaux*, *Impromptus*, duets.

Mendelssohn: concertos, *Songs without Words*, many other pieces.

Chopin: two concertos, polonaises, mazurkas, waltzes, preludes, ballades, fantasies, studies.

Schumann: a concerto, *Carnaval*, *Noveletten*, *Études symphoniques*, *Kinderszenen*.

Liszt: two concertos, sonatas, ballades, Hungarian rhapsodies, piano transcriptions of works by other composers (including Beethoven's symphonies).

Franck: *Variations symphoniques*, solo pieces.

Brahms: two concertos, sonatas, ballades, intermezzos, capriccios, variations on themes of other composers.

Saint-Saëns: five concertos, studies, other solo pieces.

Tchaikovsky: three concertos, more than 100 solo pieces.

Grieg: a concerto, *Norwegian Dances*, *Lyric Pieces*.

Fauré: *Fantasie*, *Impromptus*, *Nocturnes*.

Albéniz: *Ibéria*.

WOLFGANG AMADEUS MOZART
(1756–1791)

Debussy: 24 preludes, *Images*, and others.

Scriabin: concerto, poemes, etudes.

Granados: *Danzas espanolas*.

Rakhmaninov: four concertos, *Rhapsody on a Theme of Paganini*, preludes.

Schönberg: *Drei Klavierstücke*, op.11, a concerto, a suite, other solo pieces.

Ravel: Concerto in G, Concerto for the left hand, solo pieces.

Falla: *Nights in the Gardens of Spain*, *Four Spanish Pieces*.

Stravinski: Sonata and Concerto.

Bartók: three concertos, a sonata, *Microcosm* - a set of 153 piano pieces for children.

Szymanovski: three sonatas, *Symphonie concertante*.

Webern: variations, short serial pieces.

Hindemith: *Ludus Tonalis*.

Prokofiev: five concertos, nine sonatas.

Milhaud: two sonatas, other solo pieces.

Sessions: three sonatas and a concerto.

Poulenc: a concerto, *Trois mouvements perpétuels*, other solo pieces.

Copland: a concerto, *Piano Variations*, other solo pieces.

Shostakovich: two concertos, two sonatas.

Messiaen: *Le Reveil des Oiseaux*, *Oiseaux exotiques*, *Vings regards sur l'enfant Jésus*.

Boulez: three sonatas, *Structures I, II* for two pianos.

Cage: *Music of Changes*, works for prepared piano.

LUDWIG VAN BEETHOVEN
(1770–1827)

PERCUSSIONS

Timpani (Kettledrums)

IT.: TIMPANI, FR.: TIMBALES, GER.: PAUKEN, SP.: TIMBALES, RU.: LITAVRY

Resembling two large cauldrons with different diameters, the timpani are the backbone of the percussion section of the opera and symphony orchestra. The shell is made of copper, brass or a light metal, and the membrane (formerly of skin, now of plastic) is stretched across a metal hoop on top. An opening at the bottom of the shell allows the air to escape.

19th-century machine timpani.

1. DRUM HEAD
2. TUNING GAUGE
3. SHELL
4. SUPPORTING STRUTS
5. CROWN
6. FOOT PEDAL CHANGES PITCH OF DRUM
7. BEATERS

Timpani are played with two reed or wooden beaters with felt, leather, wood, or rubber heads, the different materials producing different shades of sound. The "batter" area begins about 2 cm from the rim, and extends for some 8 – 12 cm; the center and the outer area of the membrane are not used. The timbre can also be modified by placing a piece of soft cloth on the opposite side of the membrane.

Berlioz made imaginative use of timpani, using four of them tuned to a chord in his *Symphonie fantastique*. In the *Tuba mirum* movement of his *Grande messe des morts* he called for as many as 16. A larger number of drums allows not only for a louder, more dramatic sound, but also for the playing of melodic figures.

S Y M P H O N Y   O R C H E S T R A

Timpani are retuned by tensioning the membrane: the tauter the membrane, the higher the tone produced, and vice versa. Timpani are subdivided into hand-screw timpani, rotary timpani, and pedal timpani, according to the tuning mechanism used. Pedal timpani are used in the modern symphony orchestra, as this method of tuning leaves the player's hands free for quick retuning.

Timpani have been part of the opera and symphony orchestra since the mid-18th century. In the Classical period, two timpani were used to emphasize the main harmonies and were tuned to the tonic and dominant respectively. Beethoven broke with convention and extended the role of percussion instruments, giving them greater prominence within the orchestral fabric. Percussion instruments were also affected by the general tendency to divide instruments within all sections of the orchestra into high, medium, and low. Timpani are divided into large, medium, small, and piccolo, with respective ranges of E – c/d, A – e, c – f/g, and g – c¹.

Bass Drum

IT.: GRAN CASSA, FR.: GROSSE CAISSE, GER.: GROSSE TROMMEL, SP.: BOMBO, RU.: BOL'SHOY BARABAN

The lowest-pitched membranophone in the percussion section of the symphony orchestra, the bass drum consists of a cylindrical shell with a skin or plastic membrane stretched on a wooden hoop at each end. The tension is adjusted by means of screws. A single-head bass drum of large diameter but very little depth, with a membrane stretched over only one of its ends, is also used in the modern symphony orchestra.

The drum is sounded by a beater with a felt- or leather-covered end. The beater is held in the right hand, while the left hand stops the vibration of the skin when necessary. The bass drum can also be sounded by two beaters, one on each head. Mozart, Mahler, and other composers suggested the use of a smaller beater in the left hand, similar to the stick used to strike the Turkish davul (a bass drum).

Side Drum, Snare Drum

IT.: TAMBURO PICCOLO, TAMBURO MILITARE, FR.: CAISSE CLAIRE, GER.: SOLDATENTROMMEL, KLEINE TROMMEL,
SP.: TAMBOR, CAJA MILITAR, RU.: MALY BARABAN

The side drum is a double-head membranophone of indefinite pitch. Its construction is the same as that of the bass drum, but it differs in size, in the way it is played, and in the size and shape of the beaters. The lower or snare head is crossed by strings or spiraled wires, which muffle the sound and give the instrument a distinctive timbre with a characteristic crack.

The upper head is the batter head. The side drum is played with two beaters made of hardwood (ebony, rosewood, or hornbeam), that taper to a round or egg-shaped head. The sound of the side drum is short and crisp, and is suited to playing a variety of rhythmic figures. Its roll is particularly impressive. As in the case of the bass drum, the sound may be muffled by draping the batter head with a cloth. Most side drums have a mute (sordino) inside, that makes the instrument sound hollow and grim. Of all the percussion instruments, the side drum is the most popular and a member of a variety of ensembles, from military bands to rock groups.

Glockenspiel

IT.: CARIGLIONE, FR.: CARILLON, JEU DE TIMBRES, GER.: GLOCKENSPIEL, SP.: CARILLON, RU.: KOLOKOLCHIKI

A set of metal idiophones of varying sizes, the glockenspiel is tuned in a chromatic scale. The metal bars can either be arranged like a piano keyboard and struck directly with hammers (hammer glockenspiel) or encased in a cabinet resembling a small piano and sounded with piano-like keys (keyboard glockenspiel).

Metal idiophones tuned to a particular note, the chime-bells are a chromatic set of metal bars that, depending on their arrangement, are divided into two types:

Keyboard glockenspiel.

Hammer glockenspiel:
The metal bars are arranged in two rows in a specially designed frame, and are played with two metal hammers. The range is two to three octaves, but can be larger depending on the size of the instrument. In a variant of this instrument, the bell lyre, the frame and the rows of metal bars are vertical. Shaped like an ancient lyre and richly decorated, the bell lyre is used in military bands and has an ornamental as well as a musical function.

1. FRAME
2. METAL BARS
3. METAL BEATERS
4. STAND

Keyboard glockenspiel. This is equipped with a more elaborate mechanism, similar to that of the piano. The sound of this type of glockenspiel is weaker than that of the hammer glockenspiel, but it allows for the playing of faster and more complicated figures. A damper is provided to stop the vibration when necessary. When this type of glockenspiel is used in the modern symphony orchestra, it is played by a pianist.

SYMPHONY ORCHESTRA

Xylophone

IT.: XILOFONO, FR.: XYLOPHONE, CLAQUEBOIS, GER.: XYLOPHON, HOLZHARMONIKA, SP.: XILÓFONO, RU.: KSILOFON

The xylophone is an instrument consisting of tuned wooden bars (42 – 48) arranged in two rows on a frame of trapezoidal shape. The bars are usually made of very hard, heavy wood, such as ebony, rosewood, walnut, acacia, or cedar, though they may be also made of plastic. They are threaded on a cord, with rubber discs between them to provide free vibration. The threaded bars are laid on five bundles of straw, felt, or rubber, isolating them from the frame and allowing for the free vibration of the whole instrument.

1. STAND
2. WOODEN BARS
3. RESONATORS
4. BEATERS

The xylophone is played with two beaters, that have spherical ends of wood or plastics. Its range is either four octaves, from c^1 to c^5, or three and a half, from f^1 or g^1 to c^5 but modern xylophones may reach a range of five octaves. Each tone produced is of very brief duration. In the two-row xylophone the bars are arranged like piano keys, and the playing technique is identical to that of the other two-row percussion instruments.

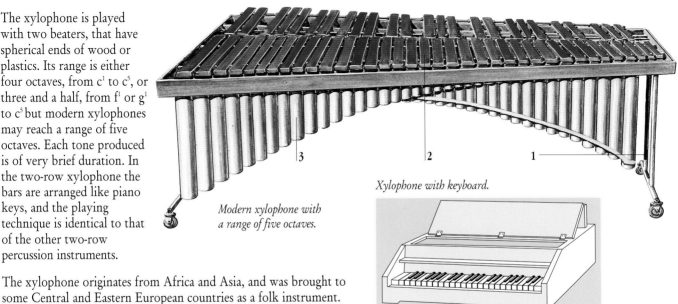

Modern xylophone with a range of five octaves.

Xylophone with keyboard.

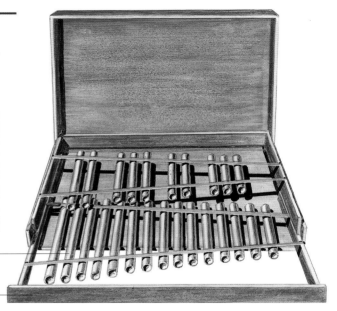

The xylophone originates from Africa and Asia, and was brought to some Central and Eastern European countries as a folk instrument. It was introduced into the symphony orchestra by Humperdinck in his opera *Hansel and Gretel* and by Saint-Saëns in his *Danse macabre*.

Tubaphone

IT.: TUBAFONO, FR.: TUBAPHONE, CLAQUEBOIS, GER.: TUBAPHON,
SP.: TUBAFONO, RU.: TUBAFON

The only difference between the xylophone and the tubaphone is that in the latter the xylophone's wooden bars are replaced by between 12 and 36 metal tubes, laid out in four or two rows. Each tone produced is longer and more melodious sounding than those of the xylophone. The instrument was created in the 20th century. A fine example of its use is in Khachaturian's Sabre Dance from *Gayane*.

1. BOX
2. METAL TUBES
3. BEATERS

Marimba

IT.: MARIMBA, MARIMBAFONO, SILORIMBA, FR.: MARIMBA, MARIMBAPHONE, SYLORIMBA,
GER.: MARIMBA, MARIMBAPHON, XYLORIMBA, SP.: MARIMBA, RU.: MARIMBA, MARIMBAFON, KSILORIMBA

The marimba is a more advanced version of the xylophone. It is similar to the vibraphone, except that the bars are made of wood rather than metal and the tubular resonators have no fans inside.

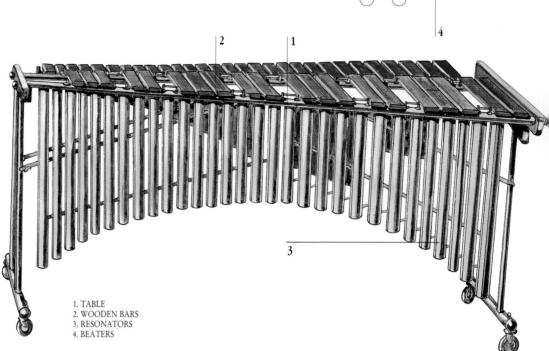

The instrument covers four chromatic octaves (c – c^4). The marimba was created in the U. S. in 1910, on the model of an African folk instrument of the same name. The earliest models were known as "marimbaphones." The marimba made its way into symphonic and chamber music around the time of World War II, but was not used very frequently. It is found in Messiaen's *Chronochromie*, Tippett's Symphony no. 4, Milhaud's Concerto for Marimba, Vibraphone, and Orchestra, and in a number of works by Henze. The marimba is occasionally used in jazz.

1. TABLE
2. WOODEN BARS
3. RESONATORS
4. BEATERS

Celesta

IT.: CELESTA, CELESTE, FR.: CÉLESTA, GER.: CELESTA, SP.: CELESTA, RU.: CHELESTA

A keyboard metallophone, the celesta looks much like a harmonium or a small piano. Its construction resembles that of the piano, but instead of strings it has metal (or sometimes glass) bars. Initially, this instrument was known as a "Mustel piano" after its creator Victor Mustel. Later, it was perfected by Mustel's son Auguste, who called it celesta.

The celesta's range is c^1 – c^5, its music notated an octave lower than it sounds. The celesta is one of the gentlest-sounding instruments in the symphony orchestra. It was introduced into the orchestra by Tchaikovsky, in *The Dance of the Sugar-Plum Fairy* in *The Nutcracker*, and was later used by Richard Strauss end Bartók.

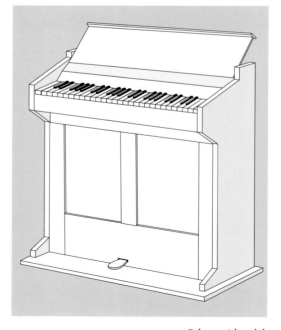

Celesta with pedal.

Vibraphone

IT.: VIBRAFONO, FR.: VIBRAPHONE, CARILLON À LAMES, GER.: VIBRAPHON, SP.: VIBRÁFONO, RU.: VIBRAFON

This is an instrument of tuned metal (aluminium) bars on two long axles, similar to the piano keyboard. Under each bar there is a metal tubular resonator, in the upper end of which a fan is rotated by a noiseless electric motor. The instrument is played with two beaters 35 – 40 cm long, with rubber- or felt-covered ends. The fans rotating in the resonators produce a vibrato effect from which the instrument takes its name. A set of dampers is operated by a pedal and is used to stop the vibrating sound. In some cases the vibraphone is played without the motor for a softer, harder sound.

Electric vibraphone.

The instrument's range is f – f³, and two, three, or four tones may be played simultaneously, depending on the quality of the beaters. Designed in the U. S. by Winterhoff in 1921, the vibraphone was first used for sound effects but gradually developed as a solo instrument.

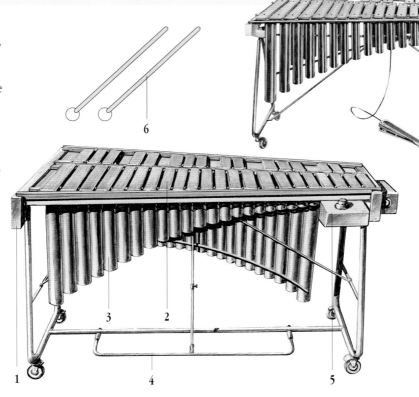

1. TABLE
2. METAL BARS
3. METAL RESONATORS WITH FANS
4. DAMPER PEDAL
5. ELECTRIC MOTOR
6. BEATERS

The first classical work to use the vibraphone was Berg's opera *Lulu*. Milhaud wrote a Concerto for Marimba, Vibraphone, and Orchestra. The vibraphone also appears in the works of Messiaen, Stockhausen, Bernstein, Britten, and Vaughan Williams. It is particularly popular in jazz, mainly in combos.

Cymbals

IT.: PIATTI, FR.: CYMBALES, GER.: BECKEN, SP.: PLATILLOS, RU.: TARELKI

Cymbals consist of a pair of identical discs made of copper, bronze, or a special alloy. They are domed at the center and are held by straps that pass through holes in the boss.
The instrument may be sounded in two ways: by clashing the two discs together, or by striking one of them (often hanging horizontally from a stand) with a beater.

Like the triangle, cymbals were first introduced into the symphony orchestra by Haydn in his "Military" Symphony. They are particularly popular in military, school, and brass bands. Modern jazz has contributed significantly to the instrument's wider use.

Cymbals come in various sizes: small (with a diameter of 25 – 35 cm), medium (37.5 – 45 cm), and large (47.5 – 60 cm). They also vary in thickness: thin, medium, and relatively thick. They are suspended either on a stand with the bass drum or on a stand of their own, and struck at the rim, at the middle, or on the dome with tenor drum beaters, timpani beaters, triangle rods, or wire brushes. A variety of sounds can be produced, depending on the point at which the cymbals are struck. Less frequent are so-called Chinese cymbals, which have a turned-up rim and a diameter of between 30 and 60 cm.

Tam-tam and Gong

IT.: TAM-TAM, FR.: TAM-TAM, GONG, GER.: TAM-TAM, GONG, SP.: TAMTAM, GONG, RU.: TAM-TAM, GONG

A bronze idiophone, the tam-tam is made of a special alloy, created according to a secret formula known only to the Chinese. It is a large bronze disc, thicker at the rim and with a central boss, suspended on a leather strap from a special stand. It is sounded with a spherical hardwood beater with a felt-covered end. The tam-tam is larger in size than the gong, and while the gong is of definite pitch, the tam-tam is not tuned to a particular tone.

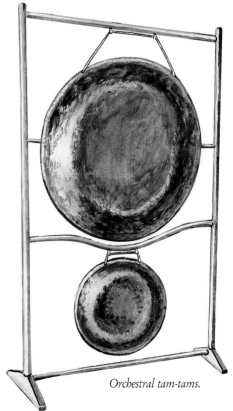

Orchestral tam-tams.

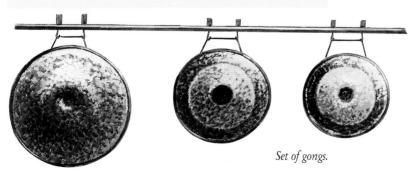

Set of gongs.

This instrument has been used by the composers Gossec, Meyerbeer, Debussy, Rimsky-Korsakov, Mahler, Stravinsky, and others. Stockhausen wrote his *Mikrophonie I* for it.

Bells, Tubular Bells (Chimes)

IT.: CAMPANE, CAMPANE TUBOLARI, FR.: CLOCHES, CLOCHES TUBULAIRES,
GER.: GLOCKEN, RÖHRENGLOCKEN, SP.: CAMPANAS, CAMPANÓLOGO, RU.: KOLOKOLA

Tubular bells in a chromatic set of 13 to 20 are used in the modern opera and symphony orchestras. The instrument consists of tubes of varying length suspended vertically from a frame, in two rows, like the white and black keys of a piano. A pedal damper is used to deaden the vibrations.

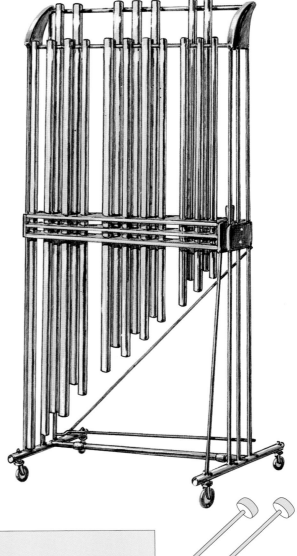

Tubular bells are played with special wooden beaters with leather-covered ends for a mellower sound. The positioning of the tubes allows for the sounding of three or four notes at once. The usual range is $c^1 - f^2$, notated at pitch. In Italy, the so-called Italian or Roman tubular bells have the range $f - c^3$, sounding an octave lower. Church bells (tower bells) are cup-shaped idiophones of definite pitch. They are cast in bronze that is composed of roughly 78% copper and 22% tin, though the exact proportions used by a particular maker are a jealously guarded secret.

Natural bell.

Originating in the East, the bell came to Europe in the 6th century, where it gained great cult significance. A bell's vibration is strongest at the rim where it is hit by the brass beater. As the overtones are not harmonious, bells are sounded in succession rather than simultaneously.

When the sound of a bell is intended to stand out from the orchestra, a church bell is used rather than tubular bells. The type of bell required is specified in the score. Bells have been put to effective orchestral use by Rossini, Berlioz, Wagner, Tchaikovsky, Mussorgsky, Verdi, Puccini, Ravel, and many others.

Sleigh Bells

IT.: SONAGLI, FR.: GRELOTS, CLOCHETTES,
GER.: SCHELLEN, SP.: CASCABEL, RU.: BUBENCHIKI

The bells are mounted on a strip of leather or a piece
of wood with a protruding handle. The bells themselves
are round or slightly flattened, with pellets inside that jingle
when shaken.

Sleigh bells are very popular as
folk instruments. They are used
in religious rites, in dances, and
as an adornment for horses, and
livestock. Their use in the opera
or symphony orchestra is fairly
rare.

Cowbells

IT.: CAMPANACCI, FR.: CLOCHETTES SUISSES, GER.: KUHGLOCKEN, ALMGLOCKEN
SP.: ESQUILA, RU.: ALPYSKIE KOLOKOLA

These bells are 20 – 40 cm
long, slightly flattened,
narrow at the lower end
and bulging at the top, and
have no clapper. Several
differently tuned bells are
suspended from a frame
and struck with wooden
beaters, producing a dull,
muffled sound.

In its modern version, the
cowbell is a longer cone 10 –
15 cm in length, sometimes
slightly flattened and made of
nickel, chromium, or a copper
alloy. Several differently
tuned bells, with or without
clappers, may be suspended
in two rows from a frame,
and either struck with wooden
beaters or shaken.
This instrument was used
by Mozart, Mahler, Richard
Strauss, and various other
composers.

Triangle

IT.: TRIANGOLO, FR.: TRIANGLE, GER.: TRIANGEL, SP.: TRIÁNGULO,
RU.: TREUGOL'NIK

A steel rod bent into a triangle that is open at one corner,
the triangle is suspended by a nylon cord from a stand.

It is played with one or two metal
beaters, though a wooden beater may
be used for a softer, more muffled
tone. Haydn was the first to include
this instrument in the symphony
orchestra, in his Symphony no. 100,
Military, Beethoven used it in his
Symphony no. 9.

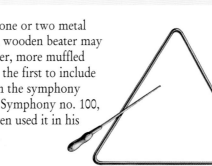

Sistrum

IT.: SISTRO, FR.: SISTRE, GER.: SISTRUM, SP.: SISTRO, RU.: SISTR

This is a metal idiophone of ancient origin. It consists
of a metal frame bent to form a long loop with a handle.
Some 4 – 8 bronze rings are strung on rods and jingle when
shaken. Modern sistrums are of simpler construction.

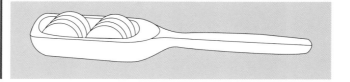

Castanets

IT.: NACCHERE, FR.: CASTANGNETTES, GER.: KASTAGNETTEN,
SP.: CASTAÑUELAS, RU.: KASTANJETY

Castanets consist of two shell-shaped pieces of hardwood (ebony, rosewood, pear, etc.), the hollowed sides of which are clapped together. When used by dancers they are loosely joined by a string that is looped over the thumb, leaving the fingers free to strike the shells against the palm of the hand. Smaller castanets are worn on the right hand, and larger ones on the left hand.

When used in the orchestra castanets are mounted on either side of a wooden handle that is held by the player and shaken. Castanets were brought to Europe by the Moors, and are immensely popular in Spain and Latin America. In ballet, opera, and symphonic music they are used to accompany Spanish dances.

Tambourine

IT.: TAMBURELLO, TAMBURIN, FR.: TAMBOUR DE BASQUE, TAMBOURIN,
GER.: TAMBURIN, SP.: PANDERO, RU.: TAMBURIN

This is a membranophone of indefinite pitch, consisting of a small wooden (sometimes metal) frame, with a skin membrane stretched over one side. Pairs of jingle discs, like miniature cymbals, are fixed in slots around the frame. In another variant of the instrument, tiny bells are hung on cross-wires on the inner side of the membrane.

The tambourine was brought to Europe by the Arabs and rapidly gained popularity in Italy and Spain. It is most often held in one hand and struck with the other, though it may also be sounded by rubbing the rim with the thumb or by shaking the instrument. The tambourine was introduced into the symphony orchestra in the 19th century. Usually, a single tambourine is used, though Berlioz opted for two in the overture *Le carnaval romain*, as did Richard Strauss in his opera *The Egyptian Helen*.

Flexatone

IT.: FLESSATONO, FR.: FLEX-À-TONE, GER.: FLEXATON, SP.:FLEXATÓN
RU.: FLEKSATON

The flexatone is a metal idiophone of definite pitch, invented in France in the mid-1920s for use by variety artists. The instrument consists of a flexible steel blade bolted onto a metal handle, with a metal, rubber, or wooden ball on a straight spring attached on either side. When the instrument is shaken, the balls strike the blade.

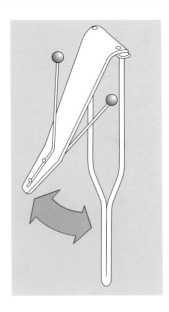

A characteristic feature of this instrument is the tremolo between the tones from which it takes its name: the Latin word "flexus" means curve, or voice change, while the Greek "tonos" means tone. Composers who have written for the flexatone include Schoenberg (*Variations for Orchestra* and the opera *Moses and Aaron*), Berg (*Three Pieces for Orchestra*), and Khachaturian (*Piano Concerto*).

Anvil

IT.: INCUDINE, FR.: ENCLUME, GER.: AMBOSS, SP.: YUNQUE, RU.: NAKOVAL'NAYA

Intended to reproduce the sound of the forge, this instrument consists of either a metal bar struck with a hammer or a genuine anvil. Verdi called for it in his opera *Il trovatore*, as did Wagner in *Siegfried*. The instrument is also occasionally used in avant-garde European jazz.

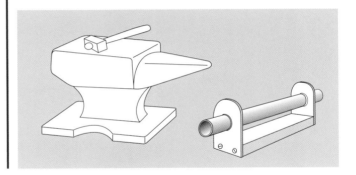

Rain Machine

IT.: EFFETTO DI PIOGGIA, FR.: PRISME DE PLUIE, GER.: REGENPRISMA,
SP.: SIMULADOR DE ILUVIA, RU.: DOZHDIVAYA MASHINA

A large rotating prism or drum with pellets inside, supported on a stand. Additional partitions may be placed inside the drum to enhance the effect. The sound produced may be louder or softer, depending on the speed of rotation, thus creating the effect of either heavy or gentle rain.

Wind machine

IT.: EFFETO DI VENTO, FR.: XÉOLIPHONE, GER.: WINDMASCHINE,
SP.: SIMULADOR DE VIENTO, RU.: VETRODUJ

The wind machine, rain machine, and other devices imitating natural phenomena are known as effects. With the advent of electronic instruments, their role was taken over by the synthesizers. The original wind machine consists of a rotating drum. Its frame is made of wooden laths, and its diameter may reach 75 cm. Richard Strauss used this instrument in *Don Quixote*, and Vaughan Williams, in *Sinfonia Antartica*.

Thunder Sheet

IT.: EFFETTO DI TUONO, FR.: TONNERRE,
GER.: DONNERBLECH,
SP.: SIMULADOR DE TORMENTA,
RU.: SHUMOVAJA MASHINA

A thin steel sheet suspended from a tall frame, shaken at the lower end or struck at the upper end with a light, soft-ended beater.
The larger its size, the lower the sound produced.

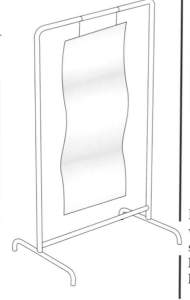

Slapstick

IT.: FRUSTA, FLAGELLO, SFERZA, FR.: FOET, GER.: PEITSCHE, KNALLBÜCHSE,
SP.: FUSTIGAR, RU.: BICH, KNUT, KHLOPUSHKI

This instrument originates from the East and consists of two wooden boards, connected at one end by hinges or by a piece of leather. The boards have handles on the outside, and when struck together produce a sharp sound like the cracking of a whip.

In the orchestra, a simplified variant is used: a strip of wood with a handle, to which a smaller strip is attached by a spring. When shaken rapidly, the smaller strip moves away from the larger one but is brought back against it by the spring, producing a loud slap.
This instrument was at one time used to imitate the clapping of hands. It was introduced into the symphony orchestra by Adam, and was later used by Mahler, Richard Strauss, Ravel, Mussorgsky, Hindemith, and various other composers.

Rattle

IT.: RAGANELLA, TABELLA, FR.: CRÉCELLE, GER.: RATSCHE, SCHNARRE,
SP.: CARRACA, RU.: TRESHCHOTKA

A thin-walled wooden box containing flexible wooden blades that snap against the teeth of a rotating wooden cogwheel. The cogwheel is turned either by a handle or by swinging the box around its axis. The wooden box serves as a resonator.

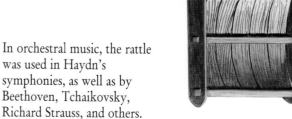

In orchestral music, the rattle was used in Haydn's symphonies, as well as by Beethoven, Tchaikovsky, Richard Strauss, and others.

ENSEMBLES AND ORCHESTRAS

THE WORD ORCHESTRA is of Greek origin. It derives from the ancient theater where it denoted the space between the stage and the audience where the chorus danced. Forgotten for a long time, the term was revived during the Middle Ages. It was used in instrumental music in Hamburg to indicate the place of musicians in the theater. (In 1678 one of the first popular opera theaters was opened in Hamburg, 41 years after the opening of the first European opera house in Venice.)

Depending on their function and their composition, orchestras cover a very wide range of types. In addition, the development of the art of music, its democratization and its transformation into a means of communication for large social groups around the world, constantly give rise to new formations and instrument combinations. Today, alongside the classical string, wind, and dance ensembles, exist many newer ones such as jazz bands, big bands, rock groups, electronic and electro-acoustic ensembles. Half-forgotten terms are again in vogue: "academy" (orchestra), "consort" (an ensemble of instruments of the same family), "camerata" (chamber ensembles), and so on. An immense variety of traditional folk ensembles also continues to flourish. Together, they form the colorful picture of the orchestra family which has its specific place in every European country's musical life.

CHAMBER ENSEMBLES AND ORCHESTRAS

A chamber ensemble is a group of instrumentalists performing in a relatively small hall. It consists of a rather small number of uniform or different instruments. They play mainly soloistically and with a single player on a part, without the clearly established "tutti" sections, complex organisation, or size of the symphony orchestra. Chamber music was established at royal courts and in aristocratic salons. It was performed before a small audience, in a more intimate atmosphere than that of a concert hall. This kind of music was also known in ancient Greece and Rome: singing to the accompaniment of the lyre, the lute, or some other stringed instrument. In the early Middle Ages, the tradition was continued by the trouveres of southern France, the German minnesingers, the Scottish bards, the Scandinavian skalds, and so on. Amateur domestic performances of madrigals and other vocal forms during the Renaissance also fall into the chamber music category.

It was only with the rise of instrumental music in the Baroque period, however, that chamber music became firmly established as an institution, accompanied by the emergence of the sonata as the most sophisticated chamber genre. The early sonata was scored for two high-pitched instruments and a bass instrument (the so-called "trio" sonata). Examples of such pieces were written by Arcangelo Corelli in the last two decades of the 17th century, scored for two violins and a cello accompanied by a harpsichord . The line from which bass and keyboard instruments played in music of this period was known as the basso continuo (continuous bass). In a Baroque orchestra the basso continuo might be performed by a variety of instruments, including the cello, double bass or contrabass viola da gamba, violone, bassoon, lute, theorbo, harpsichord, and organ. Of these, the plucked stringed instruments and keyboard instruments would play not only the bass line itself, but also chords indicated by figures printed below the line. By Mozart's time, sonatas for violin and piano were already being written in which the two parts were of equal importance: a major step in the evolution of chamber music.

Instruments of an 18th-century chamber orchestra.

At the French court in the 17th and 18th centuries there were three types of ensemble: one to perform sacred music (de la chapelle), another to play outdoors (écurie), and the third one to perform in the royal chambers (musique de chambre). These were clearly differentiated from orchestral and theatre music. In the 300 years since its emergence and establishment chamber music has come to be seen as the apogee of musical culture and creative genius. The string quartet medium that came to dominate the chamber repertory in the time of Haydn is still popular today.

Concert. Engraving by Johann Rudolf Holzhalb, 1777. Detail.

Chamber ensembles perform music of the 17th, 18th, and 19th centuries, as well as works written specially for them by modern composers. The composition of the chamber ensembles is quite flexible, consisting of instruments either of a single family (most often strings) or of different families in a variety of combinations. The musical world currently enjoys a wealth of chamber ensembles, many of which are immensely popular.

The instrumentation of a classical string quartet.

The instrumentation of Stravinsky's Octet for Wind Instruments of 1923.

The instrumentation of Schubert's Octet.

REPERTORY

Haydn composed the first of his many works for four stringed instruments in the early years of his career (c. 1757 – 1764). Mozart's 27 string quartets include some of his best works, and Beethoven wrote some of his most deeply felt music in this medium, culminating in the five famous quartets of the last years of his life. After Beethoven and the string quartet (two violins, a viola, and a cello), many composers were attracted to chamber music by its intensity of expression, its succinctness, and the opportunity for contrast offered by the relative independence of its movements.

JOSEPH HAYDN
(1732 – 1809)

Chamber music flourished in the 19th and 20th centuries as an important area of musical activity. New instruments were added to the conventional string formation, enriching its timbre. Popular chamber works include an octet by Schubert in which a clarinet, a horn, a bassoon, and a double bass are added to the classical string quartet. Mendelssohn's Octet (for double string quartet) is one of his most remarkable works. In time, woodwind and even brass instruments found their way into the chamber ensemble alongside the strings. Stravinsky's Octet requires a flute, a clarinet, two bassoons, two trumpets, and two trombones. Masterpieces of chamber music were also composed by Verdi, Brahms, Tchaikovsky, Sibelius, Debussy, Ravel, Bartók, Shostakovich, Poulenc, Milhaud, and many others.

MILITARY AND BRASS BANDS

Military and brass bands are made up of various combinations woodwind, brass and percussion instruments. Though they evolved in the industrial age, military commanders have always known about and made use of the power of music to inspire or to intimidate. The drums and shrill surnas of the bands of the invading Ottoman imperial army filled the Europeans with fear.
In Napoleon's army the band had a similar function, but, in keeping with the more civilized character of his military doctrine, it was also assigned the task of signaling the rhythm of attack, of keeping up morale during marches, and of conveying commands. Scotland's national instrument, the bagpipe, is widely used in the Scottish army. Russia adopted the Western European band model.

Turkish surna.

Tenor drum.

Scottish bagpipe.

Throughout antiquity and the Middle Ages, the military musician served as a herald in times of peace and as a signaler in times of war.
Nowadays, the function of military bands is not only to keep up morale within the army but also to give public open-air concerts. This type of band is usually composed of woodwind, brass, and percussion instruments.
Until World War II, the size and composition of military bands was related to the organization of the armed forces.
For example, the cavalry band consisted entirely of brass, while the infantry band was composed of woodwind, brass, and percussion.
Military bands frequently perform at traditional and state ceremonies as well as at large international sports events.
The march is the main genre of military music. Haydn, Gossec, Beethoven, Wagner, Rimsky-Korsakov and various other composers wrote pieces for military bands.

A military brass band.

In 1755, in Moscow, the first orchestra consisting entirely of hunting horns was formed: 37 horns, each playing only a single note. The idea proved infectious, such orchestras increasing in size to 60 players, each playing two or three notes at most. The practice was transferred to Europe, but quickly gave way to the opportunity of using increasingly refined instruments.

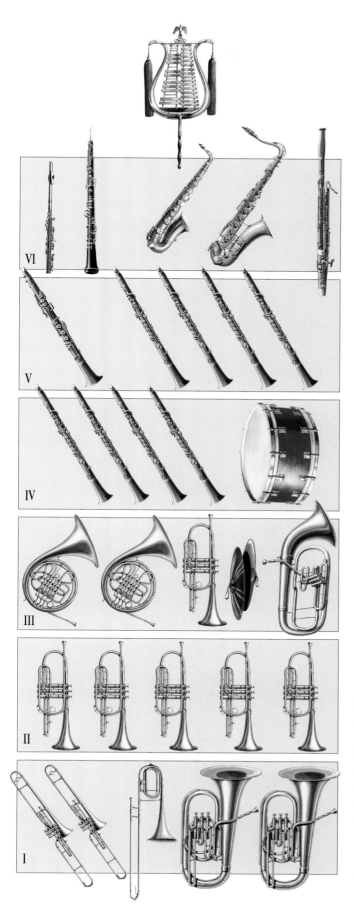

In the late 1870s, there was a transition from vocal to instrumental forms in the music of African-Americans. Their instrumental music began as an imitation of vocal sound (the so-called vocalization of sound). This determines the instrumentation of the first black orchestras, consisting as a rule of one or two cornets, a clarinet, a trombone, tubas, and percussion instruments. Civic bands flourished in the southern states of the U. S, performing at carnivals, processions, celebrations, parades, and funerals.

In the late 1880s and early 1890s they started playing dance music as well, combining French, Spanish, and Creole melodies. These groups became known as marching bands, and it was from them that the first jazz bands developed. The civic status of brass bands made them immensely popular both in Europe and in the U. S. They provided a way for schools, militarized civil services, institutions, and civic associations to participate actively in the cultural life of their town. The functions of the bands expanded and the performance of dance music and open-air concerts were added to the parades and outdoor celebrations. Players from large symphony orchestras took part in bands consisting of brass, woodwind, and percussion instruments that gave concerts, made recordings, and participated in festivals.

Playing in a marching band is difficult because of the need to march and play at the same time. The bands vary in size, and the arrangement of instruments within them depends on established traditions, on the conductor's idea of how the ensemble should sound, and on the desire for better sound projection in all directions. Some conductors arrange the band in a fashion similar to the symphony orchestra configuration; others place the brass instruments in front of the woodwind. Here is one of the possible arrangements, row by row:

   I : 2 tenor trombones, 1 bass trombone, 2 tubas
  II : 5 cornets in B flat
 III : 2 horns, 1 cornet in B flat, cymbals, 1 euphonium
 IV : 4 clarinets in B flat, 1 bass drum
  V : 1 piccolo clarinet in E flat, 4 clarinets in B flat
 VI : 1 piccolo flute, 1 oboe, 1 alto saxophone,
      1 tenor saxophone, 1 bassoon

Each band is equipped with a bell lyre, either at the front or at the back, depending on the arrangement of the instruments.

In modern practice, small, medium, and large bands are created for concert purposes, but they invariably consist only of woodwind, brass, and percussion. In such bands the function of the string section is performed by the flugelhorn or, more recently, by the saxophone group.

Instrumentation of the marching band.

Flugelhorn

IT.: FLICORNO, FR.: COR DE CHASSE, GER.: FLÜGELHORN, SP.: CORNETÍN,
RU.: FLYUGELGORN

Differing from the trumpet in its wider bore and deeper
mouthpiece (and respectively a fuller tone), the flugelhorn
is built in B flat or C, with a range and fingering identical
to those of the trumpet. It is most frequently used as a solo
instrument in jazz, but it also appears in a few symphonic
works.

Tenor Drum

IT.: CASSA RULLANTE, FR.: CAISSE ROULANTE, GER.: RÜHRTROMMEL,
SP.: REDOBLANTE, RU.: FRANTSUZSKI BARABAN

Midway between the bass drum and the side drum, the
tenor drum has a deeper shell made of wood and does not
usually have a snare. The sound it produces is muffled and
sinister, and in symphonic works it is used to create either
a funeral or a warlike atmosphere.
Around the middle of the 16th century it was introduced
by royal decree into the French army and musketeer corps.

Bass Drum

IT.: GRAN CASSA, FR.: GROSSE CAISSE, GER.: BASS-TROMMEL,
SP.: BOMBO, RU.: BOL'SHOY BARABAN

In military bands, a cymbal
is attached to the bass
drum. The player holds
a beater in his
right hand and with
a second cymbal in his left
hand, sounds the cymbal
attached to the drum.

Bell Lyre

IT.: CARILLON, FR.: CARILLON,
GER.: GLOCKENSPIEL, SP.: CARILLÓN,
RU.: KOLOKOLCHIKI

Shaped like an ancient
lyre and richly decorated,
this instrument is used
in military bands and has
an ornamental as well
as a musical function. It is
designed for playing on
the march, supported by
a strap around the player,
stabilized by one hand,
and played with a small
beater held in the other.

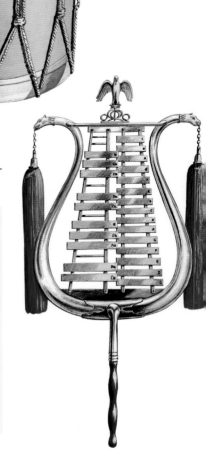

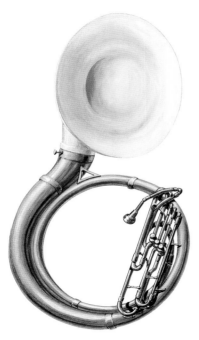

Sousaphone

IT.: SOUSAFONO, FR.: SOUSAPHONE, GER.: SOUSAPHON,
SP.: SOUSAFÓN, RU.: SUZAFON

A popular instrument in American military bands, the
sousaphone has a large forward-pointing bell. It was created
at the end of the 19th century by the American bandmaster
John Philip Sousa, and was quickly adopted
by New Orleans marching bands in the pre-classical
period of jazz.

Helicon

IT.: ELICONE, FR.: HÉLICON, GER.: HELIKON,
SP.: HELICÓN, RU.: GELIKON

For easier playing on the
march, the helicon variety
of tuba was developed in
a circular shape. Unlike the
tuba, the helicon can be
placed over the head to rest
on the left shoulder
and under the right arm.

Bugle

IT.: CORNETTA SEGNALE, FR.: BUGLE, GER.: BÜGELHORN,
SP.: FISCORNO, RU.: ROZHOK

The bugle is a simple brass instrument made of copper or,
less often, of silver alloy. The mouthpiece is cup-shaped with
a conical bore. Most bugles are made in B flat or C. Their
characteristic feature is that they play only the overtones
of a single tone; for example, a bugle in B flat sounds only
the pitches B flat, b flat, f^1, b flat^1, and d^2.
The instrument first appeared in European military bands
in the 18th century and was used for transmitting signals.
In the 19th century it was adopted by the U. S. army.
Later, a trumpet-like valved version was developed,
but despite its improved features it was never widely used.

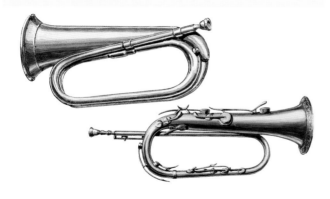

Euphonium

IT.: BOMBARDINO, FR.: EUPHONIUM, GER.: EUPHONIUM,
SP.: BOMBARDINO, RU.: EVFONIYA

The euphonium is a brass
instrument of the bugle
family (wide-bore valved
instruments tuned with a
tone that is powerful though
less noble than that of the
narrow-bore type). It is
usually built in B flat, though
instruments in C are also
found. It reads from the bass
clef, sounding as written over
its three octaves range. The
euphonium was invented by
Sommer of Weimar in 1843,
used in German and Russian
military bands, and later
adopted into American
military bands.

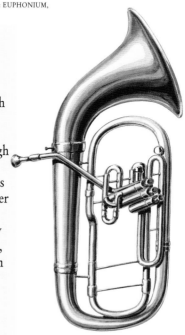

DANCE ORCHESTRA

Dance orchestras vary considerably in their instrumentation, in the number of musicians involved, and in their musical style. Common to all of them, however, is their dependence on the trends of a given time, though they, in turn, can also influence those trends.

Up to the beginning of the 20th century, the dance orchestra repertory was dominated by European music, by its traditions and its stylistic variety. The 1920s, however, described by the American writer F. Scott Fitzgerald as "the golden era of jazz," had a profound influence on European dance music and its orchestras (as on many other things). The relatively soft, discreet, and sophisticated salon orchestras were replaced by noisy jazz bands, while the waltz, the quadrille, the polka, and the mazurka gave way to the foxtrot, the tango, the one-step, and other such dances. Later, the large swing bands were swept away by rock music in all its varieties. Electronic sound has gained the upper hand in recent years and had a strong impact on "live" band performances.

Instrumentation of a salon orchestra.

The jazz band reflects a strong American influence. It was in the jazz band that a separate rhythmic group consisting of percussion, a piano, a double bass, a banjo and later a guitar was first formed. The term "jazz band" was first used in 1915 in a poster for Tom Brown's Dixieland Band. By the early 1920s, the term had spread throughout the U. S. and Western Europe, to some extent as a result of the tours and the first recordings of another band from New Orleans: the Original Dixieland Jazz Band. From the end of the 1930s the term gradually fell out of use and is now encountered only occasionally in reference to ensembles playing traditional jazz.

The salon orchestra developed from the chamber ensemble and included the entire stringed family (violin, viola, cello, double bass) as well as the piano. It established the practice of playing background music in hotels, restaurants, and cafés. In luxury restaurants the salon orchestra performs while the guests are served, being replaced later in the evening by a "hot orchestra" playing dance music. It is the "hot orchestra" that combines the European tradition and the American model, consisting of percussion, woodwind, and brass instruments, a guitar, an accordion, and so on.

Instrumentation of a typical jazz band.

The big band marked a new stage in the development of the dance orchestra, becoming a symbol of the swing era of jazz. It was in the big band that the instruments were clearly divided into two major groups, rhythmic and melodic, the latter being further subdivided into reeds (saxophones and often a clarinet) and brass (trumpets and slide trombones). The usual composition of the big band was four trumpets, five saxophones (two alto, two tenor, and a baritone), and a rhythm section. The number of instruments may vary to an extent in certain types of big band. In modern jazz, the big band may also include an oboe, a flute, a bass clarinet, a horn, a tuba, a vibraphone, an organ, and strings. The big band emerged in the 1920s, in the period of transition from traditional jazz to swing. The earliest bands included those of Fletcher Henderson (1923) and Duke Ellington (1928), followed by the bands of Don Redman, Luis Russell, Chick Webb, and others.

From that point on, the dance orchestra has been characterized by immense variety, though the rhythm section has remained its basis. Improved electronic instruments and amplifying equipment changed the dance orchestra profoundly, but have been willingly adopted by all traditional formations.

Instruments of a classical big band.

Instruments of a rock group.

Rock group. In its earliest version, the rock formation derived from the rhythm section of the large swing orchestra, through rhythm-and-blues and early rock-and-roll. The electric guitar appeared in rock as early as in urban blues and rhythm-and-blues. In the early 1950s, the Fender company developed the prototype of the electric guitar. In the 1960s, another American producer, Gibson, also launched similar guitars. The appearance of the bass guitar was decisive for the crystalisation of the standard rock formation, first on the West Coast, then in the so-called "Mercy sound" and British rock in general. The search for a fuller and more massive electric sound resulted in the combination of two guitars, a bass guitar and percussions, the most popular formation since the early 1960s. The instrument set was then expanded with a variety of keyboards, later with synthesizers, computers, and other technological innovations. Although not as hyperbolized as in the late 20th century, that sound became a recognized means of expression and com-munication for the younger generation. Initially known as beat-music, it was quickly renamed rock, and the quality, loudness, and expressiveness of its sound gave rise to a wide range of styles, under the complex influence of generation differentiation, fashions and behavior models, and to the benefit of show business.

THE HUMAN VOICE

The human voice is the most natural of musical instruments as well as the most ancient. The singing voice, like the speaking voice, is produced by the vocal organs, and has the specific characteristics of the so-called singer's formant: a range from 500 to 3000 Hz, a vibrato of six variations per second, sufficient volume, and so on. The breath, the larynx, and the resonators are the three main factors that determine the production of the vocal tone.

Even today, Orpheus remains a symbol of perfection in vocal art.

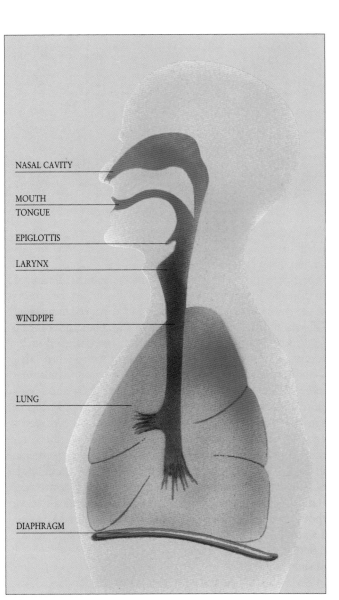

NASAL CAVITY

MOUTH
TONGUE

EPIGLOTTIS

LARYNX

WINDPIPE

LUNG

DIAPHRAGM

Anatomy of the respiratory organs that are involved in the production of sound and in the technique of vocal art.

Correct breathing is the basis of the art of singing. It differs from ordinary breathing and from the breathing involved in the speaking process. Trained singers use as the most efficient form of breathing, a combination of chest and abdominal breathing where the diaphragm plays a major role as a "supporting" organ. It helps to prolong both the inhalation and the exhalation of breath and therefore to produce a smooth and coherent vocal phrase.

Vocal sound is produced when nerve impulses from the brain cause air to pass through the vocal cords, which have the capacity to lenghten and contract. The vibration of the cords produces a sound, the pitch of which depends on the frequency of vibration as well as on the length, elasticity, and tension of the cords. In men, the length of the vocal cords is usually 20 – 25 mm, while in women it is around 15 – 20 mm. Lower voices are generally produced by longer vocal cords, though there are exceptions to that rule. Enrico Caruso for example, had long vocal cords, which are not usual in tenors.

The moment of phonation is known as the attack. There are three types of attack: harsh, mild, and aspirate. In the case of the harsh attack, the vocal cords are caused to vibrate by a sudden onslaught of air. In the mild attack, the air touches the vocal cords gently. In the much rarer aspirate attack, the vibration and the sound are preceded by an expulsion of air. Part of a singer's training is the mastering of the mild attack which makes the sound soft and supple. The harsh attack is very hard on the vocal cords and can cause serious damage.

According to its timbre, compass, and tessitura, a voice is classified as one of several principal types: soprano, mezzo soprano, and contralto for female voices, and tenor, baritone, and bass for male voices. The normal compass of a voice is about two octaves, though it may be much wider. Within the soprano and tenor voice types there are further subdivisions into lyric, lyrico-dramatic, and dramatic. Within the soprano category, there is also coloratura soprano, which is higher in compass and capable of great technical virtuosity. Basses are divided into high (cantante) and deep (profondo). The compass of children's voices increases with age to reach about an octave and a half. The part of the compass of the human voice (or of a musical instrument) that consists of a series of tones of uniform timbre is known as a register. Natural registers are used by untrained and folk singers as well as by some rock singers; in classical singing, they were used until the 19th century.

In order to achieve a uniform tone quality across the entire compass, vocal training applies the method of "shading" or "rounding": vowels are articulated through oval lips ("A" through "O", "O" through "OO"), with the correct breathing and "tuning" of all resonating cavities.

The main function of the lips is to form consonants and vowels. In singing, the consonants differ very little from consonants in speech, though they may be more forceful and so produce a more intelligible diction. Vowels, however, differ considerably both in the way they are formed and in their acoustic characteristics. Caruso once remarked that the Italian language was rich in the vowels and vowel combinations that are responsible for the tone color or timbre, and that this is why it is known as the language of singing. According to Caruso, Italians thus possessed naturally something that singers of other nations had to work very hard to achieve.

The chest is an important resonator, which amplifies the vocal tone. The right use of all cavities helps to project the tone.

The Evolution of Vocal Art

For thousands of years, singing has been related to a variety of human activities. In syncretic folk art, it is inseparable from poetry, dance, and gesture. In ancient Greece, singing gradually became independent of dance and developed into an art form in its own right. The first professional singers, the aoidoi, were given a special education. The performance of the epic works of ancient Greece seems to have consisted of endless repetition of reciting figures whose tonal range was no more than a fourth or a fifth. Some scholars suggest that "Homer," the author of the *Iliad* and the *Odyssey*, was actually the collective pen-name of a group of aoidoi.

In Greek mythology the Sirenes lured sailors to their deaths with singing. To hear the Sirenes safely Odysseus tied himself to the mast of his ship and stuffed the ears of his crew with wax.

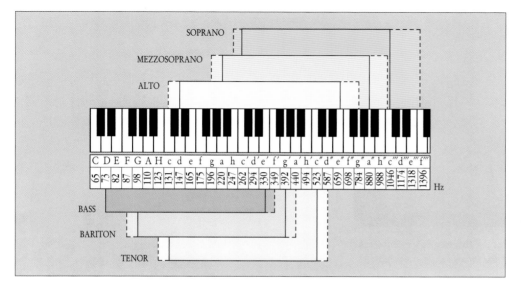

The compass of traditional vocal registers, illustrated on the piano keyboard. According to statistical data, outside vocal art, the most common respectively female and male vocal registers are the soprano and the baritone. In the opera art, the most valuable voices are the high soprano and the tenor.

The development of drama and more particularly of tragedy fostered the evolution of choral art. Before the work of Aeschylus, tragedy was based on individual artistic performance; only later did the chorus gain popularity. Christian communities in Greece and Rome introduced a new type of music. Singing developed in the early centres of the Christian faith: Syria, Alexandria, and Jerusalem. The first Christian chants were borrowed from synagogical songs. The chants were the cornerstone of Christian worship. Bishop Ambrose of Milan (c. 340 – 397) and Pope Gregory the Great (pope from 590 to 604) are both important figures in the early history of the Christian church. St. Ambrose systematically introduced chants borrowed from the East, while Pope Gregory arranged sacred chants into a strict liturgical order, establishing music as an element of the divine worship. It is from him that Gregorian chant takes its name, a style of choral singing that is closer to recitative than to song. Training in singing continued to be an essential part of general musical education up to the 17th century. Only then did singing acquire a significance of its own. From around the middle of the 17th century, the vocal style known as *bel canto* flourished – a singing method focusing on the beauty of tone. The school of Bologna was quick to gain popularity, though other centres also emerged – in Rome, Naples, and Florence. A major development was the rise of the aria, which functioned as a vehicle both for artistic expression and for the display of virtuosity . The 17th century also saw the beginning of the "golden age" of the castrato. By the beginning of the 18th century, castrati played an important role in musical performance throughout Europe, with the single exception of Paris. The most famous castrato of all time was Carlo Broschi (1705 – 1782), better known as Farinelli.

Choral singing first appeared as an element of Christian service.

Carlo Broschi (1705 – 1782) – the castrato known as Farinelli or Il Ragazzo, famous for his soprano voice with a compass a-d³, virtuoso technique and close friendship with Giacomo Casanova.

Enrico Caruso (1873 – 1921) – the Italian tenor who became a star in the United States owing to the development of sound recording.

Feodor Shalyapin (1873 – 1938), – the Russian bass who in the 20th century introduced new criteria in the opera art and brought artistic presence to perfection.

The bel canto vocal style developed in two main directions: the slow cantabile style of singing, with little ornamentation, and the coloratura style that became popular in Europe in the 18th century.

Bel canto singing involved the use of chest breathing, and the chest and head registers. Much attention was paid to the correct use of all resonating cavities, and the crisp articulation of consonants and vowels.

Europe's gradual liberation from the domination of the Italian opera and the emergence of national operatic styles in France, Germany, Russia, and elsewhere promoted the development of other schools of singing.

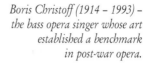

Boris Christoff (1914 – 1993) – the bass opera singer whose art established a benchmark in post-war opera.

Maria Malibran (1808 – 1836) – a French soprano who made her debut early and had a brilliant career in London and New York.

Maria Callas (1923 – 1977) – the soprano whose artistic presence created a new notion of the opera diva.

The rapid development of music in the 20th century, the success of popular music, the emergence of jazz, the experiments of avant-garde composers, and the rise of electronic music, all helped to expand the notion of singing and of the potential of the human voice. While popular music adhered closely to the principles of "beautiful singing" in its earlier phase, the tide of rock-and-roll and ethnic music revived natural singing. Alongside a few fine folk examples that preserved a quasi-medieval authenticity, these 20th century forms created a new attitude to the human voice. Although the end of the century was marked by a variety of taste among young people, electronic sound seems to enjoy the greatest popularity. At the same time, a growing interest in older musical forms, instruments, and singing styles is indicative of the fact that humanity will always regard with some nostalgia the natural, more human sound, including natural vocal expression.

Frank Sinatra (1915 – 1998) – the pop singer with a career of record length.

Luciano Pavarotti was the first famous singer to erase the dividing line between popular and opera music.

Pop-music and jazz promoted a specific formation, the vocal group. In jazz, vocal groups first appeared in the 1920s. One of the first such groups was the Rhythm Boys Trio, working with Paul Whiteman's orchestra. In Germany, Comedian Harmonists gained immense popularity by the early 1930s. Post-war jazz promoted new names: Four Freshmen, Singers Unlimited, as well as a few European formations, for example those founded by the American Ward Swingle in France. Swingle arranged for vocal performance works by Bach, Vivaldi, Handel, Mozart, Beethoven, Chopin, Tchaikovsky and other composers, seeking to "make voices sound like musical instruments." Fascinated by this revolutionary idea and the group's enormous success, similar formations mushroomed throughout Europe. The American response was The Manhattan Transfer, a group which is still a leader in vocal music today.

The Manhattan Transfer vocal group won great popularity in the 1970s and the 1980s owing to their co-operation with leading jazz musicians.

Glossary

Accent
Emphasis or stress on a tone or a chord.

Aleatoric
An avant-garde style involving chance or unpredictability in composition or performance.

Antiphony
The principle of responsory singing in religious choral singing.

Cantilena
A smooth, flowing lyrical passage of vocal or instrumental music.

Chord
A combination of three or more tones sounded together in harmony.

Chromaticism
Using or progressing by semitones.

Chromatic instruments
Instruments that are capable of playing all tones of the chromatic scale.

Chromatic scale
A musical scale made up of a succession of semitones.

Counterpoint
The technique of combining two or more distinct lines of music that sound simultaneously. It developed in the early period of polyphonic music, from the 9th to the 13th century.

Diatonic
Using a scale of seven tones within the octave.

Dissonance
Sounds which are outside the range of tone combinations accepted by composers as implying repose. The notion of which chords and intervals constitute consonance and dissonance has altered during the history of music.
A chord that sounds incomplete or unfulfilled until resolved to a stable harmony.

Dominant
Tone or harmony based upon the fifth tone of a diatonic scale.

Drone
A single low tone, sustained by a pipe or string.

Duration
The amount of time that a note is sounded. In written music, the note shape reflects the tone's duration: from a thirty-second note to a whole note.

Dynamics
Degrees of loudness or softness in the performance of music.

Figured bass
A system of shorthand notation of chords developed in Italy in the late 16th century. Figures (numbers) denoting the interval from the bass note to the other chord notes were added to the bass parts.

Fingerboard
A strip of ebony or hardwood fixed to the neck of a stringed instrument, against which the strings are pressed with the fingers to shorten them, thereby producing different pitches.

Fingering
1. A technique of applying the fingers to the strings, keys, etc. of an instrument to produce the tones. 2. Indication above notes to show which fingers are to be used.

Frequency
A scientific way of describing the highness or lowness of a tone in terms of the number of periodic vibrations or waves per unit of time.

Fret
A narrow lateral ridge fixed across the fingerboard of stringed instruments to regulate the fingering. In accordance with the laws of acoustics, the distance between the frets is larger by the pegbox.

Head
The membrane stretched across the end of a drum.

Homophony
Music characterised by a leading melody and subordinate parts providing rhythmic and harmonic support.

Interval
The difference in pitch between two tones. Measurable by the number of semitones that separate the tones.

Major
Designating an interval one semitone larger than the corresponding minor interval.

Manual
A keyboard.

Maqam
Scales used in the Middle East. There are over 70 maqams, each having its own name.

Melody
A sequence of single tones organized to make a musical phrase.

Meter
The rhythmic organization of long and short durations of tones.

Minor
Designating an interval one semitone smaller than the corresponding major interval.

Modulation
A transition in a piece of music from one tonality to another.

Monody
An early vocal style having a single voice part with chordal accompaniment.

Monophonic
Music characterized by a single, unaccompanied melodic line.

Motif
The smallest unit of a melody to be elaborated on in a piece of music.

Mouthpiece
A part of a woodwind or brass instrument held in or to the mouth. In brass instruments, it is cup-shaped and may vary in size. In woodwind instruments, it contains a single reed (clarinet, saxophone) or a double reed (oboe, bassoon).

Narrow-bored instruments
Brass wind instruments in which the note sounded without the use of valves is their keynote (e.g., trumpet, cornet, and trombone). The tapering is not uniform and the ratio between the narrowest and the widest part of the tube may range from 1:4 to 1:3.

Natural instruments
Brass instruments with no valves, producing only tones of the natural overtone series by overblowing.

Octave
The interval of eight diatonic degrees between a tone and its next occurance (e. g., c – c¹)

Opus
Latin noun meaning "work." Any of the musical works of a composer, numbered in order of composition or publication. This numbering was introduced about the end of the 16th century. Since Beethoven many composers give their works opus numbers.

Overtone
Any of the attendant higher tones heard above the fundamental tone produced by a string or column of air, having a frequency of vibration that is an exact multiple of the frequency of the fundamental tone.

Plectrum
A thin piece of metal, bone, plastic, etc. used to pluck strings.

Polyphony
A number of independent melodies or voices sounding simultaneously.

Polyrhythm
The simultaneous combination of contrasting rhythms in a musical composition.

Polytonality
The simultaneous occurrence of two or more different tonalities (or keys).

Position
On stringed instruments where the left hand is constantly shifted along the neck, the points on the fingerboard where the strings are stopped by the fingers are referred to as "positions."

Range
The distance between the lowest and highest tone, playable on a given musical instrument. Can be divided into registers (low, medium, high).

Reed
A thin strip of cane placed against the opening of the mouthpiece in certain wind instruments so as to leave a narrow opening; when vibrated by the breath (air column), it produces a musical tone.

Register
Division of an instrument's range into smaller sections where the tones have an uniform timbre.

Scale
A series of tones arranged in a sequence of rising or falling pitches in accordance with a system of intervals.

Scordatura
The retuning of one or more strings in order to extend a chordophone's range or to facilitate playing. It was first applied on lutes in the 17th – 18th century, and later on the modern violin family.

Semitone
Half of a whole tone. The basic interval in the chromatic scale.

Serial music
A 20th-century compositional technique based on a pre-selected, reccuring series of tones called a tone row. The same process can be applied to duration, dynamics, and tone color (timbre).

Slide
Movable tubing that changes the total length of tubing to create different tones. Used on the slide trombone.

Timbre
The characteristic quality of sound, or tone color, that distinguishes one voice or musical instrument from another. It is determined by the overtones of the sound.

Tone
A sound, usually corresponding in frequency of vibration to one of the semitones of the chromatic scale.

Tonality
The organization of tones around a central tone. Each tone can be used to build a major or a minor key. The tonality is designated by the keynote (tonic) and major/minor (e. g. C major /C minor).

Transposing instruments
Instruments for which the music is written higher or lower than it actually sounds.

Valve
A device in certain brass wind instruments for varying the tube length in order to change the tone.

Wide-bored instruments
Brass wind instruments such as the flugelhorn and the tuba, with a conical bore of a ratio 1:20 from the mouthpiece to the bell.

Index

Picture credits

The publisher has made every effort to trace all owners of reproduction rights. Any persons and institutions wishing to claim rights in connection with illustrations used in this book are requested to contact the publisher.

p. 2: © Hulton Getty Picture Collection, London.

p. 7: © Hulton Getty Picture Collection, London.

p. 15: Rapho, Paris.

p. 16: in: Musikgeschichte in Bildern vol. 2, VEB Deutscher Verlag für Musik, Leipzig, 1961 (Photo: Museum Hildesheim).

p. 18: in: Musikgeschichte in Bildern vol. 2, VEB Deutscher Verlag für Musik, Leipzig, 1961.

p. 19: in: Musikgeschichte in Bildern vol. 1, VEB Deutscher Verlag für Musik, Leipzig, 1989 (Photo: Gerhard Kubik).

p. 20: in: Musikgeschichte in Bildern vol. 2, VEB Deutscher Verlag für Musik, Leipzig, 1961.

p. 25: in: Musikgeschichte in Bildern vol. 1, VEB Deutscher Verlag für Musik, Leipzig, 1982.

p. 30: in: Musikinstrumente von den Anfängen bis zur Gegenwart by Alexander Buchner, Artia, Prag, 1971 (Photo: A. Buchner, Prague).

p. 31: in: Musikinstrumente der Völker by Alexander Buchner, Artia, Prag, 1971.

p. 32: in: Musikgeschichte in Bildern vol. 2, VEB Deutscher Verlag für Musik, Leipzig, 1961.

p. 36: in: Musikgeschichte in Bildern vol. 2, VEB Deutscher Verlag für Musik, Leipzig, 1961.

p. 37: © Pitt Rivers Museum, Oxford.

p. 39: in: Musikinstrumente der Völker by Alexander Buchner, Artia, Prag, 1968 (Photo: V. Solc, Prague).

p. 42: in: Musikinstrumente der Völker by Alexander Buchner, Artia, Prag, 1968 (Photo: Harald Schulz).

p. 43: in: Musikgeschichte in Bildern vol. 2, VEB Deutscher Verlag für Musik, Leipzig, 1967 (Photo: Ferdinand Anton, München).

p. 45: in: Musikgeschichte in Bildern vol. 2, VEB Deutscher Verlag für Musik, Leipzig, 1970 (Photo: Ferdinand Anton, München).

p. 48: in: Musikgeschichte in Bildern vol. 2, VEB Deutscher Verlag für Musik, Leipzig, 1970 (Photo: Ferdinand Anton, München).

p. 54: in: Musikgeschichte in Bildern vol. 2, VEB Deutscher Verlag für Musik, Leipzig, 1970 (Photo: Ferdinand Anton, München).

p. 56: © Smithsonian Institution, Bureau of American Ethnology, Washington D.C.

p. 59: in: Musikgeschichte in Bildern vol. 1, VEB Deutscher Verlag für Musik, Leipzig, 1965 (Photo: Jacques Villeminot).

p. 61: in: Musikgeschichte in Bildern vol. 1, VEB Deutscher Verlag für Musik, Leipzig, 1965 (Photo: Jacques Villeminot).

p. 62: in: Musikgeschichte in Bildern vol. 1, VEB Deutscher Verlag für Musik, Leipzig, 1965 (Photo: Ethnomusikologisch Archief Universiteit, Amsterdam).

p. 67: © Museum für Völkerkunde zu Leipzig: Playing of the musical bow, New Guinea.

p. 69: in: Musikinstrumente der Völker by Alexander Buchner, Artia, Prag, 1968 (Photo: Neues China, Presseagentur, Peking).

p. 70: in: Musikinstrumente der Völker by Alexander Buchner, Artia, Prag, 1968 (Photo: Musée Cornuschi).

p. 72: in: Musikinstrumente der Völker by Alexander Buchner, Artia, Prag, 1968 (Photo: International Institute for Comparative Music Studies and Documentation, Berlin).

p. 80: in: Musikinstrumente der Völker by Alexander Buchner, Artia, Prague, 1968 (Photo: Vaniñs – Sis, Prague).

p. 87: in: Musikinstrumente der Völker by Alexander Buchner, Artia, Prague, 1968 (Photo: Gesellschaft für internationale Kulturverbindungen, Tokio).

p. 89: in: Musikinstrumente der Völker by Alexander Buchner, Artia, Prague, 1968 (Photo: Gesellschaft für internationale Kulturverbindungen, Tokio).

p. 93: © Hulton Getty Picture Collection, London.

p. 95: © British Museum, London.

p. 97: in: Musikgeschichte in Bildern vol. 2, VEB Deutscher Verlag für Musik, Leipzig, 1981 (Photo: Subodh Chandra, Bombay).

p. 99: in: Musikinstrumente der Völker by Alexander Buchner, Artia, Prag, 1968 (Photo: A. Buchner, Prague).

p. 101: © Hulton Getty Picture Collection, London.

p. 103: in: Musikinstrumente der Völker by Alexander Buchner, Artia, Prag, 1968.

p. 104: in: Musikinstrumente der Völker by Alexander Buchner, Artia, Prag, 1968 (Photo: Irakisches Kulturministerium, Bagdad).

p. 105: © Smithsonian Institution, Freer Gallery of Art, Washington.

p. 110: © The British Museum, London.

p. 112: © Bodleian Library, Oxford.

p. 117: © Hulton Getty Picture Collection, London.

p. 119: in: Musikinstrumente von den Anfängen bis zur Gegenwart by Alexander Buchner, Artia, Prag (Photo: A. Buchner, Prague).

p. 123: Courtesy, Museum of Fine Arts, Boston. Reproduced with comission. © 2000 Museum of Fine Arts, Boston.

All Rights Reserved.

p. 126: in: Musikinstrumente der Völker by Alexander Buchner, Artia, Prag, 1968 (Photo: Zentralstelle für Volkskunstschaffen, Bratislava).

p. 128: in: Musikinstrumente der Völker by Alexander Buchner, Artia, Prag, 1968 (Photo: Sáez , Bilbao).

p. 130: in: Musikinstrumente der Völker by Alexander Buchner, Artia, Prag, 1968 (Photo: A. Buchner, Prague).

p. 139: © National Board of Antiques, Finland.

p. 143: © Scanpix, Sweden.

p. 149: in: Musikinstrumente der Völker by Alexander Buchner, Artia, Prag, 1968.

p. 151: in Lexikon Musikinstrumente, ed. Wolfgang Ruf, Meyers Lexikonverlag, Mannheim, 1991.

p. 159: © bpk bildarchiv preussischer kulturbesitz, Berlin.

p. 161: in: Musikinstrumente der Völker by Alexander Buchner, Artia, Prag, 1968 (Photo: A. Buchner, Prague).

p. 162: © Alinari, Firenze.

p. 165: in: Musikinstrumente von den Anfängen bis zur Gegenwart by Alexander Buchner, Artia, Prag, 1971.

p. 167: © The National Museum of Fine Art, Stockholm.

p. 172: in: Musikinstrumente von den Anfängen bis zur Gegenwart by Alex. Buchner, Artia, Prag, 1971. (Photo: T. Honty, Prague).

p. 173: in: The Violin by Yehudi Menuhin, Flammarion, Paris, 1996 (Photo: Bibliothèque nationale, Paris).

p. 174: © Staatliche Museen Kassel.

p. 180: © Magyar Nemzeti Múzeum (Hungarian National Museum), Budapest.

p. 189: in: Musikinstrumente von den Anfängen bis zur Gegenwart by Alexander Buchner, Artia, Prag, 1971.

p. 197: © Národni Muzeum – Muzeum ceské hudby (National Museum), Praha.

p. 198: © Staatliche Kunstsammlungen, Dresden.

p. 202: © Gallerie dell' Accademia, Venedig.

p. 207: © Rijksmuseum Amsterdam.

p. 211: © bpk bildarchiv preussischer kulturbesitz, Berlin.

p. 213: © The National Museum of Fine Art, Stockholm.

p. 229: © Hulton Getty Picture Collection, London.

p. 239: © Martin Georgiev, Sofia.

p. 248: in: Russolo: L'arte dei Rumori 1913 - 1931, Catalogo a cura di G. Franco Maffina, Regione Lombardina, 1978.

p. 249: © Hulton Getty Picture Collection, London.

p. 251: in: Union Media Magazine, Sofia, March issue, 1996 (a photo from the concert in the Royal Albert Hall, London on 29. 02. 1996).

p. 255: © Stoyan Grebenarov, Sofia.

p. 257: in: Yearbook of the Munich symphony orchestra 1993/94.

p. 261: in: Djaz – iztoki, techenia, poiski (Jazz – sources, trends, quests) by John

S. Wilson.

p. 263: in: Records and Recording magazine, London, July, 1978 (Photo: W. Neumeister).

p. 271: © Boris Razakliev, Sofia.

p. 273: © Ognyan Panov, Sofia.

p. 274: © Martin Georghiev, BTA, Sofia.

p. 277: in: The Violin by Yehudi Menuhin, Flammarion, Paris, 1996 (Photo: Roger-Viollet).

p. 279: © Viktor Viktorov, Sofia.

p. 280: in: The Violin by Yehudi Menuhin, Flammarion, Paris, 1996 (Photo: Stars and Stripes/Sygma).

p. 283: © Ognyan Panov, Sofia.

p. 287: © Hulton Getty Picture Collection, London.

p. 302: Zentralbibliothek, Zürich.

p. 304: © The Military Picture Library, Aldershot/England.

p. 310: bpk bildarchiv preussischer kulturbesitz, Berlin.

p. 311: in: The Penguin Historical Atlas of Ancient Greece by Robert Morkot, Penguin, London, 1996 (Photo: Michael Holford).

p. 312: Detail from Luca della Robbia's "Cantoria" – Museo dell Opera del Duomo (from the cover of MUSIC by Frederic V. Grunfeld, Newsweek Books, New York, 1974).

p. 312: Farinelli – in: Storia della Musica, vol. XIII, Fratelli Fabbri Editori, Milano, 1964.

p. 312: Caruso – in: Music of the World by Alan Blackwood, Facts on File, Oxford, 1991.

p. 312: Shalyapin – in: Maska i dusha (Masque and Soul) by Feodor Shalyapin, Souz Teatre Publishing House, 1989 (Photo: Private collection of V. Teleshev).

p. 313: Boris Chrisroff – in: Boris Christoff by Atanas Bojkov, Musika, Sofia, 1985.

p. 313: Maria Callas from the cover of a gramophone record of EMI Electrola GmbH, Köln (Photo: Kristian Steiner).

p. 313: Maria Malibran - in: Storia della Musica, vol. 6, Fratelli Fabbri Editori, Milano, 1964.

p. 313: Pavarotti – Courtesy of Virginia Records/Universal Music.

p. 313: Sinatra – in: Sinatra by Lew Irwin, Running Press, Philadelphia, 1997 (Photo: Frank Teti/Neal Peters Collection).

p. 313: Manhattan Transfer Photos Courtesy: Manhattan Transfer.